Adoption

ADOPTION

The Essential Guide to Adopting Quickly and Safely

RANDALL HICKS

A PERIGEE BOOK

A PERIGEE BOOK
Published by the Penguin Group
Penguin Group (USA) Inc.
375 Hudson Street, New York, New York 10014, USA
Penguin Group (Canada), 90 Eglinton Avenue East, Suite 700, Toronto, Ontario M4P 2Y3, Canada
(a division of Pearson Penguin Canada Inc.)
Penguin Books Ltd., 80 Strand, London WC2R 0RL, England
Penguin Group Ireland, 25 St. Stephen's Green, Dublin 2, Ireland (a division of Penguin Books Ltd.)
Penguin Group (Australia), 250 Camberwell Road, Camberwell, Victoria 3124, Australia
(a division of Pearson Australia Group Pty. Ltd.)
Penguin Books India Pvt. Ltd., 11 Community Centre, Panchsheel Park, New Delhi—110 017, India
Penguin Group (NZ), 67 Apollo Drive, Rosedale, North Shore 0632, New Zealand
(a division of Pearson New Zealand Ltd.)
Penguin Books (South Africa) (Pty.) Ltd., 24 Sturdee Avenue, Rosebank, Johannesburg 2196,
South Africa

Penguin Books Ltd., Registered Offices: 80 Strand, London WC2R 0RL, England

While the author has made every effort to provide accurate telephone numbers and Internet addresses at the time of publication, neither the publisher nor the author assumes any responsibility for errors, or for changes that occur after publication. Further, the publisher and author do not have any control over and do not assume any responsibility for third-party websites or their content. The publisher does not have any control over and does not assume any responsibility for the author's website.

First edition: October 2007

Library of Congress Cataloging-in-Publication Data

Hicks, Randall, 1956–
    Adoption: the essential guide to adopting quickly and safely / Randall Hicks.
        p. cm.
    ISBN 978-0-399-53368-6
    1. Adoption—United States—Handbooks, manuals, etc.   2. Adoption—Law and legislation—United
States—Popular works.   I. Title.

    HV875.55.H53 2007
    362.7340973—dc22

PRINTED IN THE UNITED STATES OF AMERICA

10   9   8   7   6   5   4   3   2   1

PUBLISHER'S NOTE: This publication is designed to provide accurate and authoritative information in regard to the subject matter covered. It is sold with the understanding that the publisher and the author are not engaged in rendering legal, accounting, or other professional services. Laws and procedures discussed herein can change or be interpreted differently. If you require legal advice or other expert assistance, you should seek the services of a competent professional.

To my parents,
Robert and Carolyn Hicks.

If I live my life with even half
of your character and kindness, I will
consider myself a lucky and successful man.

ACKNOWLEDGMENTS

If I were to add up all the individual adoptive and birth parents I've had the honor of working with as an adoption attorney over the last twenty years, they would total more than 3,000. So first of all, thanks to all of you for granting me such a fulfilling career and for giving me the privilege of being a tiny part of your families.

Taking my experience as an attorney and putting it into book form required the help of others. Big thanks to my assistant, Tammy Rendon, who went beyond the call of duty; my daughter, Hailey; my agent, Barret Neville; my editor, Marian Lizzi, and her assistant, Katie Wasilewski. Thanks also to the many adoption professionals and researchers who offered insight into different sections of the book: Mark McDermott, Mark Eckman, William P. Rosen III, Diane Michelsen, Sharon Roszia, Susan Caughman, and Lindsay Biesterfeld.

CONTENTS

Adoption

I want to help you adopt.

I've been an adoption attorney for more than twenty years and completed adoptions for more than 900 families. I believe that what I've done for them, I can do for you. More important, by the time you've finished reading this book, *you* will know that you can adopt as well.

I want to show you how to adopt quickly.

The key to success in any endeavor is *knowledge*. Adoption is no different. I will give you that knowledge in an easy-to-understand, step-by-step approach. In addition to the basic knowledge you'll need, I'll give you a strategy for success. And not just success, but *quick* success. I promise to give you more information than you thought was possible about how to succeed in adopting a child. This is true whether you wish to adopt a newborn child, an older child, a child with special needs, or a child from another country. Some of these strategies you won't find anywhere else. But don't take it on faith. In less than one hour of reading from now you will know this to be true.

I'll show you more options than you ever knew existed.

The biggest mistake adoptive parents make is to limit themselves to adoption attorneys and agencies in their home county. Did you know that about half of our states permit you to adopt in their state *even if you don't live there*? This allows you to take advantage of states with better adoption laws and options than your home state. But how do you find the "best" states? I've provided a state-by-state review with each state's unique laws and procedures, listed their key state adoption offices to contact, even listed how many adoptions occur in their state each year. Do you know some states complete more than 10,000 a year, while others complete only a few hundred? That some states make a birth mother's consent irrevocable the moment it is signed, while others give her months to change her mind? Or that some states permit you to assist a birth mother with pregnancy-related costs to encourage adoption and some don't? How about that some states require pre-placement home studies and some don't? Do you know some states finalize adoptions in only weeks, while others take a full year? These are just a few of the vital facts given for each state to help you decide in which state you want to hire an attorney or agency and where you want to finalize your adoption. Whether you elect to do everything in your home county, or expand your quest into every state in the nation, I'll show you how to optimize your chances and find success.

I'll show you how to find the right attorney or agency to assist you.

The state-by-state review also lists *every* licensed private adoption agency in the nation (more than 1,200) and also provides their city, phone number, and website. It also lists every member of the American Academy of Adoption Attorneys, including their addresses, phone numbers, websites, emails, and something you won't find anywhere else—a biography of their experiences and services. (How many years have they been in practice? How many adoptions have they completed in their career? How many last year? Do they help their clients get matched with a birth mother?) But how do you take all that information and narrow it down to find the best attorneys or agencies for your unique needs? Here's how: I know the real questions to ask to find the best adoption professionals and separate the legitimate ones from the shady profiteers. For example, in selecting an attorney, I've provided a detailed list of more than forty questions to ask, or things to do, to get the information you need and *really* find out how good—or bad—they are. There is a similar detailed list for selecting an agency or an international adoption program. By the time you are done, you will have complete confidence in who you have hired.

I'll give you sample documents to duplicate, not just theory.

If you are planning a newborn adoption, you will likely prepare a photo-résumé letter and cover letters. Ninety percent of the photo-résumé letters I see contain easily avoidable mistakes, often fatal to being selected by a birth mother. I'll give you a point-by-point review of what your letter needs to say, and how to say it. I'll also talk about what makes a great photo for your letter. Before we are done, you will have a veritable road map on highly creative and effective ways to use your photo-résumé letter to maximize your exposure to birth mothers—strategies most other adoptive parents aren't using simply because they don't know them.

I want to show you how to adopt safely.

Every endeavor in life has risks, and adoption is no exception. I believe the biggest key in avoiding a failed adoption is to never start a risky one. Will there still be risks? Yes. Adoption is fraught with emotions, for both you and the birth family, so risks can't be eliminated entirely. However, I'll show you the red flags to watch out for in order to greatly minimize risk, and to allow you to proceed into your adoption with confidence.

I want to show you how to adopt economically.

I don't practice law in Beverly Hills or in Manhattan. The adoptive parents I work with are hardworking, middle-income people: teachers, fireman, electricians, accountants. They can't risk spending their money unwisely or where it will not produce results. Sadly, however, more and more adoptions in our country involve high costs. In this book I'll show you that it need not be that way. Beginning with key steps like finding the right attorney or agency and getting free medical coverage for the birth mother's pregnancy, I'll show you how to reduce or even eliminate many typical adoption costs. Thanks to the $10,000 federal adoption tax credit we will explore later, some people may even end up with a "free" adoption.

I'll talk bluntly about international adoption.

International adoption is becoming more and more popular, to the tune of 23,000 a year by Americans. But international adoption involves not just finding the right program but the right country from which to adopt. Unfortunately, however, few people are willing to say anything negative about international adoption for fear of being politically incorrect. I've not only done international adoptions myself, I've been overseas to visit orphanages and meet foreign adoption professionals. I know how things really work. Some countries are better than others simply because they nurture their children more while in orphanages or foster care. This is a critical part of your adoption, as that early care will affect your child—and your family—in many ways for your and your child's lifetime. Also, I know how some international adoption programs prey on your ignorance, leaving you with unexpected high costs. Luckily, there are many fantastic international programs with honest, straightforward fees. I'll tell you how to "check out" each program and determine in advance the real cost of your adoption and spot the ones with hidden costs.

I want to show you how to adopt ethically.

Although this is a "how-to" and "strategy" book, make no mistake that I believe the most important thing in every adoption is to not just do it legally, but with high morals as well. Shortcuts backfire. Illegality corrupts. Immorality taints. Run from people who tell you otherwise. Adoption is how you bring your child into your home. His or her unique adoption story will be a part of your family history, to be lovingly shared with your child as he or she grows. You want to look back at how each step was accomplished with pride. Your child's adoption can be, and should be, one of the most wonderful and rewarding journeys of your life.

Let's make this journey together.

CHAPTER 1

Are You Ready to Adopt?

Your readiness to adopt is the first critical step in your adoption. If you are not emotionally ready, all the knowledge in the world won't make adoption the right family-building option for you. Instead it will be the proverbial "house built on sand," destined to fail. You owe it to yourselves, and your future child, to be sure you are ready.

Readiness to Adopt

People often confuse being ready to *adopt* with being ready to *parent*. They are two vastly different things. Just because you are ready to parent does not mean you are automatically ready to adopt. Adoption means a full recognition that you are making someone else's biological child your own, as if born to you. This is an issue that can't be denied or ignored. Adoption can't be a healthy option if an adoptive parent views the lack of biological connection as a negative characteristic in their child. The biological diversity of an adopted child must not just be accepted but embraced. As stated by Sharon Kaplan Roszia, one of the nation's leading authorities on the subject and the coauthor of *The Open Adoption Experience*, "Children reflect both *nature* and *nurture,* although the exact interplay between those factors is a mystery. Children have a connection to both the birth parents and the adoptive parents, because each has made a significant contribution to the child's development. This dual responsibility for who a child is, and who he or she becomes, also creates a connection between birth parents and adoptive parents. Through them, a human life is created and nurtured."

As an adoptive parent you must recognize that your child may look different from you (even if of the same ethnic group), or genetically be predisposed to different interests and skills. Of course, even biologically conceived children often have looks and interests different from their parents or siblings. Oddly, those differences are never questioned in biologically created families, just taken for granted as an extension of each person's individuality. In adoption, however, some people examine such differences with inappropriate scrutiny.

Another issue related to readiness to adopt, assuming you are adopting due to infertility, is that you must have come to terms with infertility. For this reason, counseling is a normal and highly recommended part of the infertility process. For some, it is hard to give up the dream of a biologically conceived child, while others have little difficulty with the concept of adopting a person who is genetically from another family. For those who have difficulty with abandoning the dream of their own biologically conceived child, it is critical to come to terms with this issue before starting an adoption. To not do so would be like marrying someone while you are still in love with someone else. Everyone will suffer as a result, no matter how good your intentions.

Readiness to adopt means you have to look into more than your heart. You have to look into your mind. Are you adopting because you want be a parent? To have a family? If so, those are natural, healthy reasons to adopt. Some adoptive parents, however, are motivated by the desire to "save a child." Don't get me wrong; this is a good-hearted motivation by likely a wonderful person. It is the wrong reason to adopt, however.

Let me use marriage as an example again. If you were to marry someone to "save" them, perhaps from a life of loneliness and poverty, think how doomed that marriage would be. Either consciously or unconsciously, you would expect gratitude, and you would not get it. Instead, you would eventually get resentment. You'd feel they were ungrateful, and now we've got two people feeling resentment. Adoption is no different. The fact may be, particularly in older-child and international adoption from some impoverished nations, that you are physically saving a child from a poor start in life and giving them a brighter future. Adoption, however, is about creating a *family*—a parent and child relationship—not living an act of charity. There are many honorable and much-needed ways to help children besides adoption, such as foster parenting, mentoring, volunteering time, and donating money. Let's leave adoption for true family creation, however, not human charity.

How Will You Talk with Your Child About Being Adopted?

You might be asking a valid question right now. Why are we discussing talking with your child about adoption when you don't even have a child yet? Good point. There is a valid reason to bring it up now, however. A couple of reasons, actually. First, let's look at the practical side of it. If you are planning a newborn adoption, where the birth mother will likely be meeting with you prior to deciding if you are the right parents for her baby, a common question for a birth mother to ask you is, "How are you going to tell your child that he's adopted?"

If this is a question to which you've never given any thought, and you stumble out something simplistic and antiquated about the child "being special," you likely will not have impressed that birth mother. In fact, many birth mothers have already been given information, or met with a counselor, and learned about how and when adoption should be discussed with a child, meaning she already knows what the answer to this question should be. You want her to look at you as more than nice people who will be great parents; you want to be great *adoptive* parents. That means you took the time to be ready for these issues because you care about the subject, that you have not left it to deal with at some uncertain point in the future. Failure to fully educate yourself on such vital issues means you might not be "birth-mother ready" when you are selected by a birth mother. She may come away unimpressed after meeting you and might select another adoptive family. And you've lost what could have been your placement.

You also owe it to your future child to do this kind of thinking in advance. It's just what adoptive parents *do*. It's part of the fantasy every future parent has, whether that family is created biologically or through adoption. As we look forward to parenthood, we all have fantasies about our child taking her first steps, playing catch on the lawn, opening presents at Christmas or Hanukkah, and sitting on Grandpa's lap to hear the same stories we were told as children. The only thing different is that adoptive parents need to have a few additional fantasies, and talking to their child about how she entered the family is one of them.

Some adoptive parents feel very comfortable in discussing adoption with their child, while others have some anxiety. All adoptive parents, however, have one thing in common. They understand that not only does their child need and deserve knowledge of how their family was created through adoption but also that this knowledge must be provided in a way that will give their child the pride and self-respect every person needs as a foundation in life.

What do you say and when do you say it? Every child and family situation is different, but there are many common themes that the adoption community has come to embrace. The practice followed by some parents many years ago of hiding any information about adoption until the child was "old enough" has been rejected. Although that policy may have been followed with good intentions, many problems resulted. Many children would accidentally learn from others that they were adopted, instead of from their parents, creating confusion and parent-trust issues. Other children would wrongly assume their parents' silence was due to embarrassment about the adoption, creating shame in the child, unjustly believing something must be "wrong" with adoption.

Now, openness is embraced. Although your child grew in your heart and not physically in your body, you don't want to deny your young child the great joy every child experiences when hearing about the anticipation of his or her arrival into a family and how cherished and important a part of the family he has become. How your child views him or herself—and adoption itself—will depend almost exclusively upon you.

If you are adopting a newborn, talking about adoption starts at birth. True, the baby won't understand you, but that doesn't stop you saying "I love you," does it? You say "I love you" because you enjoy the giving and receiving of emotion the words bring. You don't wait until you are sure your child can understand the meaning of those words. Using the word *adoption* in a context such as, "The day we adopted you was the happiest day of our lives," makes the word a comfortable part of your family's vocabulary for the time when the words are understood. And your child will know, even before the word *adoption* has any meaning, that is must be a "good" word, because Mom and Dad are always smiling when they say it.

Learning about adoption is a gradual process, like many things we need to teach our children about, such as "the birds and the bees" and "stranger danger." We don't sit down our babies or toddlers and give them a detailed lecture on those subjects. Neither do you do so when discussing adoption. Instead, you slowly lay the groundwork, and give information as your child is mature enough to understand it.

When you are adopting an older child, either in a domestic or international adoption, your child will enter your home knowing she is adopted. In these cases, the focus is on why you have brought her into your home and that you are going to be her parent forever. Many older children come from disrupted families, often filled with unreliable— sometimes even abusive—parents. Even if raised in foster care, your child may have been moved often, unable to form normal attachments.

Regardless whether you are adopting a newborn or older child, it will help your child to know other adoptive parents and their children and to be made aware that there are millions of other people out there who entered their families in just the same way. Some of these people will be your friends and neighbors, or people in your community, like your dentist or minister. They can also be some of the many public personalities, such as adoptive parents Steven Spielberg (director), Magic Johnson (basketball player), and Nicole Kidman (actress), who are very public about their adoptions. Famous adoptees (adopted persons) include Aristotle (philosopher), Charles Dickens (writer), Edgar Allan Poe (writer), Faith Hill (country singer), Halle Berry (actress), George Washington Carver (inventor), and Mark Twain (writer). And why stop there? The Bible tells us Moses was adopted, not to mention Jesus (by Joseph). The comics give us Superman, a superhero adopted by his Earth family. Even two U.S. presidents were adopted (Bill Clinton and Gerald Ford). This knowledge creates a subtle message, allowing your child to think: "I'm not different. I'm like everyone else. I just entered my family differently than some, but exactly like many others." For an extensive list of famous adoptive parents, birth parents, and adoptees, visit http://celebrities.adoption.com (the list includes stepparent adoptions).

This chapter is short, but don't think that is because these issues are not important. To the contrary, they are critical to your long-term success and that of your family. One book can only do so much, however, and my goal is to help you adopt. Issues related to emotional readiness to adopt and talking to your child about adoption are best covered by those who specialize in those fields. These subjects need, and deserve, entire books to adequately cover them. By touching upon these subjects, however, I hope I have demonstrated their importance and that you will choose to explore them. I firmly believe that a small investment in an adoption library is the best money you will spend in your entire adoption process. Appendix A lists recommended books and magazines in each of these subjects:

- Are you ready to adopt?
- Being an adoptive parent
- Talking to your child about adoption
- Older-child and special-needs adoption issues

CHAPTER 2

The Fourteen—Yes, Fourteen!—Types of Adoption

The normal approach to teaching about adoption would be to give you a detailed outline of how each major type of adoption—independent, agency, and international—works. Sorry, I'm not going to do that. Instead, I'm going to approach this backward and show you fourteen subtypes *first*. Why? I want you to see right from the beginning that there are more types of adoption—meaning more options for you— than you ever imagined. It is in these subtypes, many of them greatly underused, where success lies for adoptive parents. Many adoption professionals don't even know about them.

I'm also doing it this way to eliminate some preconceptions. I find many adoptive parents take their first steps into the adoption process armed with a basic understanding of adoption, and think they already know the best route to find, and adopt, their future child. You might be like that, firmly believing a traditional independent, agency, or international adoption is the route you'll follow, and you just need help getting there. Don't be surprised if by the time you peruse this overview you see there are types you didn't even know existed, and that one of them may be the best option for you. This is true whether you are seeking to adopt a newborn baby or an older child, or do an international adoption.

Want an analogy? Let's say a traditional adoption quest is like a cross-country road trip. So you get a sedan, a reliable car, suitable for most situations. But maybe the path to your adoption actually requires a SUV to get up a sandy hillside for the adoption waiting on the other side. Without the SUV, that adoptive placement is lost to you and goes to another family who knew where to look and was prepared to get there. In fact, you drove right by, never knowing you came that close to the opportunity. Or, maybe you need a subcompact to squeeze through a narrow roadway. The by-the-book sedan won't fit, so again you pass by, unaware of the great adoption opportunity down that road. It's kind of like that classic Cary Grant movie, *An Affair to Remember*, where he's waiting on top of the Empire State Building for his true love, but he passes by her on the street, thinking he was stood up. Turns out she was right there; he was just looking in the wrong direction.

To succeed in adoption, you need to be looking down every road, with the right equipment at your disposal. Where you live—a small town in Alaska with no adoptive placement options, an East Coast state where independent adoption is not permitted, or a region with no qualified adoption attorneys or agencies—makes no difference. You are not limited by your city, county, or even state. Your only limitation is how open you are to exploring options that may be different from your initial concept of how adoptive matches are made.

Of the fourteen subtypes of adoption, ten involve domestic (American-born) children and four concern international children. The majority is centered on the adoption of newborns, while others deal with older children. Before we review them, however, it will be helpful to have a basic adoption vocabulary.

Domestic adoption: Adopting a child born in the United States.

International adoption: Adopting a child born overseas, born to a citizen of that country.

Birth mother: The biological mother of the child being placed for adoption.

Birth father: The biological father of the child being placed for adoption.

Birth family: A general term referring to all biological relatives of the child, such as the birth parents, siblings, grandparents, etc.

Adoptive parents: The parents who will be adopting the child and becoming the child's legal and permanent parents.

Adoptee: The child being adopted.

Networking: The outreach effort to find women with unplanned pregnancies who might be considering adoption, and in turn have them consider you as adoptive parents. You can network on your own following my suggestions, or rely upon your adoption attorney or agency to do it based on their special relationships with health-care professionals, and other strategies.

Independent adoption: An adoption typically initiated by an attorney, who helps "match" you with a birth mother and does the legal work required. Virtually all independent adoptions involve only newborns.

Private adoption agency: Private agencies can elect to serve the general public or a selected group (usually based upon religious affiliation). They can help "match" you with a birth mother and perform your home study, as well as other functions. Most of their placements are of newborns, but some may also work with older children.

Public adoption agency: Virtually every county in the nation has a government-operated adoption agency, usually a division of the state's department of social services. Although some county adoption agencies handle newborn adoptions, most have the duty of finding homes for older children, many of them dependents of the court due to their forced removal from their biological parents. Usually the agency's services to adoptive parents are free or low cost to encourage the adoption of waiting children.

Now let's take a quick look at the fourteen types of adoption. Thereafter, we have an entire book together to prepare you to look at them in more detail, analyze the pros and cons, determine which ones are right for you, and map out a strategy for quick, safe, economical, and ethical adoption.

Independent Adoption via an Attorney Located in Your Home State

This is the most popular option for those seeking to adopt a newborn baby born in the United States. You select an attorney located in your home state. He or she helps match you with a birth mother, or supervises your efforts to do so, then does the legal work thereafter all the way through finalization of the adoption in court. Your home study is done by an agency, social worker, or state adoption office, depending upon the regulations of your state. (All states permit independent adoption except Colorado, Connecticut, Delaware, Massachusetts, and North Dakota.) In Chapter 4 we will be exploring this type of adoption in more detail. Chapter 15 provides a state-by-state review, detailing the exact laws and procedures governing independent adoption in your state.

This is a great method if:

- Your state has a large enough population base resulting in a sufficient number of birth mothers making adoptive placements.
- The qualities you possess as adoptive parents are those local birth mothers will find appropriate for their expected child. (For example, if you are Catholic and live in a state like Utah, with a predominately Mormon population, the birth mothers will most likely be Mormon, and less likely to pick you as a non-Mormon.)
- Your region or state has attorneys who are well qualified and charge reasonable fees.
- Your state's laws are fair to adoptive parents and not unduly restrictive.
- You are seeking to adopt a newborn.

Independent Adoption via an Attorney Located Outside Your Home State (An "Out-of-State" Adoption)

Instead of hiring an attorney who is located within your home state, you select one out of state. This could be in a neighboring state, or across the country. This attorney will usually be networking in his or her state for birth mothers, with the baby generally born in the attorney's state.

Does this mean you have to stay six or eight months out of state with the baby until the adoption is completed? Not at all. When the child is born, after the necessary interstate approval, you return home with the baby, later finalizing the adoption in your home state's court. You would also be using a local in-state attorney for these proceedings, as normally many of your home state's laws will apply. In addition to the more detailed information about out-of-state independent adoption in Chapter 4, the state-by-state review gives each state's unique laws and procedures, allowing you to determine the most advantageous ones in which to possibly start your adoption.

This is a great method if:

- There are not sufficient birth mothers in your state, perhaps due to a low population, or adoption is not a promoted or popular option.
- You live in a state that you feel is overrepresented with waiting adoptive parents compared to the placements available.
- There are not enough well-qualified attorneys in your state.
- You belong to a particular ethnic or religious group and want to adopt a child matching your characteristics, but they are underrepresented in your state, meaning few birth mothers to select you.
- Your state's adoption laws are unfair toward adoptive parents (such as giving the birth mother too long to change her mind and reclaim a child), some of which can be avoided by an out-of-state birth.
- Your state might be satisfactory, but you want to expand your options by including efforts in additional states.
- You don't mind traveling out of state, typically one or more times (certainly for the birth, but likely also for your initial meeting with the birth mother).
- You are seeking to adopt a newborn.

Independent "Nonresident" Adoption

This is one of the most important types of adoption, and one of the least known. As with the above type of adoption, it involves hiring an attorney in a state other than your own. However, instead of finalizing the adoption under your own state laws and in your local court, you complete virtually the entire adoption in the attorney's state, where the child was born, under that state's laws.

As with *out-of-state* adoption, you can bring the child back to your home state after birth and reside there, having to return to the birth state later for a brief court appearance to finalize the adoption, just as you would need to do in your own city. The only service needed in your home state would usually be a local agency or social worker doing your home study and reporting that you are caring for your child properly. More than half the states in the country permit nonresidents to adopt in their state, only requiring that the baby be born there. These states are Alabama, Alaska, Arkansas, California, Hawaii, Iowa, Indiana, Kansas, Louisiana, Maine, Maryland, Michigan, Missouri, New Hampshire, New Jersey, New Mexico, New York, North Dakota, Ohio, Oregon, Pennsylvania, South Carolina, Texas, Utah, Virginia, and Washington. Chapter 4 provides more information about this critically important type of adoption, and the state-by-state review details the laws of the above twenty-six states that permit nonresident adoption.

This kind of adoption is ideal for adoptive parents for the same reasons as those listed above regarding out-of-state adoptions, as well as the following:

- The laws of a particular state are attractive to you, as the birth state's laws will almost exclusively apply when you are also finalizing there.
- Adoption costs in your state are extremely high, and some of them can be reduced or avoided by completing the adoption in another state.
- You don't mind an additional trip out of state, as you will normally be required to return about six months after birth for the final court appearance granting the adoption.

Private Adoption Agencies Located in the Adoptive Parent's Home State

This is the second most popular type of newborn adoption in the country. You select a private adoption agency located in your home state. The agency will help match you with a birth mother or supervise your efforts to do so, do your home study, and write a report for the court. Then either an in-house attorney does the legal work thereafter through finalization in court, or they refer you to a local attorney to do so. This method is very similar to an independent adoption via an attorney in your home state, except you are selecting an agency, rather than an attorney, to be the primary entity. Chapter 5 explores the dynamics of an in-state agency adoption. Chapter 15 reviews the laws governing agency adoption in each state, as well as lists every licensed private adoption agency in your home state.

This is a great method if:

- Your state has agencies that are well qualified, reasonably priced, and you meet their eligibility requirements.
- Your state has a large enough population base in your region resulting in sufficient birth mothers making adoptive placements.
- The characteristics you present as adoptive parents are those which local birth mothers will find appropriate for their expected child, such as religion and ethnicity.
- Your state's laws are fair to adoptive parents and not unduly restrictive.
- You are seeking to adopt a newborn (although some agencies do older child placements).

Private Adoption Agencies Located Outside the Adoptive Parent's Home State

Instead of hiring an agency located within your home state, you can select one out of state, either in a neighboring state or thousands of miles away. This is very similar to an independent out-of-state adoption, except you are retaining an agency rather than an attorney. The agency will usually be networking in its state for birth mothers, meaning the baby will likely be born in the agency's state. You can bring the child home shortly after birth, process the adoption primarily under your home state's laws, and finalize it in your local court. Your in-state agency will do your home study and prepare the report for the court. Chapter 5 gives more details about how out-of-state agency adoption works. Chapter 15's listing of every private adoption agency in each state allows you to easily find and contact agencies throughout the nation. It also explains the laws within those states.

This is a great method if:

- There are not sufficient birth mothers in your state, perhaps due to a low population, or adoption is not a promoted or popular option.
- You live in a state that you feel is overrepresented with waiting adoptive parents compared to the placements available.
- You are not pleased with the qualifications or fees of agencies in your state, or they have requirements making you ineligible.
- You belong to an ethnic or religious group and want to adopt a child matching your characteristics, but they are underrepresented in your state, meaning few birth mothers to select you.
- Your state's adoption laws are unfair toward adoptive parents.
- Your state might be satisfactory, but you want to expand your options by including efforts in additional states.
- You are seeking to adopt a newborn (but toddlers and older children are available too).

Private Agency "Nonresident" Adoption

Just as nonresident adoption can be done with attorneys, it can also be done via adoption agencies. You retain a private adoption agency located in another state and finalize the adoption there, under that state's laws, where the child was born or the agency having custody of the child and making the placement is located. It is not required that you stay in the child's birth state during the entire adoption. Instead, after interstate approval, you can return home with your child until it is time to finalize the adoption, when you normally return to the birth state. Usually the only services required within your state will be a home study by a local agency or social worker, who will write reports to the out-of-state agency confirming that you are caring for your child properly.

Thirty-one states and the District of Columbia permit nonresident agency adoption when an in-state agency is the custodial agency. These states are Alabama, Alaska, Arkansas, California, Colorado, Delaware, District of Columbia, Hawaii, Iowa, Illinois, Indiana, Kansas, Louisiana, Maine, Maryland, Massachusetts, Michigan, Missouri, New

Hampshire, New Jersey, New Mexico, New York, North Dakota, Ohio, Oregon, Pennsylvania, South Carolina, Texas, Utah, Vermont, Virginia, and Washington. You may have noticed that this list of states permitting nonresidents to adopt is a bit larger than the list provided when *independent* nonresident adoption was discussed earlier in this chapter. The reason is that some of these states (Colorado, Delaware, and North Dakota) are "agency-only" states and do not permit independent adoption, meaning nonresidents can only adopt there if doing so via agency adoption. Also, some states do not allow nonresidents to adopt simply because the child is born in the state, but do allow it if the agency having custody of the child is located there. Chapter 5 gives more information on this popular type of adoption and the state-by-state review provides the laws and procedures of each of the above states.

This kind of adoption is ideal for adoptive parents for the same reasons as those listed above for out-of-state adoptions, as well as the following:

- The laws of a particular state are attractive to you, as the birth state's laws will almost exclusively apply when you are also finalizing there.
- Adoption costs in your state are extremely high, and you wish to reduce or avoid some of them by completing the adoption in another state.

Public/County Adoption Agencies

Almost every county in each state has a public adoption agency to serve both the children and adoptive parents in their region. This "public" or "county" agency is primarily supported by taxes, and services to adoptive parents are either free or greatly discounted. Although sometimes newborns are available via this method, in most cases the county adoption office has the imposing duty of finding homes for the older children in its care. Many of these children have been involuntarily freed through the courts due to inappropriate parenting, including neglect, abandonment, and abuse. For more information about adopting through your local public agency please refer to Chapter 5.

This is a great type of adoption if:

- You like the people and procedures of your local county adoption agency, as normally it will be the sole "public" option in your county.
- You are looking for a free adoption, or one that has very minimal costs.
- You are seeking an older child, a sibling group, a child with special needs, and/or a child of an ethnic minority, as most, but not all, children will be in at least one of these groups.
- You want to share your love with a special-needs child but worry about the possible financial strain on your family. The existence of a possible monthly stipend even after the adoption is complete makes the adoption feasible for you.
- You want an adoption where everything is likely to be done in your home region.
- You possess the emotional qualities and training necessary to provide the extra nurturing a child from a disrupted family will require.
- You are open to a child who has been exposed to drugs during the pregnancy.

Adoption Exchanges

In addition to each county serving their own local children, there are state, regional, and national adoption *exchanges*. They list waiting and special-needs children in an effort to find them homes. Most exchanges welcome adoptive parents from any state, not just the state in which the child is located. For example, this would allow a Texas child with special needs, and no local adoptive parents available to meet those needs, to be matched with the perfect family who lives in New York. Although it is true that most of the children served by exchanges have been deemed to have special needs of some type, it may not always be a physical or mental challenge, as you may initially imagine when hearing the term "special needs." Some of the children have received that designation for no reason other than their age being past the toddler years, being part of a sibling group to be adopted together, or being of an ethnic group for which there are not enough adoptive parents. You might find you owe it to yourself, and the children waiting, to check out this virtually free option.

As discussed in more detail in Chapter 5, each state has its own adoption exchange. There are also regional exchanges and one national exchange. Generally, the exchanges charge no fees. Most exchanges have photo listings so you can see the actual children available online right from your home. In fact, you could do it right now if you want. The state exchanges, and their phone numbers and websites, are listed in the state-by-state review. I'd suggest starting by checking your state exchange, the registries of some of your neighboring states, then the national exchange. The national and regional exchanges, and their phone numbers and websites, are listed in Appendix B. Here's a tip few people know: Although you can check the exchanges from your own computer, many states require a password known only to licensed agencies to see all the children listed. Accessing most exchanges on your own may only grant access to some of the children, often the longer-waiting children. The opportunity for full access makes a trip to a local agency worthwhile.

Adopting through an exchange is ideal for the same reasons as those listed for public/county adoptions, as well as the following:

- You don't mind traveling several times to another region or state to meet, and slowly bond with, a child.

The Foster Parent Shortcut

In the above two types of adoption (local county agencies and exchanges), the children are normally legally free for adoption when they are shown to you. This also means they are older and have waited longer to get to that point, perhaps having gone through one or more foster homes, and the potential trauma of multiple placements.

You can sometimes get to the "front of the adoptive parent line" by being a foster parent, caring for a child who may not yet legally be free for adoption. This often means the birth parents still have their parental rights yet have been denied custody, and it is believed the child is destined for adoptive placement. For example, the birth mother may have abandoned the baby in the hospital, or been under the influence of drugs at the time of birth, requiring the county agency to step in and take care of the child. In most situations the court will give the birth parents a limited time to prove they can be adequate parents and regain custody, but if they fail to do so, will terminate their parental rights. For this reason, the foster parent shortcut can be risky, as only some placements starting out as foster care turn into adoptions. Chapter 5 provides more information about fost-adopt placements.

This kind of adoption is ideal for the same reasons as those listed for public/county adoptions, as well as the following:

- You have the emotional constitution to be content with helping a child by giving him or her a loving home as a foster parent, knowing it may not turn into an adoptive placement as you hope.
- You feel you want to live with a child for an extended period and see if the family emotionally jells as you anticipate, prior to moving into adoption planning.
- You want to adopt but can't afford any legal or agency costs, and need the slight additional income provided as a foster parent prior to the adoption being finalized, to fully meet your child's needs.

Identified Adoptions

An "identified" adoption is a hybrid between an independent and a private agency adoption. Some people call them "designated" adoptions. These are adoptions where an adoptive parent likes some elements of an attorney-initiated independent adoption, but also likes the formality of an agency adoption, and combines the best elements of the two. In the most typical identified adoption, the adoptive parents retain an attorney to help find a birth mother and do the legal work, then when a birth mother is "identified," they use an agency to provide counseling to her, assist with her relinquishment of parental rights, and conduct the adoptive parent home study.

This type of adoption can be combined with other subtypes of adoption. For example, you might select an out-of-state attorney to help find a birth mother and get the adoption going, but hire an agency in your home state to do the rest and complete the adoption in your home state. In so doing, you've now created a hybrid of sorts: an "identified out-of-state adoption." When you include the many hybrids possible, there are actually *more* than fourteen types of adoption available to you. Identified adoptions are discussed in Chapter 5.

This is a great option for you if:

- You want the flexibility of the characteristics of both independent and agency adoption.
- You want the option to do an in-state, out-of-state, or nonresident adoption, determined primarily by the laws of the state where you elect to hire your adoption agency and/or attorney.
- You seek to adopt a newborn.

Facilitators

A facilitator is not so much a *type* of adoption (so it is not being counted as one of the fourteen types of adoption) as it is a *method* to start a newborn adoption. A facilitator is a person or business being paid a fee for adoption services, but which is not a licensed attorney or agency. They are the subject of a great deal of controversy. Some consider facilitators as "infantpreneurs," profiting from the placement of children, because unlike attorneys and agencies, they are not licensed to do legal work or conduct home studies. In fact, some states make it a crime to facilitate an adoption for a fee.

Most would agree a facilitator's primary function is to find birth mothers, usually via yellow page and Internet ads. Those who support facilitators argue they are a viable, although often expensive, route to finding a birth mother. Also, remember that once you find a birth mother via a facilitator, you will still need to complete your adoption via either the independent or agency adoption method and select an attorney or agency to assist you with those legalities, so you will have those costs as well. For more information about facilitators, and the potential risks in using them, please refer to Chapters 6 and 8.

This might be an option for you if:

- The state in which you are working permits facilitators.
- You are comfortable with the facilitator's methods of networking for birth mothers.
- You are content that the facilitator's fees might be more than that of an attorney or agency.
- You understand the risk of working with an entity not licensed as an agency or attorney.

- You understand that in addition to paying a facilitator, you will still normally require an attorney and/or agency to complete the adoption.

Private Adoption Agencies with International Adoption Programs in the Adoptive Parent's Home State

Some of the private adoption agencies in your home state will offer international adoption programs rather than domestic placements. A few agencies do double duty, handling both domestic and international adoptions, although most international agencies focus only on that specialty. You will find that each agency normally has specific countries from which it makes adoptive placements. One agency might have a program only in Russia, while another might work in multiple countries, like China, Guatemala, and the Philippines. Hiring an in-state international agency means that one entity can handle your domestic requirements, such as your home study, as well as supervise the overseas portion of the adoption.

The state-by-state review not only lists every agency within your state but also indicates which agencies have international programs and in what countries. Chapter 7 explores international adoption in great detail.

This is a great method if:

- You want to adopt a non-newborn (usually from six months to sixteen years, depending upon the country).
- You want one agency to do everything: your prebirth home study as well as the international aspects of the adoption.
- Your state has qualified international agencies with programs in the countries of interest to you, and you meet the eligibility requirements of the agency and the child's country.
- You are comfortable adopting a child where sometimes little medical history is available.
- You are willing to travel to the child's country and stay there for at least several weeks (although some countries use escorts to bring the child to you).
- You understand that your child, if of speaking age, will initially speak another language and not know English.

- You are aware that at the time of the placement your child will usually be 10 percent underweight and about two months per each year of age regressed in physical and emotional development compared to other children due to lack of sufficient stimulation and nurturing in orphanages. (Most of these children can and will quickly catch up to their peers, however, if there are no other health factors causing the lack of development.)
- You understand a child raised in an orphanage or similar institutional setting may suffer from some degree of attachment disorder due to lack of prior nurturing or bonding with a parenting figure.
- You want a "closed" adoption, as usually you will have no contact with the birth family.

Private Adoption Agencies with International Adoption Programs Outside the Adoptive Parent's Home State

As with domestic adoption, you might find that the agency with the best program, working in the country from which you want to adopt, is located in another state. No problem. In fact, this is very common. The out-of-state agency will handle the international aspects of your adoption (which is the critical part of an intercountry adoption) and will ask an agency in your local region to do the required home study. For more information on out-of-state agency international adoption, please refer to Chapter 7 and the state-by-state review listing all agencies and their intercountry specialization.

The factors favoring this kind of adoption are the same as those listed above for private international agencies within your state, with these additional considerations:

- You feel there are no qualified international agencies in your state with programs in the countries of interest to you, or you don't meet their eligibility requirements.
- You don't mind working with two agencies: one to do your pre-placement home study, and one to handle the international aspects of the adoption.

Adoption Attorneys with International Adoption Programs in the Adoptive Parent's Home State

Most international adoption programs are operated via private adoption agencies. (It is the reverse of domestic adoption, where the majority is via attorneys.) Still, there are some attorneys who operate international programs. To some degree, every international adoption is an "agency adoption," as each one requires a preplacement agency home study, and most all require a few postplacement visits as well. When we talk about international adoption programs, however, we are talking about much more: satisfying our federal laws governing international adoption, preparing a dossier to present overseas, having translators and drivers in the child's country to guide you during your visit, and much more. Attorneys can do this as well as agencies. Most foreign countries prefer to work with agencies, but in some attorney programs are common. For more information on international adoption please refer to Chapter 7 and the attorney biographies in the state-by-state review, which lists attorneys who practice international adoption.

The factors favoring this kind of adoption are the same as those listed above for private agencies within your state, with the addition of the following:

- You will be working with two entities: a local agency to do your preplacement home study and the attorney for the international aspects of the adoption.
- Attorneys generally have less, or no, adoptive parent eligibility requirements regarding such factors as religion, as do some agencies.

Adoption Attorneys with International Adoption Programs Outside the Adoptive Parent's Home State

You might like the idea of working with an attorney outside your home state if he or she has an excellent international program in the country you prefer. This is usually no problem. You will need an agency in your local region to do the required home study, but the out-of-country work required in the international program can be done equally well whether you select someone in or out of your home state. After all, most of the work in the adoption will likely be occurring 10,000 miles away, in the child's country, so having an attorney in another state is usually not a big factor.

The factors favoring this kind of adoption are the same as those listed above for out-of-state international and in-state attorney international adoption.

As you can see, there are many, many doors open to you. Fourteen distinct types of adoption—more actually, when you count the many possible hybrids. And we've only touched the tip of the proverbial iceberg in learning about them. To find the right door, however, we need to explore each method in depth. We will be doing that by devoting individual chapters not only to independent, agency, and international adoption but also to describing how to find the right attorney or agency. So much time is spent on this issue because success in adoption means finding the right method to accomplish your personal goals in adoption and the right professional to help you make it happen.

CHAPTER 3

Selecting the Right Attorney

Here's what most people do to find their adoption attorney:

They open their local yellow pages and select one.

And there you have the reason why most people fail at adoption or take longer to succeed.

Think about it. If you're married, did you find your spouse in the town where you grew up? Did you buy your house down the street from your mom and dad's place? Did your find your career job around the corner from your high school? I'm betting the answer to several of these questions is "no." So why should you think the best attorney for you and your unique needs would happen to be in your local phone book, just a short distance from your home?

That doesn't mean there isn't a well-qualified adoption attorney right in your region. For most people, however, if that is the beginning and end of their search, the adoption is doomed from the start. Let's look at why that is and the right approach to take.

Let me start with the basics of why you need an attorney. The attorney's role is to explain every aspect of the adoption process to you in advance so you fully understand what is ahead, then guide you through it. If you are planning a traditional *agency* adoption (Chapter 5), you may not need an attorney at all, or for only minimal services, depending upon the laws of the state in which you complete your adoption and the services of your adoption agency. However, if you are like the majority of adoptive parents seeking to adopt a newborn through *independent* or *identified* adoption (Chapter 4), the selection of your adoption attorney is critical.

In addition to their obvious legal function, many adoption attorneys also have networks leading to birth mothers being referred to their offices, creating adoptive matches. Simply doing one of these two functions is of great importance. Doing both is monumental, making the selection of your attorney likely the most important decision in your adoption.

You might already have a general practice attorney in mind to assist you. This might be an attorney you previously used for a nonadoption purpose, such as drafting a will. Or perhaps a friend has recommended their family law attorney who does "some adoptions on the side." In most cases I think selecting such an attorney is a mistake. We live in an era of specialization. The world in general, and law in particular, is so complex it is almost impossible to be a "jack of all trades." Not a good one anyway. Would you consider consulting a dermatologist for a bad back? Or an orthopedic surgeon to examine your eyes? So why would you trust the formation of your family to someone who "dabbles" in adoption?

Finding the right attorney is not a difficult task if you know how to approach it. There are specific steps to follow to find not just a great attorney but one who is right for your unique needs and desires. Let me list these steps, then we will look at each one individually:

1. Compile a list of possible attorneys.
2. Fine-tune your list.
3. Come up with specific questions to ask the attorney.
4. Test the attorney's knowledge.
5. Determine if the attorney's personality and approach to adoption matches yours.

Compile a List of Possible Attorneys

There are tens of thousands of attorneys in the country, and several hundred who specialize in adoption. My advice is start with a wide net, then narrow down your findings to attorneys who are not only well qualified but with whom you feel personally comfortable. You may be looking only for an attorney in your home state, or in states other than your own. Regardless of the number of attorneys you will elect to hire to start your adoption quest, let's look at creating your list.

• *Only consider attorneys in your preferred geographical states.* Your selected regions or states from which to adopt will be unique to you and different from other adoptive parents. You might live in a well-populated region in a state with advantageous adoption laws and a good percentage of birth mothers. If so, you will likely select an attorney in your home region and state. Another adoptive family may live in a state with very poor adoption options, so they've selected several states they feel are best for them and will consider attorneys in those states.

To determine the right states for you, consider the many in-state and out-of-state options we discussed in Chapter 2 and the information provided in the state-by-state review in Chapter 15. Depending upon where you live, and the kind of adoption you want, different states will be better for each adoptive family. It is within only these states that you need focus your search for the best attorneys.

• *Consider members of the American Academy of Adoption Attorneys (AAAA).* This membership organization has more than 300 members nationwide and is limited to attorneys with demonstrated skill and expertise in adoption. The completion of fifty adoptions, twenty of them within the last two years, is a minimum requirement to become an AAAA member. Most have completed hundreds, however. Members are listed in the state-by-state review, including their biographies detailing important information about their background and experience, as well as contact information. Additionally, the AAAA website, www.adoptionattorneys.org, lists all members by state, with full contact information.

Sometimes people fear a "specialist" will charge more. This can be true (although it is usually well worth it for the extra knowledge and experience), but the reverse is also true. Often hiring a specialist is actually less expensive. This is because a nonspecializing attorney will not know the needed procedures and documents to prepare and will charge you for that research time. The experienced adoption attorney typically already knows the needed information and has prepared the required documents hundreds of times, meaning less work hours are required and, therefore, less time for which you are billed.

Are there good adoption attorneys who are not in the AAAA? I'm sure there are, and we will get to how to find them in a moment, but the AAAA remains an excellent starting point. It is there you will find most of the nation's premier adoption attorneys. As the only national adoption attorney organization, why would an adoption attorney *not* be a member? The AAAA is more than a membership organization where attorneys pay a fee just to get a fancy plaque for their wall. There is a great deal of information sharing between members, and attendance at periodic national educational conferences is required. Some attorneys apply for membership but are denied, or are removed from the organization due to their failure to meet or maintain the organization's high standards.

What if there isn't an AAAA member in your area, or you don't feel the closest member is right for you, but you want an AAAA attorney handling your adoption? Don't worry. First of all, as was discussed in Chapter 2, you don't necessarily need an attorney right in your home area, or even your own state. True, you will likely be finalizing your adoption in your local courthouse, unless you do a nonresident adoption, but that is the simplest part of the entire adoption. It's the equivalent of the "graduation ceremony" after years of college. The difficult work is in getting there. The smart thing to do is to find the best attorney for you, whether they are close or distant. Then, if need be, that attorney can use another attorney right in your hometown to make the final court appearance, often at a token fee.

• *Check your local yellow pages under "adoption," or perhaps "attorneys—adoption/family law."* Although many of these attorneys may lack the qualifications you need and deserve, you might get lucky and find an excellent attorney who is not an AAAA member. This applies to your local yellow pages as well as those in other counties or states you are considering. Out-of-region yellow pages can usually be found at your library. You can also access the same information anywhere in the nation via Internet sites like www.yellowpages.com.

• *Join or visit local adoptive parent support groups.* Many of the people attending these meetings have "been there, done that." They've completed the process you are just starting. They can tell you about their experiences with local attorneys, both good and bad, and perhaps some outside your region as well. To find out if there is an adoptive parent support group in your area, try calling local adoption agencies and attorneys who might know of some. Because these support groups are small, and sometimes just meet in members' homes, they are often not listed in the phone book.

Other resources listing adoptive parent support groups in each state are the *Adoptive Families* magazine's website, www.adoptivefamilies .com (just click on "Parent Support Groups" on the home page), and the Child Welfare Information Gateway (a federal government site, formerly known as the National Adoption Information Clearinghouse), www.childwelfare.gov. (The site is gigantic. To find the adoptive parent support groups, go to "Adoption," then "Overview," then "National Adoption Directory," then "Search by State.")

For more information about *Adoptive Families* magazine and the Child Welfare Information Gateway, please see Appendix C.

• *Join Resolve, or attend one of their meetings.* Resolve is a well-established and respected national infertility organization with regional chapters throughout the country. Part of their focus on infertility includes adoption. Many of their members are in the process of, or have completed, an adoption, and can talk about attorneys they used. To find a Resolve chapter near you, visit www.resolve.org.

For more information about Resolve, please see Appendix C.

• *Call your local bar association.* Some bar associations have referral services based upon the attorney's specialty. Although this will possibly lead you to a good attorney, be aware that a local bar association "referral" is not as impressive as it may sound. Most local bar associations are merely voluntary associations that attorneys pay a fee to join (unlike the state bar, which is mandatory). Many of the attorneys being "referred" to you have done nothing more than fill out a form to be included in their list of recommendations. There is usually no requirement of demonstrating expertise or experience in adoptions. It is often the equivalent of a yellow page ad, but provided over the phone. Still, it is worth checking into when starting your list.

• *Call your local court.* Each court has a different department that accepts Petitions for Adoptions (the document that starts the legal process in court) for filing. In some states this might be the probate court, or perhaps the family law court. Call the court's main number and ask to speak to one of the clerks who handle the filing of Petition for Adoptions. When you reach the correct person, explain that you are planning to adopt and are compiling a list of possible attorneys. Ask which attorneys file a lot of petitions within your county. Some clerks will be willing to share some names with you, and some won't. Remember, although the cases filed are confidential, you are only asking for the names of attorneys they see a lot in court on adoption-related matters. There is nothing confidential about that. The clerk's only remaining concern will be if he or she will be perceived as giving a recommendation by passing along some names (which they are barred from doing). Explain that you are not asking for a recommendation, simply the names of attorneys who are busy in their courthouse doing adoptions.

• *Talk to other adoptive parents.* The more you start talking about adoption, the more you will find that people you already know have adopted. Often they have not previously volunteered the information, as there was no need to do so. But upon hearing you share that interest, they are happy to share their adoption experiences. There are millions of successful adoptive parents out there. You will find them everywhere: at work, in your neighborhood, at your place of worship. Ask who their attorney was and other attorneys they've heard about from their friends who have adopted. Generally, adoptive parents tend to know a lot of other adoptive parents.

• *Talk to any attorneys you know.* You may have used an attorney to draw up a will or handle a car accident, or you just know some socially. Although they may know nothing about adoption law, they may know of other attorneys who specialize in adoption. Sometimes these referrals are more to "friends" than necessarily the best attorney. Still, sometimes these leads can be viable.

• *Visit the* Adoptive Families *website. Adoptive Families* is the pre-eminent adoption magazine in the United States and their website is quite helpful. One feature is a state-by-state listing of adoption attorneys at www.adoptivefamilies.com. Be aware that attorneys pay a fee to be listed in the *Adoptive Families* directory, so many well-qualified attorneys may elect not to be listed.

• *Talk to people you know in the health-care industry.* Adoption attorneys constantly work with doctors, counselors, and hospitals regarding the care of the birth mothers they are working with. For this reason, some health-care professionals may be able to tell you about attorneys with whom they have had contact in prior adoption situations.

You will be surprised how quickly you can compile a list of possible adoption attorneys, and how large the list becomes. Don't worry if it seems unmanageably large. We will be paring it down fairly quickly.

Fine-Tune Your List

Depending upon the scope of your search, you might have only a dozen attorneys on your list, or more likely, many times that, and they will be located in one or several states. Now it's time to contact each one and get more information. Although nothing is wrong with calling and asking questions to each law office, I'd recommend you initially start by asking for their written materials. There are two reasons for this. One is that there is so much information for you to obtain about each attorney, it is almost impossible for any busy law office to verbally give all that information to every person calling. Remember, they have work to do and clients to serve. The other reason is that looking at the materials they send you is your first chance to see a sample of the attorney's work.

To fine-tune your list, and make it a manageable size, we now need to do some fact-finding. Just because an attorney does some adoptions, perhaps even specializes in it, does not mean he or she is the right attorney for you. Different qualities are important to different people, and the best adoption attorney for one adoptive family may not be the best one for you. Here are some recommended steps to take, or questions to ask, to narrow down your list:

- Examine the written information provided to you by the attorney. Is it clear and concise? Does it give you bona fide information about the adoption process, the attorney's qualifications, and the likely fees? Or is it a "puff piece" featuring a cute baby on the cover of a brochure, but little hard information? If the attorney can't provide you with professional, clear information to convince you to become a client, imagine how bad he or she will be once you've become a client and they've already got your money. Also, you are seeing your first sample of the attorney's work product. Is it well written, neat, and professionally presented? If not, why would you expect their court documents prepared on your behalf, or correspondence to important people in your case, to be any better?

- When you ask for written materials, the attorney's staff may tell you the same information is available on their website. If so, by all means, check out the website. I still recommend, however, that you ask for their written materials. That is because the website is likely the work of a web professional. You want a chance to see the work of the attorney and/or his staff, and their written materials will give you that.

- In your initial phone call to the attorney's office, do you get a good feeling from the receptionist or secretary? Is he or she professional and friendly? Remember, this will be the same person a potential birth mother will likely get on the phone on her initial call. If the receptionist is not warm and friendly, why would a birth mother be interested in staying on the line to speak to the attorney? That would mean fewer birth mothers to be considering you as adoptive parents through that office.

- Call the state bar association where the attorney practices, or visit its website. (Each state has a mandatory state bar association.) In most states, records are available to the public regarding any discipline against the attorney for inappropriate conduct or malfeasance. Discipline by the state bar can result in disbarment, temporary suspension of the attorney's license, or a public reprimand. Even the least severe discipline, a public reprimand, is seen as a quite serious among most attorneys. The state-by-state review provides each state's bar association phone number and website address. Be aware, however, that a "clean record" for an attorney is only confirmation he or she has not been disciplined for something. An attorney may still be a very poor practitioner, yet have managed to refrain from committing any indiscretions requiring sanctions by the state bar.

Don't be surprised if you quickly eliminate half the attorneys you are considering just from the steps above. Does this surprise you? Sadly, the legal profession is no better than similar fields. Think of all the doctors you've met whom you didn't really care for and would not trust to treat you again. How about all the great, and bad, teachers you've had in your life? Attorneys are no better or worse. Just be glad you can so quickly eliminate some and not waste more of your time on the ones not right for you.

Come Up with Specific Questions to Ask the Attorney

Now it's time to pare down your list to just a few attorneys and learn the questions that will lead to hiring the right one. Some of the following questions may be answered by the attorney's advance materials you have received, or provided by other materials, such as their biographies in the state-by-state review, or the attorney's website. Some questions, however, you will have to ask the attorney in a phone call or in a personal consultation. For adoptive parents seeking an attorney to provide legal services and help them be matched with a birth mother to start a newborn adoption, all the following questions will be relevant. If you already have your own birth mother, or don't feel you will need an attorney's guidance in being selected by one, some of these questions will not be necessary.

• *How many years have you been an attorney?* There is no perfect answer here. For example, an attorney with fifty years experience is impressive, but are they so advanced in years that a birth mother will not be able to relate to them? What about an attorney with only a few years experience? Likely they are younger and can work more effectively with seventeen-year-old birth moms, but do they possess enough experience? So what's the answer? It's a combination of things and requires answers to the next few questions, so keep reading.

• *Is your practice limited to, or does it primarily consist of, adoption?* The more specialized an attorney is, the more likely he or she is to be up-to-date in every aspect of adoption law, on both a state and federal level, as both can have an impact on your adoption. If an attorney handles a few adoptions a year, as well as a few dozen bankruptcies, some divorce work, and the occasional drunk-driving case, he shows an admirable diversity, but will he have the same depth of knowledge as the attorney who focuses exclusively, or primarily, on adoption?

Let me revisit the comparison of doctors and attorneys. If you needed surgery on your spine, would you go to a general practitioner who also delivers babies and helps the local teenagers with their acne? I'm guessing no. You'd be seeking a specialist. In almost every case, the more specialized the professional is, the better trained he is within that narrow specialty. A general practice attorney who confidently tells you: "Adoptions are simple; there's no need to specialize in them," is only proving to you how little he or she knows about the field and what can potentially go wrong. They just don't know enough to know it. In a few moments I'll even give you some "test questions" to ask attorneys, as a way to determine their knowledge.

• *How many adoptions have you done in your career?* The years of experience are important, as is their degree of specialization in adoption. More than anything, however, it comes down to numbers. Does this mean more is always better? Not necessarily, as long as the attorney has completed a significant number of adoptions to have sufficient experience. You will find some attorneys, particularly those in major metropolitan areas, who have completed hundreds and hundreds of adoptions, maybe even more than a thousand. That's impressive. However, that by itself does not make the attorney better than one who has completed only 150. That is still an impressive number of adoptions, and enough to have seen most possible situations come up and have experience handling them.

• *How many adoptions do you complete each year? How about last year?* These questions are particularly important for you if you are hiring an attorney to do the legal work of the adoption and to help match you with a birth mother. You will find that most adoption specialists complete from fifteen to seventy adoptions a year. Generally, the larger number is for attorneys in large cities. A high number of adoptions each year, particularly the most recent year, is impressive. As you will see in the next few questions, however, that information by itself can be misleading.

• *How many adoptive parents waiting to be matched by a birth mother do you work with at one time? Is there a maximum number you work with at one time? How many do you have at this moment?* These questions are all related, and critically important if you are looking to your attorney for his or her birth mother matching skills. Let's say attorney Bob completes sixty adoptions a year, and he works with one hundred adoptive parents at one time waiting to be matched with a birth mother. Attorney Susan only completes twenty, but she limits her number of clients waiting for a match to ten. Mathematically, Susan actually has a more successful ratio, as her clients on average are waiting six months for an adoptive match, while Bob's clients are averaging a wait of almost twice that long. Plus, assuming Susan isn't filling her time with other nonadoption cases, her smaller caseload may indicate she has more time to work on each case and to get to know each client. (Sometimes bigger is better, and sometimes it isn't. There is no simple answer, which is why there are so many factors to consider.)

• *What is the average wait for an adoptive match? What is a soonest versus longest estimate of waiting time to be picked based upon prior clients?* On your own, you can "do the math" of a typical waiting time for an adoptive match based upon the attorney's estimates of the number of adoptions done annually divided into the waiting number of clients. Still, it is helpful to hear it from the attorney. For example, if the attorney does fifty adoptions a year and works with one hundred waiting clients (one hundred divided by fifty equals two), that tells you the average wait is about two years. If that same attorney tells you his clients' average wait is five months, something is wrong. Either the attorney is not being honest about some of those figures, or there is an explanation for the disparity. Ask the attorney to explain any confusion.

• *Are most of the adoptions you help arrange "open" or "closed?"* Sometimes the issue of an adoption being open or closed is due to state law on the subject. Other times, it is due to the mind-set of the attorney who consciously or subconsciously feels one type of adoption is best, and that feeling is picked up by birth mothers and adoptive parents working with him or her.

As a general rule, most newborn adoptions in the United States are to some degree open. Usually this means meeting in person and sharing identities. Slightly more open will include the adoptive parents sending the birth mother an annual picture and updating letter about the child until adulthood. Still more open might be where it is agreed the birth mother will have some continuing face-to-face contact with you and the child. Make sure that the attorney's philosophy, and his or her typical cases, matches your preferred degree of openness.

• *Do some adoptive parents who hire you never get picked by a birth mother, or have to wait several years? Do you find these adoptive parents have any ethnic, religious, or other qualities in common?* There are two reasons to ask these questions. One is that if the attorney finds some families don't get picked by a birth mother, or have a much harder time being picked, you want to know if you fall into that category. For example, if you are a Hispanic couple seeking a Hispanic child, and you are hiring an attorney who is in a predominantly Caucasian region, there will be fewer birth mothers of your ethnicity to select you. It would likely make more sense for such couples to select an attorney in a border state, like California or Texas, with a higher percentage of Hispanics. This would make more sense than hiring an attorney in Idaho, for example.

The same issue can arise regarding religion. Parts of Utah, where the Mormon religion is quite prevalent, would be an example of this. A non-Mormon family would likely find that attorneys practicing in Utah would be less effective for them. America is a very heterogeneous nation, however, and many adoptions cross cultural and ethnic lines. Still, the reality is that many birth mothers and adoptive parents' first choice is to stay within their ethnic group. If an attorney isn't suited for your particular individual characteristics, it is best to know it right away.

The second reason to ask an attorney if some of their clients don't get picked is to judge their honesty. The reality is that some adoptive parents desiring a newborn child won't get picked by a birth mother, just as some wonderful people out there will never find the love of their life and get married. Life is not always fair. To me, if an attorney tells you *every* client gets picked, this either means he or she has only handled a small number of adoptions over a short period of time, or the attorney is exaggerating his or her success. There is nothing wrong with an attorney telling you some adoptive parents fail. The key is how often it happens and why. If only a small percentage of adoptive parents are not picked, such as less than 5 percent, the 95 percent success rate is actually incredibly successful. (Later we will discuss strategies to almost guarantee you will not end up in the small percentage of adoptive parents who do not succeed.)

• *Does the state in which you practice allow you to find birth mothers for adoptive parents and create a match?* Several states either bar attorneys from "finding" birth mothers to create an adoptive match, or may permit it but forbid the attorney to charge for it. These states include Connecticut, Georgia, Illinois, Maryland, Minnesota, New Jersey, and New York. If you live in one of these states (and plan to finalize your adoption in your home state, as most do), it should not discourage you if your attorney can't introduce you to birth mothers. Although it is great when an attorney has the added benefit of finding a birth mother for you, let's not forget that an attorney's primary role—and a critical one—is to give you legal advice at all stages of your adoption. This is an especially important role in your home state. If you want an attorney to be networking for you, in addition to your own networking efforts (or in place of it), you can consider retaining an out-of-state attorney in addition to your home state attorney, as discussed elsewhere in this book.

• *What methods do you use to find birth mothers, or to help us do it, resulting in a birth mother selecting us?* There are many strategies you, as well as your attorney, can use to find women facing unplanned pregnancies and wanting to start an adoption. Later, I'll be sharing my most successful networking methods, including some unusual ones. Every attorney has his favorite methods, and you need to make sure you agree with the methods your potential attorney plans to use.

Some attorneys practice in states where it is not legal for them to attempt to find birth mothers (the state-by-state review tells you which these states are). Accordingly, in those states, the attorney will give you advice on what techniques he or she thinks are best. You will want to make sure that you see eye to eye on the methods to be used, as either you or the attorney may not feel comfortable with some types the other plans to use. Some networking strategies are very aggressive and public, which some adoptive parents might find uncomfortable. There are also many subtle and more private techniques. Regardless of the kind of networking campaign you plan to employ, you want to make sure the attorney shares your view.

• *What percentage of the birth mothers you find are in state, as compared to coming from another state?* If you don't care which state your birth mother resides in (affecting your travel costs, easy access to the birth mother prebirth and at birth, and the state law that will apply), this may not be an important issue for you. However, if you are retaining an attorney in, let's say, Washington State, because you want a Washington State birth mother, or you want to do a nonresident adoption there, why would you want to retain an attorney who finds all his or her birth mothers via a method leading to out-of-state birth mother contacts, such as out-of-state yellow page or Internet advertisements?

• *When birth mothers contact you, how are we and other adoptive parents shown to her, giving us a chance to be selected?* Some attorneys show all their waiting adoptive parents, while some favor those who have waited the longest, showing those families at the exclusion of his or her newest clients. Others only show a few adoptive parents, selected to match characteristics of the birth mother.

I believe the best approach is to show every adoptive family to every birth mother, unless the birth mother has characteristics not desired by the adoptive parents (ethnicity, drug usage, projected expenses, open or closed adoption, etc.). The reason I favor that wide approach, rather than the subjective thinking of the attorney selecting the "right" families, is it assumes the attorney knows what the birth mother is truly looking for. The reality, however, is that often opposites attract. The "spark" of attraction is impossible to define.

Furthermore, the more adoptive families the birth mother has to choose from, the more likely she will be truly happy with her decision. For example, is she more likely to find a family she truly likes, and therefore follow through on her adoption plan, if she chooses from two families or twenty? What would our chances for a successful marriage be if we had only two or three prospective spouses from which to choose? Adoption is no different.

• *What percentage of your clients find a birth mother through your efforts, as compared to your clients finding a birth mother on their own?* If one of the key things you hope to accomplish in hiring an attorney is to have his or her help in finding a birth mother to in turn select you as adoptive parents, you will want to know how effective the attorney's efforts are. For example, an attorney may complete an impressive fifty adoptions a year, but if 80 percent of the adoptive parents found their own birth mother, it is not as impressive as an attorney completing twenty-five, all of which resulted from his or her own birth mother networking efforts.

• *Does your fee include your networking efforts to help us get picked by a birth mother, or is it a separate fee?* If the attorney is networking for birth mothers, leading them to contact his or her office to in turn select one of the waiting adoptive families, a lot of money is being expended by the attorney in that effort. This might take the form of mailings to health-care professionals, yellow page advertising, Internet promotion of their website geared to birth mothers, contributions of time and/or money to organizations, which indirectly lead to referrals, etc. Just like with any attorney expenses, these costs are passed on to you as the client benefiting from those efforts. The question is if it is part of their standard fee, which includes their legal work, or a separate fee specifically designated for networking efforts.

It does not matter which of the two payment options the attorney uses. What does matter is that you know what you are paying for. For example, if one attorney's fee includes networking efforts, and he or she has demonstrated success with those efforts in the past leading you to believe an adoptive match is likely for you, it is understandable his or her fees will be higher than an attorney who does not offer those services. Sometimes this makes it hard to compare fees, as the services vary. However, as you start contacting many attorneys and agencies, you will soon get a feel for what is a reasonable cost for birth mother networking efforts in a particular region. This might range from a few hundred to several thousand dollars. The issue of networking, and its costs, is discussed in more detail in Chapter 8.

• *Can we be listed with other attorneys and/or agencies while we are working with you, and proceed with whichever attorney or agency finds an adoptive placement first?* The goal of every adoption agency and attorney should be to help you adopt. To that end, if you wish to hire more than one attorney to obtain your goal as quickly as possible, you need attorneys who will work within that philosophy. Most will be agreeable. Some attorneys, however, require you to only work with them. I believe this is wrong, as the attorney is making him or herself the central person in the adoption, not you. In reality, the adoption is about you and the child you will be adopting, not the attorney.

• *Do we pay for your services as we work through the adoption, or do we pay it all in advance?* Some attorneys, especially in matters like criminal cases, charge their entire fee in advance, or require a retainer for their anticipated total fee, then bill against that and return any unused portion. Adoptions tend to be billed differently. For example, if you are waiting to be matched with a birth mother, it is not yet even known if you will *have* an adoption. For that reason, many adoption attorneys charge their fee in stages, so you are only paying for the services as they are provided.

Other attorneys may charge their entire fee in advance, but you should only accept such a fee arrangement if the unused portion is held in a trust account and any unused portion will be returned to you with a written accounting of all expenses. Be very cautious of attorneys who require a disproportionate payment in advance, particularly if it is non-refundable. While you might be led to think that paying more means you are getting more, this is often not the case. Often you will find the best, most ethical attorneys charge the most reasonable fees.

• *What are typical birth mother expenses we will be expected to pay?* Almost all states allow adoptive parents to help with the adoption and birth expenses. Often this includes medical bills and the birth mother's living costs while she is incapacitated due to the pregnancy. Some birth mothers have few or no expenses (they have insurance and are employed, or live at home), while others may have significant expenses. This question is important because some attorneys either practice in an area with a higher cost of living, or choose to operate their practice in a way that results in higher birth mother costs. As a general rule, expenses for a birth mother ranging from a few hundred to several thousand for total living costs during the pregnancy is not unusual.

When you get into significantly higher amounts, however, it is a sign for potential caution. For example, does the attorney "bribe" birth mothers to work with him or her by offering them an ocean-view condo (at your expense) at quadruple the rent of a typical apartment? Does the attorney entice out-of-state birth mothers to travel to meet with you by providing them a first-class plane ticket rather than coach? Needless to say, such behavior is not conducive to a successful adoption or finding the right kind of birth mother.

• *What is the fee for your initial consultation?* Some attorneys offer free consultations. You know this because you see them offered on TV, right? Other attorneys charge you for their time, and considering legal fees range from $150 to $300 hourly depending upon where in the nation you live, a two-hour consultation with an adoption specialist will cost you approximately $300 to $600. A good consultation will completely educate you about the adoption process, not just the basic legal aspects. This would include strategies to be used to find a birth mother, screening birth mothers, what happens when meeting a birth mother in person, the hospital experience, potential risks (the birth mother's time in which to change her mind and revoke her consent, etc.), birth fathers' rights, permitted expenses, interstate adoptions, the Indian Child Welfare Act, the home study, finalization in court, and the federal adoption tax credit. The initial consultation will let you determine if you like the attorney. Does he or she explain things thoroughly? Can you imagine the attorney meeting with birth mothers and making them comfortable?

Let's get back to the enticement of free consultations. Sounds good, and in some cases, it may be. Generally speaking, however, while some attorneys, such as personal-injury attorneys, are in the habit of offering free consultations, well-qualified adoption attorneys, or any specialist for that matter, are not. Usually free consultations are offered only when the attorney's practice is lacking in clients (not that they'd admit that's the reason). Think about it. Would a successful and established heart specialist, copyright attorney, or dental surgeon sit down with you and spend two to three hours for no compensation? And then do it again for the next family after you? And the family after that? No. You generally get what you pay for. Well-qualified professionals get paid for their time, and to expect otherwise is not reasonable.

• *Do you encourage counseling for birth mothers?* Placing a child for adoption will be one of the most emotional moments of a birth mother's life. The more prepared she is, the more likely it is she can make the placement as planned. Counseling is one major tool to help prepare her for the birth and the emotions to follow. Both she and you deserve the benefits she will receive from pregnancy/adoption counseling. Some state laws require counseling and some do not. If an attorney feels counseling is not important, or in any way discourages birth mothers from receiving it, I believe it indicates a lack of not only empathy but a basic understanding of the emotions at work and the making of a successful adoption.

The answers to these questions should give you an excellent idea of the full scope of the attorney's services, fees, personality, and view of adoption. Do they match your vision of how an adoption should be handled? Do they make you feel comfortable and confident? Likely your list of possible attorneys is getting smaller and smaller, and those on it are getting better and better.

Test the Attorney's Knowledge

No, I'm not suggesting you hand your prospective attorney a number 2 pencil and a written exam. Nor am I suggesting you make it obvious—and perhaps offensive—that you are testing the attorney's knowledge. What I am recommending you do is ask about certain areas likely to arise in an adoption, which are normal questions to ask. The key here is that by the time you have finished this book, you will be savvy enough to know a good answer from a bad one.

Let's say you've narrowed down your list to just a few attorneys. It's now time to meet them in person, to see if you want to work with them. You might get some to speak to you on the phone if you explain you've read their materials and just have a question or two. For more than that, however, you will need to schedule a consultation.

Here are some recommended questions:

- *I've heard about something called the Indian Child Welfare Act. Can you explain what that is?* As we will discuss later in Chapter 12, this is a federal law, normally superseding state law. It provides that if a child is a member of an Indian tribe, or eligible for membership, the tribe must be given notice and certain procedures followed. If the attorney is unfamiliar with the Indian Child Welfare Act, or says it never applies in their state, beware. More and more adoptions are at least potentially touched by the Indian Child Welfare Act, such as where the birth mother is not actually a member, but has a small degree of tribal heritage that could make her a member. Noncompliance with the Indian Child Welfare Act can potentially invalidate an adoption, a high cost to pay for an attorney's ignorance. It is not necessary for the attorney to know every aspect of the law off the top of his or her head, but they should be aware of its importance and general terms.
- *We may do an interstate adoption. Can you explain to me how the Interstate Compact works?* As we will discuss in Chapter 12, more and more adoptions are interstate, where you live in a different state than the state in which the child is born. The Interstate Compact on the Placement of Children provides that prior to a child being transported across state lines by adoptive parents, certain procedures will apply, such as a preplacement home study of the adoptive parents, and approval from both states' Interstate Compact administrators. This is fundamental knowledge every attorney should have.
- *What are the birth mother's and birth father's rights? Can they change their minds, and if so, for how long?* These issues are the most fundamental and important of all, so the attorney should

know these issues forward and backward regarding their own state. Do not, however, expect them to know this information for other states without some research, as each state has different laws.

• *Is there a federal tax credit for adoptive parents?* If the attorney does many adoptions, he or she should certainly know about the federal tax credit. In basic terms, if the adoptive parents have a modified adjusted gross income of less than $170,820 in the year in which the adoption is completed, they are eligible for a tax credit of $11,390 per child adopted. It is not reasonable to expect an adoption attorney to know the detailed tax repercussions of adoption. That is for a professional tax advisor. However, they should know the existence and basics of the tax credit.

The above questions are just a sampling of what an attorney needs to know, but they are diversified enough to give you an idea of an attorney's knowledge. Those particular questions may not even be applicable to your individual adoption, but it doesn't matter. The questions are an excellent indicator of what your attorney knows or doesn't know. If he or she is ignorant about these issues, the same is likely true regarding other important adoption issues. If you find you know more than the attorney simply by reading this book, look for the door.

Determine If the Attorney's Personality and Approach to Adoption Matches Yours

Doing an adoption is a very emotional process with many emotional highs and, potentially, some lows. Although high legal qualifications are mandatory in the attorney you choose, they are not enough. You want someone who views adoption the same way you do. Like a marriage, you need to be on the same page for things to go smoothly.

Remember, you've got an entire nation of attorneys out there. Tens of thousands of them in fact, with several hundred being adoption specialists, offering the exact service for which you are looking. And if you end up not being satisfied with the attorney options, there are more than a thousand licensed private adoption agencies to choose from, as discussed in Chapters 5 and 6. Start your search in your own home county, expand from there to different counties within your state, and from there into different states after viewing the state-by-state review and determining which states appeal to you. Your options are limited only by your own time and effort.

For now, however, let's explore how independent adoption works and if it is right for you.

CHAPTER 4

Independent Adoption

The majority of newborn adoptions completed in the United States are done via *independent* adoption. You will often hear it referred to as *private, direct, attorney-assisted,* or *open* adoption. Why independent adoption is so popular with both birth mothers and adoptive parents can be seen in its characteristics. In some ways it is very similar to private agency adoption, but in others it is distinctly different. The most popular elements of an independent adoption are:

- Almost all adoptions involve newborns.
- A preplacement home study is not required in all states.
- There are no formal eligibility requirements.
- There is less bureaucracy.
- A match can often be made faster than via agencies.

In many states, independent and agency adoptions are almost equally popular, while in others, like California, a whopping 85 percent are independent. To see the percentage in your home state, or states from which you are considering adopting, please refer to the state-by-state review in Chapter 15. Forty-five states permit independent adoption, while five require all adoptions to be done via only the agency method. Those states are Colorado, Connecticut, Delaware, Massachusetts, and North Dakota.

Here are the basic steps in an independent adoption:

1. Retain an adoption attorney (preferably one who has his own outreach program to find birth mothers to create adoptive

matches and/or who has experience advising adoptive parents on the networking strategies they will be employing on their own).

2. Wait for the attorney to create an adoptive match for you (or find a match through your own networking efforts).
3. Have your attorney screen the birth mother to be sure it looks like a safe placement and examine the case for potential legal problems.
4. Have a preplacement home study done if one is required by your state. Your state law may provide that the home study be done by a social worker, adoption agency, or state adoption office.
5. Get to know your birth mother personally so she has confidence in you, and you in her.
6. Help her with medical and other pregnancy-related expenses, assuming she has any, and if permitted by your state.
7. Be present at the hospital to share the birth experience.
8. Bring home the baby from the hospital.
9. The birth mother consents to the adoption (some states require this before the child is released to you from the hospital).
10. The birth father consents to the adoption, waives notice, or has his rights terminated because he can't be found or fails to object.
11. Do your postplacement home study (six months in most states).
12. Have your attorney complete all necessary documents and satisfy all legal obstacles to make sure the child is fully free for adoption.
13. Go to court to finalize your adoption.
14. Receive a new birth certificate naming you as the child's biological parents, as if you gave birth to him or her.

There are a lot of choices in how you do an independent adoption. That, in fact, is one reason for its popularity. The fact that it is flexible, however, does not mean it is simple. To the contrary, there are many potential false steps in every adoption. Becoming aware of independent adoption's ins and outs and how to best use its flexibility to serve your goals are important steps to achieving success.

Eligibility Requirements

Asking what the requirements are for independent adoption is a bit of a misnomer. Why? Because there usually *are* no requirements. The restrictions commonly seen in many agency adoptions, such as your age, marital history, religion, financial status, number of children, and proof of infertility, have little relevance in independent adoption. This is because there are usually no agency guidelines that must be satisfied. Instead, the birth mother personally selects the adoptive parents based upon factors *she* deems important. If she elects to choose a single woman as the adoptive parent, fine. If she wants to choose adoptive parents where both are fifty years of age, fine. If she chooses an adoptive family where the adopting father is Caucasian and Jewish with two children from a prior marriage and the adoptive mother is African-American, Catholic, and restricted to a wheelchair, fine. It's like choosing a spouse; everyone is attracted to different kind of people.

Does this mean anyone can adopt via independent adoption? No. You still have to be approved via a home study, but its requirements will almost always be very basic, generally establishing two things: your present and past life indicates you can and will be good parents, and you were honest in telling the birth mother about yourself, so she can make an informed consent about who is adopting her baby. We will discuss the home study in more detail shortly.

The Role of the Adoption Attorney

An attorney. Do you need one? And if you do, does it have to be an adoption specialist? That's up to you. Technically, you can do an independent adoption without an attorney. You could find your own birth mother, make sure there are no legal obstacles or risks (and solve them if there are), do all the routine legal work required, select a proper agency or social worker as required in your state to do your home study, prepare your final documents, and finalize your adoption in court. Yes, it's possible, but do you want to try? The creation of your family is on the line.

Some adoptive parents think of adoption attorneys only as a route to be introduced to a birth mother to select them as adoptive parents. That is a valid reason for selecting one. Sometimes, however, finding a birth mother is the easiest part of your adoption. The real work is in screening potential adoptions, looking for legal risks (outlined in Chapter 12), noting red flags indicating risks beyond legal issues (Chapter 10), and doing the legal work needed in the adoption. By the time you've finished this book you will see how much analysis and work goes into each adoption, and why the chances of your adoption being successful increase dramatically with a qualified adoption attorney at the helm. To me, attempting an adoption without an attorney is like doing dental work on yourself. Rarely a good idea. As you learn more about independent adoption, you will see it is the adoption attorney who makes things happen in an adoption, and helps make them happen when and how they are supposed to. Because finding the right attorney is so important, Chapter 3 details forty-four individual steps and inquiries leading to finding the right attorney to best serve your unique needs.

The Home Study

The home study required in an independent adoption is usually considered less intrusive and time-consuming than in a typical agency adoption. In agency adoptions there are always two stages in a home study: preplacement (before a child is placed with you) and postplacement (after a child is placed with you). In independent adoptions, however, approximately half the states do not require a preplacement home study. The state-by-state review tells you which states waive this requirement. Surprisingly, a few states not only don't require a preplacement home study but the court can waive even a postplacement home study, meaning there is no home study at all. These states are Hawaii, Mississippi, and Wyoming.

The fact that often no home study is required before a child is placed with you, and only occurs postplacement, might sound quite odd. The rationale behind it makes sense, however. In an agency adoption, as a legal matter the birth mother is technically placing the child with the agency, and the agency uses its judgment to place a child with selected adoptive parents. Whether or not the birth mother had a role in selecting the adoptive parents, it was the agency that officially made the placement, typically making it legally responsible. To protect itself from that liability, a home study is their safeguard. In independent adoptions, it is usually the birth mother who is personally making the placement, based upon her judgment of the adoptive parents, not those of an intermediary agency. Even if she met the adoptive parents through an attorney, as is typical in independent adoption, it is the birth mother who is the "placing person." Not an agency. Not the attorney.

As a practical matter, it is very, very rare for adoptive parents in an independent adoption to be denied due to their home study. Virtually all adoptive parents know from the beginning what their home study will entail for them and don't attempt to start a process they know will not be approved. Plus it also helps that the standard is very basic, simply showing that you will be a secure and loving parent, and that you were honest in describing your life situation to the birth mother, without the sometimes subjective approval of a private agency.

Each state has different regulations and procedures regarding who may perform an independent adoption home study. In some states a special state adoption office, usually a division of its social services office, has been staffed to perform all independent adoption home studies. Other states allow private agencies, social workers, or people approved by the court to perform it.

Home study fees vary. If a preplacement home study is required, the cost may vary from state to state, between $500 and $2,500, and the study usually takes four to ten weeks to complete once started. The postplacement is lengthier (usually six months) and frequently costs between $500 and $6,000. Most fall in the middle. If you live in a state where private agencies are the designated entity to do your independent adoption home study, the agency fee is usually significantly less than if the same agency were performing a full traditional agency adoption, where it would be performing more services for you and the birth mother.

A typical independent adoption home study will include the following:

- Your completion of forms describing your life history (health, employment, marital history, existence of other children, religion, age, etc.). Unlike a private agency, however, which may exclude you based upon your answers, the independent adoption home study entity is simply collecting the information to provide to the court and share with the birth mother when appropriate.
- You will be fingerprinted for a criminal and child abuse check.
- A basic physical, usually with your personal physician. (If you

have a physical impairment, or one spouse has a reduced life expectancy, this will not necessarily disqualify you in an independent adoption, but is a fact that will need to be shared with the birth mother.)

- Several letters of reference from friends/neighbors, whom you select.
- Verification of marriage (if married).
- Verification of the existence of health insurance, or a plan to deal with medical costs if you don't have insurance.
- Verification of employment. (The issue is simply that you can meet your family's needs, not reach a designated high-income level.)
- Proof that any prior marriages were terminated by a court of law (via a certified copy of the divorce decree).
- Reports from your child's pediatrician that you have been properly caring for the child.
- Verification of assets and any past bankruptcies. (The only concern here is if you show an inability to properly manage your resources, which could therefore put your family at financial risk. A prior bankruptcy, followed by financial stability, would rarely be seen to demonstrate financial instability.)
- Home visits by your social worker. Most states require between two and four, usually over a six-month period. If a preplacement home study is required, both adoptive parents must usually be present at home at the same time. In the postplacement home study, both adoptive parents and the child are usually expected to be present. In almost all cases these visits are by appointment, not "surprise" visits.
- Inspecting your home. Unlike becoming a foster parent, or even an adoptive parent in an agency adoption, an independent adoption home study will usually not need to meet the same safety levels imposed upon foster or agency adoptive parents. The reason traces back to the rationale that in those placements the agency is usually liable for any injuries to the child that might result from an accident. In independent adoptions, the birth mother is making the placement directly, usually without an intermediary taking over her role as the "placing person." For example, in a

foster parent home study, the agency might require them to have latches on all toilets and cabinets, even if the child to be placed is, at present, a baby and unable to move from his crib. In an independent adoption, many states will only require that the adoptive parents make changes that are necessary for the child's safety at the present time and simply recommend alterations to be considered when needed as the child grows. This is closer to the decision-making freedom parents have when conceiving a child themselves.

The Children Available

Virtually all children available through independent adoption are newborns. They are of all ethnic groups, typically mirroring the ethnicity of the community in which they live. If you live in a region that is mainly Caucasian, most birth mothers will be Caucasian, meaning Caucasian placements. If your region is predominantly Hispanic, expect most of the placements to be Hispanic.

It is understandable why so many adoptive parents select independent adoption as their chosen method of adoption, but why do so many birth mothers do so? There are several reasons. Many birth mothers may feel a stigma about approaching an adoption agency and feel better about contacting a private attorney. (This stigma is unfair to most agencies, as most are staffed by nonjudgmental, caring people, but the stigma still exists in the minds of many birth mothers.) Also, adoption attorneys are often more aggressive in their networking efforts to reach birth mothers, resulting in more referrals. Furthermore, independent adoption has the reputation of being more open and direct, which is pleasing to most birth mothers.

Waiting for a Child

There is no absolute guarantee of adopting quickly, even in an independent adoption. The vast majority of adoptive parents, however, report they successfully adopt a baby within eighteen months via this method. For many lucky couples the waiting time can be only a few weeks or months (and I will later tell you how you can be one of them). One reason for this is that there are usually no "waiting lists" employed in independent adoption, where the adoptive parents must wait to get to the top of a list to be considered for an adoptive placement. Instead, most independent adoption attorneys show all their waiting adoptive parent families and leave the decision of who is the best family completely up to the birth mother (assuming the adoptive parents want to be shown to that particular birth mother). Also, many states do not require a preplacement home study, allowing you to start the process instantly, rather than waiting several months or more to complete a home study, therefore reducing the waiting time for a placement.

Even if you live in a state that requires a preplacement home study for independent adoption, you can still normally start networking for, and meeting, birth mothers immediately. You would just concurrently start the preplacement home study, as typically it must be completed before a baby is placed with you. Even if you met a birth mother almost immediately, she will likely not be due before you could complete the home study. (Compare this to most agency adoptions, where you usually cannot start working toward a birth mother match until the preplacement home study is complete.)

The Openness of the Adoption

Many people think of independent and "open" adoption as being synonymous. This is confusing as *open* adoption is a vague term and can mean many things. When used to describe independent adoption, it usually refers, at minimum, to the fact that most adoptive parents and birth mothers meet in person (or at least by phone if they live in different states), and share first, or more commonly both first and last, names. Each state has different requirements and traditions about openness. The state-by-state review tells you what to expect in your state.

For birth mothers, personally meeting and selecting you can be emotionally rewarding, as she can develop complete confidence in you as adoptive parents, greatly enhancing her likelihood of placing the baby for adoption as planned. She can visualize you as the child's parents and the child being nurtured by you. She can also take pride in her active role in personally creating your family, rather than relinquishing that role to an agency.

You also benefit from becoming acquainted before the birth. You can learn more about your child's biological mother in person, rather than reading about her from an impersonal written analysis. You will be able to share important information with your child about how the adoption occurred and why his birth mother felt adoption was her most loving option for the child—issues of great importance to a child as he grows.

A small number of states allow for confidentiality in independent adoption, as is done in some agency placements. Usually this is done by the use of an intermediary, such as an attorney, who will provide information about the birth mother and adoptive parents to each other, allowing each individual to withhold their identities if they so desire. This practice is rare, however, and even when states permit it the birth mother and adoptive parents often voluntarily opt for sharing full identities.

This open relationship can continue postbirth. The overwhelming majority of postbirth arrangements call for the birth mother to receive pictures of the child and updating letters from you once or twice a year (often the child's birthday and Christmas) and a promise from you that you will be raising your child with the knowledge that he was placed with you out of love by his birth mother. It is not uncommon for her to give you a photo of herself and perhaps a letter to the child describing why this was the best way for her to show her love.

Sometimes, even if you and the birth mother have become well acquainted before the birth, some birth mothers elect to have complete privacy after the birth and wish no further contact. Not all are comfortable with openness. Only about 5 percent feel this way, however. An equally small number wish to stay in contact with you, but expand that contact to what is usually called "cooperative adoption." A less technical term would simply be "a very open adoption." This would be where you and the birth mother agree that you will send pictures and letters and also maintain a face-to-face relationship, perhaps getting together one or several times a year. Some adoptive parents embrace this openness, while others feel uncomfortable. Talking about the issue with an adoption counselor, as well as your attorney, and reading some of the many books on the subject (see Appendix A) will help you determine what is right for you and your child. Regardless of what you decide, the degree of openness your adoption will have should be discussed with the birth mother before the birth to be sure you all have matching expectations.

Fees and Costs

There are several areas of possible expenses in an independent adoption. The major ones are:

- Attorney fees
- Home study costs
- Possible medical and pregnancy-related expenses for the birth mother

An attorney is usually considered a necessity in an independent adoption as there is no adoption agency overseeing the entire process. Even if adoptive parents find their own birth mother, there are many legal issues to be addressed requiring an attorney's skill and knowledge. Although the attorney's degree of involvement will vary from case to case, thus affecting the cost of the adoption, most adoption specialists charge between $1,500 and $9,000 to handle all aspects of an uncontested, independent adoption, depending upon many factors. The three biggest factors are the extent of the services offered, their location, and reputation. Attorneys in more populated cities and highly commercial states tend to have higher fees than small-town counterparts. And, of course, attorneys with established reputations and a history of success, like in any profession, are going to charge more than those lacking those qualities. Also, some attorneys expend a great deal of time and money in networking and outreach efforts to locate birth mothers, who in turn select their waiting clients. This can greatly increase the attorney's overhead costs, so expect to pay a few thousand dollars more if your attorney is also performing that service.

For their fee attorneys typically do the following:

- Fully educate you on the laws and procedures in adoption, and advise you on how to plan a successful adoption.
- Use an established outreach program to find birth mothers, or advise you on how to effectively do it on your own.

- Screen birth mothers to eliminate inadvisable situations.
- Obtain necessary background and health information about the birth parents.
- Provide physician, counseling, and hospital referrals to the birth mother.
- Examine the case for potential legal or practical difficulties.
- Attempt to contact the birth father and give any legal notices required.
- Handle any legal problems that may arise.
- Help the assigned social worker process the home study by providing what is needed.
- Manage an attorney-client trust account to provide expenses to the birth mother or other parties (doctors, landlord, etc.) on behalf of the adoptive parents.
- Prepare the necessary legal documents.
- Appear in court to finalize the adoption.

Expenses for the birth mother may exist. If she needs assistance with expenses related to the birth, such as her medical costs or her living expenses, you can usually assist her by paying some or all of those expenses. Such assistance allows a birth mother to stay in her own residence when she would otherwise be short on rent, rather than relocating to an agency-style maternity home, which may not be comfortable for her. Or she may be without a place to stay and you can help get her into an apartment. Each state has different regulations regarding what assistance may be provided and for how long. A small number of states forbid adoptive parents to provide any expenses other than medical and legal costs, not permitting help with such expenses as food and rent. Generally, however, if the expenses are *pregnancy-related*, they are permitted. Financial assistance can usually be provided not only during the pregnancy if she is unable to provide for herself but also after the birth for a month or two, while she recuperates.

Of course, in some cases, there may be no pregnancy-related expenses. For example, if a birth mother has health insurance (perhaps through her parents' policy or her own employment) or state-provided Medicaid, there may be no medical costs for you. Similarly, although some birth mothers are impoverished and desperately need financial help to pay for basic food and rent during the latter stages of the pregnancy, there are many birth mothers who require absolutely nothing, as they have adequate employment or live with their parents or partner with no rental expenses.

Other less-substantial expenses may involve the purchase of some maternity clothes and arranging for adoption counseling to prepare for the birth and adoption experience. These expenses usually total several hundred dollars.

Many adoption professionals estimate the total cost of most attorney-assisted independent adoptions, including attorney fees, home study fees, and medical and living expenses (if any), to range between $4,000 and $20,000. Usually costs only go significantly higher if there are medical complications not covered by insurance. Particular expenses, as well as suggestions to reduce or eliminate such critical expenses as medical fees, will be addressed in subsequent chapters.

Bringing the Baby Home

One of the nicest parts about independent adoption is that it normally allows you to bring the baby home directly from the hospital. There is virtually never an intermediate foster parent placement while you wait for the birth mother's consent to become irrevocable, or other procedural steps to be satisfied. (The popularity of immediate placements in independent adoption has caused many private agencies to duplicate the practice in their adoptions.) Most states allow the birth mother to release her child directly into your physical custody immediately upon the hospital's discharge of the baby, usually when the baby is two or three days old.

There is a great benefit to you in taking your baby home immediately. Every new parent, adoptive or otherwise, knows the early days of a child's life are precious and irreplaceable. Naturally, the child also benefits from being with you immediately as his or her future parents, rather than foster parents. But there is also a disadvantage. There is always a possibility you will bond to a child the birth mother has not yet permanently released for adoption and that she may seek to reclaim. This rarely occurs, but you have to be aware it is a risk.

As is discussed in Chapter 12 and the state-by-state review, each state law is different regarding when a birth mother signs her consent and when it becomes permanent. Some states' laws permit the birth mother to sign her official consent to the adoption while she is in the hospital, or within several days of the birth. Other states take her consent weeks or even months later. Although the adoptive parents are normally permitted to bring the baby home during the interim between birth and the signing of the consent to adoption, this leaves a window of risk where the birth mother could change her mind about the adoption and seek to reclaim the baby. Many adoption experts agree, however, that in professionally arranged adoptions fewer than 5 percent of birth mothers seek to stop an adoption once the child is placed. In some ways, it seems incongruous that adoption is viewed as risky, considering that approximately 15 percent of pregnancies result in spontaneous miscarriage. Oddly, this makes adoption a less risky venture than pregnancy itself.

Identified Adoptions

An *identified* adoption (sometimes called a *designated* adoption) is a hybrid of an independent and an agency adoption. Sometimes adoptive parents like some aspects of an independent adoption and other aspects of an agency adoption. Combine them, and what you have is an identified adoption.

An identified adoption typically involves your selection of an adoption attorney to network for birth mothers, screen potential birth mothers, create your adoptive match, then refer the birth mother to an agency to provide counseling, do your home study, and perhaps witness her consent. Depending upon the laws and procedures of your state, the attorney and agency will divide their legal duties to you, working together to get you into court and have your adoption approved. Essentially, identified adoptions start as an independent adoption, but are finalized as an agency adoption.

What is the advantage of this type of hybrid adoption? Usually it is increased speed or safety. Let's say for example that you think an attorney will be more effective in quickly matching you with a birth mother and spotting potential legal risks in the adoption. This makes independent adoption attractive. But maybe you live in a state that has different procedures for how a birth mother gives up her rights in each type of adoption. For example, maybe the state gives a birth mother seventy-two hours to change her mind and reclaim her child in an agency adoption, and the same state gives her thirty days in an independent adoption. You want to reduce the at-risk time you face postbirth, so you want to complete the adoption as an agency adoption. Presto, a hybrid—identified adoption.

Working with an Out-of-State Attorney

The majority of adoptive parents will do every aspect of the adoption in the state in which they live. This is true whether they are doing an independent or agency adoption. They will hire an attorney there, the birth mother will live and give birth there, and the adoption will be finalized in their local court. If you live in a state with great attorneys from whom to choose, good adoption laws making you feel secure, and a sufficient number of birth mothers in your region or state, why leave your own state?

Many adoptive parents aren't so lucky. What if you don't like what the local attorneys have to offer? Perhaps there are few adoptive placements in your region or state. Maybe you are concerned that your state has laws that give a birth mother an excessively long period in which to change her mind. Or it could be that your state is fine, but you want to expand your options to increase the likelihood of being picked for an adoptive placement quickly. Clearly, there are many reasons to either do your adoption out of state or work in both your home state and another state concurrently. Let's look at the two primary ways to do this.

Interstate adoption. Let's say you've found an exceptional attorney, but he or she is located in another state. Does that mean you can't work with that attorney because you are in a different state? No. In fact, it is getting more and more common to have an interstate aspect to adoptions. For example, you can hire the out-of-state attorney to help you find a birth mother and create your adoptive match, arrange for birth mother counseling, assist with her signing her consent to adoption, and have the child discharged directly to you from the hospital. Then, very shortly after birth, when the initial paperwork is done and you get interstate approval to bring the child across state lines (discussed in Chapter 12), you return home and raise the child there. Depending upon the laws of your home state, you would probably also have an in-state attorney and agency. The agency would do your home study and write the final report to the court to complete the adoption, and the attorney would do any legal work needed in your home state. Doing an adoption involving two states sometimes creates a conflict between state's laws, although rarely does this become a problem. This issue is discussed in Chapter 12.

A twist on the above is if the out-of-state attorney finds a birth mother for you and creates the planned placement, but perhaps the birth mother doesn't wish to stay in that state. Perhaps she has no place to live and has recently lost her job. To get to know you better and have you close for the moment the birth occurs, you can discuss having her relocate for the birth to your home state. After the birth she may return to her original state, relocate elsewhere, or decide she likes what your state has to offer and stay. In an adoption such as this, your local attorney and/or agency would be performing all the needed legal functions, other than creating the initial act of creating the adoptive match.

You might worry that using an attorney out of state and another attorney or agency in your home state would double the cost. That is not true, however. As discussed in more detail in Chapter 9, many attorneys and agencies only charge for the services they perform. Accordingly, if they are dividing their duties, their fees should be proportionally less. Not every adoption professional will work that way, but most will.

Nonresident adoption. Some adoptive parents want to do virtually the entire adoption outside their home state. You might choose to do this because your state allows a birth mother a long time to change her mind and the birth state's laws only permit a few days. Maybe you recognize birth mothers are more likely to start adoption planning if you are permitted to help them with their pregnancy-related costs, and your state does not permit them, but the laws of the birth state do. Or perhaps your adoption can be finalized in court much faster out of state. For these reasons, you might want to adopt from a state permitting independent nonresident adoption.

Many states permit independent nonresident adoption. They are Alabama, Alaska, Arkansas, California, Hawaii, Iowa, Indiana, Kansas,

Louisiana, Maine, Maryland, Michigan, Missouri, New Hampshire, New Jersey, New Mexico, New York, North Dakota, Ohio, Oregon, Pennsylvania, South Carolina, Texas, Utah, Virginia, and Washington. You can learn more about each state's laws and the attorneys and agencies within that state in the state-by-state review. It also provides the number of annual adoptions completed in each state, giving you an idea of the chance of success of adoption within that state. This can range from more than 10,000 adoptions in one state to only a few hundred in others.

A nonresident adoption is basically just like the interstate adoption discussed above. You selected an out-of-state attorney to help match you with a birth mother. That attorney, however, continues to do virtually everything in the adoption, rather than transferring everything to your home state. After creating the adoptive match, he or she can offer counseling for the birth mother, make sure the child is placed with you directly from the hospital, arrange for the birth mother to sign her consent to adoption, and arrange for your adoption to be finalized in its local court. An agency in your home state will only be needed to do any required home study work as determined by the laws of the state of where the child is born and the attorney is located. Unlike interstate adoptions, where there can be a potential conflict of laws between the two states, in nonresidency adoption generally only the laws of the birth state will apply, as everything was done there. Nonresident adoptions can also be done working with an agency in both states, rather than an attorney, making the adoption an agency, rather than an independent, adoption.

When Independent Adoption Is Not Permitted in Your State

Five states do not permit independent adoption, requiring that all adoptions be completed only by agencies. These states are Colorado, Connecticut, Delaware, Massachusetts, and North Dakota. If you live in one of these states, you must either do an agency adoption in state or work with another state. If you elect to do an out-of-state adoption, you may still be able to initiate the adoption with an attorney, as long as your home state completes it as a full agency adoption. Because each region within these states may differ on this policy, however, it is best to check with the agency that will be doing your home study and writing the final report to the court, to be sure they foresee no problems with your plan. Alternatively, you can do a nonresident adoption, which will virtually eliminate your state and its laws from the adoption. Even there, however, the out-of-state authorities will want to see a home study of you from an agency in your area, so check in advance to be sure they will cooperate in that plan. Usually, there are no problems.

CHAPTER 5

Agency Adoption

There are two basic types of adoption agencies: private and public. Despite sharing the term "agency" adoptions, they are actually quite different. This is true in the services they offer, the fees they charge, and the children they place. In fact, most private agency adoptions are more like independent adoptions than they are like public agency adoptions.

In Chapter 2, we looked at fourteen different types of adoption in capsule form. Of those, nine types are fully or partially agency adoptions:

- Private adoption agencies performing services in your home state.
- Private adoption agencies located outside your home state, but able to create matches for you, with the adoption to be finalized in the court of your home state.
- Private adoption agencies located in states permitting nonresidency adoption, allowing you to retain an out-of-state agency and finalize the adoption in the state where the child was born, under that state's laws.
- Identified adoptions, where an attorney and agency are working together, using elements of both an independent and agency adoption.
- Public adoption agencies.
- The foster parent shortcut.
- Special-needs registries.
- International adoption by agencies located in your state.
- International adoption by out-of-state agencies.

Some of these methods can only be done via private agencies, while others fall into the domain of public agencies. To better understand these many options, we need to explore how agencies work and how they can best be used to help you accomplish your adoption goals. It is interesting that only a few decades ago, almost all adoptions were done through agencies. As time went on, independent adoption became the most popular type (for newborn adoption). Agency adoption, however, remains a very viable adoption method, and in some states is still the most common way to complete an adoption.

Comparing Public and Private Agencies

Private agencies are privately operated businesses. They are licensed by the state in which they operate to conduct adoptive parent home studies and/or place children for adoption. Some agencies only do one or the other, but most do both. Some additionally help match adoptive parents with birth mothers and may even actively network and advertise to make birth mothers aware of their existence. Most agencies only do domestic adoptions, but some do international adoptions. (International adoption is separately discussed in Chapter 7.) Adoption agencies are principally supported by the fees they receive from adoptive parents. A listing of virtually every adoption agency in the nation is provided in the state-by-state review in Chapter 15, with notations regarding whether they focus on domestic or international adoption.

Public adoption agencies are completely different than private. Public agencies are operated by the county or state in which they are located and are supported by tax dollars. The main function of public agencies is to find homes for children for whom the county or state has assumed responsibility. These agencies, usually referred to as public adoption agencies, are often a branch of your state social services department. You can find your local public adoption agency in several ways. The state-by-state review provides each state's central adoption office, which can direct you to the public adoption agency serving your area. You can also check your local phone book and look under government listings for your county under "adoption."

Although public adoption agencies are usually licensed to accept birth mothers' relinquishment of newborns, their most important function has evolved in recent years to finding homes for "waiting" children (in foster care and free for adoption) and children with special needs or hard-to-place characteristics. For this reason, unlike private agencies, they rarely network or advertise their services in an effort to reach birth mothers.

Free Seminars

A nice thing about adoption agencies, both public and private, is that they typically offer free seminars to learn about their services. Compare this to attorneys, who will almost always charge you for an initial consultation. The difference, however, is that the typical agency free seminar is in a group setting scheduled at a time dictated by the agency, while attorney consultations are private and scheduled at a time you have agreed to. When you attend agency seminars, I strongly encourage you to bring a question list so you leave fully informed. The seminar is your chance to learn exactly what their services are and what they can and can't do for you, as well as at what cost.

The Agency's Licensing Status

Both public and private agencies are licensed by the state and a failure to perform their services properly can result in the revocation of their licenses. Agencies are also licensed to do different things. Virtually all are licensed to perform home studies. Some will be licensed to perform either domestic or international home studies, while a smaller number does both. Domestic agencies may also be licensed to place children for adoption, acting as a state-approved intermediary of sorts between the birth mother and adoptive parents. Agencies that do home studies *and* make adoptive placements are often called "full service" agencies. In some states all agencies are full service, while other states issue separate licenses for each permitted service. For these reasons, you need to ask each agency:

1. Are they licensed by the state as an adoption agency?
2. Are they licensed to perform services in your county? (Many states require agencies to be approved on a county-by-county basis, with some being statewide and others approved in only one county.)
3. What services are they permitted to perform?

Clearly, there is no benefit to you in hiring an agency if they can't perform the duties you need done, so the above are threshold questions. The first inquiry about asking if they are "licensed as an agency" may sound unnecessary, but that is not the case. The reality is that you must verify the agency you are considering is licensed as an actual *licensed adoption agency* by the state in which it operates. Some individuals or organizations use names that sound like adoption agencies, when in fact they are not. Instead, they are generally what are referred to as *facilitators*. Facilitators are those who render the limited service of finding a baby for a fee. Chapter 8 addresses the risks of facilitators. To verify an agency's present valid licensing status, the state-by-state review provides contact information for the state office, usually called the state's Department of Social Services, or a similar title, and located in the state capital, and a department within that office will be responsible for overseeing adoption agencies and their licensing.

Religious Affiliation

Private agencies can be divided into *denominational* and *nondenominational* categories. Denominational agencies are those affiliated with a particular religious faith. Generally, these agencies are easy to recognize based upon the agency's name (e.g., Catholic Family Services, Church of Jesus Christ of Latter-day Saints Social Services, Jewish Family Services, etc.). However, the name can't solely be relied upon, as some agency names bear little relation to the religious entity to which they are affiliated.

The opposite is also true. Some private agencies employ religiously oriented names with no official association with that faith, perhaps thinking it will boost business with birth mothers or adoptive parents by associating itself with that religion. For these reasons it is necessary to look beyond the name and question individual agencies to determine their status.

An important fact about denominational agencies not known by most people is that some denominational agencies do not require adoptive parents to be of the faith with which the agency is affiliated. This may be beneficial when you live in a region where there are few agencies from which to choose, or if you find the policies of one particular agency matches your desires, even though the agency is affiliated with a different religion.

Public adoption agencies are different. They are forbidden to have any religious ties, or to use religion to determine the general eligibility of adoptive parents.

Eligibility Requirements of Adoptive Parents

Each agency, whether private or public, sets eligibility requirements for you as adoptive parents. These can vary from state to state, and even from agency to agency within a state. Speaking very generally, however, here are some typical guidelines followed by many agencies:

- Be no more than forty years of age older than the child you will be adopting. If you plan to adopt a newborn, this means that you could not be older than forty. If you were seeking to adopt a child age five, your maximum age would be forty-five. Be aware, however, that although there continues to be some age restrictions, more and more agencies are eliminating the age requirement and taking more of a "whole person" view of the adoptive parents in finding the right parents for each child. The more "conservative" states, however, have held on to this requirement.
- Marital status. If you are married, you must be pursuing an adoption in conjunction and with the agreement of your spouse. Almost all agencies will now permit singles to adopt.
- If married, be married a minimum number of years (usually two).
- Don't have what the agency may consider to be an excessive number of prior marriages. Some agencies will permit only one prior marriage per spouse, while others will allow several.
- Live in a home suitable for a child. The days of requiring home ownership are largely gone. Usually renting either a house or an apartment is acceptable, as long as the housing will be safe and appropriate for a child, and he or she will have his or her own bedroom. An agency social worker will visit your home to make sure it appears safe for a child. These visits are almost always by appointment, not the "surprise" visits that are part of agency adoption lore. The agency has the right to require certain safety precautions prior to a child being placed (safety gates, drawer latches, etc.).
- Be of reasonably good health with the expectation to live at least until the child becomes an adult, and do not have any contagious diseases that could put a child at risk.

- Be medically unable to conceive a child, or show it is physically unsafe to give birth. The agency goal here is to be sure you are not adopting for an inappropriate reason, such as a goal to not gain weight during a pregnancy, or the "save a child" mentality that will result in the unreasonable expectation that a child should be grateful for being adopted.
- Have no more than one child already. (Many agencies are eliminating this requirement.)
- Have at least one spouse securely employed with sufficient income to support a family. Being newly employed is usually fine if there is a history of employment.
- Some agencies require one spouse to be a full-time, stay-at-home parent, although most have eliminated this requirement and both parents can be employed. Almost all agencies, however, encourage one parent to stay at home—rather than put the child in the care of day-care providers—as one of many factors contributing to the best interests of a child.
- No criminal record or child abuse history. This is a serious issue. In fact, most states' fingerprinting is so in-depth that it will show even sealed and expunged adult criminal records. This does not mean that you can't adopt if you have made a mistake in your life. If a crime was of a nonviolent nature (e.g., shoplifting or intoxication), and it was an isolated incident where many years have gone by without a repeat of such behavior, it might be overlooked. If the arrest was for a violent crime, however, that single offense will almost always be deemed grounds to deny you.
- No history of serious financial mismanagement. The agency will want to be sure you manage your resources well, so your family will be financially secure. A history of financial problems, such as bankruptcies or repossessions, can lead to denial. Often a single bankruptcy, if followed by a significant period of financial stability to show it was an aberration, will not be deemed a reason to deny you.

Remember, these are *general* requirements. Your state, or certain agencies within your state, might be stricter or more lenient. Also, be aware that even within a single agency, their requirements might differ. Because they recognize the difficulty of finding homes for special-needs or hard-to-place children, many of the eligibility requirements (other than a criminal background) might be more flexible. For example, the agency will often allow adoptive parents to have more than a forty-year age differential. Single parents are also considered where they otherwise might not be. In fact, some states report one of every five agency adoptions is by a single parent. Couples who already have several children, or who are not infertile but wish to adopt, are often also welcomed. Those not interested in adopting a special-needs child can still apply to adopt through the public adoption agency, although often long waits are reported by those waiting for a newborn, with some never receiving a placement.

If you find the agency you hoped to work with, but it will not work with you because you do not meet their requirements, it's no cause for concern. You still have many options. You can work with more flexible agencies within your state. You can work with an out-of-state agency. Or, you can do an independent or international adoption.

Fees and Costs

Like other businesses, private adoption agencies offer services for a fee and must make a sufficient profit to remain in operation. Most agencies are *nonprofit* agencies. Nonprofit agencies may receive financial assistance from charitable entities. A small number of agencies are operated on a *for-profit* basis. As long as the agency is licensed by the state as an adoption agency, there is usually little difference between the services of a nonprofit and for-profit agency, although some view nonprofit agencies as more altruistic and reliable. Often, for-profit agencies charge higher fees, as they are solely supported by the fees earned from adoptive parents. Most states require all agencies to be nonprofit.

The term "nonprofit" causes confusion for many. To most people it implies the people working there are doing so merely out of dedication for no pay, like a volunteer. To the contrary, however, virtually every key employee is earning a salary, just as they would at any job. The designation of a business as nonprofit is principally a tax designation.

Fees can vary tremendously among private agencies. Depending upon the type of agency, the services being offered, and the state in which it is located, fees may range from approximately $500 to

$25,000. The average fees fall between $4,000 and $15,000. Some agencies don't use flat fees and instead adjust their fee based upon your income and use a sliding scale. This sliding scale fee typically varies from 8 percent to 12 percent of your joint pretax annual income.

The fee usually covers the adoptive parent preplacement home study, adoption education and counseling for you and birth parents, the postplacement home study and evaluation of the adopted child's progress in the adoptive home, and the final court report showing your approval for the adoption to be granted. Not all agencies offer these complete services, however, so each agency you are considering must be questioned. Usually a portion of the agency fee is paid when the preplacement home study is started, with the balance due when the child is placed in the adoptive home. Most private agencies request additional funds from you if the birth mother needs assistance with her medical expenses or other birth-related costs, just as in independent adoption. Other agencies may include such costs in their agency fee and forbid any such expenditures directly by you. Usually these agencies refuse to incur many pregnancy expenses, however, and offer little flexibility to a birth mother. For example, if she needs a place to live, they are more likely to insist she stay in their maternity home, rather than rent her own apartment. Many birth mothers don't like the rigidity and go to another agency or attorney.

The same fee flexibility can be seen in the agency's networking services, if it offers them. Some agencies will include birth mother outreach efforts in their flat fee. Others will make it a separate optional program. It doesn't matter which method is used, as long as you know what you are getting for your money.

Public agencies have a completely different fee structure than their private counterparts. Many offer their services for free, while some may charge a very minimal fee, often approximately $500. The expenses of public agencies are paid via taxes like other government services. The reason public agencies basically underwrite the adoptions they do is because:

1. Virtually all of the children are presently in foster homes and would benefit from a permanent adoptive home.
2. Most of the children waiting for placement are in a hard-to-place category (physical or mental challenge, age, being part of a

sibling group to be adopted together, being of an ethnic minority where there is a shortage of adoptive parents).

3. The continued placement of the children in foster homes until age eighteen would cost the government even more money than underwriting the adoption.

4. The best interests of the children will be served by having the permanency of an adoptive home, benefiting not just the child but society in the long run.

Adoptive parents often wonder if they can use a "free" home study from a public agency, and use it toward an independent or private agency adoption, thereby saving themselves the cost of the preplacement home study. The answer is almost always no. Remember, the entire purpose of the public agency financially underwriting adoptions is to help encourage the adoption of the children in their care desperately needing homes. To provide their manpower and services at no cost, only to have adoptive parents turn around and use those services for a private newborn or international adoption, would not serve the purpose for which the public agencies exist.

In addition to the lack of any significant fees, there are almost never any costs associated with a birth mother's medical or living expenses. This is because most children come into the county agency system after having been freed for adoption through the courts. Even the few voluntary newborn adoptions the public agencies might handle usually permit no payment by the adoptive parents for a birth mother's pregnancy expenses. This usually means the public agency will either pay those costs, make sure the birth mother is eligible for government aid to cover her costs (such as Medicaid and food stamps), decline working with the birth mother, or refer her to a private agency or attorney where such expenses can be provided.

There are other limits in working with a public agency. The ability to "shop around" as with private agencies is usually not possible in the public sector. Virtually all public agencies will only accept applications from you if you reside within the county or territory they serve. Also, public agencies will normally refuse to offer their services to you if you have located your own birth mother and want the public agency to handle the adoption and take advantage of their low fee. This is because their function is to find homes for children for whom they are already responsible.

The Home Study

All agency adoptions, whether they are through a private or public agency, require a home study. Home studies are in two parts. Before the child enters your home, there is a preplacement home study to confirm you will be appropriate parents for the type of child you hope to adopt. (The agency will consider the needs of a newborn versus an older child, and those of a child in excellent health versus a child with special needs.) The satisfactory completion of the preplacement home study is a prerequisite to having a child placed in your home.

An agency social worker will be assigned to do the preplacement home study and will want to have several meetings with you, some of which will be in your home. Home visits are required to see the potential environment for a child. These visits are almost always arranged by appointment, not surprise visits.

The vast majority of agency social workers are friendly professionals who are anxious to help you succeed at adoption, although a small number may be judgmental and take advantage of the power they have over whether a child will be placed with you. To avoid such an unpleasant experience, a list of suggested questions to ask potential agencies is provided in Chapter 6.

Because most agencies operate with almost unlimited discretion regarding with which of their waiting families they will place a child for adoption, it is important to show the agency you are the best waiting adoptive parents. Many adoptive parents waiting for a placement do not realize in many ways they are "in competition" with the agency's other waiting adoptive parents. To impress your agency, and make them extra motivated to specifically help you, consider doing these simple things:

- Return your required paperwork quickly, and complete it accurately and thoroughly. (You'd be surprised how many people take weeks or months to return their applications or subsequent paperwork.)

- When the agency seeks to make appointments with you for visits to your home or their office, don't ask the social worker to alter his or her busy schedule to fit yours. Show the meeting is important to you by agreeing to the soonest time they have available. Reschedule any conflicting and less important matters. They will think, "If you can't prioritize your life around a planned adoption now, how can you do it when a child's life will require it tenfold?"

- Attend all seminars offered by the agency to teach you about adoptive parenting and related issues. This includes nonmandatory seminars as well. They have valuable things to teach you about the uniqueness of parenting through adoption. Go because you want to, not because you have to.

- When asked by the agency why you wish to adopt, be honest regarding your motivation, instead of saying what you think they want to hear. For example, many social workers report that they question the motivations of adoptive parents who profess to be interested in adopting only out of humanitarian desires to make a home for a child. This motivation may be one of many appropriate factors when discussing adoption, particularly concerning children waiting for a home, such as children with special needs. Even in those cases, however, many social workers feel the primary motivation for adoptive parents should be the desire to share their love with a child and be a parent.

- Read recommended books regarding adoption and share what you learn with your assigned caseworker and others on the agency's staff you deal with. It is tremendously impressive to the caseworker if you have read respected adoption books, especially if you have done so voluntarily before the agency even begins your home study. Your advance reading shows you are strongly motivated and truly desire to learn all you can about the most important thing in your life—adoption. Appendix A provides recommended reading.

These basic suggestions for establishing a beneficial relationship with your agency may seem absurdly simple. Surprisingly, however, many caseworkers complain that a large number of their agency's waiting families fail to show their sincerity and readiness to adopt by such simple acts. Remember, an agency's goal is to find the best homes for the children they place. The more educated and prepared you show yourselves to be can only serve to impress your agency. When a waiting list is not used, the agency has sole discretion regarding with which waiting adoptive parents it will place a child. Make their discretion benefit, not hurt, your chances to adopt quickly.

Usually there is little difference between a private or public agency home study. The only exception is usually time. In most cases, private agencies can start and complete your home study faster than can public agencies. This is just the reality between the private and public sector. The people employed in your local public adoption agency may be the best and most dedicated social workers in the area. Still, as part of a governmental office, they will have a higher level of bureaucracy for you to work through. Also, because they are offering their services for free, or close to it, they don't want to start home studies until they are sure you plan to stick to your decision to adopt through the public agency (and not stop the process after many hours have been spent on your behalf). This means they often "put you through the paces," to test your mettle. That, in turn, often means a longer wait to start a home study. Still, if they offer the services you want, it will be worth the wait.

So far, we've only discussed home studies as they relate to agency adoptions. Considering this is a chapter on agency adoptions, that makes sense. You should be aware, however, that in many states private agencies can perform home studies for adoptions created via independent adoption. This can occur in an "identified" adoption (discussed in Chapters 2 and 3), where the placement begins via an attorney and is then converted to an agency adoption. Some states also give adoptive parents doing an independent adoption several choices in where they get their home study done, perhaps getting to choose between a private agency or social worker, or a state adoption office specifically available to do independent adoption home studies. Many agencies have different fee structures to distinguish such adoptions from ones where they helped create the match and spend additional time and effort in that part of the adoption. For this reason, you need to be very specific when you call agencies to inquire about home study services and fees.

The Children Available

The children available for adoption through private agencies handling domestic adoptions range in age from newborns to older children and are of all ethnic groups. Most of the adoptive parents retaining private agencies, however, will do so with the goal of adopting a newborn, often of their same ethnic group. Some private agencies additionally handle the adoption of *waiting* and *special-needs* children. The adoption of these latter two groups usually originates via county/public agencies, but sometimes is completed via the assistance of a private agency, as I'll describe later in this chapter.

Public agencies handle the vast majority of children in the *waiting* and *special-needs* categories. A "waiting" child refers to a child who has already been born and is awaiting a home, likely in foster care. Although all children in the foster care system are *waiting* children, not all waiting children are designated as special needs. For example, a healthy young child would be termed waiting, but not special needs. A "special-needs" child is usually a child the agency feels may require extraordinary parenting due to a physical, emotional, or mental challenge. Special-needs children may also include children without disabilities, but who fall into a category the agency believes will make an adoptive placement difficult. Some prefer the term "hard-to-place" for children in this category. This could include a large sibling group to be adopted together, a child over a particular age, and children of certain ethnic minorities where there is a shortage of adoptive parents.

Many of these children have been freed for adoption through the court system due to parental abandonment, abuse, or severe neglect. These children are of all ethnic groups and of varying ages, although ethnic minorities are often overrepresented. Some of these children will need extraordinary parenting due to the problems suffered prior to the adoption, whether emotional, physical, or intellectual difficulties.

There are approximately half a million children in America presently in foster care, and a large number of them are either immediately available for adoption or destined to eventually need an adoptive home due to their biological parents' inability to care for them. Oddly, many Americans who consider international adoption (where many of the children are toddlers or older) won't even consider adopting one of our own nation's waiting children. Sometimes this is because they want a child of a particular ethnic group and they feel that need can't be met in the domestic foster care system. In some cases, that may be true and international adoption can best fit their needs. Sometimes, however, this preconception is incorrect.

Just who *are* these waiting children? The U.S. Department of Health and Human Services has provided the following information about children in our country presently awaiting adoptive homes.

AGE OF WAITING CHILDREN

Under age 1	2%
Ages 1–5	37%
Ages 6–10	26%
Ages 11–15	23%
Ages 16–18	3%

ETHNICITY OF WAITING CHILDREN

Caucasian	32%
African-American	51%
Hispanic	11%
Native American	1%
Asian	1%
Unknown	4%

As will be discussed later in this chapter, it is easy for you to see the children waiting in your home state, as well as other states. Thanks to adoption *exchanges*, you can visit your state's photolisting website, and within a few clicks, see pictures and learn about thousands of waiting children.

Waiting for a Child

Historically, all agencies maintained *waiting lists*. Adoptive parents would simply wait their turn to reach the top of the list for their turn to adopt, and waiting several years was not uncommon if a newborn or very young child was desired.

Waiting lists have largely been discarded, however, and now most agencies will only consider which of their available adoptive parents could most effectively meet the needs of the child to be adopted. This evaluation may include judging the emotional readiness of the adoptive parents and matching the ethnicity, religion, and physical characteristics of the child and the adoptive parents. If all things are equal between waiting adoptive parents, often only then will the longer-waiting family get the nod. If the child is a newborn, and the birth mother has relinquished the selection of the adoptive parents to the agency, the agency will additionally honor any specific requests from the birth mother regarding the kind of adoptive parents she would like the child to have.

Because of these variable factors, and the ratio of placements that individual agencies may have at a given time compared to the number of their waiting adoptive parents, the wait for a child might be only months or it could be years. Remember, adding to this time is how long it will take to complete your preplacement home study, as most agencies will not show you to birth mothers to be considered as adoptive parents until you are fully approved (unlike independent adoption where you can normally start being shown right away). For this reason, it is important to ask any agency not only how long it takes to *complete* a home study with them but also how long must you wait to *start* the home study. If the home study will only take two months, but they can't start it for six months due to a backlog, factor those eight months of forced inactivity into your timetable. Of course, not all agencies are backed up to this degree and many can start immediately.

In the past, if you were working with an agency, the birth mother matches could only come via the agency, not due to your own networking or other outside efforts. This was partially due to the agency tradition of not sharing identities between birth mothers and adoptive parents, which could not exist if you found the birth mother on your own. With a greater sense of openness, however, and agencies welcoming that new tradition, it has opened up the options you have. This means most private agencies will allow adoptive parents to speed up the process of being matched with a birth mother by using their own contacts and initiative. This might include you hiring an attorney who is active in networking, or by planning your own networking campaign (discussed in Chapter 8). In these cases the adoption would then be completed as an agency adoption, even though they met outside the agency, making it an "identified" adoption.

Identified adoptions are becoming a very common type of agency adoption. These terms are derived from the fact you have brought your own "identified" birth mother to the agency, rather than the agency finding her for you. If your adoption agency is willing, they may also be willing to let you start your campaign to locate a birth mother before your preplacement home study is completed, as they know your efforts may take several months to be successful, as long as any actual placement of a child will not occur until the preplacement home study is completed.

Public agencies usually offer a shorter or longer waiting time for a placement than private agencies, depending upon the type of child you hope to adopt. If you are interested in adopting a child with special needs, often there is a substantially shorter waiting period for the placement, as many such children are already awaiting an adoptive home and few adoptive parents are available. Many public agencies are also willing to waive some of their normal restrictions regarding adoptive parents, creating a double benefit for you. With newborn placements, however, normally there is a much longer waiting time than with private agencies or independent adoption. This is because few birth mothers elect to place with their local public agency (they often view it as a "county facility" like a welfare or public health office) and prefer the private sector. Also, in many regions, a large percentage of the few newborn placements that do end up being handled by public agencies are those involving substantial drug abuse during the pregnancy. In fact, this is often why the public agency is involved, because Child Protective Services was contacted by the hospital at birth due to a positive drug test and the child was not permitted to leave with the birth mother. Prenatal drug usage can occur in any type of adoption, but it is more commonly found in the placements finding their way to public agencies.

Unlike private agencies, public agencies will normally not allow you to find your own birth mother, either on your own or through an attorney, then have the agency perform the home study and needed services. This is true even if the placement happened accidentally, not through any effort on your part. For example, if you were waiting with your local public agency in good faith for an adoptive placement, and before it occurred you were approached about a voluntary adoption, the agency will usually decline to have any role because their role is to find homes for the waiting children they are dedicated to serve. They will normally refer you to a private agency or attorney to complete that adoption and terminate your pending public agency application.

Postplacement Procedures

Private and public agencies handle postplacement procedures (after the child is placed with you) differently. Historically, both operated similarly. Once the child was born, the agency would require the child be placed in a foster home until the birth parents had irrevocably relinquished the child, or the child was freed for adoption through a court action. The reason for the delayed placement was to eliminate any risk to adoptive parents of the child being reclaimed. This was a worthy goal, but the downside was it meant the child had to stay with foster parents, instead of bonding with his or her future parents. This foster home period could be days, weeks, or even months, depending upon the circumstances. Adoptive parents did not like this policy. Birth parents didn't like it. Most child welfare professionals didn't like it.

As a result, over the last few decades more and more private agencies began to change their policies and agree to place newborns with the adoptive parents immediately upon the child's discharge from the hospital. In so doing, the adoptive parents were agreeing to a trade-off. Some would be taking children into their homes before the consent was irrevocable, but would have the benefit of bonding with their children from birth. (To see how soon the consent becomes irrevocable in the states of interest to you, see the state-by-state review.) Presently, most all private agencies agree to immediate placements.

Public agencies have been slower to follow this trend and many continue to follow the more old-fashioned, conservative path. It remains common for them to delay the adoptive placement until the child is irrevocably free for adoption. With older children this is less of an issue, as usually they have been legally free for a long time, allowing an immediate placement once adoptive parents are located. For newborns, however, the issue remains one of conflict.

Luckily, an increasing number of public agencies have started to make placements before the child is irrevocably free for adoption. They usually term these placements "fost-adopt." A fost-adopt placement is one where a child is placed with the intended adoptive parents, but technically designates them initially as "foster parents." Then, when the child is irrevocably free for adoption via a consent or court action, their official status is altered to "adoptive parents."

Some agencies prefer to term these placements "at-risk" placements, rather than fost-adopt. Regardless of the labels used, however, the bottom line is that this allows you to have the baby in your home immediately, usually right from the hospital. Because the potential benefit outweighs the risk, most adoptive parents prefer such placements rather than having the child in foster care for the interim period.

Once a child is placed with you, whether through a public or private agency, there will be several postplacement home visits by the agency social worker to monitor the child's progress in your home. The number varies by state, but most range from two to four. Usually about six months after the child's placement with you (depending upon the laws of your state), the agency will be ready to recommend the adoption be granted, allowing the court to finalize the adoption.

Many agencies will require you to retain an attorney to prepare the necessary legal documents and appear with you in court, as legal proceedings are usually outside the scope of most adoption agencies' duties and are not covered by agency fees. Because the attorney is only handling a small part of the adoption, the cost is usually a small fraction of their usual "full adoption" fee. Some agencies have an in-house attorney, however, and he or she will prepare your needed documents, and appear with you in court, as part of the agency fee. Chapter 12 discusses what happens in court when the adoption is formally granted.

Placements via Foster Parenting

Adoptive placements resulting from traditional foster parenting are different from the fost-adopt situations discussed above. Each county or state licenses foster parents to care for children for whom the government has temporary legal custody. Generally, these children have been removed from their families by Child Protective Services due to parental abandonment, abuse, or neglect. These children range from infants to older children.

The purpose of placing these children in foster homes is to provide a safe environment for the child while allowing the child's parents an opportunity to put their lives in order and prove they can provide appropriate parental care. Depending upon the law of the state you live in, the birth parents may be granted up to eighteen months to establish their ability to be adequate parents. Failing to do so, the court may terminate their parental rights and request the county or state adoption agency to find an adoptive home for the child.

Some states wisely recognize the emotional bonds that can form between foster parents and their foster children and thus give special consideration to foster parents wishing to adopt the children they've been caring for. In such cases, they are given priority status over other adoptive parents and can adopt the child they have been caring for. Other states do not provide much special treatment or many rights to foster parents. In fact, some foster parents are asked to sign a document promising they will not try to adopt their foster children. This might seem unfair, and often is, but the rationale is that the county or state desperately needs foster parents and doesn't want to lose any. (Some adoptive parents have successfully challenged such restrictions by court action.)

As you can see, foster parenting is not a guaranteed route to adoption. For this reason, foster parenting should not be done with adoption as the only, or even the primary, goal. This will only lead to your disappointment and perhaps failure to effectively meet the child's needs. However, for those families who would enjoy caring for a child and knowing they are providing much-needed affection and stability in a child's time of need, it can be a rewarding option. It can also be a learning experience for those individuals who are considering whether adopting an older child is right for them. Both you and the child can benefit from the temporary living arrangements, and if it ends up turning into an adoption situation, you all benefit.

Foster parents are paid by the county or the state an amount deemed sufficient to care for the child's needs, ranging from a low of $250 monthly in some states to more than $800 in others. Most average about $500. Almost every state provides for a one-time reimbursement of expenses to purchase needed items for the child, such as clothes, etc. Most states set this amount at approximately $1,500.

Adoption Exchanges and Special-Needs Children

Because of the importance and difficulty of finding homes for hard-to-place children, special *adoption exchanges* and *photolisting books* have been created to assist both public and private agencies in placing these children. An exchange is simply a means to get information about as many children as possible to as many adoptive parents as possible. Every state has its own exchange (each is listed in the state-by-state review), made up of the waiting children within the state. Normally the state exchanges have almost *all* the waiting children in the state available for adoption, virtually all of them presently in foster care under the county's care. Most of the state exchanges have websites with photos and information about all these children. Some states prefer that the adoptive parents be from the same state when they feel it will serve the child's best interests. For example, the child might have extended family in the area and it would be detrimental to lose those extended family bonds. In many cases, however, adoptive parents from other states will be welcomed, giving you fifty databases to consult.

There are also regional exchanges, each covering many states. These exchanges do not list all the children available from every state, however, only some. Typically, most states will only submit children to their regional exchange when they are having difficulty, or anticipate difficulty, in finding an adoptive home locally and need to expand their search. You do not need to live in one of the states covered by a particular regional exchange to be considered for the children listed. The regional exchanges are:

- National Adoption Center
- The CAP Book (Children Awaiting Parents)
- Northwest Adoption Exchange
- The Adoption Exchange

There is also a national exchange, established by the federal government (Department of Health and Human Services), found at www.adopt uskids.org. This is the nation's largest photolisting of available children, usually totaling approximately 5,000 children. As with the regional exchanges, however, many of the children in the state exchanges are not submitted, as they do not anticipate the need for a national search for adoptive parents, or the child may simply be new to the system and his or her caseworker has not yet taken the time to submit them. In fact, the 5,000 children on the national exchange is only a small fraction of the total children available when adding all the individual state exchanges. Appendix B gives contact information for the national and regional exchanges. (The federal government's contract with AdoptUsKids expires December 31, 2007. It is unknown at this time if the contract will be renewed, or if another entity will be selected to handle the national exchange. If this happens, the name of the exchange will be changed. Should that occur, any of the regional exchanges listed on page 85 could direct you to the website for the new national exchange.)

Ideally, the sharing of information will allow an adoptive parent who is working with a public or private agency in San Francisco to learn of a waiting or special-needs child available for adoption through an agency in New Orleans. The two agencies, with the assistance of the exchange, will then work together to make the placement. Initially, only public agencies were involved in the placement of waiting and special-needs children via registries, but more recently many private agencies have become involved as well. Not all private agencies handle these adoptions as part of their services, however.

Adoption exchanges will normally speak directly with you about a particular child, but for any real advancement to be made in a possible placement, they will want to speak to a caseworker at your agency who can provide your home study and further information about you. When a placement seems appropriate, a "go slow" approach is advised to make a smooth transition for the child. Moving to a new home, into a new family, is as major a change in a child's life as can occur. Often the adoptive parents will travel to see the child on multiple occasions, then the child might visit with them in their home. When both you and the child feel comfortable, the child can move in with you and the adoption can formally begin.

Your search for a waiting child will usually start on a local level, as each individual public adoption agency has its own children to serve as its first duty. So if you live in Orange County, California, Orange County Social Services may begin by showing you the local children in their care awaiting homes. The next step would be to visit the California state exchange and see which children are available statewide. Next, the national and regional exchanges, and individual state registries, could be explored.

There are normally no fees charged to you by the exchanges. You will be required to have a home study, however. If you obtained this through your local public adoption agency, it was likely provided to you for free, or at a minimal cost (such as $500 or less). Some states will require you to hire an attorney for the final court appearance and any needed legal work. This can cost from several hundred dollars to more than a thousand. Other states arrange for the public agency to prepare your final court papers for you, eliminating that cost.

If you have a home study from a private adoption agency, then later elect to adopt a child in the county system, or via one of the exchanges, in most states you can use your existing home study. There is normally no need to do the home study process all over via the public agency. Sometimes, however, the public agency or exchange may require you to take special parenting classes dealing with adopting a waiting child and how best to meet that child's needs, if your private agency did not include that training as part of your preparation to parent.

To offset the financial expenses of adopting a special-needs child (future medical care, possible counseling for some children, etc.), the federal government has created an *adoption subsidy* program (some states refer to it as *adoption assistance*) for eligible children. The subsidy gives the adoptive parents monthly support to offset the child's expenses, even after the child is adopted, until the child reaches age eighteen (some states go as high as age twenty-one). Additionally, the child can be deemed eligible for Medicaid, regardless of the adoptive parents' income, covering most medical costs. If your child is found to not have sufficient special needs to be eligible for the federal subsidy, or is ineligible for another reason, most states have their own subsidy programs to encourage special-needs adoption. The reasoning behind the subsidy, in part, is that since the government would be paying foster parents anyway, paying an equal or slightly lesser amount and encouraging the child's existing foster parents or other adoptive parents to adopt the child make more sense, both fiscally and for the welfare of the child. This benefits the child by having a permanent family via adoption, as opposed to him or her remaining until adulthood under county supervision in foster care.

It is the job of your agency to help you with these subsidy options and your child's eligibility. Not all children will be eligible for the federal or state adoption subsidy. Just because a child is a *waiting* child (such as a young, completely healthy child) does not make him or her a *special-needs* child. Additionally, there is a highly respected national organization, the North American Council on Adoptable Children (NACAC) that offers information and assistance to adoptive parents, or prospective adoptive parents, about adopting a waiting child and subsidy availability. Information about NACAC is provided in Appendix C.

There is also a tremendous tax benefit in adopting a special-needs child. A federal adoption tax credit of $11,390 is available for adoptive parents whose modified adjusted gross income is less than $170,820 in the year in which the adoption is completed. This is not a *deduction* (like a mortgage payment). A *credit* is much better. It is a dollar-for-dollar elimination of tax owed, virtually giving you up to $11,390. In the adoption of a child who is not deemed to have special needs, you can only take the credit to the extent you had actual adoption expenses. In other words, if you did an independent adoption and paid $2,000 for a home study, $4,000 for an attorney, and the birth mother had $1,500 in medical costs, you could take a credit of that amount, $7,500. If your adoption expenses were $15,000, you would be permitted to take the credit of $11,390 as the maximum amount.

You might be thinking that it appears there may be no expenses in a special-needs adoption, as public agencies and exchanges generally charge no fees. That means there are no expenses, so no tax credit, right? Wrong. When the adoption is of a child confirmed to have special needs (talk to both your agency and tax preparer to confirm that your child will apply), you are eligible for the entire tax credit, *even if you had no adoption expenses.*

You still have to show your adjusted gross income qualified by being under $170,820, and of course you have to have some tax liability to be able to take the credit against it. In addition to the federal tax credit, some states offer special tax credits or incentives to adoptive parents adopting a special-needs child. The existence and scope of the tax credit can change annually, so talk to your tax preparer. The federal adoption tax credit is discussed in Chapter 12.

Adopting a waiting or special-needs child can be a wonderful opportunity to bring a child into your home who desperately wants and needs a family. Every child deserves a family, but the reality is many won't ever get to be a part of one. It takes special preparation and education to be sure you are ready to meet the needs of these special children. In addition to the classes and educational opportunities that your local agency or exchange should make available to you, there are many great books to help you determine if such a child is right for you, and you for the child, and how to meet the needs of these children now and throughout their lives. These books are listed in Appendix A. For some real "hands-on" learning, you might consider talking to other adoptive parents who have adopted waiting and special-needs children. In addition to meeting them through your local agency, the North American Council on Adoptable Children lists adoptive parent support groups on its website, www.nacac.org. These families have adopted waiting and special-needs children, so they may be an excellent resource for you. More information about the North American Council on Adoptable Children is provided in Appendix C.

The Openness of the Adoption

Years ago most private and public agencies arranged only *closed* adoptions, while independent adoption was viewed as the *open* adoption alternative. A closed adoption is one where the adoptive parents and birth mother would never meet and identities were not disclosed. Although some private agencies still do closed adoptions, many now arrange open adoptions, typically in newborn placements. Although the term "open adoption" can mean many things, normally it refers to an adoption where the birth mother and adoptive parents personally meet and exchange personal information before the birth to be sure each wishes to go forward.

Depending upon the policy of the agency and the desires of the birth and adoptive parents, full identities may or may not be disclosed. The openness may continue after the birth in a variety of ways. In many cases the adoptive parents and birth mother maintain contact by sending pictures and letters once or twice a year up to the child reaching age eighteen, often using the agency as an intermediary. In a small number of adoptions the adoptive parents, birth mother, and the child maintain face-to-face contact as mutually desired. Such a relationship, called *cooperative* adoption, is found in about 5 to 10 percent of recent adoptions. Some birth mothers prefer the other extreme and want no postbirth contact at all.

Many adoptive parents have a knee-jerk reaction against open adoption, often thinking it will "complicate" their lives or undermine their role as parents. Although you as parents have the right to select the kind of adoption you prefer, you might want to ask yourself the following questions:

- If our child ever needs bone marrow or something like a kidney transplant, who will we be contacting?
- We will be raising our child from birth with the knowledge that he or she was adopted, and that adoption was a loving act by his or her birth parents. Won't it be natural that at some point our child will want to meet these people?
- If the birth parents' rights have been terminated and the adoption is finalized, and we are our child's only legal parents, do we really need to feel worried and insecure about the continuing existence of a birth parent?
- We have a lot of distant relatives who we see once or twice a year. They are part of our family, but have no right to interfere in our child-raising decisions. Is there a reason that a birth mother (or father) can't have a similar role?
- Can a child be loved by too many people?
- We know as our child grows we won't be able to fill every need our child has. Sometimes he or she will turn to a teacher or a friend. Maybe at some point only a birth parent can address a particular issue. Do we want a relationship where we can call a birth parent if we ever had a unique need that no one else could fill?
- We believe the birth mother placed her child for adoption with us because she wanted us to be his or her permanent parents, and she only wants the best for us and our child, so is there any reason to fear her?

Although private agency adoptions have become quite open, those through public agencies still tend to be completely closed. This is often due to the fact that a high number of the children they assist in placing for adoption were freed through court action due to inadequate or improper parenting and continued contact would not be deemed to serve the best interests of the child. Furthermore, the selection of the adoptive parents and the placement of the child with them was done completely by the agency. The birth parent had no role, as usually their rights were completely terminated by that time. Even in the small number of voluntary newborn adoptions that a public agency may handle, traditionally these adoptions remain closed as well.

Working with Out-of-State Adoption Agencies

Most adoptive parents will do every aspect of the adoption in the state in which they live. They will hire an agency there, the birth mother will live and give birth there, and the adoption will be finalized there, in the local court. If you live in a state with great agencies from which to choose, good adoption laws making you feel secure, and a sufficient number of birth mothers in your region or state, why leave your own state?

Many adoptive parents aren't so lucky. What if you don't like what the local agencies have to offer? Or you want to work with them, but you don't meet their eligibility requirements? Perhaps there are few adoptive placements in your region or state. Maybe you are concerned that your state has laws that give birth parents an excessively long period in which to change their mind. Or it could be that your state is fine, but you want to expand your options to increase the likelihood of being picked for an adoptive placement quickly. There are many reasons to either do your adoption out of state, or work in both your home state and another state. You have several ways to do this.

Interstate adoption. Let's say you've found a great agency but it is located in another state. No problem. You can hire the out-of-state agency to help you find a birth mother, offer counseling to her, help with her signing her relinquishment of parental rights, and arrange for the child to be physically placed in your care. Very shortly after birth, when the initial paperwork is done and you get interstate approval to bring the child across state lines (discussed in Chapter 12), you return home with your child. A local in-state agency that you've selected does both the pre- and postplacement home study and writes the final report to the court to complete the adoption. You complete the adoption in your local court, primarily under your home state's laws. (Sometimes the other state's laws can apply, as discussed in Chapter 12.)

A twist on the above is that the out-of-state agency finds a birth mother for you and creates the planned placement, but perhaps the birth mother has no place to stay or has recently lost her job. She has no reason to stay in that region and would welcome the chance to get to know you better and have you close for the moment the birth occurs. You agree, and you would like the chance to go to doctor appointments with her and not risk missing the birth due to living so far away. The answer? She can relocate to your home state, where you can find her someplace to stay (assuming your state permits assistance with living costs, as discussed in the state-by-state review). After the birth she may return to her original state, relocate elsewhere, or decide she likes what your state has to offer and stay. Regardless, in this scenario, your local agency would be performing all the needed agency functions, other than creating the adoptive match. They, rather than the out-of-state agency, would counsel the birth mother (or share in that duty with the other agency, at different points of the pregnancy), assist with her signing her relinquishment of rights, as well as do their usual home study duties.

You might fear using two agencies would double the cost, but that is usually not true. As discussed in more detail in Chapters 6 and 9, many agencies will only charge for the services they perform. Accordingly, if they are dividing their duties, their fees should be proportionally less. Not every agency will work that way, but most will.

Nonresident adoption. How about if we take all the reasons why you might be considering an out-of-state agency from the section above, and add one thing? What if the state in which you hired the out-of-state agency allowed nonresidents to adopt, assuming the baby is born there? Perhaps you might want to finalize the adoption under that state's laws. Why? Maybe your state allows a birth mother thirty days to change her mind and the out-of-state agency's state laws only permit seventy-two hours. What if it typically takes a year or more after birth to finalize an adoption in your state, compared to the out-of-state agency's usual time of three months? There are many other legal comparisons to be made between each state regarding such issues as birth father's rights, permitted birth parent expenses paid by adoptive parents, the adoption being open or closed, etc.

States permitting agency nonresident adoption are Alabama, Alaska, Arkansas, California, Colorado, Delaware, District of Columbia, Hawaii, Illinois, Indiana, Iowa, Kansas, Louisiana, Maine, Maryland, Massachusetts, Michigan, Missouri, New Hampshire, New Jersey, New Mexico,

New York, North Dakota, Ohio, Oregon, Pennsylvania, South Carolina, Texas, Utah, Vermont, Virginia, and Washington. You can learn more about each state's laws and the agencies and attorneys within that state in the state-by-state review.

In a nonresident agency adoption you start with the exact same scenario as we discussed for interstate adoption. You selected an out-of-state agency to help match you with a birth mother and that agency continues to do virtually everything in the adoption. After creating the adoptive match, it provides counseling for the birth mother, assists with her relinquishment, arranges for the baby to be released into your care, and makes the arrangements for your adoption to be finalized in its local court. The agency in your home state will only need to do your pre- and postplacement home study. Generally, only the laws of the birth state where the out-of-state agency is located will apply, so there is less chance of a conflict of laws as compared to an interstate adoption. These potential conflicts are discussed in Chapter 12.

CHAPTER 6

Selecting the
Right Agency

Just as selecting an attorney is the central element of an independent adoption, choosing the right agency is the key ingredient in the success of an agency adoption. Despite the importance of this decision, the vast majority of adoptive parents give much less thought to this decision than they should. In most cases they call a few agencies in their region and select the best of those few. You can choose to be like everyone else, or you can choose to succeed.

Considering there are more than 1,200 private adoption agencies in the nation (this is not even counting the equally high number of public/county agencies), you are clearly cheating yourself if you don't thoroughly consider agencies beyond those in a small radius of your home. There are many supremely qualified agencies located all around the country. There are also many to be avoided that fall short of what a good agency should do for you.

Adoption agencies are no different than any other business. You will see the same differences in quality of service as with other professionals you've hired, some great, some barely competent. The good news is that you can easily find an excellent agency by following some basic steps:

1. Select between private or public agency adoption.
2. Narrow your list of possible agencies.
3. Verify that the agency is licensed.

4. Determine whether the agency is able to perform the specific duties you need.
5. Find out if you meet the requirements of the agency.
6. Fine-tune your list.
7. Specify questions to ask the agency.
8. Test the agency's knowledge.
9. Determine if the agency staff's personality and approach to adoption matches yours.

Select Between Private or Public Agency Adoption

Chapter 5 illustrated how different private and public agency adoption are. If you are planning a public agency adoption, you are normally restricted to working with your local county adoption office. In other words, you can't "shop around" like you can when selecting a private agency. That doesn't mean you are limited to your local region as far as eligible children are concerned, however, as your public agency can work with national registries and other public and or private agencies on placements (usually children in the *waiting* and *hard-to-place* categories).

The good news is that if you plan a public agency adoption, your search for an agency is already complete. All you do is find your county's public adoption agency and you're done. It's sort of a good news/bad news scenario as you've got a choice of one agency. No choices, no options. If you can't find your local county adoption office in your phone directory, you can find it on the federal government's adoption website (the Child Welfare Information Gateway), www.childwelfare.gov, or you can call the state adoption office as listed in the state-by-state review in Chapter 15, and that office can give you the needed contact information.

If you plan on adopting through a private agency, however, as you will likely be doing if you plan on adopting a newborn, or doing an intercountry adoption, your choices are staggering. The remainder of this chapter is for you.

Narrow Your List of Possible Agencies

How do you start with more than 1,200 private adoption agencies and end up with one? Sounds daunting, but it's not. Obviously, you won't be looking at a thousand-plus adoption agencies. It's helpful to know they are out there, however.

You may be looking only for an agency in your home state, or wish to consider out-of-state agencies. I'd recommend you start locally and expand from there as needed. Who knows, the right agency might be only twenty miles away. For others, it might be a county away, in a neighboring state, or even on the other side of the country. The answer is dependent upon the region and state in which you live, the type of adoption you choose, the kind of child you hope to adopt, and the services you will require.

Compiling your list of agencies will be done in the opposite way as compared to compiling an attorney list. This is because we are *subtracting* in compiling an agency list, and *adding* to an attorney list. What do I mean? When you compile a list of attorneys, there is no complete list of every attorney doing adoptions. True, there is the American Academy of Adoption Attorneys, and that's an excellent place to start, but there are many attorneys doing adoptions besides those several hundred. This means you need to build your list, then whittle it down. Compare this to agencies, where the state-by-state review lists *every* private agency in the nation. In other words, they are all here, right in this book. Now your task is narrowing down this list and deciding which ones to contact. Let's explore how to do this.

• *Only consider agencies in your preferred geographical regions or states.* Your selected regions or states from which to adopt will be unique to you and different from other adoptive parents. You might live in a well-populated region in a state with advantageous adoption laws and a good percentage of birth mothers. If so, you will likely select an agency in your home region and state. Another adoptive family may live in a state with very poor adoption options, so they'll select several states they feel are best for them and will consider agencies in those states.

To determine the right states for you, consider the many in-state and out-of-state options we discussed in Chapter 2 and the information provided in the state-by-state review. Depending upon where you live, and the kind of adoption you want, different states will be best for each adoptive family. It is within only these states that you need focus your search for the best agency.

• *Call adoption attorneys.* You might think that most adoption attorneys are "in competition" with agencies, and so would not recommend any. In most cases, this isn't true. Most attorneys, even in states where independent adoption competes with agency adoption, work regularly with adoption agencies. Adoption is a small world and the good professionals in the same region usually know and associate with each other.

Although you might not succeed in directly reaching the attorney him- or herself, usually speaking to a staff person is sufficient as they will know who the attorney commonly works with or avoids. Some might have a relationship with one particular agency causing them to unjustly favor one over others; that's okay, since you are hoping for a consensus, hearing one or more agency names several times from different sources.

• *Join or visit adoptive parent support groups.* If you live in an area with a large enough population base, it is likely you have a local adoptive parent support group. These are valuable people for you to contact as they've completed the process you are just starting. They can talk to you about their experiences with local agencies. Not only can they tell you why they hired the one they did, but why they didn't hire the others.

There are several ways to find adoptive parents support groups. *Adoptive Families* magazine has a very helpful website, www.adop tivefamilies.com (just click on "Parent Support Groups" on the home page). The Child Welfare Information Gateway (a federal government site, formerly known as the National Adoption Information Clearinghouse), also includes this information on their website, www.childwel fare.gov. (To find the adoptive parent support groups, go to "Adoption," then "Overview," then "National Adoption Directory," then search by state.) For more information about *Adoptive Families* magazine and the Child Welfare Information Gateway, please see Appendix C. You can also call local adoption agencies and attorneys and inquire if they know of any adoptive parent support groups. Some agencies have their own support groups. These might be valuable to attend, although not quite as unbiased as if the group was assembled by a neutral entity.

• *Join* Resolve, *or attend one of their meetings.* Resolve is a very established and respected national infertility organization with regional chapters throughout the country. Part of their focus on infertility includes adoption. Many of their members are in the process of, or have completed, an adoption, and can talk about agencies they used. To find a Resolve chapter near you, visit www.resolve.org. For more information about Resolve, please see Appendix C.

• *Talk to other adoptive parents.* The more you start talking about adoption, the more you will find that people you already know have adopted. Most of these families feel no need to volunteer personal information about their family being formed by adoption unless there is a reason to do so. In most cases, upon hearing you share that interest, they are happy to share their adoption experiences. There are millions of adoptive parents out there. You will find them everywhere. You can ask which adoption agency they used and how they would rate their services. Also, ask if they can put you in touch with other adoptive parents who might have information to share with you about their adoption experiences. You will find that adoptive parents tend to know a lot of other adoptive parents.

• *Talk to people you know in the health-care industry.* Many adoption agencies work with doctors, counselors, and hospitals regarding the care of the birth mothers they are working with. For this reason, some health-care professionals may be able to tell you about agencies with whom they have had contact in prior adoption situations.

If you previously read Chapter 3 ("Selecting the Right Attorney"), you have likely noticed that some of the recommended steps in compiling a list of possible agencies are the same as when inquiring about adoption attorneys. If you are like many adoptive parents just starting the process, perhaps unsure at this point if you will be doing an independent or agency adoption, clearly it makes sense to concurrently inquire about *both* agencies and attorneys when you speak to the people and groups recommended above.

Don't forget that your inquiries about adoption agencies need to be in the region where the agency has its office. That means that if you are inquiring about a local agency, let's say, in your hometown of Chicago, you would be contacting Chicago professionals and support groups to ask about them. But let's say you were considering an agency in another city and state, perhaps Los Angeles. You will need to inquire about it with its local entities. That means finding the appropriate professionals and organizations the same way you did as described above, but in Los Angeles, and see what they tell you.

Verify That the Agency Is Licensed

What you are really asking here isn't so much if the agency is licensed, rather *is it an adoption agency at all*. In many states, if you start your search for an adoption agency by opening your local yellow pages, or turning on your computer and searching on the Internet, many of the ads you will see are for what you will assume are adoption agencies. They have names that sound like agencies, and they do adoptions, so what could they be but a licensed adoption agency? Right?

Wrong. In the majority of states, these entities are not agencies but *facilitators*. A facilitator is a person or business that helps arrange adoptions for a fee, but is not licensed as an agency or attorney. They can't do home studies. They can't witness relinquishments. They can't prepare legal documents or give you legal advice. They can't write a court report approving the adoption. What *do* they do? They find birth mothers to make adoptive matches. Is this a bad thing? Not necessarily. Finding a birth mother is an important part of newborn adoptions. Make that finding the *right* birth mother. And therein is part of the problem in dealing with facilitators.

A good agency or attorney is educated, trained, and licensed to do the job. Furthermore, they are monitored by a state office, and if they don't perform their services correctly, they risk losing their licenses. To be a facilitator, however, most states simply require getting a business license. How easy is that? Go spend twenty-five dollars or so for your license, make up a name, let's say, Baby Love USA, and presto! You're in business. Now you can run your ads proclaiming "Number 1 in adoptions!" Or, perhaps, "Christian adoptive parents waiting for your baby!" (Sadly, you will often see a religious theme used as what sometimes appears to be a marketing tool, as the business rarely has any official tie to any religion.)

I would have fewer problems with facilitators if their ads clearly stated: "We are not a licensed adoption agency or attorney." The reality, however, is most ads imply to adoptive parents, and especially to less sophisticated birth mothers, that they are an actual licensed agency with the protections that brings. A good question to ask facilitators is, "If you are truly dedicated to the field of adoptions, why don't you become a licensed agency?" The answer in many cases is that either they would be deemed ineligible, or they wish to continue to operate without the legal restrictions placed on legitimate licensed agencies. And a good question for you, if you are considering hiring a facilitator, is if the ads of the facilitator are incomplete and misleading, what makes you think that they will be completely forthright in other matters with you?

Another example of providing misleading information is in the advertisements many facilitators use. Most of them advertising out of the state in which they are located will not provide any information about their actual whereabouts. They will provide a toll-free number and no address. Why? To entice birth mother and adoptive parent calls from all around the country and only later reveal that they are located in a different state. By then, they likely hope, they have convinced the person to work with them, when initially the birth mother or adoptive parent may have never made the call if it was known their office was so far away. The average facilitator charges large fees, often more than most agencies and attorneys, despite the fact that agencies and attorneys provide more services. Despite this, some adoptive parents elect to hire facilitators. That's fine, I just want to make sure you know what you are getting for your money, and what you are not.

Facilitators are not the only entities that omit important information like their actual whereabouts from their ads. Some legitimate agencies and attorneys have also been known to do this, and I think caution should be exercised with them when they do as well. The practice seems to be most used by facilitators, however.

Determine Whether the Agency Is Able to Perform the Specific Duties You Need

Each adoption agency is licensed to perform particular functions or chooses to so limit itself. Some do domestic, others do international. A small number do both. Some are licensed in multiple states while most are licensed in only one. Even within a state, some might be licensed only in one county, while others are statewide. Of those doing domestic adoptions, some might be licensed only to perform home studies. Others are additionally licensed to make adoptive placements. Among those who make adoptive placements, they are further distinguished by those that have outreach programs, networking for birth mothers to contact their agency to select adoptive parents. Other agencies are more passive and do little or nothing to create adoptive matches, leaving you to do that on your own or via an adoption attorney.

With this wide diversity in services, it is critical for you to find the right agency offering the services you need. If you are hoping to be matched up with a birth mother to adopt a newborn, you will want an agency that actively networks and places children for adoption in addition to doing home studies. If you will be using another source to find a birth mother, such as an attorney or your own networking efforts, you might only need an agency that does home studies. If you are planning an international adoption, does the agency only perform home studies that are accepted for international adoption? Does it have a program in the country from which you plan to adopt? (Because international adoptions involve procedures that differ from domestic agency adoption, they are separately discussed in Chapter 7.)

Find Out If You Meet the Requirements of the Agency

So far, we've talked about you choosing an agency. The reality, however, is that they are also choosing *you*. Private adoption agencies can set their own guidelines regarding which adoptive parents they will work with. Some agencies have a religious affiliation, usually obvious from their name, such as Jewish Family Services. Some of these religious-affiliated agencies will welcome adoptive parents of all religious backgrounds, but most will only work with adoptive parents of their designated faith. Others will set their own unique requirements regarding your age, the number of existing children you have, whether you are married or single, length of your marriage, existence and number of any prior marriages, if one spouse must be a full-time parent, and similar factors.

Public agency adoptions have fewer restrictions. For example, as a government institution they can't exclude you based upon your religion. (They could, however, give preference to those with a religion that matches the preexisting religion of a child to promote stability and the best interests of the child.)

The one thing both private and public agencies will have in common in their requirements is that you show you can provide a secure and loving home for a child. In this regard, the existence of any evidence of child abuse, criminal activity, or consistent financial instability is grounds for denial with both private and public agencies.

Fine-Tune Your List

You've likely eliminated a large number of agencies on your list simply by determining they don't offer the services you want or that you do not meet their eligibility requirements. You should still have a large list of possible agencies (and if you don't, maybe you should be expanding your list to include other regions in your state or other states). How do you further eliminate the "wrong" agencies and get the right one for you? Here are my recommended steps:

- Request each agency's written materials describing all their services, fees, and requirements. Besides receiving the information in writing (which is more definitive than information over the phone), it also gives you a chance to see the quality of the materials they present. An adoption agency will be preparing and processing many important documents for you. If they can't put together a professional-looking informational packet, that tells you something about the quality of their work and attention to detail. When you receive their information, carefully read what they have sent you. Does it give you all the information you need about them? Be cautious if the information is nothing but baby pictures and fluff. Creating your family is an important decision and warrants thorough information. Good agencies recognize this.
- Visit their website. This is one more chance to learn about their services. I still recommend, however, that you ask for their written materials. That is because the website is likely the work of a web

professional. You deserve the opportunity to see the work of the agency, which is more likely to be seen in their written materials.
- When you first called the agency, did you get a good feeling from the person who initially answered the phone? Was he or she professional and friendly? Was it a person employed by the agency or an answering service? Remember, this will be the same person a potential birth mother will likely get on the phone in her initial call. If the receptionist is not warm and friendly, why would a birth mother be interested in staying on the line to speak to a social worker? That would mean fewer birth mothers to be considering you as adoptive parents through that office.

You will likely be immediately impressed or not with the materials you receive, allowing you to quickly shorten your list. We still have a ways to go, however, to get down to the best agency for you.

Specify Questions to Ask the Agency

Some of the following questions may be answered by the written materials from the agencies or their websites. If not, these are important questions to ask. Since most agencies offer periodic free seminars to learn more about their services, that would be an excellent, and free, chance to get your questions answered. Depending upon the type of adoption you are planning, not all of the following questions may be required.

- *How many years has your agency been in business?* (You've already verified they are an actual licensed agency, as discussed earlier.) There is no real detriment if the agency you are calling has only been in business a few years as long as they appear to be doing their job well. Generally, however, the stability of a long-established agency is impressive.

- *How many adoptions has your agency done?* An agency's extensive experience is impressive, but only as it relates to how many adoptions it has done. You can't ask for much more than the combination of an established reputation combined with a significant number of completed adoptions.

• *How many adoptions do you complete each year? How about last year?* This is particularly important to you if you are hiring an agency to not just do your home study and assist with the birth mother's relinquishment but to help match you with a birth mother. Some agencies might only complete a couple dozen a year, while others complete hundreds. (Generally, those doing in excess of fifty are usually found in high-population areas.) A high number of adoptions each year is impressive. As you will see in the next few questions, however, that information by itself can be misleading.

• *How many adoptive parents waiting to be matched by a birth mother do you work with at one time? Is there a maximum number you work with at one time? How many do you have at this moment?* These questions are what really put things in perspective. If an agency completes 100 adoptions, but has 300 waiting families, that means only one in every three couples are being picked in a year. An agency completing 50 adoptions with 50 waiting adoptive families being shown to each birth mother may only be completing half as many adoptions, but they appear to be making placements three times faster.

• *What is the average wait of your clients for an adoptive placement? For what kind of placements? What is a soonest versus longest estimate for a placement based upon prior clients?* When you ask these questions, you need to be clear about the type of adoption you want. For example, if you want to adopt a Caucasian or African-American newborn, then ask that specifically. It won't help you any to find out the average wait for a placement is fourteen months, and 90 percent of those were Hispanic toddlers. Obviously that sounds like the perfect agency for those seeking a Hispanic toddler adoption, but not if that isn't your choice of placement.

• *Are most of your adoptions "open" or "closed"?* Although each state has different laws and customs regarding how open or closed an adoption may be, often this is an area where the agency asserts its discretion, as they may elect to make adoptions more closed than independent adoptions in the same state. Assuming you want to adopt a newborn, find out if you meet the birth mother in person. If so, at what point of the pregnancy? Do you share first names? Last names? Can you be at the hospital for the birth? Hold the baby? What about post-birth contact with the birth family? If so, will it be pictures and letters one or two times a year, or face-to-face get-togethers? There is no right or wrong answer here. Adoptions are like marriages. They can all be different and yet work wonderfully. You simply want to make sure that your view of the degree of openness or closedness matches the agency's expectations.

• *Who selects us as the child's adoptive parents, the agency or the birth mother?* Some states, and the agencies within those states, continue to do adoptions as they were done fifty years ago, with no contact at all between the birth mother and adoptive parents. Overall, in the United States, this is becoming rarer and rarer in newborn placements. You might be one of the small number of adoptive parents who desire that degree of closedness, however.

• *Do some adoptive parents who hire you never get an adoptive placement, or have to wait several years? Do you find these adoptive parents have any ethnic, religious, or other qualities in common?* You want to know if the agency is creating adoptive placements that match your goals, for people with the qualities you offer. For example, if you are a member of an ethnic group seeking to adopt a child of that same ethnic group, why retain an agency located in a geographical area where that ethnicity is not represented?

• *Do you have an outreach program to find birth mothers to select us as adoptive parents, or do you just help us do it ourselves?* Some agencies are active in networking and create many matches for their waiting adoptive parents. Others do little or no networking, focusing on preparing home studies for adoptive parents who have found their own birth mother, or who are adopting older children already freed for adoption. Chapters 8 and 9 are dedicated to teaching you strategies to find a birth mother and proceed with a newborn adoption. It is helpful, however, if your agency is working toward this goal as well.

• *What percentage of the birth mothers you find are in state, as compared to coming from another state?* You may not care if your birth mother lives in or out of your home state, as you just want to get picked. Other families want to stay in state, perhaps worrying about travel costs, easy access to the birth mother prebirth and at birth, and the laws of the state where the birth will occur. If you want a birth mother from a particular state, there is no reason to hire an agency that appears to find birth mothers from other states.

• *When birth mothers contact you, how are we and other adoptive parents you are working with shown to her, giving us a chance to be selected?* Few agencies use waiting lists where they would only be showing the longest-waiting families to each birth mother. Still, agency procedures can differ. Some show all their waiting adoptive parents, while others only show a few adoptive parents, selected to match characteristics of the birth mother that the agency feels are important.

Other than cases where a birth mother has characteristics not desired by the adoptive parents (ethnicity, drug usage, open or closed adoption, etc.), you want to make sure you will be shown often and without delay, with the birth mother given a broad choice in adoptive parents. Why do you want her to have a "broad choice," rather than just you and one or two other adoptive families? A couple of reasons.

One is that if they only show a few adoptive parents each time, think of all the times you are *not* being shown. A perfect birth mother match for you may never even get to see you. The other is that even when you are shown to her, you want her decision to be solid. The more adoptive families she has to choose from, the more likely she can be truly happy with her decision. If she had only two or three families from which to choose, she might be choosing the best family available, but without a diverse enough group to be truly excited about who she is selecting. This will be one of the toughest decisions of her life. She needs to be truly impressed and emotionally attracted to the family she chooses.

• *What percentage of your clients find a birth mother through your efforts, as compared to your clients finding a birth mother on their own?* If one of the key things you hope to accomplish in hiring an agency is to have them help you find a birth mother, you will want to know how effective their efforts are. For example, an agency may complete forty adoptions a year, but if 90 percent of the adoptive parents found their own birth mother, it is not as impressive as an agency

completing only twenty-five, all of which resulted from their own birth
mother networking efforts.

• *Does your fee include your networking efforts to help us get
picked by a birth mother, or is it a separate fee?* If the agency is networking for birth mothers, leading them to contact the agency to in
turn select one of the waiting adoptive families, a lot of money is being
spent by the agency in that outreach effort. This might include yellow-
page advertising and Internet promotion of their website geared to
birth mothers, contributions of time and/or money to organizations
that indirectly lead to referrals, etc. Just like with their other expenses,
these costs are passed on to you as the client benefiting from those
efforts. The question is if it is part of their standard fee, which includes
their agency services, or a separate fee specifically designated for networking efforts.

Either payment option is fine, as long as you know what you are
paying for. Just like with attorneys, you can often expect to pay several
thousand dollars or more for an effective networking campaign.

• *What if we want to adopt a toddler, older child, or a child with
special needs? Do you work with other agencies and exchanges in other
states to help make a placement?* Some agencies primarily focus on the
children relinquished through them, but many will work with agencies
from all around the nation, as well as registries, to find the right child
for you. If you want a child in this category, it is really essential that the
agency takes full advantage of the information sharing between agencies and states or your options will be severely limited.

• *If we adopt a toddler, older child, or a child with special needs, is
there any special funding programs to assist us with future costs?* You
want to find out if these children are available for an adoption subsidy
program or other benefits that might be unique to your state, if that is
important to you.

• *Can we be listed with attorneys or other private agencies while we
are working with you and proceed with whichever attorney or agency
finds an adoptive placement first?* The goal of every adoption agency
and attorney should be to help you adopt. To that end, if you wish to

hire more than one agency to obtain your goal as quickly as possible, you need agencies and attorneys who will work within that philosophy. Most all will be agreeable. Some agencies, however, require you to only work with them. I believe this is wrong, as the agency is making itself the key figure in the adoption. In reality, the adoption is about you and the child you will be adopting, not the agency.

• *Do we pay for your services as we work through the adoption, or do we pay it all in advance?* A few agencies charge their entire fee in advance, but this is quite rare. That's because their services are usually clearly divided, as it makes little sense to charge fees before each stage of service is reached. For example, all agencies will require a preplacement home study. That's one fee. When an adoptive placement is made there will need to be services provided to the birth mother, such as counseling and assisting with her relinquishment. There will be a fee for that. Then there will be a postplacement home study, and a fee for that. Why would they charge that in advance when it is not known when, or if, that postplacement home study will even be needed? Furthermore, why charge some of these fees if another agency (perhaps out of state) or an attorney is providing some of those services? With these facts in mind, you should be very cautious in working with an agency requiring full payment for the entire adoption in advance.

• *What are typical birth mother expenses we will be expected to pay?* Almost all states allow adoptive parents to help with the adoption and birth expenses, although some states make different rules for independent or agency adoptions. Standard costs may include medical bills and the birth mother's living costs while she is incapacitated due to the pregnancy. Some agencies have, or are affiliated with, unwed mothers' homes. This is often an inexpensive way to meet a birth mother's food and rent needs (often about half what an apartment would cost), but many birth mothers don't like living in a group setting and are used to living on their own.

Some birth mothers have few or no expenses (they have insurance and are employed, or live at home), while others may have significant expenses. If your birth mother will have any expenses, you want to know in advance what they are, and for how long. As a general rule, expenses for birth mothers needing full assistance will range from

$600 to $1,200 per month for food and rent. Much is dependent upon where the birth mother lives, as apartment rent might be a few hundred dollars in a small southern town but triple that in New York City. When you get into high living costs, however, it is a sign for potential caution. For example, if an agency improperly encourages birth mothers to work with them by offering them a luxury apartment (at your expense) at several times the rent of a typical apartment, or similar gratuitous inducements, it borders on bribery. And bribery is not conducive to a successful adoption or finding the right kind of birth mother. To learn more about permitted living expenses, see the state-by-state review and Chapter 12.

• *Do you provide counseling for birth mothers?* Placing a child for adoption will be one of the most emotional moments of a birth mother's life. The more prepared she is, the more likely she can make the placement as planned. Counseling is one major tool to help prepare her for the birth and the emotions to follow. Both she and you deserve the benefits she will receive from pregnancy/adoption counseling. Some state laws require counseling and some do not. If an agency feels counseling is not important, or in any way discourages birth mothers from receiving it, I believe it indicates a lack of not only empathy but a basic understanding of the emotions at work and the making of a successful adoption.

By the time you have received answers to these questions, you will have a definite "yes" and "no" pile for agencies you are considering. However, we still need to whittle down your list a bit to find the best agency for you.

Test the Agency's Knowledge

Just as I recommended in the independent adoption chapter that you "test" an attorney's knowledge, I recommend you do the same regarding agencies. The problem is that this is harder to do with an agency. This is because with an attorney, you have one person—the attorney—who will be doing all the work, and you know who to question. With an agency, however, there are different people involved. Perhaps one social worker will be doing your preplacement home study. Another will be doing your postplacement home study. Yet another might be working with the birth mother, providing counseling and assisting with her relinquishment. It is possible none of these social workers deal with the procedural and legal side of the adoption. It could be the director, an in-house attorney, or a private-practice attorney hired as needed for legal work.

Regardless, just as the agency will need to be aware of these issues when a birth mother calls and they begin processing the adoption, someone should be prepared to answer your questions about important issues such as interstate adoption requirements, permitted expenses for birth mothers, the Indian Child Welfare Act, birth father's rights, etc. If the social worker answering your questions says such issues are not in her or his area of responsibility, ask to speak to the person who *does* have that responsibility. Asking hypothetical questions about how problems are solved is not at all unreasonable. If they can't answer those questions now, how can they solve them if they occur? As with attorneys, you will quickly see some agencies really know their business, while others struggle to keep up.

Here are some recommended questions:

- *I've heard about something called the Indian Child Welfare Act. Can you explain what that is?* As we will discuss later in Chapter 12, this is a federal law, normally superseding state law, which says if a child is a member of an Indian tribe, or eligible to be a member, the tribe must be given notice and certain procedures followed. If the agency is unfamiliar with the Indian Child Welfare Act, or says it never applies in their state, beware. More and more adoptions are at least potentially touched by the Indian Child Welfare Act, such as where the birth mother has a small degree of tribal heritage that could make the child a member. Noncompliance with the Indian Child Welfare Act can potentially invalidate an adoption, a high cost to pay for an agency's ignorance.
- *We may do an interstate adoption. Can you explain to me how the Interstate Compact works?* As we will discuss in Chapter 12, more and more adoptions are interstate, where you live in a different state than the state in which the child is born. The Interstate Compact provides that prior to a child being transported across state lines by adoptive parents, certain procedures will apply, such as a preplacement home study of the adoptive parents

and approval from both states' Interstate Compact administrators. This is fundamental knowledge every agency should have.

- *What are the birth mother's and birth father's rights? Can they change their minds, and if so, for how long?* These issues are the most fundamental and important of all, so the agency should know these issues frontward and backward regarding their own state. Do not, however, expect them to know this information for other states without some research, however, as each state has different laws.

- *Is there a federal tax credit for adoptive parents?* The agency should certainly know about the federal tax credit. In basic terms, if the adoptive parents have an adjusted gross income of $170,820 or less in the year in which the adoption is completed, they are eligible for a tax credit of $11,390 per child adopted. It is not reasonable to expect an adoption agency to know the detailed tax repercussions of adoption. That is for a professional tax advisor. However, they should know the existence and basics of the tax credit.

There is much more to an agency adoption than the above questions, but they are diverse enough to give you an idea of an agency's knowledge. Those particular questions may not even be applicable to your individual adoption, but it doesn't matter. The questions are an excellent indicator of what your agency knows or doesn't know. If they are ignorant about these issues, the same is likely true regarding other important adoption issues, and you know to look elsewhere.

Determine If the Agency Staff's Personality and Approach to Adoption Matches Yours

Deciding if an agency's "personality" matches yours is more difficult than with an attorney. That's because with an attorney you will be working almost exclusively with one person. True, he or she will have a secretary or paralegal, but the attorney has the primary responsibility for everything. For better or worse, most agency adoptions are more of a "by-committee" undertaking. As mentioned earlier, there might be different social workers for the pre- and posthome study, yet another one for birth mother counseling, and perhaps even an attorney hired by the agency for legal work. Some small agencies may have one person do virtually all the work.

Regardless of the size of the agency and how they assign personnel to handle your adoption, you can only do your best to get a general feeling from the staff, especially the social worker you are most likely to have contact with. It is not unreasonable to call the agency and ask who the social worker would be in the event you started a home study immediately with them. If that person is not available to meet at the agency's free introductory seminar, it does not seem unreasonable to ask to speak to him or her before hiring the agency.

CHAPTER 7

International Adoption

International adoptions—the adoption of a child who is born outside of the United States to a citizen of another country—have become increasingly popular. In fact, approximately 21,000 international adoptions are now being completed by Americans every year. To give you the full picture of how international adoption works, and how to find the right program and country for you, I'm going to do the following:

1. Provide an overview of international adoption.
2. Discuss the pros and cons compared to domestic adoption.
3. Walk you through the entire process step-by-step.
4. Statistically break down and compare the most popular countries (children available, costs, adoptive parent requirements, visits/time overseas, etc.).
5. Discuss keys to finding the best international agency.

Overview

Not every country permits its children to be adopted by foreign citizens. Why do some countries allow it, even welcome it, while many don't? The answer lies in a mixture of cultural, political, and financial factors. The bottom line is that some countries have an inability to care for their parentless children, or lack the ability to create adoptive homes for them within their nation. As a country we should be grateful for the opportunity to adopt these children, fulfilling a need that their own countries can't fully satisfy. The United States has approximately half a million children in foster care, many of them available for adoption. It may be far simpler for adoptive parents to adopt these children, rather than travel 10,000 miles away, but the majority of the adopting parents adopting overseas feel America's waiting children do not meet their criteria (often citing issues like age, ethnicity, and freedom from concerns over possible birth parent objections).

According to the U.S. Department of State, the ten most popular countries from which Americans adopted in 2006, and the number of adoptions from each country are:

China (Mainland): 6,493
Guatemala: 4,135
Russia: 3,706
South Korea: 1,376
Ethiopia: 732
Kazakhstan: 587
Ukraine: 460
Liberia: 353
Colombia: 344
India: 320

The remaining countries, in order of number of children adopted, are Haiti, Philippines, China (Taiwan born), Vietnam, Mexico, Poland, Brazil, Nepal, Nigeria, and Thailand.

You might be wondering why "major" countries such Canada, Australia, and England are not listed. After all, it would be easier to travel to a country where English is spoken by everyone and that is more "tourist-friendly." The reality, however, is that most industrialized nations all face the same problem as Americans—there are more couples waiting to adopt than there are children available for adoption. For that reason, if you travel overseas to adopt, you can expect to meet other adoptive parents who have traveled there from countries like Canada, England, France, Germany, Italy, and Sweden, to name just a few.

Most of the countries with children free for adoption are countries facing economic problems or social conditions leading to some women being unable to parent, and countries unable to provide adoptive homes. Unlike America, where foster homes are used, most foreign nations place children in orphanages (common in Russia and other eastern European countries), while only a few fully or partially use foster homes (Guatemala, Korea, and, more recently, China). These countries recognize that neither orphanages nor even foster care can match the love and nurturing a child will receive in an adoptive home.

There is also a very important legal reason why international adoptions from the countries listed above are so popular. The United States government will only issue an immediate "relative" visa, allowing the adopted child to enter America, if the child is given "orphan" status. These specially designated children are given unique consideration in being granted immediate entry into America, as well as automatic citizenship when adopted. Only children who have been abandoned, been relinquished for adoption to a governmental entity (such as an orphanage or through the courts), or whose parents have died or the sole surviving parent has irrevocably released the child for adoption can receive "orphan" status and the right to immediate entry to the United States when adopted. The children must also be under the age of sixteen when the adoptive parents file the orphan petition. A direct and voluntary placement of a child, as is common in domestic adoption, does not meet the U.S. government's designation of an "orphan."

The "orphan" limitation is about to change, however. It is estimated that in late 2007 or early 2008, the Unites States will complete its readiness to implement what is called the Hague Convention. This is an agreement between many countries to permit adoptions between member nations without the child meeting the "orphan" designation, meaning more direct and open adoptions will be permitted. The orphan requirement will still only exist when the country you are adopting from is not a Hague member country, even if the United States is a member. To see the most up-to-date list of countries that are members of the Hague Convention, visit www.jcics.org/hague.htm (website for the Joint Council on International Children's Services), or ask your international adoption program.

The children available. The age of the children being adopted via international adoption varies country by country. The U.S. Department of State issued statistics on this subject most recently in 2003. Here is the age and gender breakdown:

Under one year of age: 9,726 (46%)
Age one to four: 8,852 (41%)

Age five to nine: 1,680 (8%)
Over age nine: 1,059 (5%)
Male children: 7,435 (35%)
Female children: 13,882 (65%)

Both the gender differential and age breakdown are significantly affected by China. In 2003, 6,859 children were adopted from China. Almost all of them were females, owing to Chinese customs that value male children to a higher degree. Also, China's laws allow children to be freed for adoption sooner than many other countries' (whose regulations may not free them until they are toddlers or older), meaning most of the 6,859 children from China were under one year of age. Accordingly, to get a more accurate picture of international adoption generally, here are the same figures from above when removing China:

Under one year of age: 2,867 (20%)
Age one to four: 8,852 (61%)
Age five to nine: 1,680 (12%)
Over age nine: 1,059 (7%)
Male children: 7,435 (51%)
Female children: 7,023 (49%)

Although many adoptive parents hope for a child "as young as possible," for understandable reasons (bonding from an earlier age, less time in a less-nurturing environment, such as an orphanage), this is not always possible in international adoption. As the above statistics show, when excluding China, the vast majority of children are in the one-to-four age bracket.

The legal basics. International adoptions are potentially much more legally complex than domestic adoptions in that each one involves three sets of laws, not just one as would be the case if you were doing a domestic in-state adoption. An international adoption involves the laws and procedures of your home state, our federal government, and the country from which you adopt. Does this mean an international adoption is three times more complicated? No. To the contrary, they are sometimes simpler than a domestic adoption because the path to many countries is so established that the process becomes almost automatic. In fact, some adoptive parents can actually adopt faster internationally than domestically.

That being said, international adoption *can be* complicated. The potential complications, however, demonstrate the importance of working with a quality international adoption program with an excellent support staff overseas.

The procedures you must follow will be determined by many factors: the eligibility restrictions on the adoptive parents set by the adoption program you select and the child's country of origin (your age, marital status, etc.), the laws of the child's country governing adoption, the adoption laws of your state governing international adoption, and the U.S. Citizenship and Immigration Services' (USCIS) requirements concerning the admission of the child into the United States and eventual citizenship. (The USCIS was previously known as the INS—the Immigration and Naturalization Service.)

All international adoptions require a preplacement home study by an agency licensed to do international home studies by the state in which it is located. In that sense, every international adoption is an "agency adoption." However, the home study requirement is only a very small part of what makes up a completed international adoption. The critical part is the completion of the adoption itself overseas.

In most states, international adoption programs may be operated by either agencies or attorneys, or in some cases even facilitators (businesses not licensed as an agency or attorney). The overwhelming majority of international programs are run by agencies, however. When the Hague Convention becomes enforceable in the United States, any adoption agency, attorney, or person who makes or supervises international adoption placements must be approved by our government. Nonprofit agencies must be "accredited," and all other entities, including attorneys and for-profit agencies or individuals, are "approved." Because of the increased bureaucracy and government approval fees, it is expected that international adoption programs operating in Hague countries will need to increase their fees approximately 10 percent or more to offset these costs. If the country you are adopting from is not a Hague member country, there is no need that your adoption program be accredited or approved.

Comparing countries. Table 1 provides a helpful chart listing the top countries from which most Americans adopt. It provides each country's eligibility requirements (if any) for adoptive parents, the typical age and gender of the children available, whether escorts are used

TABLE I

	Any special requirements for adoptive parents	Average waiting time for child after submitting dossier	Usual "in-country" costs: hotel, food, local travel, gifts, orphanage donation*	Typical orphanage donation*
China	Age up to early 50s; single women accepted but only 8% permitted; few single men accepted.	13–15 months	$2,000–$7,000	$3,000
Russia	None, but may be harder for single men.	6–9 months for child under age two, 4–6 months for older children.	$5,000–$8,000	$2,000–$4,000
Guatemala	None.	3 months	$20,000, for attorney, court costs.	None.
Korea	Usually under age 45 and married 3 years.	12–18 months		
Ukraine	None.	6–14 months	$4,000–$8,000	$500–$3,000
Kazakhstan	Married and single women accepted.	6 months	$9,000	$3,000
Ethiopia	Married and single women; the youngest spouse must be age 43 or less.	4–8 months	In-country attorney required; cost varies.	

* Some of these costs are included in the fee of the international program you've selected, not an additional cost for you.

Must the adoptive parents travel to the child's country or is escort used?	Number of visits to child's country required	Usual in-country time required	Common age range and gender of children	Any specific health or care-taker issues/ problems
Travel required, but only one spouse must go.	1	10–13 days	9–13 months; the vast majority are girls.	General health good, but often little health history known. Check lead exposure (treatable).
Travel required; both spouses must go for final visit (court hearing) only.	2; in rare cases 3	7 days each trip.	Rarely under 12 months, many are toddlers or above; slightly more boys than girls.	Fetal alcohol syndrome with some; possible effects of institutional (orphanage) care.
Travel not required, escorting possible.	1 (often voluntary)	4 days, if elect to travel there.	Under 8 months; more boys that girls.	Misc., but no major issues. Foster homes are common.
Escorts used in most cases.	1 (voluntary)	3–4 days, if elect to travel there.	5–20 months; both boys and girls.	Misc., but no major issues. Foster homes are common.
Travel required, both spouses.	2	9–15 days each visit.	Most toddlers and above; slightly more boys.	Same as Russia.
Travel required, both spouses.	1	3 weeks	Rarely under 12 months, most toddlers and above; slightly more boys.	Same as Russia.
Escorts used in most placements.	1 (voluntary)	4 days, if elect to travel there.	6 months and up to older children; both boys and girls.	Treatable skin problems and parasites (e.g., ringworm).

to bring the child to the United States or if you go to the child's country, the number of visits and length of stay if visiting the country is required, the usual waiting time for a child, the common in-country costs, and common health problems.

Pros and Cons

Domestic and international adoptions have tremendous differences, both in the way the adoptions are completed and the characteristics of the children being adopted. What is a "pro" for one family might be a "con" for another. Why might you prefer international adoption over domestic? There are several reasons:

- You do not want to adopt a newborn, and feel the waiting children available in the United States are not right for you. (Some countries make children under age one available for adoption, but even in these nations, you can't have custody of a baby from the moment of birth, as can occur in a domestic adoption.)
- You might worry that you will be ineligible or unable to adopt domestically due to various factors (age, marital status, etc.), which are frequently not issues internationally (although some countries do have requirements).
- You may be worried that even if you are eligible for a domestic adoption, you may wait a long time for a birth mother to select you. You want a definite timetable to have a child in your home, which may be more likely in international adoption than in domestic.
- You wish to adopt a Caucasian child and believe such a child might be difficult to adopt locally.
- You wish to adopt a child of your ethnic group and there are few adoptive placements locally.
- You have humanitarian concerns for the children living overseas in orphanages who desperately need homes, and this is more compelling for you than the domestic scenario, with many adoptive parents vying for the babies available. Be aware, however, as was discussed in Chapter 1, that adopting to "save a child" by itself is actually seen as an inadvisable reason to adopt. Also, don't forget there are about half a million children here in the United States

in foster homes, either free for adoption or able to be freed upon someone's desire to adopt them.

- You may not be comfortable with the typical open nature of most domestic adoptions. Not everyone feels comfortable in working closely with a birth mother and possibly having continued contact. You may prefer to work with a foreign government that has already severed the parental rights to a child and complete a closed adoption. (A few countries, such as Guatemala, have some openness at the time of placement. With other countries, even though initially closed, some adoptive parents voluntarily seek out birth parents at some point in the future for some degree of openness.)

- You may have extreme anxiety about the fact that most birth mothers in most domestic newborn adoptions have a certain time in which to change their minds, often even after the child has gone home with you, and you refuse to take that risk (even though the percentage of failed adoptions is quite low).

There are also potential disadvantages to international adoption:

- Most countries require you to travel to the child's country (usually once or twice). Although some countries bring the child to the United States via an escort, the norm for most countries is to require you to visit and finalize the adoption in their court.

- You will be traveling to a country where you will most likely not speak the language and where few people speak English.

- Winters in some countries popular for intercountry adoptions can be quite severe (such as all the eastern European nations).

- Although many of the countries from which you can do international adoptions are not third-world nations, they are still going to be quite a bit less developed than you are used to.

- Depending upon the country you adopt from, your out-of-country time may range from a few days to two months (typically several weeks), usually with both adoptive parents present for some or all of the process.

- Things can still go wrong just as in domestic adoption. A small number of adoptive parents complain they arrived in the foreign country only to find the child was not yet free for adoption, or that other adoptive parents were promised that child. Sometimes they discover the child's photos they were shown may have been years old. Luckily, both of these occurrences are rare, particularly with well-established programs.

- You will be dependent upon a translator and guide, and in some cases a foreign attorney, to navigate the complicated legal system in the child's country. They will be speaking a foreign language and you will have to trust them to accurately relay important information about the child's health history, the procedures and problems, etc.
- Health histories may not be available or guaranteed to be accurate.
- Most children are raised in orphanages and many of these institutions lack the resources and staff to fully nurture a child, emotionally and physically, meaning the longer a child stays there, the more likely he or she is to be negatively affected by his or her environment. Orphanages can range from excellent to terrible, with most falling in the middle. Some countries, however, have reputations for more nurturing orphanages.
- Even in the best orphanages or foster homes, where children are loved and nurtured, the care can't equal the one-on-one attention and love of a traditional parent-child relationship. For this reason it is not unusual for some children to initially be slightly to moderately underweight and physically underdeveloped compared to other children their age raised in traditional families. The good news is that most of these children physically "catch up" quite soon.
- Children raised in orphanages are more likely to suffer from "attachment disorder," sometimes more severe the longer they stay in the orphanage. In basic terms, a child with attachment disorder has difficulty bonding with you as parents due to never having a loving and trusting parent-child relationship previously. He or she has simply never learned through experience and observation that it is natural to get love and give it back. Instead, if a child was neglected or abused, he or she can become distrustful of adults, hampering the ability to fully bond with you, no matter how loving you are. Not all children suffer from severe attachment disorder simply because they lived in an orphanage, however. Many

adoptive parents report they see little or no sign of it once the child has adjusted to his or her new home.

- There is always the risk that the country you are adopting from will change its requirements in the middle of your adoption, requiring you to redo extensive paperwork and applications, or shut down entirely.
- Some countries have traditions we as Americans find distasteful and which would be illegal in our country, but are customary there. "Expediting fees" or gifts are sometimes demanded by officials who know that without their assistance, you can't complete your adoption. Fortunately, your adoption program can tell you in advance if such expectations will occur in the country you are adopting from, and if so, how it is handled. When we are faced with such improper conduct here in America, we have a legal system in place to demand justice. In some countries, however, it is the justice system itself that sometimes demands the very fees or gifts that we believe to be improper. Often these costs (and headaches) are handled by the international program and are built into your prepaid program fee, and are not issues you have to deal with directly.

You can see there are both good and bad elements unique to an international adoption. Most adoptive parents instinctively know right from the beginning if domestic or international adoption is right for them. Likely that is how you feel: either emotionally drawn to the concept or not. Some of the negative issues can be avoided by carefully choosing the international program you will work with. This means not just choosing the right agency or attorney operating a top-quality international program but the right country from which to adopt.

Step-by-Step

To fully understand why some international adoptions can go smoothly while others become mired in complications, it is necessary to see how the entire international adoption process works. There are two methods to use in doing an international adoption. The USCIS, which oversees part of the process, in a rare display of governmental humor calls one "the fast way" and the other "the other way." First you will want to have selected the country you want to adopt from and the program to help you do it. Once that decision is made, here is a step-by-step review of "the fast way":

- You must obtain a home study from a licensed adoption agency or social worker specially approved to perform international adoptions. This typically takes about two to three months. The usual home study cost for this preplacement evaluation usually varies from $500 to $3,000, depending upon your state. Most states charge about $2,000. If you are adopting from a Hague member country, after the implementation of the Hague Convention, you will want to make sure the agency is Hague accredited.
- *Concurrent* to starting the home study, you should file a USCIS form called the I-600-A (Application for Advance Processing of Orphan Petition). The purpose of the I-600-A application process is to receive the USCIS's preapproval for your international adoption, a required element in every international adoption. The I-600-A can be downloaded by visiting the USCIS website at www.uscis.gov. When you file the I-600-A, you are basically saying to our government, "I want to adopt a child overseas. I don't know who that child will be yet as I have not been assigned a child, but I want all my paperwork done and all my approvals in hand and ready, so when my child is finally identified I am ready to ask for my child's visa to bring him or her home." It is expected the USCIS will have a new form for Hague country adoptions, but at this point the form has not been created. It will be very similar to the I-600-A, however, and serve about the same purpose.
- The I-600-A form must be sent to the USCIS office serving your home region, along with either your birth certificates or passports (if they have at least five years of validity remaining), marriage license or divorce decree, if any, and the USCIS's fee (which is presently $545 but changes frequently). You, and any other adults living in your home, will later be fingerprinted as part of the I-600-A application process.
- It is wise to file the I-600-A at the same time as starting your home study, because although the USCIS does not require a copy of the home study when the I-600-A is filed, it does require the home study at some point before approving the I-600-A. This

allows you to start the two processes at once, rather than one after the other. Once the USCIS has received your final document (the home study) and has processed your fingerprints, it will issue you the I-171-H letter, which shows you have been approved for advance processing of your Orphan Petition. Once all your paperwork is completed, approval usually takes from two to eight weeks, depending upon the speed of your local USCIS office.

- Each foreign country requires a *dossier* of the adoptive parents. This is a compilation of all the documents required by you. A typical dossier will contain ten to fourteen documents, including such items as the home study, your formal approval from the USCIS (the I-171-H), birth certificates, marriage certificate and divorce decree, if applicable, letters verifying employment/income and good health, and application forms that are unique to each foreign country. All these documents must then be *authenticated* or *apostilled*, based upon the foreign country's requirements. These are simply different ways of verifying the authenticity of the notarization or certification of the document by the state secretary of state.

- When the dossier is complete and fully authenticated, it must be translated into the language of the foreign country, then those translations must usually be authenticated. Depending upon the requirements of the country from which you are adopting, the cost of the authentications and translations for a complete dossier will usually be from $1,500 to $4,000.

- Depending upon the policies of the country from which you adopt, the dossier may be mailed to the foreign country's officials for approval, hand-delivered by a representative of your adoption program who is in the country, or in rare cases it may be hand-carried by you when you travel there to do your adoption.

- The time for the foreign country to approve your dossier and offer you a child to adopt can vary tremendously. In some countries this is only months, while in others it can take a year or even more. This delay can be due to either their government's bureaucracy or a shortage of available children to meet your desires.

- Most countries will send you a photograph and health history of a child they believe matches your stated desires (age, gender, existence of any special conditions, etc.). Some countries will instead show you children when you arrive in country (Ukraine is the only popular country doing this presently, but may soon change its policy). Sometimes you can adopt more than one child at once, particularly if siblings are involved, as most nations recognize the importance of not separating siblings. Countries differ on what happens if you decline the adoption of the child assigned to you. Some will require you to go home and await the assignment of another child, while others will offer you another placement while you are there.

- Although a small number of countries allow the child to be brought to you via an escort, most countries require you to go to their country, meet the child, and then finalize the adoption in their own court. Naturally, these nations want to be sure their children are being properly adopted under their laws.

- A good international adoption program will have a skilled translator (as well as a car and driver, to meet your travel needs). This person will translate for you with foreign officials, interpret health records, and accompany you to the many places you are required to go in completing the adoption (which you could never find alone): government offices, the orphanage, the court to finalize the adoption, the birth certificate bureau for the child's original and new birth certificate, and the passport office to obtain the child's passport.

- When the adoption is finalized overseas, you are typically given a new birth certificate with you listed as parents, and with the child's new name, as you wish it to be. If an escort was used to bring the child to America, the court of the child's home country will usually name you as the child's guardian, later giving approval for the adoption to be finalized in the United States, usually after receiving several satisfactory reports from the supervising adoption agency.

- Before the child can enter America, a foreign doctor specifically approved by the U.S. government, called a *panel physician*, must conduct a basic examination of the child. The goal is to be sure you know everything possible about the child's health. Again showing the varying quality of different country's orphanage systems, the U.S. government requires extensive testing for the children of some countries. With others, however, the U.S. government seems to have such confidence in the health system and records of the foreign orphanages that the examination is cursory.

- The foreign court's order granting the adoption and new birth certificate is presented to the American embassy in the child's country, along with additional USCIS forms, to obtain the needed permission for the child to be given a *green card* and to enter America as a *legal resident alien*. One of these USCIS forms is called the Petition to Classify Orphan as an Immediate Relative (the I-600). Note the absence of the letter "A" at the end of the form compared to the I-600-A form discussed earlier. The "A" in that form designates "advance" processing. This means that because you previously filed your I-600-A, the embassy can virtually immediately approve your I-600, which identifies your adopted child. It is usually not necessary that you have a detailed understanding of the workings of these various USCIS forms, as a good international adoption program will be guiding you through this.

- If your child was fully adopted overseas, and both adoptive parents (or the single parent) saw the child before the court hearing, the child is a citizen upon entering the United States. If the adoptive parents did not see the child before the hearing, or an escort was used and only a guardianship or similar status was granted overseas, citizenship can be applied for after the adoption is granted in court.

- Even when the adoption is finalized overseas, many adoptive parents elect to *refinalize* the adoption in their home state court, called a "readoption." Depending upon the state in which you reside, this readoption home study may be only a single-visit home study, multiple visits, or may not be required at all. Some international adoption programs include the cost of the legal work in the refinalization. Separate from any domestic requirement for postplacement home studies, most countries require a few postplacement visits by an adoption agency to confirm the child is adapting well. There is no reason, however, that you can't do "double duty" with your home visits, and use them to satisfy both purposes at once.

Clearly, international adoption is an intricate process. The good news, however, is that virtually all of the above detailed steps are the job of your international adoption program. So, your first job is to find a program. A good program will know the ins and outs of working with the USCIS and foreign governmental officials. The program should also know the exact eligibility requirements of the country with which they are working and what, if anything, you would be required to do in the child's country to legally complete the adoption and bring the child home.

Fees can vary in international adoptions as much as in domestic adoptions. Most programs charge between $10,000 and $30,000, varying tremendously by the country you adopt from and the services provided. You need to be very careful to find out what is covered in the program fee. Some programs do not cover the cost of your home study, your translator/guide overseas, car and driver while you are overseas, the translation and authentication of your dossier, or the orphanage donation. These services can each cost thousands of dollars. The better, more straightforward programs will include most or all of these costs, leaving only the cost of your own airfare, hotel and food costs while in country, and USCIS fees. Most programs estimate you should plan to spend $150 per day while in country for your hotel and meals, although costs vary.

Keys to Finding the Best International Program

As was discussed in Chapter 2, you are not limited to agencies and attorneys with international programs in your home state. Let me repeat: *you want to find the best program, not the closest*. A significant number of adoptive parents retain an international program located in another state. This opens a lot of doors. To find potential international adoption programs and learn about different countries and what they have to offer, you can do the following:

- Talk to everyone you know who has adopted, including those who did domestic adoptions. Adoptive parents share information with each other and tend to have a wide informational net. They can either tell you about their own experiences with one or more international programs, or tell you about other adoptive parents they know who can. Don't just ask for a list of international adoption programs; try to meet people who have adopted from different countries to learn more about what the children and procedures are like from that country. Only you know what is most important to you. For some adoptive parents the key question is where they should go to adopt the youngest possible child. For others it is where they should look to find the healthiest and most nurtured children. For still others the goal may be finding a child who looks like them.

- Call local agencies and attorneys, even if they only do domestic adoptions, and ask for recommendations. The adoption community is a small one. They can often point you to a good intercountry program.
- Join or visit adoptive parent groups. Some of those participating have done international adoption. To find them, visit the websites of *Adoptive Families* magazine and the federal government's Child Welfare Information Gateway, provided in Appendix C.
- Join or visit Resolve and attend their adoption support groups. To learn more about Resolve, see Appendix C.
- Read *Adoptive Families* magazine and peruse their advertisements.
- Go online and find international adoption chat rooms and resources, selecting search words with the countries you are considering (e.g., "China adoption, health issues," "Russia adoption, adoptive parents," etc.).
- Read the state-by-state review and contact those agencies that have international adoption programs or perform international adoption home studies, as well as attorneys who have international programs.

Once you have your list of potential international programs, consider the following questions to help find the best agency or attorney:

- *Are you a licensed agency or attorney?* As discussed previously, some entities that have names like adoption agencies are actually facilitators—not licensed agencies or attorneys—and are viewed with suspicion by many in the adoption field. This is particularly true in international adoptions. I suggest you only work with an international adoption program that is operated by a licensed agency or an attorney who is a member of the American Academy of Adoption Attorneys. When the Hague Treaty is ratified and enforceable, you will want to ask if they are accredited or approved under the Hague Treaty and if their services include making or supervising the placement when you are adopting from a Hague member country.

• *With which country or countries do you work?* Some agencies or attorneys work with a dozen or so countries, while others specialize in just one country. You might want to be a bit cautious with programs that list a large number of countries from which they do adoptions. Sometimes working with an excessive number of countries indicates the agency or attorney does not have their own staff in those countries, and rather are subcontracting from another agency.

• *Does your overseas staff work directly for you as one of your employees, or are they contracted through another agency or attorney's program?* If you learn they subcontract another agency's labor overseas, it is not necessarily a reason to stop working with that program. However, you do want to be extra cautious when checking out other aspects of the agency, and inquire why, if they have a viable program in that country, they have not invested the time and money to hire their own staff there. Another concern with subcontracted employees is that their loyalty (and perhaps the best placements) may go to the adoptive parents in the program that directly employs them. You may also be paying a higher fee, as the agency or attorney's employees who your program is using may be charging your program a fee, which is passed on to you.

• *I am interested in hiring your agency/law office, but you are located in a different state than the one I live in. Will that cause any problems, delays, or extra costs?* Often the answer is no. You will need a home study by a local agency, but that will be required regardless of the state where the intercountry program is located, so that is not an extra cost. And unlike domestic interstate adoptions, where you either finalize the adoption in the child's state of birth or your home state, most international adoptions are finalized in the child's country, having nothing to do with the state in which you live or where the agency or attorney is located. Even if you do not complete your adoption overseas, and instead have your child brought to the United States, you will usually finalize the adoption in your home state.

• *How many adoptions has your program done this year with the country we want to adopt from? How about last year?* You want to see a record of reasonable success. However, you may wish to be cautious of those programs that boast of completing hundreds of adoptions a year. An adoption is not an assembly-line function. Bigger is not always better.

• *What are the children available for adoption in that country like (age, ethnicity, health, gender, etc.)?* You want to make sure that the children available in a particular country meet your goals before you start a program. Some vary tremendously in age and health issues. You can also learn about a particular country by calling the U.S. embassy that processes orphan petitions in that country. Ask what most children who are being adopted by Americans over the last year are like. Be cautious if their information differs greatly from what a program tells you.

• *So we are fully informed, what specific health tests are given to the child before we consider him or her for adoption? HIV? Hepatitis B? Syphilis?* Some countries have good orphanages that provide regular physical checkups and screening for various health problems. Other countries do much less, and it will be up to you when you arrive to either have a private physician do it (which can be difficult sometimes if a child is in an orphanage), or wait until the *panel physician* does the exam as required by the U.S. embassy before your child enters America.

• *Are there children waiting for immediate placement? What is the average time to complete an adoption, measured from the very start of the process to bringing a child home?* Although your first goal should be to find the right child from the right country, you will want to know what your possible timetable looks like. Some countries have children waiting and you will be invited over soon after receipt of your dossier. Other countries have more applications than they have children, meaning a backlog exists and it might be a long time before you are invited.

• *What are the procedures to adopt from the country we will be working with? Do we go to the country to bring the child home or does an escort transport the child to us? How many visits do we make? Both of us, or just one? How long will each visit be?* Some adoptive parents look at their visit, or visits, to the child's country as a great adventure and look forward to it. Others, whether because of limitations in how much time they can take off from their jobs, difficulty in leaving home because they already have a child to care for, or simply the costs of repeated trips overseas, have limits on how many times they can leave the country, how long they will stay there, and if one or both adoptive parents need to go each time.

• *What is the full program fee? Does it include the authentication and translation of our dossier? The home study? A translator and car and driver to meet us at the airport and bring us to all our official meetings? The translator's and driver's food and lodging? Are we expected to give the orphanage a donation to help the remaining children there, and if so, how much is it? What about the translation of the foreign court documents for our embassy overseas? The cost of a lawyer doing our child's readoption for us when we get back? If it's not included, what will those fees be?* Intercountry adoption program fees can be very misleading. Knowing all the required elements of your intercountry adoption in advance, as you are now learning, will allow you to figure out the true total program fee. An intercountry program that looks like a bargain at $12,000 may soon become overly expensive when you add several thousand dollars each for your dossier, your translator and guide overseas, in-country car and driver fees, the orphanage donation, expediting fees, overseas court costs, and attorney costs in your readoption at home. A program that is significantly more expensive—let's say $30,000—but that includes all of those fees might actually be less expensive in the long run. Regardless of whether the fee structure includes everything or breaks it up into several separate fees, either type of program might be excellent. The key is avoiding any programs that attempt to mislead you with a "low" fee, glossing over the extra costs to come later. Remember too, just like in domestic adoption, bigger is not always better, nor is the most expensive necessarily the best.

• *Is the adoption completed and approved by the court in the child's country or are we only given guardianship?* Some countries will only grant guardianship, thus requiring you to adopt the child under your state law when you return home.

• *Do you have get-togethers of adoptive parents who have already adopted, so we can meet them and their children? If not, can you give me the names of at least six adoptive families who used your program in the last year whom we can call to ask about their experiences?* Meeting other adoptive parents who have been where you are going, assisted by the same people who will be assisting you, is very important. They can give you the lowdown on what it was like from their perspective. No matter how honest the staff of an international program is, they will still see their program through their professional eyes. This is different from how an adoptive parent, doing all this for the first time in a strange foreign country, likely felt.

These questions, coupled with the general questions regarding attorneys and agencies provided in Chapters 3 and 6, should help you find an excellent program, whether inside or outside your state. Remember, every year about 23,000 international adoptions are completed by Americans. There is no reason you can't add to that number.

CHAPTER 8

Strategies to Find a Baby to Adopt

This chapter is dedicated to one thing—finding a birth mother to choose you as the adoptive parents for the child she is expecting. According to the National Center for Health Statistics, there are more than three million unplanned pregnancies in the United States each year. Three *million*. Of these, more than a million will elect to terminate their pregnancies. About 130,000 will plan adoption. The others will parent the child or place with a relative. So the question is: how do you find these women, to get information about you in front of them so they will not only choose adoption, but pick you?

In previous chapters we've discussed the most important action: hiring an adoption attorney or agency, either in or outside your state, whose services include showing you to birth mothers contacting their office to start adoption planning. Often hiring the right adoption professional is enough in itself to result in creating your adoptive match. My advice, though, is don't stop there. The more you do, and the better you do it, the higher your chances of success. Plus, we don't want just *any* adoptive placement, we want the right one for you—the right birth mother placing for the right reasons—so wouldn't it be nice to have a *choice* of adoptive placements? Not just one? If you want to achieve that, be prepared to use some originality and effort to obtain it. I'll provide the originality if you'll provide the effort. Deal?

While your attorney and/or agency is doing their best to match you with a birth mother, you are doing the same. Here's a key difference,

however, and why you want to be active on your own behalf in various networking strategies. When your attorney or agency is contacted
by a birth mother seeking the right adoptive parents for her expected
baby, she will be shown the many waiting families your adoption professional represents. This means your chances might be one in ten, one
in forty, whatever. But when you find your own birth mother, and then
have your attorney or agency get involved to make sure it looks like an
appropriate and safe placement, you are normally the only considered
adoptive parents. After all, your hard work should pay off for *you*, not
other waiting adoptive parents.

I'm going to suggest some tried-and-true networking methods, and
some you have likely not heard of before. The key is to exhaust these
methods. Don't look for an excuse to do nothing and go after your
adoption halfheartedly. Do it with double the intensity you did for
other important aspects of your life: getting an academic degree, finding the right job, choosing your dream house, battling infertility.

Before I list these networking strategies, let me say one thing:

It only takes one.

I know from personal experience in working with more than 900
adoptive families that they are quick to disparage certain methods, saying, "too many people already do that," or "if I send my photo-résumé
letter to doctors, they will just throw it away."

It only takes one.

You may be right. Of the letters you send out, the calls you make,
the people you talk to, 99 percent of that effort may be wasted. Actually, let's be brutally honest: 99 percent *will* be wasted. Doctors will
toss away your photo-résumé letters without a glance, as will most
health-care professionals when given to them in the traditional way.
Even your friends, without the right approach, will not know what to
do with them.

So what.

*You only need one letter to be passed on to a birth mother to be
successful at adoption.*

It only takes one.

But to find that *one*, you need to get in the game, and use every
opportunity to get yourself out there, waiting to be discovered by a
birth mother. And more than that, you've got to do everything in the
most effective manner, using original techniques.

Prepare a Photo-Résumé Letter

This is the foundation of your search for a birth mother. For a birth mother to seriously consider you, she will want to initially see what you look like and read what your life is like. This is the heart of a photo-résumé letter. Because we are going to use it for so many things, and because most are prepared poorly, I want you to recognize the importance of creating the best possible letter. It is the essence of your quest. A typical photo-résumé letter will have a photo of you and a letter describing what your life is like, giving a birth mother a chance to visualize what a child's life will be like with you.

Your Photo
Nothing is more important than your picture. You could have the most eloquent letter accompanying it, but if the birth mother does not find the photo attractive, she won't even bother reading the letter. That's just reality. Take it from someone who has sat next to hundreds of birth mothers and watched them go through a stack of photo-résumé letters.

Let me digress here for a moment, because it is just about here that most adoptive parents go into a panic, fearing they don't have the "right" look. I've heard it all: I'm overweight, we're too old, my husband is balding, etc. The reality is all of us are insecure about some aspects of our lives, particularly our appearance, and for some reason most adoptive parents assume every other adoptive parent in the world looks like Julia Roberts and a young Paul Newman, and that every birth mother will end up with them.

The reality, however, is that adoptive parents come from all walks of life, duplicating the general population. They will be skinny or obese, tall or short, black or white, Christian, Jewish, or agnostic, college educated with a fancy job or a high school graduate working in manual labor. You get the idea.

Here's the key thing to make you relax and stop worrying if you feel you will not be attractive to a birth mother: rarely does a birth mother elect adoptive parents based upon physical attractiveness or professional job status. True, they want their child to be raised in a financially secure home and be presented with options in life, but that exists with most middle-income families.

Here is the reality of who birth mothers choose as adoptive parents: they select adoptive parents they can *identify* with. This means people they feel comfortable with, who make them feel good about themselves when they meet. Comments I frequently hear from birth mothers when explaining why they selected one family over a stack of others are:

- "The adoptive mom reminds me of my favorite aunt."
- "They look like they love to laugh."
- "I can tell they really love each other."
- "They like to do the same kind of things I do."

What I *don't* hear from birth mothers in choosing adoptive parents are such comments as:

- "She's the most beautiful woman I've ever seen!"
- "Wow, the adoptive dad has impressive muscles!"
- "I bet they're millionaires!"
- "With all those college degrees, they must be geniuses!"

Okay, I'm being a bit silly, but you get the point. But now you are thinking, if the above is true, then why did I say if a birth mother does not like the look of your photo, she will not read your letter? This sounds shallow and seems to contradict what I've just said about why birth mothers pick certain families. However, it's not. Here's why.

When most birth mothers look at photo-résumé letters, they will either get a spark, or they won't. A good example is when you are young and single, and you're walking across campus, or in the mall, and your eyes and mind are open to finding someone special. Maybe your head would be turned by a few people, but the rest go by unnoticed. Even you might be unable to explain why one person caught your eye and you hoped to engage them in conversation. It was just a gut feeling. The reality is that everyone is interested, and attracted to, different types of people. Even we don't know why we are so attracted to someone. Just look how different all your friends' spouses are from each other. Everyone finds different things attractive. For some, it is finding someone who is our complete opposite. Or it may be someone who is just like ourselves. Birth mothers are no different. And because birth mothers come from all walks of life, as do adoptive parents, there is someone for everybody.

Now that we've tossed away your insecurities, let's discuss preparing your photo for your photo-résumé letter.

• Take an accurate picture. Making yourself look like a fashion model, then walking in the door for your meeting with a birth mother looking completely different serves no purpose. If you are not who she thought you would be, the meeting will likely go for naught. Just as bad, another birth mother who would have picked you if you looked "normal" didn't, because she wasn't interested in someone looking like a fashion diva.

• Don't hire a professional photographer. Many will disagree with me, but I recommend you have a friend take your picture, or use the self-timer on a good-quality camera. Why? Studio photos tend to look artificial, and they look like you are trying too hard. Plus, since you will be duplicating your photo for many, many photo-résumé letters, most professional photographers copyright their photos and won't give up their negative, charging you an exorbitant fee for duplicates. Better to get copies at your discount drugstore for a fraction of the cost.

The biggest reason for not using a professional photographer is that you want to emphasize the personal aspect of your presentation. You want it to smell of *home* and *family*, not slick commercialism. You want the picture to be a casual one, emphasizing the fact you will be a fun and loving family.

• Some adoptive parents use just one photo of themselves, while others use five or six and make a collage. Neither is better than the other, assuming that if a single picture is used, it is a great picture. The only time I think it is definitely advantageous to use a collage is when the adoptive parents already have one or more children. It can be difficult to get a young child to cooperate and get that one "perfect" picture with all of you, and a collage lets you mix and match to give an accurate view of your family. If you do elect to use a collage approach, don't use multiple pictures of the same thing: you standing in front of the fireplace; you standing in front of your house; you standing in front of your fountain in the backyard. Instead, use the collage to show a full view of your family: a picture of both of you; a picture of the extended family (so a birth mother can see beaming future grandparents, aunts and uncles, etc., at a family event), one or both of you doing one of your favorite activities, such as hiking in the mountains, on a ride at Disneyland with your existing child or a favorite niece or nephew. By the time she sees all the pictures, a birth mother should feel she really knows you.

• Smile! I can't tell you how many times I look at my clients' possible photos and see picture after picture with the wife showing her glowing smile, and next to her a husband with a toothless version of a smile. For some reason, even the happiest and most motivated husbands have a tough time showing a nice, toothy smile. I'm not saying to show a false smile, but I am saying that if you are not smiling in your photo, why would a birth mother pick you? She will assume if you can't smile to be picked for adoption, you never smile.

• Inside or outside? I recommend outside photos. Inside pictures are usually filled with distraction, the backgrounds containing the corner of a doorway, the corner of a painting, etc. If you are outside, you can select a bright and beautiful background. This might be the beach, the mountains, a local park with beautiful flowering shrubs, a local restaurant with a gorgeous Mexican tile fountain, a historic building, etc. One caution with outside pictures, though: avoid bright sunlight. You don't want to be squinting in your pictures, and you definitely don't want your eyes hidden behind sunglasses.

Whether inside or outside, I'd avoid using holiday pictures. For example, a photo of you standing in front of a Christmas tree is nice for December, but untimely when a birth mother sees it in July.

• Wearing casual clothes is preferable to something formal like a suit and tie. This is not an Easter picture to give to your parents. This is to show a birth mother what you are like. Successful but casual clothes, like a polo shirt and slacks for men, is perfect. For women, a casual dress or pants is fine.

• Make sure your faces are easily recognizable. For example, you might have a great picture of you on vacation standing in front of a volcano in Hawaii, but if you are so tiny that your bodies are an inch tall in the picture, with your face a fraction of that, no one can see what you look like. Instead, either have your faces fill the picture, or go with a full-body shot (sitting on a bench, standing arm in arm, etc.).

• Choosing the right picture is the key. How do you do it? Start by taking *lots* of pictures. Don't just go through your existing pictures and use one of those. You might be lucky and find a perfect, recent picture, but I find this to be rare when looking for that single, great photo. Instead, most adoptive parents take pictures specifically for their photo-résumé letter. Because it is hard to create the photo that best personifies you, and because so much is riding on it, I recommend you take three or four rolls of film, about seventy-two exposures. Take a dozen in one location in one position, then another dozen in another position. Then off to yet another location. Maybe some with pets, some without. Try a few clothing changes. Play "model for a day." Don't be shy about showing affection in your picture. Standing with your arms around each other or holding hands only emphasizes your affection.

If you are a single person, your main picture will be of you alone, but a collage is the perfect chance to show the significant others in your life. This visual demonstration of the support of family and friends is important for birth mothers to see.

The odds are, even after taking all these pictures, you will only find one or two that satisfy you. In fact, it is not uncommon for adoptive parents to not like any of the pictures and use the first round of photos as a learning experience, and do better the next time around. Perhaps you notice you are squinting in the sun, framed the pictures poorly, the clothes you selected did not photograph well and distract the viewer from your faces, the background was not attractive, etc. In your second go-round you can correct any such mistakes.

In addition to the fact that your photo is the most important part of your being selected by a birth mother, it is also the least expensive part of the process. Even if you repeated the process three straight weekends to come up with the perfect picture, what would the cost be? A few hours of your time and fifty dollars? Accordingly, it is time and money well spent.

• If you are using just one picture, the size is usually three by five or four by six. You can scan the picture into the letter, use a color copier, or have prints made and staple one to each letter. Any of these three options are acceptable. If you are using a collage approach, most of the photos will likely be quite a bit smaller, and will almost certainly be scanned or copied onto the résumé letter, as trimming and stapling multiple photos would be too time-consuming and not very visually appealing.

In deciding on issues like the size of the picture, and whether to staple an actual snapshot (which has a nice homey and personal aspect to it), or go with the more convenient scanned photo or color copy, it is best to decide in advance how you will be using the letters. For example, if your preference is to give out your letters in person, or mail several at a time in one large oversized envelope, there is no problem with using letters with a snapshot of any size stapled to your letter. But if you are going to be mailing individual letters folded in a traditional business-sized number ten envelope, if your picture is four by six, or if it is positioned vertically, you will have to fold the snapshot in every letter. You would not have this problem with scanned or color-copied résumé letters, or an attached three-by-five snapshot positioned horizontally at the top or exact center of the page. Below I will be discussing different networking techniques in using your letters, and if you know which methods you plan to use in advance, you can make the mailing of your photo-résumé letter more convenient and economical.

One warning: if you are attaching a photo to letter, don't paperclip it. Pictures have a habit of becoming separated from letters, and when they get reattached, your face might be on someone else's letter. A staple or glue gun is usually best. (Glue sticks seem to lose their adhesiveness quickly.)

• If you scan the photo into your letter or use a color copier, it is critical to use top-quality equipment. Nothing is worse than blurred or distorted photos. Before paying your local copy store to make a large quantity of your letter, have them print one and check out the quality.

• If you already have a child, or children, feature them in your photos. This may sound obvious, but some adoption "strategists" advise you to hide the fact you have children, and present yourselves as childless. Their reasoning is that some birth mothers are less likely to select you if you already have one or more children. While there is some truth to this statement, to hide the existence of your children is not a good strategy. You want to honestly represent yourselves to a birth mother. Either she will like you for who you are, or she won't.

Hiding the existence of your existing children is doubly ridiculous as at some point the birth mother will be told about important facts about you: your profession, length of time married, number of children if any, etc. So what is gained by hiding the fact initially? What viable birth mother will be attracted to childless adoptive parents, then discover they didn't bother to mention what should be the most important part of their lives—their children—and still want to select them? And the birth mothers who may have liked the fact that the adoptive parents had children because they wanted their child to be raised with siblings didn't consider them because they appeared to be childless. So not only is this dishonesty unfair and offensive to birth mothers, but it potentially hurts your chances of success.

The Résumé Letter

I think the ideal résumé letter should be long enough to describe yourselves, but not so long as to start boring the reader. Remember, the photo-résumé letter is just a first look at you. It is not expected to tell a birth mother every fact about you. It is to have a birth mother say, "I like what I see and I want to learn more." Let's talk about what to include and what to leave out.

- How do you start out your letter? Many times I see the salutation "Dear Birth Mother." I'd suggest you don't use it. I believe it is so impersonal that it strikes the wrong tone right from the start. But decide for yourself. When you get mail addressed "Dear Homeowner," is it greeted with enthusiasm and anticipation? No, I didn't think so. I believe starting out "Dear Friend," "Hi," "Hello," or with a similar greeting is better. Actually, there is no need to even have a salutation at all. Why not just start out your letter getting right to the point: "We are Carol and Mike and we are hoping to adopt."
- Your names. Depending upon the custom in your state, and on the advice of your agency or attorney, you will list either only your first names, or your last name as well. (If you are going to

use your photo-résumé on the Internet, I strongly suggest omitting your last name.)

- Just as with your picture, you want to show a birth mother that a child will be loved in your home and that you have a life filled with activities of interest. For one couple it might be quiet activities: reading the Sunday paper in bed together with a box of donuts; Friday nights spent renting old movies and popping popcorn. Others might be active and like hiking, scuba diving, and skiing. Just like we discussed above about appearances, birth mothers are all different in what attracts them to certain adoptive parents. Some birth mothers will identify with quiet couples, while others are into active people and sports. The point is, you don't need to be anything but yourself, as there is no perfect description in the eyes of most birth mothers, beyond wanting a loving and secure home for their children.

- Talk about your jobs, or if one of you will be a stay-at-home parent, but keep it brief. For example, writing that you have been a fourth-grade teacher for five years is sufficient. You don't need to add that you were voted teacher of the year, have guaranteed job security based upon seniority, and are the only teacher in your district with a Ph.D. in childhood psychology. I'm not saying a birth mother is not interested in those impressive facts, but save them for later. Don't risk boring her.

- Your hobbies and interests are what define you in many ways, and they are what a birth mother will identify with. Either she has the same hobbies, or dreamed of doing them but never had the opportunity, and wants her child to have the chance to experience them. I think you can't list too many hobbies, as long as they are genuine interests. Such activities might be scrapbooking, gourmet cooking, church, aerobics, movies, softball, tennis, reading, and countless more. More is not always better, however. Just be honest and describe yourselves.

- Where you live is important to birth mothers. You may choose to list the city and state, or just the general area. Some birth mothers like the idea of doing the adoption in the same state where she lives, so she will prefer in-state couples, while others might visualize a family on a distant coast as the best place for a child to be raised. When you mention where you live, talk about why you like it: "We go to Dodgers games every weekend and love the museums the city has to offer"; "We like the mountains so we can hike in the summer and ski in the winter"; "We really enjoy our house in the suburbs. We have a lot of kids on our street and a great park just around the corner. It's very safe and all the kids ride their bikes to school."

- Your pets are part of your family; don't forget to mention them. When describing dogs, particularly large breeds, it is a good idea to mention their gentleness and experience around children.
- Your letter should be typed, not handwritten, in an easy-to-read font. I recommend that the letter, including the photos, should be no longer than one page, or one double-sided page. The last thing you want is for a birth mother to get a short, well-written letter from every other couple when yours is a long, rambling treatise. She is likely to put it on the bottom to be read last and find someone she falls in love with before she gets to it.
- The paper you use is important. This is not a job résumé. You aren't going to use plain, boring paper. Your target audience of this letter is female, and young females at that. You want your letter to be *pretty*. Either choose a nice color, or perhaps stationery with a nice border. Alternatively, you might dress it up with some stamped images, or punch holes and intertwine a ribbon. You are showing the birth mother receiving it that you care about what you are doing and have invested time and emotion into it.
- There is no need to volunteer something negative in the letter. For example, you may be concerned that you have several prior marriages, a bankruptcy many years ago, or one or both of you are older than you look. In most all states, a birth mother is entitled to know these facts prior to consenting to the adoption (and I find almost all are very open-minded about such information), so you know she needs to be told these things. The question is whether or not to put it in your photo-résumé letter.

To me this situation is different from the wrongness of initially omitting that you have existing children. Having children is something you should be proud of and be shouting from the rooftops. A fact that some might see as negative is different, as a birth mother might unfairly dismiss you when a little more knowledge might keep her interested. I advise that whoever gets the birth mother's initial call about her interest in your letter—whether that is you, or more likely your adoption attorney or agency—*immediately* tells her about those negative facts before she invests the time and emotional commitment to meet you. This gives you, or your attorney or agency, the chance to fully inform the mother and put the fact or incident in perspective. She can then decide for herself if she wants to take the next step and meet you or not.

- Be yourselves. There is no need to strike a false chord in your letter. If you are funny, great, be funny. I've even had couples make funny "Top Ten" lists enumerating reasons why they'd make great parents. If you are a quiet, thoughtful couple, that's fine too, and your letter should reflect that in its style and tone. Birth mothers come in all sizes and personalities, just like you.

- Don't dwell on your infertility or personal heartbreak in trying to conceive a child. The birth mother is facing her own personal crisis with the pregnancy and doesn't want to read letters from people sharing their heartbreak. Mentioning you are adopting due to infertility is fine, but don't try to gain a birth mother's sympathy. Keep your letter positive and uplifting and fun to read.

- Mentioning or not mentioning your religion is a difficult decision. A birth mother is entitled to know it, but do you want to put it in your letter? For Christian adoptive parents, there is usually no downside to mentioning it. In fact, in most cases it will be beneficial. For adoptive parents who have no religious affiliation, writing "we have no religion," strikes a potentially negative chord in what is supposed to be a positively toned letter. And what if you practice a nonmainstream religion, such as Seventh-Day Adventism? Perhaps reading that would cause a birth mother to unfairly dismiss you from consideration, knowing nothing about the religion due to her young age and lack of exposure to many faiths. Instead, if the birth mother is told about your religion when she expresses an interest in you, and immediately receives some information about it, she is much more likely to be open-minded and consider you.

- Your letter must have a contact phone number. It can be your number, or that of your attorney or agency. If you are networking with your photo-résumé letter outside of your region, a toll-free number is helpful, and most attorneys and agencies have one for that purpose. As mentioned before, I recommend if you are dispersing your letter on the Internet, don't use your home number. If you want to use your own number, rather than your attorney or agency's, consider a temporary extra phone line or cell phone.

• Each letter should be hand-signed so it looks personal, not mass-produced. After the letter has been photocopied, sign your first names at the bottom of each letter.

Okay, you've got your photo-résumé letter. Now the question is how many copies to make. The answer will depend upon how you use it. If your attorney or agency is networking for you, they will want some copies—from dozens to hundreds, depending upon how they plan to use them. To maximize the exposure you will get from them, however, the largest distribution of the letters should be through your own networking efforts, supplementing your attorney's or agency's efforts.

We will start with the most basic strategies and advance to some lesser-known techniques. It is not necessary to do all of them. You will likely find that some methods appeal to you more than others. The more you do, however, the wider your outreach and the better your chances of quickly finding the right birth mother. (In the next chapter, we will continue with strategies for success, as I explain the Power of Three.)

Traditional Networking

There is no limit to how broad your networking attempts will be through *traditional networking* with your photo-résumé letter. Traditional networking involves compiling lists of people in the health-care industry, who may come into contact with a woman with an unplanned pregnancy and give them your photo-résumé letter, perhaps leading that birth mother to you. This will include obstetricians, gynecologists, family practice doctors (as many women start their pregnancy care with a general practitioner before transferring to an ob-gyn), counselors and psychologists (as unplanned pregnancies lead many to counseling to deal with their decisions), and abortion and pregnancy-planning clinics.

You can elect to send these out to local professionals in these categories, throughout your state or in other states. A small traditional networking campaign would be 1,000 letters, and a large one closer to 3,000.

If a letter costs you thirty cents to duplicate (assuming you buy nice paper and are using a computer to print the letter and photo), and the envelope and postage (assuming you fold your letter into a traditional number ten envelope) is another fifty cents, the total is eighty cents. This means a general networking effort of 1,000 photo-résumé letters will cost approximately $800, not counting the cost of the mailing list itself, which I'll discuss in a moment.

Adoptive parents give me three reasons for not doing general networking:

1. *My letter will just get thrown away.* True, most of them will be immediately discarded. But remember, it only takes one letter reaching one birth mother to make the entire campaign a success. The more letters you send, the better your odds of success.
2. *Everyone sends out letters to health-care professionals, so even if my letter is kept by the doctor or counselor receiving it, it will just be lost in the mass of other letters.* Actually the overwhelming majority of adoptive parents *don't* do traditional networking. Either they don't know about it, or they convince themselves it will be a waste of time. And even among those who do it, not everyone is networking in the same regions you will select.
3. *I don't know how to compile a list of names and addresses to send the letters to.* The best way to prepare a networking mailing list is to buy it preprinted on mailing labels. You just peel and stick. True, this may make the recipient mentally lump it into the "junk mail" category before opening it, but handwriting all the names and addresses is just too time-consuming a task when talking about a minimum of 1,000 envelopes. There are two ways to counteract the impersonal appearance of an envelope bearing an address label. One is to use a personalized return address sticker or rubber stamp, like you likely already use for personal correspondence. The other is to make the label less obvious by using clear labels tending toward invisibility on the envelope, rather than the traditional white labels.

Finding mailing lists for health-care professionals, especially pre-printed on peel-off labels, is difficult. An Internet search for "mailing lists" will lead you to companies that sell this information by any guidelines you request: homeowners, shoe repair stores, etc. Accordingly, you can buy a doctor list, but be aware that a general "doctor list" will be of little assistance, as it will include dermatologists, podiatrists, etc., which are of no value to you. You want primarily obstetricians, gynecologists, and to a lesser degree, family practitioners in the medical field, as well as other health-care professionals (hospitals, counselors, abortion clinics), so if you go this route, specifically request those. As I'll explain momentarily, you may also want beauty and nail salons. An Internet search for "adoption mailing labels" may be most productive in finding retail providers of appropriate mailing lists.

Some companies can provide you with the categories you want for only the states you want, while others can't. Also remember that you don't want just the mailing *addresses* printed on mere sheets of paper, as that would require you to write all those addresses on the envelopes. You want them *preprinted on mailing labels and ready to use*, so ask if they can ship them that way. If they can't, another option for you is to have them email you the names and addresses, allowing you to format the information so that you can print them yourselves onto blank sheets of labels you've purchased. This is only recommended for those who are truly computer savvy. The website www.adoption101 .com deals specifically with adoption networking addresses divisible by state and preprinted on mailing labels (via its "Secrets to Success" section).

Nontraditional Networking

The health-care industry is the obvious place to start networking. It is not the only place, however. A lesser-known category in which to network, but one I've found to be very successful, is hair and nail salons. These are female-dominated industries, and discussing other people's business seems to be the order of the day when getting a haircut or manicure. A customer's best friend's daughter's pregnancy would not be an uncommon topic of conversation. Getting your photo-résumé letter into the right hands can in turn get it to birth mothers.

There are other reasons why including beauticians in your networking campaign is a good idea. One is that there are a lot of them. If a midsized city has ten obstetricians and gynecologists, don't be surprised if it has ten or twenty times as many hair and nail salons. This allows you to focus on a particular geographical area and not run out of appropriate recipients. Another reason is that even among adoptive parents who do elect to network, many don't think to include beauticians. This makes them an underused group of people, and few have received photo-résumé letters.

If you are networking in your own region, you may want to personally deliver some or all of your photo-résumé letters. In a hair salon, for example, you'd give one to each person working in the store, taking a moment to tell them how you hope they will help you: simply keep the letter on hand until they hear of an unplanned pregnancy situation, then to pass it along. If they like you, most will be excited to do it and be part of the creation of your family.

Besides personally delivering them, you can also purchase mailing lists of hair and nail salons, just as with health-care professionals, as discussed earlier. If you are mailing the letters, I'd advise a basic cover letter, so the recipient knows why they are receiving the letter. It can be as simple as this:

> Hi,
> We are hoping to adopt and are sending you our photo-résumé letter
> in the hope you will pass it along if you hear of a woman facing an
> unplanned pregnancy who would like to learn about us.
> Thanks!

When you create your cover letters, you could even print four "cover letters" to a page, and cut them horizontally, to reduce copying costs and give the recipient a simpler, smaller packet to review. Using a partial page for your cover letter would also allow you to staple it to your photo-résumé letter in a place allowing your photo to show through behind the cover letter. Sample cover letters for traditional and nontraditional networking are provided in Appendices E and F.

Here's a checklist for traditional and nontraditional networking:

1. Prepare your photo-résumé letters.
2. Copy the number of photo-résumé letters you will need.
3. Prepare a cover letter.
4. Copy the cover letters you will need.
5. Buy or share a mailing list of health-care professionals and other groups you think will be helpful (like beauticians) in the region you wish to network, making sure you purchase them on pre-printed mailing labels (or have the ability to create them yourself on your computer from the data provided).
6. Buy number ten business-sized envelopes.
7. Buy return address mailing labels.
8. Mail (or in rare cases, hand deliver) one cover letter stapled on top of one photo-résumé letter to each professional on your list.

Personal Networking—"One Times Five"

Traditional networking can be effective, and I recommend you do it. I'll admit, however, my favorite kind of networking is what I call *personal networking* or the "one times five" strategy. It requires no purchase of mailing lists, no huge mailings of 1,000, 2,000, or 3,000 letters, and no direct mailings to health-care professionals who may toss your letter.

The heart of personal networking is to ask people you know to *personally* give their health-care professionals, or other helpful individuals, your photo-résumé letter. The biggest advantage to this method is that because the doctor or other selected recipient is getting your letter personally from someone they have a relationship with (their patient or customer), they are much more likely to take it seriously and keep it.

Here's how you mount an effective personal networking campaign:

1. *Make a list of friends and family.* When I say make a list, I mean make a *big* list. You are not just listing your best friends, you are listing *everyone you know.* This means your friends from work, from your college days, your neighbors, people you exercise or work out with, who go to your place of worship, etc. You get the idea. Start with your Christmas or Hanukkah list and try to triple it. Try to compile a list of

at least 100 people if you can. For some, based upon where they work, this is easy. For others it is impossible. Just do your best. Some brave souls will open their church directory and presto, they've got 300 names. You may be thinking that, sure, friends will help, but why would mere acquaintances do so? Keep reading, and I believe you will see why they will participate and how effective this can be.

2. *Write a "Dear Friends" cover letter.* Unlike the cover letter used for health-care professionals or beauticians, this cover letter takes a different approach. It will be a short, typed letter stating that you are hoping to adopt and asking for the help of your friends and acquaintances by doing several *specific* things: the next time they go to their family doctor, *personally* give him or her your photo-résumé letter and mention they know you; the next time they go to their gynecologist or obstetrician, *personally* give him or her your photo-résumé letter and mention they know you. The same with their minister or rabbi. And the person who cuts their hair, does their nails, and so on. A sample "Dear Friends" cover letter is provided in Appendix F.

3. *Mail each person on your networking list five copies of your photo-résumé letter (with a traditional networking cover letter— provided in Appendix E—stapled to each one), with a single cover letter clipped to the top of the stack, explaining why you are enclosing the letters and what to do with them.* Now, your friends, who'd like to help you adopt but don't know how without specific guidance, know exactly what to do. So the next time they go to their family doctor, they bring along a letter. Their next ob-gyn appointment, they bring a letter. The next time they go to church, they bring a letter. If they can think of friends in other health-care fields working with pregnant women, such as counselors, they give him or her a letter.

Personal networking is primarily a local means of networking, as most of the people you know will live in the region where you live and work. But don't forget about friends and family out of state. Send them a packet as well.

4. *Be confident your letters will be handed out as you are hoping.* Let me ask you something. If you received a letter like this from an acquaintance, maybe not a best friend, but someone you know and

thought well of, wouldn't you enjoy the opportunity to help and maybe be the person who created the link that lead to the creation of your family? I find most people are thrilled to do this.

5. *Let the numbers work for you.* If you have 100 people on your list, and each one gives out the five photo-résumé letters you included in your envelope to them, you have now reached 500 key people. And a high percentage of them are likely to keep the letter, because they personally got it from someone they know.

I believe personal networking is *a must* in an effective adoption campaign. You may be shy about telling others you hope to adopt, but I encourage you to get past that. Your friends and relatives likely know many people who have adopted and are very comfortable with the subject. In fact, you will be amazed by how many calls you will get from acquaintances who receive your letter and have personal experience with adoption.
Here is a checklist for personal networking:

1. Prepare your photo-résumé letters.
2. Prepare a "Dear Friends" cover letter for your friends who will receive them (Appendix F).
3. Prepare (if not already done for traditional networking) a traditional networking cover letter (Appendix E) and staple one cover letter to each of the photo-résumé letters.
4. Clip one "Dear Friends" cover letter on top of a stack of five photo-résumé letters (each of which already has a traditional cover letter stapled to it).
5. Buy large nine-by-twelve-inch envelopes so you won't have to fold the photo-résumé letters, and place one packet of five photo-résumé letters inside.
6. Mail or hand deliver your packet to each person on your list containing one cover letter and five photo-résumé letters.

Advertising

Placing a classified ad in local newspapers has been a popular way to reach birth mothers for decades. About half the states permit adoption ads (the state-by-state review tells you which states permit this and which don't). Personally, I've never been a big fan of newspaper advertising, but to be fair, I must say I know many adoption professionals who have used the method with viable results.

Usually an advertisement, or "announcement" if that sounds better, is a small ad placed in the personals or classified section of a newspaper. Even when it is permitted in a state, the individual newspaper may have its own requirements, such as a letter from your attorney or agency to be sure the adoption will be done correctly.

If you elect to place an ad, as with all types of networking, you might elect to only do it locally, or go into other states. The newspapers can range from being major papers with huge circulations to small-town weeklies. Although most will be "general circulation" newspapers, the newspapers of college, special-interest, and religious entities are possibilities too. Those who employ advertising as one of their prime networking methods usually advertise in several dozen papers, and expect to do so for several months.

Typical ads might be:

ADOPTION. LOVING COUPLE IN OREGON HOPES TO ADOPT INFANT. MEDICAL BILLS PAID. 1 (800) 555-1234

ADOPTION NOT ABORTION. WE ARE A CHRISTIAN COUPLE HOPING TO ADOPT. CAN HELP WITH LIVING AND MEDICAL COSTS. CONFIDENTIAL. CALL COLLECT: 1 (212) 555-1234

PREGNANT? WE HOPE TO ADOPT AND CAN OFFER A LOVING HOME AND A WONDERFUL LIFE IN THE COUNTRY. WE HAVE A COMPLETED HOME STUDY. WE CAN COME TO MEET YOU. 1 (800) 555-1234

Newspaper advertising has been popular over the years for one simple reason: it's easy. You can reach a large number of people by simply phoning in an ad, rather than compiling mailing lists and stuffing envelopes. The cost is about the same, as running a large number of ads in fifteen newspapers for two months each often equals the cost of a networking campaign of about 2,000 letters ($25 per ad per week times eight weeks is $200, times fifteen newspapers is $3,000). Of course, you could elect to do a smaller campaign. The primary disadvantage of newspaper advertising is its impersonal nature and your lack of any control over who sees the ads. With a networking campaign, you are directing your photo-résumé letters toward people in the health-care industry, or specific people like beauticians. Also, your ad can be seen by anyone, including people who are not even pregnant and think they see an opportunity to manipulate someone.

If you feel advertising is an outreach method you wish to employ, I strongly recommend you have an adoption attorney or agency to receive any calls, and have them thoroughly screen any callers before passing them through to any contact with you. Good adoption situations can come out of adoption advertisements, but extra caution is needed at the early stages to be sure you are working with a legitimate person sincere about adoption planning. As a general rule, however, I do not find the high cost of extensive advertising to be as cost effective, or beneficial over a longer period of time, than both traditional and personal networking.

The Internet

The Internet has become our new yellow pages and an educational resource rolled into one. For this reason, some birth mothers, just like some adoptive parents, will make going online their first step toward adoption. However, I don't believe many birth mothers find adoptive parents online. I find most birth mothers are so poor they don't have computers to go online. Still, some do search the Internet.

There are several routes to being seen by birth mothers searching online. One is to retain one of the adoption professionals who advertise heavily on the Internet (some spend hundreds of thousands of dollars annually, telling you how high their income needs to be to offset those expenses). By hiring those agencies, attorneys, or facilitators, one would assume that when a birth mother contacts them, she would be shown your photo-résumé letter. You might find, however, that when using the guidelines provided in Chapters 3 and 6 regarding how to select the best attorney or agency, that these entities don't measure up to your scrutiny. As a general rule, I don't have the highest opinion of adoption entities advertising widely and forcefully on a national basis, whether they be agencies, attorneys, or facilitators. Many seem more concerned with making a large profit than with serving a limited number of people.

The other way to reach birth mothers who go online is to work with one or more of the services that showcase adoptive parent photo-résumé letters. They charge you a fee to offset their costs of Internet advertising. Sites generating a fair amount of birth mother traffic will usually charge from $100 to $300 per month for a featured spot on their site.

But how do you find a good site? I won't list any, as the Internet world changes quickly and a valid URL today sometimes doesn't exist tomorrow. That's one good reason to not invest money in long-term exposure on the Internet. Better to pay for one month or so at a time.

Remember that being visible on an Internet site is only helpful if birth mothers are actually visiting the site. So how do you know if it generates a lot of traffic? Many sites brag of high "hit" totals on their sites, but that information is hard to verify, or to know if the site visitors are even birth mothers, not other adoptive parents. As a result, my advice is this: *in your mind pretend you are a birth mother looking for adoptive parents.* Sit at your computer and go on your favorite search engines, perhaps Google or Yahoo!, and type in search terms just like a birth mother would. Clearly you will start with something basic like "adoption," and perhaps expand into other words or phrases, such as "place a baby for adoption," or a geographical search like "adoption, Illinois."

What comes up on your screen will be the same thing birth mothers will see. You want to go where she would go. Click on the URLs offered, perhaps starting on the top few that usually get the most interest, or even on one of those hated pop-ups. You will find several sites that list adoptive parent résumés for birth mothers to see and contact. With a little digging into the site, you will find out how to have your photo-résumé letter listed and what the cost is.

Another option, if you are a computer-savvy person, is creating your own website, and doing just as the adoption listing services do— paying listing fees to search engines like Google and Yahoo! to compete for a top spot with chosen search terms. This is quite an endeavor, however, and is not suggested unless you already have experience in both website construction and working with search engine companies, and understand how to bid for "pay-per-click" exposure. A new option is a site like www.myspace.com, where you can create your own page for free and hope birth mothers will find it.

Just as with newspaper advertising, the advantage to Internet exposure is a lot of potential coverage with little work. No mailing lists or envelope stuffing. The disadvantage is that you can't control the location of the people who access your photo-résumé letter. Of course, that's fine if you don't care whether your birth mother lives in California, Idaho, or Massachusetts. One advantage it has over newspaper advertising, however, is that it is a directed medium. For example, with a newspaper ad, anyone looking at the paper will see your ad, not just those with an interest in adoption. On the Internet, only those searching for adoption sites should find it. This reduces the likelihood of wasted calls or potential scams. Still, birth mothers found through the Internet, just like via the newspaper, require careful initial screening to be sure all is bona fide before getting involved. The use of a skilled adoption attorney or agency to handle these initial calls is critical.

One big disadvantage to an extensive posting of your résumé online is that you will likely get calls from less-than-reputable adoption agencies, attorneys, and facilitators, stating they represent a birth mother who saw your letter and wants to meet you. Of course, the request for money, usually to be wired to them, before your attorney or agency can fully investigate the situation, will be a part of their call. Think about it. If they were a legitimate entity—the kind adoptive parents want to work with—they would have their own adoptive parents from whom the birth mother could choose. Right? The fact that they need to troll the Internet for paying customers tells you all you need to know.

Adoption "Business Cards"

Think how often you stumble across someone's business card, perhaps left in a restaurant or on the seat of a cab. Often it is for a Realtor or mortgage broker, or other professions where people sometimes have to be aggressive to get noticed. Clearly they leave their cards everywhere to be found. Sometimes adoptive parents do the same thing. A typical adoption business card (the same size as a regular business card) might have your picture, with the caption "Hoping to adopt!" in large letters next to it. On the other side might be a very short bio, providing your first names, some bare-bones information, and a contact phone number. An example may be:

> *We are Glen and Carrie. Our dream is to start our family through adoption. We are both teachers. We can help with pregnancy-related costs. Please call to learn more about us! 1-800-555-1234.*

You then give a card to every person you interact with each day, or leave them in public places where they are likely to be found. Like with newspaper and Internet advertising, I recommend you don't use your home phone number, and having an attorney or agency screen the initial calls is a good idea.

Facilitators

A facilitator is a person or business that is not an attorney or an agency, rather an entity that finds birth mothers, usually for a fee. Usually for a large fee. Many, in fact, charge as much or more than agencies or attorneys, despite the fact that they can provide only a small portion of the needed services. As a general rule, I caution adoptive parents against using facilitators as they can't perform any of the functions attorneys or agencies can. They can't give legal advice, do legal work, or make court appearances. They can't do home studies, place children in an adoptive home, or write court reports. Some states make facilitating an adoption for a fee a crime, though most states have no legislation on the issue. Those caveats aside, however, if you are aware of what a facilitator is, and still want to use one to help you find a birth mother, it is an additional option for you.

Just like attorneys and agencies, facilitators find birth mothers in many different ways. Many facilitators rely heavily on large yellow page ads and the Internet. Some birth mothers will decline to work with a facilitator when they learn their true nature as a nonagency or nonattorney (although it is tough for anyone, especially young birth mothers, to know their true status, as facilitators usually employ names that sound like agencies). Other birth mothers, however, may prefer a facilitator to help them go outside of what many consider normal adoption channels to make an adoptive placement. Of course, that may be the very reason to avoid such a birth mother.

Despite the questionable issue of the high fees facilitators charge in relation to their limited services, the bottom line is that some do produce results. Because they are unlicensed and untrained, however, unlike attorneys and agencies, they are less able to effectively determine a good from a bad adoption. For this reason, it is particularly important that you have an experienced attorney or agency to screen any birth mothers located by the facilitator and to help you make sure you have a viable adoption.

Complicating the issue is that unlike attorneys and agencies, there is no formal database for facilitators in most states. Facilitating is a largely unregulated industry, without the strict licensing laws affecting attorneys and agencies. The simplest way to determine if the entity you are considering is a facilitator or not is to just ask if they are a licensed agency, and if so, in what state. If the answer is no, they usually fall into the general category of facilitator. To verify what they tell you, you can call the state social services office (provided in the state-by-state review) for the state in which they are located and ask the agency licensing office if they are a listed agency.

How do you spot a good facilitator from a bad one? This is a difficult question. For example, with an attorney, a prospective client could call the state bar and inquire about any disciplinary actions against the attorney, and learn where he went to law school and how long he has been in practice. With an agency you can call the state social services office and verify their status and ask about how long they've been in business. Such questions about facilitators to a similar independent government office are generally impossible. My only advice in this area is to read the guidelines for selecting a good attorney in Chapter 3 and ask the same questions. In addition, here are some specific recommendations if you are determined to hire a facilitator:

1. Ask for the full contract you will be expected to sign in advance of arranging a meeting or paying any initial fees. Have your attorney look it over to be sure it seems appropriate.

2. Don't pay a large portion of your fee in advance. I give this same advice when hiring an attorney or agency, so I'm certainly going to give it regarding facilitators. I believe you should pay for services as you go through the process. Why pay their entire fee, or a significant portion of it, before you even know if they can

indeed find you a birth mother, and if they do, if you will want to work with that birth mother?

3. Ask what methods they use to find birth mothers and make sure you agree with the methods used.
4. Ask what region or state the birth mothers typically come from. This may not matter to you, but if you only want a local birth mother in your home state, that is unlikely to happen if they rely solely on national Internet advertising, leading to most placements being out of state.
5. Ask the attorney or agency you will be working with if they agree to work with facilitators. Some work regularly with facilitators and have a good relationship. Others may view them as infantpreneurs who use questionable networking techniques and have a reputation for arranging risky and expensive adoptions, and will decline to work with them.
6. Ask the facilitator for a list of past adoptive parent clients. Don't accept referrals to adoptive parents simply "matched up" with a birth mother, or who just received a baby but the adoption is not finalized by the court. Those are adoptions "in progress," and things can still go wrong. Insist on speaking to recent adoptive parents who have *completed* their adoptions in court. They can report on the entire gamut of working with the facilitator from beginning to end. I'd also recommend you ask for a significant number of referrals, not just three or four. Even the worst professional in any business will please *some* of their clients. You want to be sure they please *most* of them. Accordingly, I'd ask for at least ten recent referrals. Most facilitators I've encountered boast of helping with a very large number of adoptive placements every year. If this is true, there should be no problem giving you a large number of referrals.

When you speak to their prior adoptive parent clients, ask:

- How long did you wait to be selected by your birth mother?
- What was she like? (See if the typical birth mother located by the facilitator is of the ethnic group you hope to adopt from, has a health and drug history you feel is appropriate, etc.) Remember that you are talking about the birth mother of the child the adoptive parents adopted, so you want to be respectful in your

questions, but thorough enough you feel confident in the information you obtain.

- Did you have any false leads prior to the placement that worked?
- What were the fees you paid the facilitator?
- Were there any fees you didn't expect?
- Did you get the chance to meet the birth mother before the birth?
- Were you given complete birth mother (and birth father, if available) health histories?
- Did the facilitator cooperate with your attorney or agency?

There are some good facilitators performing a valid service, for a fee commensurate with the limited services they are able to provide. Unfortunately for the adoption field as a whole, many are profiteers with little adoption training, and adoptive parents have little recourse when the adoption is handled improperly.

So there you have it, a wide selection of networking techniques and strategies to help match you with a birth mother. Let's review what we have so far:

- You are going to select not only a skilled adoption attorney or agency but one whose services include networking for birth mothers, helping to lead to an adoptive match, or alternatively advising you on your own networking campaign.
- You are not going to sit and wait to see when, or if, your attorney or agency will be successful in creating an adoptive match. You are going to mount your own networking campaign.
- You are going to put great effort into the best photo and résumé letter you can make, and duplicate it as needed to effectively network.
- You are going to choose not one, but several, networking strategies. These include, in my personal order of preference:
  1. Personal networking (mandatory for an effective campaign)
  2. Nontraditional networking (mandatory, at least 1,000 letters)
  3. Traditional networking (mandatory, at least 1,000 letters), if not doing nontraditional networking

4. Internet advertising
5. Adoption business cards
6. Newspaper advertising
7. Facilitators

Do you think we are done strategizing? Not a chance! Maybe the biggest part of guaranteeing you a fast, newborn adoption is in the next chapter, "A Key Factor: The Power of Three."

CHAPTER 9

A Key Factor:
The Power of Three

The routine way to do a newborn adoption is to select an adoption attorney or agency and wait for them to tell you that you've been selected by a birth mother. That's the norm across America. It's just the way it has always been done. There is certainly nothing wrong with that, particularly if you maximize your odds of success by hiring a great attorney or agency and are diligent in your networking.

Even when doing everything right, you might still find that you wait longer than you want for your adoptive match to occur. Part of the reason for this is that no matter how active you are in your adoption efforts, the bottom line is that you still have to wait for a birth mother to pick you. Adoption is a game of "hurry up and wait." You diligently hire the right professional, energetically prepare your photo-résumé letter, get your networking efforts going, and then sit and wait to be picked. You might be lucky and get picked in a fraction of the time you expected. It happens. But for every adoptive parent who gets picked in a week, there is someone else at the other extreme, perhaps waiting years. This can be true even for adoptive parents in the same geographical area, with personal and lifestyle characteristics similar to yours. It's much like dating, and like dating, it is not always a fair process. Why does one person find the perfect spouse at age twenty-five, and another person, equal in every way, never finds that special partner? Adoption has the same dynamics. Thus, the issue becomes beating the odds, and doing so quickly.

This is how you do it. As we've discussed, the key to being matched with a birth mother is hiring an attorney or agency that includes birth mother networking in their services. But who says you only have to hire one? Tradition?

Forget tradition.

I want to encourage you to hire *three* attorneys and/or agencies. That's right, three, not one. And I recommend you hire them all *simultaneously*, don't wait to hire someone new only if you become disappointed with how long the process might be taking with the first one.

Your first thought will be "I can't afford that." Wrong. You are probably assuming that hiring three adoption professionals will triple the cost. To the contrary, though it will increase the cost of your adoption, it will not even double it. Here's why. You are not hiring three adoption professionals to do the *entire* adoption for you. Instead, you are hiring them to perform the initial stage of their services: advising you on adoption laws and procedures in their region or state and showing you to birth mothers contacting their office. As we discussed in Chapters 3 and 6 regarding selecting the right attorney or agency, those with the fairest payment schedules charge as they work through the different stages of the adoption. Only a portion of that will be due initially, until you are matched with a birth mother.

So you pay each of the selected professionals their initial fee, then when one of them comes up with an adoptive match you wish to accept, you can kindly thank the other two for their services and let them know their services are no longer needed. The only fees you have thereafter will be for the attorney or agency who created your adoptive match. (If you are doing an interstate adoption, you will still need one attorney/agency in each state.)

Doing the math is simple. If the average time to be picked by a birth mother in a particular region when working with competent attorneys or agencies is fifteen months (averaging those lucky enough to be picked in days, and others waiting years), by hiring three you've mathematically reduced your average to five months. Of course, the average waiting time in one region might be more or less, but you get the idea. Because you've tripled your exposure to birth mothers, you have tripled your chances. It's that simple. It's that obvious.

By the way, the money you pay to start with to the professionals you will not end up using is not necessarily wasted. If you are like many adoptive parents, particularly if you are adopting your first child, you will likely be considering starting another adoption a few years after completing the first one. Often the retainer agreement with the "dismissed" attorneys or agencies who did not create the first match will provide that you can become "active" again with them, as you paid the initial fee and are entitled to return to that stage with no additional initial fees. This gives you the chance to start a new adoption later with virtually no money out of pocket. In other words, you're prepaid for adoption number two.

So how do you put such a plan into action? Think back to when we discussed finding the best attorney and/or agency, looking in both your home region and other states you wanted to consider. Likely you found several well-qualified attorneys and agencies and had a hard time narrowing it down to just one, particularly if you did a broad search in more than one state. Now you don't need to limit yourself to just one.

Not every attorney or agency is right for this strategy, however. Some will have fee structures that require an unreasonably large percentage of their fee up front. These attorneys or agencies are not for you, and I warn against hiring such a professional even when hiring just one. You also need to be honest with whomever you are hiring that you plan to take this approach of hiring several adoption professionals and continue only with the one who first helps create a good adoptive match. There are some adoption professionals who do not like this multiprofessional strategy and will insist on being the only entity involved in your adoption. Fine, that attorney or agency is not right for you. To me, those individuals should be avoided anyway, as their mind-set shows they consider themselves to be the center of your adoption. You, your birth mother, and the child to be adopted are the stars of the adoption process, not the attorney or agency.

Unlike the few attorneys or agencies insisting on being the one and only professional in your adoption, the vast majority will be happy to work with other adoption professionals, knowing you will proceed only with the one creating your adoptive match. In fact, you are creating a healthy unspoken competition between the entities you hired. This can only be to your benefit. Each wants to look good and produce results. Each wants to do the entire adoption and earn their fee. It's simply human nature. The knowledge that you have others out there trying to do the same thing for you can only serve to give them extra motivation to work hard and create an adoptive match for you. They realize adoptive parents share information with each other. They know you are going to be telling people, *"We hired one attorney, Rick Jackson, and an agency, Children's Family Services, both in our home state, and an attorney out of state, Helen Williams . . . and it was Rick who came through for us first."* Believe me, they want to be the one who produced results.

The key question for you when employing this strategy is whether to focus your efforts in one region, or to spread out into other states. As you know from Chapter 2, there are fourteen different types of adoption available to you. If you are like most adoptive parents, several options seemed attractive. In fact, it was likely tough for you to choose between doing everything in state and doing an interstate adoption, an identified adoption, or a nonresident adoption. Now you don't need to choose just one. You can open the door to several types and see which comes through for you first.

Here is some specific advice. Let's say you live in a large metropolitan area (Los Angeles, Chicago, etc.) in a state with good adoption laws, good adoption attorneys and agencies from which to choose, and a significant number of birth mothers making placements within the state. With all that going for you, you might prefer an in-state adoption using only local professionals. Therefore, you might want to hire all three of your professionals in your state. There is one disadvantage in this, however. All these professionals are competing over the same geographic pool of birth mothers. Some birth mothers might contact several attorneys and agencies to find the right adoptive parents, and you are getting less exposure for your investment. Accordingly, if you are hiring all three professionals in state, consider spreading them out a bit, at least into neighboring counties.

If you are open to an out-of-state adoption, either interstate or nonresident, this opens up unlimited doors for you, as you are not considering attorneys and agencies in just one state, but several—perhaps even the entire nation. Now you can really analyze the state-by-state review and determine which states appear attractive when considering their laws, available attorneys or agencies, and sufficient birth mothers making placements, and consider a nonresident or interstate adoption.

I think the best utilization of the Power of Three strategy is to mix attorneys and agencies, selecting one of one type and two of the other.

Depending upon your state, either attorneys or agencies will be the primary way adoptive matches are created. Also, even if your local agencies do not create as many adoptive matches as attorneys, if your state requires a preplacement home study from a private agency (as compared to some states that only require a postplacement home study), why not use the agency for the double duty of the required home study and trying to create an adoptive match? Due to the fact that laws and procedures vary so much from state to state, it is impossible to provide one perfect strategy for everyone. However, by the time you have finished this book and spoken to some local professionals, you will find that the best routes for you will be clear. It is just up to you to act on them.

You can also use this strategy between completely different types of adoption. So far, I've only discussed it in terms of domestic, newborn adoption. But let's say that you are open to either adopting a newborn born here in the United States, or an existing child from another country via international adoption. Let's further say you recognize that there are no guarantees with either type of adoption and you are not sure how soon a birth mother will pick you, and that delays and problems can occur with international adoption as well. You just know you want a child, and you want to start your family as soon as possible.

There is no reason you can't hire one or two attorneys or agencies to start a domestic adoption, and concurrently start an intercountry adoption from the country you choose. If you are selected by a birth mother before a child is available for you overseas, you can put the intercountry adoption on hold (perhaps until you are ready for your next child) and complete your domestic adoption. If you are not picked by a birth mother and you get the word there is a child now available to you through intercountry adoption, you can complete that adoption and put the domestic one on hold. The only thing to be aware of in this example is that the costs of intercountry adoption can often be more front-loaded, due to the costs of preparing a dossier and submitting it overseas. Also, some intercountry programs will want a commitment from you to not start another adoption once your dossier has been submitted overseas.

This is a reasonable issue as the intercountry agency or attorney would not look good in the eyes of the foreign country if its adoptive parents continuously withdraw from the process after time and energy has been expended by the foreign country. One advantage, however, at least if you live in a state requiring a preplacement home study in an independent domestic adoption, is that you can often get "double duty" out of your home study. You will need one for your international adoption to start the process overseas, so why not use it if necessary for a domestic adoption? Usually there is no reason the same agency, for a small administrative fee, can't retype the same home study in a slightly different format as required for a domestic placement.

Here are some sample scenarios and how to perhaps best use the Power of Three:

- *You live in a state with unfair adoption laws and few or no adoption options.* Hire all three attorneys or agencies in states permitting nonresident adoption, and do virtually everything in the state of birth. (You will still need a local agency for your home study, so you might want to consider that as one of the three).

- *You might be moving to another state and hesitate to hire local attorneys or agencies.* If your present state permits nonresidents to adopt, and the adoption laws are fair, there is no detriment to hiring local attorneys or agencies, as they can continue to fully serve you if you move. However, if your present state does not allow nonresidents to adopt, you should consider adoption professionals in states allowing nonresident adoption, so they can assist you regardless of where you live. Alternatively, the adoption professionals you hired before you moved can continue to network for a birth mother and do the adoption as an interstate adoption, to be finalized in your new home state.

- *You live in Connecticut, Georgia, Illinois, Maryland, Minnesota, New Jersey, or New York, states that bar attorneys from finding birth mothers to create adoptive matches, or doing so for a fee.* Hire a skilled adoption attorney in your home state, but hire two out-of-state attorneys or agencies who can network as part of their services to you. Or, you can retain an in-state agency, which unlike attorneys *can* network under these states' laws, to meet your in-state needs, *if* you feel the agency and their in-house attorney can meet your legal needs as well as an independent attorney.

- *You live in a region with good adoption attorneys and/or agencies, and in a state with fair adoption laws, so you'd like to finalize the adoption in your home state, but there appear to be few birth mother matches created locally.* Hire a local attorney or agency to handle the in-state work and court finalization, but concurrently hire two out-of-state attorneys or agencies experienced in creating adoptive matches. You can then do an interstate adoption from virtually any state, where the child will be born, but you will be completing it in your home state.

- *You just want a child as soon as possible and don't care if you adopt a newborn or an older child, via domestic or international adoption.* Hire two domestic adoption attorneys or agencies to start networking for a birth mother, and one international agency or attorney to start the overseas adoption. Since both domestic and international adoption require home studies, sometimes you can use the preplacement home study prepared for an international adoption for a domestic adoption, avoiding a waste of those costs.

Well, you can't say you don't have options! You might even complain you have too many. That's a nice problem to have. Best of all, the Power of Three strategy triples your chances of success, cuts by 67 percent the likely time of that success, and opens the door to hundreds of supremely qualified attorneys and more than a thousand agencies throughout the nation. The only limits you have are those you choose to set on yourself.

CHAPTER 10

Risky Adoption
Red Flags

I firmly believe the surest way to avoid a failed adoption is to never start a risky one. Just because you are selected by a birth mother as adoptive parents doesn't mean that you will want to accept the placement and work with that birth mother. You want to make sure she is the right person for you, doing it for the right reasons. Hard as it may be to believe, sometimes that means passing on an adoption opportunity.

How do you spot a risky adoption? It is not mystical at all. No fortune-teller is required. Looking at specific characteristics of the birth family and the motivations for adoption will give you the answer. That, and your gut instincts—the same instincts that safely guide you through life—will separate the "right" from the "wrong" placements.

The Birth Mother's Age

Many people wrongly assume that most adoptions are started by high school girls facing unplanned pregnancies. Although there is a high number of unplanned pregnancies in the high school years, fewer of these pregnancies result in adoption than those of older women, usually aged eighteen to twenty-six. What happens to all those high school pregnancies? Most of these young women will terminate their pregnancies, or raise the children themselves.

Generally speaking, the younger the birth mother is (as well as the birth father), the riskier the adoption is. There are several reasons for this. The biggest one is the lack of life experience and maturity that a young girl will have, as compared to someone more mature. A young birth mother doesn't yet know what it means to face the obligations of parenthood and life as an adult. All her needs have been met by her family. An older birth mother, however, has faced issues such as having to earn money for rent, what it feels like to be hungry because your paycheck wasn't as much as needed, coming home from work tired and having no energy to do anything, much less care for a child as a single parent. Also, a young birth mother is subjected to the peer pressure of her equally young and inexperienced friends who think it would be "fun" to have a baby, or who perhaps are young single moms themselves and want their friend to share the experience.

The biggest reason working with young birth mothers is risky is simply the narcissistic nature of most teenagers. Most care about themselves and their lives at this moment in time and little else. This may sound simplistic, but talk to the parents of the vast majority of teenagers, and you will be convinced it is true. An example we can all associate with is the first time someone breaks your heart, the girl or guy who you were sure—at age sixteen—was the person you wanted to spend your life with, and your heart aches when you lose them. At the moment of that breakup, you believe that pain you are feeling will never heal and your life is over. As adults we all know that feeling will pass, and we will go on to fall in love again. But when you were sixteen you would have done *anything* to make that pain go away if you had it within your power.

So, let's compare this to adoption. Imagine you are a very young birth mother giving birth for the first time. You face more emotions than you ever thought possible, and the pain of losing your child is unimaginable, despite common sense and parents telling you that you are too young to parent. You know adoption is the right thing, but it hurts to say good-bye to the child you just gave birth to. Hurts more than you thought it would. More than you thought possible.

What do you do if you are that young birth mother if the law grants you the right to change your mind? Unlike with failed love, you *do* have the power to relieve your pain. So do you eliminate your pain by stopping the adoption? Some will, and that is the danger of young birth mothers. Of course, any birth mother can change her mind, teenager or adult, but the younger she is, the greater the chance she will be unable to deny her emotions.

Does this mean you should never ever work with a birth mother under a certain age? And if so, what is that age? Fourteen? Sixteen? Eighteen? No, it does not mean that. I've worked with birth mothers as young as twelve (I'm sad to say) and have seen those adoptions work out fine. So what is the answer?

I think the key is not focusing specifically on a numerical age, rather the birth mother's maturity. There might be cases where a fifteen-year-old birth mother is more mature, and therefore more likely to make the placement, than some twenty-year-olds. Her maturity is going to depend on many factors: her life experience or lack thereof, how she was raised, her degree of fortitude, and similar factors. The only way to determine this is to personally get to know the birth mother and encourage her to receive professional counseling (discussed later) to help prepare her for the emotions ahead.

The Influence of Family and Friends

We are all influenced by those around us, particularly the people most important to us—our family and friends. For this reason if a birth mother is surrounded by negativity, where her closest friends and family members are trying to dissuade her from placing her child for adoption, it creates a significant risk. Remember that her family and friends are only doing what they feel is right for her and themselves. Don't take it personally, as rarely does it have anything to do with you as the adoptive parents. It is simply their hope that she will keep the child in the family.

Sadly, often it is clear to an impartial person that the birth parent should not be listening to this negative advice, as anyone can see the future for the birth mother and child will be bleak. There are millions of people in the United States, however, and hundreds of millions around the world, who live in similar, or worse, situations than she does. They face poverty, lack of education, single parenthood, and other challenges, yet they survive. We have to understand that not every decision has to make sense to us. Some families and friends will just be against adoption, despite all the reasons to the contrary.

So what do you do when that happens? One important consideration is the birth mother's age. If she is young, she is much more likely to give in to family pressure. This is particularly true if she is a minor living with her parents. In most states a birth mother under age eighteen does not need parental consent to place a child for adoption (see the state-by-state review), but she is dependent upon them for everything else. She would be hesitant, as would any of us, to alienate those she is dependent upon. Also, if her family says they will take care of the baby and do all the work required, the birth mother is more inclined to say "yes."

Situations involving negative input from family members are entirely different when a birth mother is an adult, no longer lives at home, and is not financially dependent upon her family. A disagreement over the pregnancy and how to deal with it is likely not the first time she has had disagreements with her family about how she should live. Since she is already on her own she is much less likely to be controlled by their desires. If her parents do not live locally, she may not even share the fact she is pregnant, preferring to not admit the unplanned pregnancy to her parents.

Luckily, few adoptions involve a great deal of antiadoption sentiment by a birth mother's family and friends. Most want what is best for her and have enough life experience to know raising a child under difficult circumstances will cause both her and the child to suffer. Actually, in the vast majority of adoptions I've handled, most involve overwhelming support for adoption from the birth mother's parents and family. That is why it is a significant concern when that support does not exist. It is not unusual for a birth mother to have one or two people against the adoption, but if this is just a small percentage of the people who have an impact on her life, you can be confident that she is receiving emotional support from most of her key people.

The Due Date

Birth mothers can start adoption at any time in the pregnancy. Some will call an adoption attorney or agency the minute they discover they are pregnant, perhaps only two months along. Others ignore the fact they are pregnant, wait until the last minute, and finally contact someone when they give birth. This brings up a question: is there a good or bad time to start adoption planning?

The answer is that yes, there are times when adoption planning should be avoided, or at least delayed. Starting an adoption with a birth mother early in her pregnancy, such as in the first trimester, has several risks. Let's look at the practical reasons first. There is a 15 percent chance that a pregnancy will be miscarried during the first trimester. Do you want to incur the financial and emotional costs of an adoption only to have it result in a miscarriage? You may have already gone through that heartbreak as part of the infertility that brought you to adoption. The last thing you want to do is go through it again, even indirectly via adoption, if it can be avoided.

The other reason is that when a birth mother is so early in her pregnancy, it is generally too soon for her to make a complete emotional commitment to adoption. She can *intellectually* determine it is the best decision for herself and the baby. *Emotionally*, however, she can't anticipate how she will feel about the pregnancy until she *feels* pregnant. Until she is far enough along to feel a baby inside her, and perhaps even start "showing" enough for people around her to remark on the pregnancy, she can't truly emotionally come to grips with the pregnancy. So what happens if she made a commitment to you as adoptive parents when only two months pregnant, then by the eighth month is asking how she got herself into this situation and wants a way out without hurting you? The likely answer is a failed adoption.

This doesn't mean you can't start an adoption with a birth mother two or three months along, but it does mean you acknowledge the extra risk in doing so. The safest course is to work with birth mothers who are at least halfway through their pregnancies, or even better, in their last trimesters. If a birth mother contacts your attorney or agency and she is too early to intelligently start adoption planning, the smart professional won't immediately match her up with adoptive parents, nor will he or she turn the birth mother away. Instead, he or she should begin to work with her, perhaps start counseling and get her started on paperwork that will later be necessary in the adoption (health history forms, etc.). This allows the birth mother to feel she is accomplishing something and know she has a plan in place, yet slows down the start of the adoption. Soon, a month or two will have passed and she will be far enough along to start adoption planning.

There is usually no such thing as starting "too late." Some birth mothers will even wait until they are at the hospital and they have already given birth. They may have been in denial about the pregnancy, been embarrassed, or simply not known who to call. Amazingly, I've actually had some birth mothers tell me they hesitated to call someone because they were afraid there would be a legal fee for them to pay to place a baby for adoption. Last-minute "after-birth" placements can often be the most secure, as the birth mother has gone through the one emotional moment most adoptive parents fear the most—the birth—and wants to plan an adoption. The only detriment to starting an adoption when the birth has already occurred is that you don't have the usual time to gather information, get full medical records, try to find birth fathers, etc. This means that there can be unsolved legal risks before you bring the baby home.

Health History

Your agency or attorney should have the birth mother (and birth father if he is available) complete detailed health history forms. It is my belief that the adoptive parents should be given this information prior to even meeting a birth mother. This is because some health issues, such as extensive drug usage during the pregnancy or extended family members with congenital health problems or psychological disabilities, could be so severe that they may influence your desire to even start the adoption. Even if there are no such serious conditions in the birth family, you will want to know as much information as possible to share with your pediatrician.

Knowing about your child's biological history is tremendously important. When your child's pediatrician asks you if anyone in the family is allergic to a particular medicine, is left-handed, or wears eyeglasses, not to mention more serious questions, the birth mother will not be standing next to you to answer. You need and deserve complete, written health histories. If you are adopting a not-yet-born baby, the health history you receive will likely be exclusively from the birth mother (and sometimes the birth father) based upon their family knowledge and any relatives they contact for more information. If you are adopting an older child, you should additionally have the child's existing medical records.

It is unreasonable to expect an adopted child to have a perfect health history. Every family—likely yours included—has a grandparent who had a heart attack, an aunt who battled obesity, an uncle with diabetes and other maladies. Such things are just part of life. Those problems don't make everyone in *your* genetic circle unadoptable, so why think of others that way? However, if there are potential health concerns of a major nature, you owe it to yourselves and the child to be sure you are prepared for the challenges that might lie ahead.

Adoptive parents often ask about what happens if the child they plan to adopt is born with a medical problem they did not anticipate and feel they can't handle. Do they have to complete the adoption? This question might sound hard-hearted and cruel, but it is a fair question. The answer is no. You are not the legal parents until the adoption is granted by a court. This means, as tragic as it would be, that adoptive parents have the right to abandon a placement should they feel they need to do so. Although this may sound wrong, remember that birth mothers have the same right to change *their* minds after the birth, so to some extent it is fair, as each can back away from the other.

In addition to the completion of birth parent history forms, an important part of obtaining health information is via the birth mother's doctor. It is common for the birth mother to sign an Authorization to Release Medical Information. This form waives the doctor-patient privilege and allows the medical office to release records and information about the pregnancy and fetus to the attorney or agency, or directly to the adoptive parents. In many open adoptions, the adoptive parents are accompanying the birth mother to some of her doctor appointments, so they are right there next to her to hear what is said, ask the doctor questions, and stay up-to-date. This may seem to make the need of an information release form unnecessary, but there may be instances where the adoptive parents do not accompany the birth mother to the doctor, or want to discuss information not addressed at the medical appointment.

Here's a final thought on health histories that, depending upon your mind-set, will make you feel better or worse about health issues. In many cases, the birth father cannot be found. This is due to the fact that a significant number of adoption situations arise out of one-night stands and casual relationships, meaning last names and contact information was not exchanged. Or, perhaps he is known but does not wish to be contacted, for fear of child support obligations if she was to keep the baby or other complications. The result of these common situations is that sometimes there is no birth father health history available, besides the cursory information the birth mother will know, such as his ethnicity and general appearance.

So how is this lack of birth father information in many adoptions going to make you feel—better or worse? Well, some adoptive parents worry so much over a birth *mother's* health issues that they realize the futility of such worries when the other half of the gene pool is basically unknown. For other adoptive parents, this only serves to double their anxiety. The same issues exist in international adoption, but even more so, as sometimes there is even little or no information about the birth mother.

Drug or Alcohol Usage

Sadly, drugs are becoming more and more common in our culture, so they are a reality we have to deal with in adoption. Does this mean that all birth mothers use drugs? No. Does it mean *most* birth mothers use drugs? Again, no. There is no way to definitively state the percentage of birth mothers who use drugs, but it is fair to say it is a small amount, but sizable enough that you may face the issue. (When I say this I am referring to voluntary adoptions, not county adoptions where the child was taken from the birth parents due to drug problems.)

Naturally, you want a drug-free pregnancy. Every adoptive parent does. But does that mean you should decline a birth mother who has selected you if she used drugs or alcohol during the pregnancy? Obviously, you can decline such placements, but you may be passing on what might be an excellent adoption without the risks that you believe exist.

First of all, you need to decide where you draw the line in drug usage, and that requires that you educate yourself. In addition to the assistance of your family doctor, gynecologist, and your attorney or agency, an excellent resource to learn more about the potential effects of drugs on a fetus is the Organization of Teratology Information Specialists. They have access to studies on all types of fetal drug exposure and the potential consequences and can answer hypothetical questions. "If a woman used crystal methamphetamine a few times in the first trimester, then stopped, but smoked marijuana twice a week in the last trimester to help stop nausea, what is the likelihood that could affect the baby, and if so, how?" No one can give a definitive answer, but they can tell you what is known. Their website is www.otispregnancy.org. Their toll-free number is (866) 626-OTIS.

You will be surprised to learn that some drugs do not cross the placenta, meaning they usually don't directly affect the fetus. What about drugs that *can* affect the child? Every adoptive parent will view the situation with a different comfort level. Would you consider working with a birth mother who only smoked marijuana a few times early in the pregnancy, then stopped when she learned she was pregnant? Most adoptive parents would accept that placement with no hesitation. What if the drug was crystal methamphetamine, but was again used only a few times early in the pregnancy? At this point some adoptive parents will back away, while some would stay on board. What if it was consistent usage of methamphetamine throughout the pregnancy, and she tested positive for drugs at birth? Or daily alcohol? Most adoptive parents would abandon ship right and left, leaving only a few families interested in the placement. These are personal decisions and everyone's feelings and interpretation of available research will vary.

Whatever you decide, it is important to make your decisions based on actual research, not knee-jerk reactions. Here's an example. Let's say you are presented with a birth mother who consumed a single glass of alcohol daily, perhaps more on the weekends, throughout the pregnancy. And let's also say she smoked multiple packs of cigarettes throughout the pregnancy too. You are probably ready to bail on this adoption already. You are thinking of things like fetal alcohol syndrome and the carcinogens from the tobacco. I won't even try to dispute those concerns, but here is a question for you. Ask everyone you know who is in their late forties or older if their mothers smoked cigarettes and drank alcohol on a daily basis while pregnant. In fact, ask yourself about *your* mother's pregnancy if you are in this age range. I predict a large number will answer yes to both questions. No one knew any better back then, so many women drank wine every night, perhaps cocktails on the weekend, and smoked while pregnant. Now ask yourself, do all those people who just answered yes suffer from fetal alcohol syndrome? Are they in terrible health due to their mothers' smoking? Most likely, the answer is no, and your friends in that age group are normal people, not a generation of unadoptable men and women.

Don't get me wrong. I'm not encouraging you to ignore issues like drug and alcohol usage. They are indeed important and you need to talk to your family doctor, your obstetrician/gynecologist, and resources like those provided in Appendix C. I am, however, encouraging to not pass on a placement due to what might be incorrect assumptions on your part.

The birth mother's honesty. Many worry that a birth mother may lie about important issues like her health history and drug usage. This is true; she could lie. But then, so can adoptive parents lie to a birth mother. Luckily, I find that few birth mothers lie. The reason that a birth mother plans for adoption is simple: she wants a wonderful life for her child. She is hardly doing that if she lies about important facts, hurting the child later by having hidden that information. After all, she could have terminated the pregnancy—in some ways an easier option for her—but instead she went through a forty-week pregnancy and the painful and potentially life-threatening experience of childbirth just to give that child to you. Such sacrifices do not normally jell with lying.

Still, there will always be some birth mothers who lie, and usually it will be about drug usage. This is where your attorney's or agency's approach is critical. If he or she is very nonjudgmental with the birth mother, and from the very beginning makes clear to her that there are adoptive families waiting out there regardless of whether there was drug usage or not, she is much more likely to be honest.

Drug testing. Fears over a birth mother using drugs may lead you to request drug testing. This is a possible option, but has disadvantages. For example, if you are working on having the kind of open, trusting relationship many newborn adoptions start with, and she tells you she has never used drugs, and you reply, "Of course we believe you, but take a monthly drug test anyway," her opinion of you is likely damaged. She may agree to what you want and not complain, but a bit of the unequivocal trust she needs to see in you—the future parents of her child—may disappear. A good example might be if your spouse required you to take a polygraph test before you got married, fearing you were lying about things in your past. You might agree to do so, but you'd be deeply hurt over the request and your relationship may suffer.

Another reason drug testing is not as beneficial as you might think is that they are not infallible. Certain drugs only show up for certain periods of time after usage (some only days, and some, like marijuana, usually longer), and tests can sometimes be tricked or have false readings. Blood tests generally show positive results longer than urine tests, so if you elect drug testing, doing so by blood is usually more reliable. If a birth mother is a savvy drug user, however, she likely knows exactly how long a particular drug will be in her system and when she'd be clean for a test.

Of course, the reverse could be true as well. It's conceivable that a birth mother inclined to take drugs could be dissuaded from doing so if she knows she'll soon be tested. I don't find this very persuasive, however, because if she used and then tested positive, and you declined to work with her anymore, she'd just find another adoptive family. So there goes the dissuasion theory; there's no real penalty for her if that's her true inclination. I think usually the best route is to decline to work with a birth mother you don't believe in and work with one you trust. That may sound absurdly simple, and I will admit it is not foolproof, but then neither are the above "safeguards" of drug testing. Each option has its pros and cons. I think selecting the right birth mother, then showing faith and trust in her, offers the most pros and the least cons.

Goals and Future Plans

Birth mothers who have future goals and plans are more likely to place than those who don't. Those who have no interest in getting a job, pursuing an education, finding the right man and marrying, or improving their lifestyle, are more likely to look at the baby right after birth and think that he or she can fill the void and make her life complete. Compare this to a birth mother who has dreams and goals, and can recognize that raising a child at this time, under these circumstances, will ruin or delay the goals she has for her future. This latter type of birth mother is more aware of the child's future as well, and understands how future opportunities would be diminished is she were to try to parent under her present difficult circumstances.

Feelings of the Birth Father

I consistently talk about birth mothers in this book, but don't mention birth fathers nearly as often. This is no disrespect to birth fathers, but is rather a reflection of the reality that very few of them elect to get involved in adoption planning. Every adoption has a birth father, whether he is findable or not, and that makes him potentially an important part of the adoption.

When the birth father is unknown or can't be found, or is findable but has no interest in the pregnancy, many birth mothers consider adoption. A pregnancy is viewed completely differently, however, when it results from a caring relationship with a loving partner. If he wants to raise the baby, either alone or with her, this is potentially a major disruption in the adoption on two fronts. One is that he could seek to object to the adoption on legal grounds (discussed in Chapter 12). The other is that, even if he has no plans to object in court, if he prefers that she keep the baby, he may try to influence her to change her mind. If their relationship is, or was, a solid one, this will make his feelings a significant influence on her.

Luckily for adoptive parents, a very small percentage of nonmarital birth fathers elect to object to adoption planning. Most of the pregnancies are results of one-night stands, casual encounters, or terminated relationships. This makes both birth mother and father unlikely to want to be linked to each other for life through the child and is one more reason for adoption.

Regardless of the birth father's initial feelings when he is contacted, the surest way to get him to cooperate in adoption planning is to treat him with respect. Acknowledging that he is an important part of the child's creation, asking him for a personal and health history, and extending an offer to send pictures and update letters about the child if he is interested, are important courtesies. This is particularly true with birth fathers who are initially unsure if they want to parent the baby or not. Sometimes, just like a birth mother, they need time and counseling to see the benefits of adoption and see it as a loving, unselfish act. Some wrongly initially see it as abandoning their duties as a man. The more they understand about the true nature of adoption, however, the easier it will be to let go of any antiadoption sentiments.

Legal Risks

Before starting any adoption, it is important to consider any legal risks. To some degree, every adoption has risk, such as the chance the birth mother will change her mind. I'm referring to avoidable issues, however. For example, are you aware in advance of a legal challenge that will be filed in the adoption? This could be by an objecting birth father, an Indian tribe's intervention pursuant to the Indian Child Welfare Act, or other problem. (There are several potential trouble spots in every adoption and these potential issues are discussed in Chapter 12).

It is critical is to analyze every possible complication in the adoption based upon the unique facts in your adoption. You may elect to proceed despite the possibility of a known problem, but if you do, you want to know the full extent of the risk. Will you have to go to court? How long will the court action take? How much will it cost? How likely are you to win? Have you considered the effect on you and the child if you bond, then have to give up custody after protracted litigation? Fortunately, litigated adoptions are rare. One reason for this, however, is that many cases destined to be litigated are abandoned before getting to that point.

Motivation for Adoption

There are many reasons for a birth mother to start an adoption. In a nutshell, the "good" reasons are a combination of either not wanting to parent a child, or recognizing they are not ready to be a mom, usually combined with factors like insufficient income, inadequate employment, having one or more other existing children to raise, the goals of college or a career, or lack of an appropriate relationship with the birth father. We need to be on the lookout, however, for the "wrong" reasons.

Sometimes a birth mother will either consciously or subconsciously start adoption planning as a way to spur the birth father into action. Perhaps he greeted her disclosure of the pregnancy with apathy, and he is a man she had hoped—and still hopes—to have a relationship with. She may think adoption will get his attention and nudge him into action, to mature and solidify their relationship. The only way to determine if this is her motivation is to get to know her and learn more about her feelings and changing emotions toward the birth father. Some giveaways can be that the birth mother and father had a long relationship, or are only very recently broken up. Usually it is fairly clear when she is not "over him."

Another improper motivation is if she is placating someone important to her, doing the adoption to get their approval, when it is really not what she wants. This could be the birth father who is telling her he will continue being her boyfriend, but not if she keeps the baby, or her parents who are already raising one or more of her children (and know this one will soon become their responsibility as well). In these situations, the birth mother is trying to please *them*. But if it's not what *she* really wants and feels in her heart is the right thing, she is likely to change her mind when the baby is born and her true emotions come out.

The greatest concern regarding improper motivation is money. It is understandable that a birth mother needs a safe and comfortable place to live and food to eat, both during the pregnancy and while she recovers. For this reason, most all states permit adoptive parents to provide pregnancy-related assistance. There are two areas of concern, however, in these financial arrangements. Some birth mothers will want improper financial benefits, literally wanting to be "paid" for their baby. Not only is this illegal, but it demonstrates a birth mother who is trouble in every way and is placing a child for the wrong reasons. These situations are easy to spot and avoid. (See Chapter 12 regarding permitted financial assistance and the state-by-state review.)

Questionable financial situations that are more difficult to spot are those where the birth mother is seeking assistance in categories that are legally permitted, but are grossly excessive. For example, a birth mother may need to rent an apartment. Accordingly, a standard apartment, likely one she could afford on her own when she starts working again after the pregnancy, is reasonable. Some birth mothers may insist on an apartment that might be double or triple what they would normally stay in and could not afford to live in afterward. With this kind of birth mother, you will usually see other pregnancy-related costs enhanced as well, such as food, maternity clothing, and transportation. Even if these expenses could be considered lawful as they fall within appropriate categories for pregnancy-related expenses, it is clear the birth mother is seeking to grossly escalate her lifestyle at your expense. When this becomes the motivation for adoption—turning a pregnancy into a luxury vacation—she is a risky birth mother to work with as her true motivations are suspect.

Will She Accept Counseling?

Counseling is often an important part of success in adoption. The problem is, however, that most birth mothers feel they don't need counseling, so don't embrace it when offered. (Although a few states make counseling mandatory, in many cases it is optional.) Birth mothers will often say they know what they want and don't need counseling on the subject. It could be they are correct. They could also be wrong.

What they typically don't understand, due to their young age and inexperience, is that while their decision toward adoption seems obvious to them now, things can change dramatically at, and shortly after, the birth. The emotions involved in giving birth—likely for the first time—and seeing the baby, plus the effect of hormonal changes due to the pregnancy and childbirth (you've likely heard of "baby blues" and postpartum depression), not to mention the reality that she may never see her child again, can hit her like an emotional sledgehammer.

The goal of counseling is twofold. First, it is to help her explore her options and let her reaffirm to herself that adoption is the best option for her and the baby. Second, it is to prepare her for the likely emotions of birth and separation, so she knows to expect them. Counseling can serve as a "pause button." If she is feeling more emotional pain than she anticipated postbirth and is thinking the only way to stop that pain is to stop the adoption, she can remind herself that her counselor discussed these very emotions and that her pain means she is a normal, loving human being, not that she is making a mistake. Rather than give in to those temporary emotions, she is more likely to look back to the decisions she made when she was more analytical.

Pressure to Go Forward

Earlier I discussed the dangers of pressure on a birth mother. Now I want to talk about pressure on *you*. It is possible that your photo-résumé will fall into the hands of an adoption facilitator, agency, or attorney who is less than ethical and will aggressively contact you (one more reason to put your attorney or agency's number on your photo-résumé letter, not your own). These adoption businesses may have seen your photo-résumé letter online, or received it indirectly from your networking. Many of these individuals have few or no waiting adoptive parent clients, but advertise for birth mothers. When they find one they show any available photo-résumé letters (yours), then call you to say you've "been picked" by *their* birth mother. It likely does not surprise you to hear that this revelation is immediately followed by the need for you to send money to them and/or the birth mother to "secure the placement." If you hesitate, they will say that they will have to call another family, one "the birth mother can count on."

It would be easy to recommend that you not bother speaking to businesses like these, even if they claim they are reputable because they are a licensed agency or attorney. (Yes, even some agencies and attorneys engage in such behavior, not just facilitators.) But I'm aware that is easier said than done when they are presenting you with what appears to be an excellent adoption situation. Admittedly, even "bad" agencies, attorneys, or facilitators can be contacted by an excellent birth mother. This creates a difficult situation: the birth mother is great, but the adoption entity is someone you'd normally never hire.

If you want to consider going forward in such a situation, here are some things you want to do:

- Have your attorney or agency talk to the birth mother and make sure it appears to be an appropriate placement, with no legal impediments to success.
- Have your attorney or agency talk to the entity that found the birth mother about their legitimacy, fees, and any information they have on the birth parents.
- Receive a full health history for the birth mother (and if he's available and willing, the birth father).
- Have the birth mother sign an Authorization to Release Medical Information so you can speak to her doctor to confirm the pregnancy and inquire about her medical condition.
- In most states (laws vary) it is wise to have your attorney or agency speak to the birth father to be sure he will not be opposing the adoption.
- Speak to the birth mother initially by phone; make sure she likes you and you feel confident in her. If the initial calls go well, arrange to quickly meet her in her region, or pay to have her come to you, so you can meet face-to-face to be sure the placement is right.

- If your attorney or agency is in the same region where you will be meeting the birth mother, have him or her meet with the birth mother face-to-face as well to give you additional feedback.
- Only pay the intermediary when you are confident and ready to go forward with the placement. Also, ask yourself why this business is calling you, a stranger to them, rather than making a placement with one of their own existing families. These types of questionable entities, even if they are a licensed agency or attorney, usually state they "can't keep up with so many birth mothers calling." The reality, however, with many such businesses is that the word is out on them, and they can't attract clients and must troll for them, the adoption version of an ambulance chaser. Don't forget the advice from Chapters 3 and 6 regarding how to inquire about the legitimacy of an attorney or agency. Many of them will apply to situations like these.

As you can see, risky adoptions throw up many red flags. Does this mean you should never do an adoption with a red flag? No, it does not. It means that the pros and cons in each adoption must be weighed and analyzed, by both you and your adoption professional.

Some red flags, such as a birth mother "selling" her baby, are so significant that the one such factor alone is enough to send you running away. Other factors, however, are less significant and you might only want to pass on the adoption if there are multiple cautions. This is where the guidance of your adoption professional will be tremendously helpful. Likely he or she has met hundreds or thousands of birth mothers and has a good feel for what to expect. That, combined with your own gut instinct, usually results in successful adoptions.

CHAPTER 11

Working with the Doctor and Hospital

Adoptive parents often have a great deal of anxiety over being fully informed about their future child's health. This is understandable. When you are planning to adopt a not-yet-born baby, it is the birth parents' health histories, and those of their extended families, that is sought. We've previously addressed the fact that this is accomplished by having birth parents complete detailed health histories. But what about the records and information about the fetus, the birth mother while pregnant, and the baby at birth?

Access to Medical Records

If you are like most adoptive parents, you understandably want to do more than look at health histories and review a doctor's notes (even assuming they could be deciphered). You want to simply call the doctor or his or her staff and ask prebirth questions like, "Is the baby okay?" "Does the ultrasound look normal?" "Is there anything we should know, or problems we should be prepared for?"

There are two ways to make this happen. Every birth mother should be asked to sign a form called an Authorization to Release Medical Information. This form waives the doctor-patient privilege and allows the doctor's office to speak to those named on the form. Usually the form will list you as the adoptive parents, and either the agency or attorney. If it is a closed adoption and everything will be done through an adoption agency, they will usually be the ones in direct contact with the doctor and will forward the information to you.

If you live in a state where it is the norm to have an open prebirth relationship, and you live close enough to make it feasible, it is not unusual for you to actually accompany your birth mother to several of her doctor appointments. This is great for both you and her. For you it is wonderful to share in the prenatal care, to get to know the doctor and personally ask questions, and to have special moments like seeing the fetus in an ultrasound, or hearing his or her heartbeat. From a birth mother's perspective, these moments are also important. The chance for her to see your emotion at these times helps reassure her how much you want to be parents and how excited you are about the baby. It can help forestall any subconscious doubts that you will not love the baby like your own.

Postbirth, the hospital is given the Authorization to Release Medical Information form, allowing you to have full access to medical information for both the birth mother and the baby. This not only applies to verbally asking questions, but to having a copy of the birth records sent to the pediatrician you've selected.

Regardless of how you receive the information, you will want to share it with your obstetrician/gynecologist or family doctor so you fully understand any information provided, both *before* and *after* the birth. In a well-planned adoption the goal is for the combination of the birth mother's completed health history forms (and the birth father's if available) and direct conversations with her doctor and, later, hospital staff, to leave you as fully informed about the pregnancy and birth as you can possibly be.

Each state has different procedures regarding releasing the baby to you from the hospital. This can also depend on whether you are planning an independent or agency adoption. Even within the same state individual hospitals may have different policies. As a general rule, however, in most independent adoptions the child will be released directly to you, usually requiring the written permission of the birth mother, or in some states, a judge. There is almost never a foster home intermediary placement. In some agency adoptions, an immediate placement can also be made, but in some states the agency will keep the child in foster care for a short period until the child is legally free for adoption, a process that can take only a few days or much longer. The state-by-state review in Chapter 15 provides the typical hospital release procedure for both independent and agency adoptions in each state.

The Hospital

While the child is at the hospital, many states allow you to have contact with the baby, including both holding and feeding. You can also have contact with the birth mother. In fact, in many open adoptions, the adoptive mother, sometimes the adoptive father as well, is asked by the birth mother to be her labor coach. Not only will sharing in the birth of your child be a wonderful moment for you but who better than you to take part in the birth in the eyes of the birth mother? Of course, some birth mothers are more modest and may prefer that you wait outside until the birth is complete, and those feelings are to be respected.

When you interact with your birth mother at the hospital, it is important that she sees you care about *her* as a person, not just as a means to get a baby. That means spending time with her *and* the baby. It is also a great time, if she has elected to see the baby, to take pictures of all of you together. This is a great way to one day show your child it took all of you, loving him or her, to create your family. It also shows your birth mother that you value and appreciate her, and that you will be sharing the knowledge of her critical role in your child's birth and in placing you with your child.

Some birth mothers fear seeing the baby after the birth will be too difficult for them, and if so, those feelings should be respected. Never make a birth mother do something she is not comfortable with. Most birth mothers, however, want to see the child they created and gave birth to, and to have time for a personal good-bye. Many birth mothers refer to the time with the baby at the hospital as "their time," noting you have a lifetime thereafter. Often, the issues of seeing or not seeing a baby after birth are discussed in prebirth emotional counseling.

Insurance and Medical Costs

Virtually every state allows you to pay your birth mother's medical costs, although some states require that it be paid through an agency or attorney, or that you obtain court approval first. It's nice, however, if you can avoid medical costs. It may surprise you, but it is very common in adoption that the adoptive parents don't have to pay *any* medical costs. Many birth mothers have insurance through their jobs. Others may be covered by their parents' policy, if she meets certain age and residency requirements. Regardless of which situation it might be, the coverage might be an HMO (health maintenance organization) with 100 percent coverage, or a PPO (preferred provider organization) with only 80 percent. Still, paying only 20 percent is much better than 100 percent.

Her insurance eligibility should not be affected in any way by the fact that the baby is being placed for adoption, other than coverage will usually not extend into nursery or pediatric care after you have custody. Of course, usually your health insurance coverage will pick up coverage from this point, leaving you with no uninsured period. You will want to discuss this with your health insurance provider in advance. Sometimes though, even when both you and the birth mother have insurance, there will be an interim period when neither insurer feels they should provide coverage. This is an issue your adoption professional can look into before the birth to avoid any surprises.

What about if she had no insurance? Can she use yours? The answer is virtually always no. This is because each policy holder is a determined risk by the insurer, and while they agreed to insure you, they did not agree to insure someone whose health history they know nothing about. You are the insured, not the birth mother, even if the baby is to be placed with you.

Medicaid

Not all birth mothers will have insurance. In fact, most won't. That doesn't mean you are destined to pay medical bills, however. If a birth mother is unemployed or has low-income employment, she will be eligible for her state's version of Medicaid. If the birth mother isn't already on such a program when she starts adoption planning, you can often assist her with application. Usually the only requirements are to show that she is a resident of a particular county and state, is pregnant, and is income eligible. Just as with insurance, the fact that she is placing the child for adoption should not affect her eligibility. Usually Medicaid coverage will cover 100 percent of her medical costs, although not all doctors and hospitals will accept the coverage, as frequently the payment is less than what is paid through private insurance.

Each state has different insurance regulations determining when your insurance can cover the baby after the birth. Some will start as soon as the baby (or an older child) is placed with you for adoption. A few will not provide coverage until the adoption is finalized by a court, which might be six months or more away. Since no one wants to see a child without insurance, however, normally the birth mother's coverage (if any) will apply until your coverage takes effect.

What if the birth mother has no insurance and is not eligible for Medicaid? Perhaps she makes too much money at her job, but insurance is not offered there. Well, this means you will probably be paying medical bills, so you will want to know what they will be in advance. You will usually be paying a doctor for both prenatal care and to deliver the baby, and separately the hospital for using their facility. Sometimes other doctors are required, such as an anesthesiologist if she is having a caesarean birth or an epidural. Also, a pediatrician will charge for examining the baby at the hospital.

Doctors usually charge a flat fee for both prenatal care and the delivery. Usually there is one set fee for vaginal deliveries and a higher one for caesarean births. Some doctors, if they know a patient has no insurance, will offer you a prepay discount if you pay in advance. Many hospitals are the same way. They often have a special discount rate if you pay before the patient (the birth mother) is discharged. These discounts can be huge, particularly with hospitals, sometimes as much as 50 percent. The reasoning is that when someone comes in for medical care and has no insurance, the hospital may never receive any payment, so they'll gladly accept a lesser payment if it is timely.

CHAPTER 12

Legal Issues: Step-by-Step

There are many legal steps on the road to a completed adoption. Some of them are routine steps. Others, usually arising with difficult or contested adoptions, involve issues you hope to avoid. The best way to avoid those issues, however, is to know about them from the start. That allows you to have a chance to solve the problem before becoming too involved emotionally or financially in an adoption, or to avoid the adoption entirely. Let's look at the routine procedural steps in every adoption, as well as the legal issues that can come up along the way, in the order you are likely to encounter them.

The Petition for Adoption

Every adoption requires court approval to be granted. The start of the process to obtain approval is to file a Petition for Adoption. In most cases this is filed shortly after the child is placed in your custody. Some states will require that the birth mother first sign her consent, others allow it to be signed and filed later. In some agency adoptions, particularly public adoption agencies, the child may need to be in your home for a prescribed period before the petition can be filed.

The Petition for Adoption will normally identify you as the adoptive parents and establish the court has jurisdiction to handle your case (based upon your residence, where the baby was born, etc.). It will also name the birth mother and father (if known), the date and place of the child's birth, the name of the child on the initial birth certificate and how you would like it to be changed after the adoption is granted, and list what agency, social worker, or state adoption office will be doing your home study.

Who prepares and files your Petition for Adoption? In an independent adoption it will be your attorney. In an agency adoption it will usually be either an attorney you have hired, or one on staff for the agency. The first issue is where you will file your Petition for Adoption. In most cases you will file it in the county and state in which you live. In fact, usually you have no choice and can only file in your local court. Some states, however, allow nonresidents to adopt in their state and permit you to file it in the county and state of the child's birth, the location of the placing adoption agency, or sometimes even the birth mother's residence.

Your Petition for Adoption, once filed, will be assigned a case number by the court and a file will be opened. Adoption files are normally confidential, so the only parties permitted access besides court personnel are you, your attorney, and the home study agency.

The Birth Mother's Consent to Adoption

As an adoptive parent, one of your primary concerns in your adoption is when the birth mother can sign her consent to adoption, and when it becomes permanent and irrevocable. Every state is different, not only regarding what they call the consent but also when it can be signed, who must act as a witness, and when it becomes permanent. The form used for a birth mother to give up her parental rights might be called a *consent*, a *relinquishment*, a *surrender*, or a *voluntary termination of parental rights*. Forty-eight states require a birth mother to wait until after the birth to sign her consent, while two—Alabama and Washington—allow it to be signed before the birth (although it will not become permanent until after the birth).

Most states impose a waiting time after the birth before a consent can be signed. Many states make this period seventy-two hours, while others require a longer time. Each state will also designate a specific person who can witness the consent. This is usually a judge or a social worker, or sometimes an attorney. Even within a state, the laws regarding when a consent can be signed and before whom can vary between independent and agency adoption. Please refer to the state-by-state review in Chapter 15 to see the specific procedures in the states of interest to you.

If you live in one state and your birth mother lives in another, do you execute a consent under the birth state's laws or those of the state where you live? The answer depends upon the states involved. Some states will accept the consent to adoption as prescribed under the laws of the state where the birth occurred. In other states your home state's consent forms and procedures can be used, even if the birth occurred in another state. In many cases, you end up executing double consents, one under both states' laws. Even if this is not required, it is often a good idea. This is because sometimes a *conflict of laws* issue will arise: each state has different laws, and there is a dispute regarding which should apply. The safest thing in many cases is to execute both consents, providing extra security for you. The last thing you want is to execute only state A's consent, have a dispute arise, and determine state B's laws apply. If you did not have the birth mother sign state B's consent, it may be determined she never gave up her parental rights and you will be powerless.

Some states require a birth mother to have her own attorney to advise her of her rights. Others require counseling or meetings with a social worker. The goal is the same: to protect a birth mother and make sure she knows her rights and options. In a very small number of states, if the birth mother is under eighteen, she must have the consent of a parent, or a court-appointed individual (sometimes called a guardian ad litem), to give up her parental rights. In the vast majority of states, however, birth mothers under eighteen do not require the consent of a parent or other person.

Can the Birth Mother Revoke Her Consent?

Every adoptive parent's worst nightmare is that their birth mother will place the child for adoption, then change her mind. Although some states make her signed consent permanent the moment it is signed, most give her a prescribed time in which to revoke the consent. This might be twenty-four hours, seventy-two hours, ten days, or even a month or more.

Some states make this right to revoke the consent automatic, imposing no burden upon the birth mother, other than to perhaps fill out a form. Other states require a court hearing to prove the child's best interests would be served by being with her rather than with you.

Once the revocation period is over, the birth mother has basically lost the right to change her mind and you can feel fairly secure. The principal exception would be cases where the birth mother can prove that fraud or duress was used to obtain her consent. Such a showing could invalidate a birth mother's consent after the usual revocation period has passed. Such situations are extremely rare, however, for the simple reason that adoptive parents and the adoption professionals they work with are smart enough not to use fraud or duress. Fraud, by the way, is usually considered a significant deception, not simply a small misunderstanding. For example, situations involving sufficient fraud to invalidate a consent would include the postbirth discovery that you had a criminal history that you had tried to hide, not that she thought your eyes were blue when in fact they are green. It is almost unheard of for a birth mother to challenge an adoption on grounds of fraud, even more so for such a request to be granted.

The state-by-state review provides each state's unique laws regarding how long a birth mother has to change her mind and revoke her consent to adoption and any burden she is required to prove.

When the Birth Mother Does Not Consent

If the birth mother refuses to sign a consent and wants to stop the adoption, normally she has the automatic right to stop the adoption and reclaim her baby. There are some circumstances, however, where an adoption can proceed without the birth mother's consent, although they are not commonly used. Such situations can arise when the birth mother disappears after placing the child with you but before signing her consent, or where she refuses to consent, yet does not seek custody and wants the child to stay with you.

Every state has some kind of provision to involuntarily terminate parental rights in order to protect a child's best interests. One such action is *abandonment*. Typically, if a birth parent fails to fulfill her parental responsibilities, specifically not having any contact with the child or providing financial support, a court can terminate her rights and allow those who have been caring for the child to adopt. The required length of time to constitute abandonment differs, but is usually six months. Abandonment situations are rare in independent or private agency adoptions, and are more common in the adoption of older children via public agency adoptions.

The Rights of the Birth Father

When a pregnancy results from an established, caring relationship, even outside of marriage, the expecting parents usually elect to keep the baby. Adoptions rarely come from these situations. Instead, they are usually the result of one-night stands, short relationships, or relationships that soured with news of the pregnancy, leading the birth father to distance himself (often fearful of a lifetime of child support and parental obligations). For this reason, many birth fathers welcome the news of adoption and elect to cooperate.

Determining the rights of birth fathers, and the proper way for them to show their consent, can be a complicated legal issue. This is because not only does each state have different laws regarding birth fathers rights in adoption but each state will also distinguish between different categories of birth fathers.

Escalated fathers' rights. Some birth fathers will have escalated rights due to a special relationship with the birth mother or the child. This usually includes a man who is married to the birth mother, or who has lived with or supported the child prior to the adoption. Usually for an adoption to proceed with a birth father in this category you will need to obtain his consent. If he refuses to give it, you may be unable to adopt the child, unless a situation such as abandonment exists. Sometimes this creates tragic results. For example, a birth mother may honestly tell you of fleeing her spouse because of his physical abuse. That birth father will be subject to both criminal and civil penalties for that behavior, but it will be almost impossible for you to use that as grounds to adopt his biological child without his consent.

Putative fathers. Most birth fathers do not fall into the escalated category above. In fact, they are quite rare in adoptions. As you likely assume, most birth fathers in adoptive placements have only a casual relationship with the birth mothers, or perhaps were dating for some time but now have no desire to take responsibility for a child. Most states label this category of birth fathers as "putative" (and some use the term "alleged"). The overwhelming majority of men in this category not only support adoption, but are thrilled about it, as it will end their anxiety over potential child support obligations if the birth mother were to keep the child. Be cautious, however, of the few birth fathers who may seek to challenge the adoption against the desires of the birth mother.

States fall into two general categories in determining the rights of these types of birth fathers. Some states are "notice" states, and put the burden on you as the adoptive parents and require your attorney or agency to give written notice to the birth father, informing him about the pregnancy and adoption. Usually he will have a set time in which to object, and if he doesn't, his rights can be terminated in a fairly simple court proceeding. Many states even allow putative birth fathers to waive their rights *before* the baby is born, usually by signing a simple form, and a court can usually terminate their rights shortly after the birth.

Sometimes the birth father can't be found. He may have moved and not given the birth mother his new address, or their relationship was so short that phone numbers and addresses were never exchanged. He could even be hiding out of fear of his potential obligations and court proceedings. In these situations your attorney or agency will need to show due diligence was used in trying to find the birth father. This might include a property records check, a phone book search and a motor vehicles bureau inquiry. Some states will require publishing the notice of paternity and adoption in a local newspaper, usually buried in the back with the classified ads.

If he can't be found with due diligence, typically the court can sever his rights and the adoption proceeds without difficulty. Sometimes a birth mother will not even know the birth father's last name. In those cases, search efforts are usually impossible (you can't do a search for "John in Cleveland"), so his rights are terminated as an "unknown father."

What if a putative father receives his notice and is one of the few who wishes to object and seek custody? Each state will define his rights differently, but most will require a judge to examine his behavior and lifestyle and ask questions like: "Did he take responsibility for the pregnancy and help the birth mother with her expenses and other needs during the pregnancy?" "Can he emotionally and financially care for a child?" "Would the child's best interests be served by being with him, or the adoptive parents?" Accordingly, if the birth father acted "like a man should" with a baby on the way, he may be tough to defeat in court. If he avoided responsibility, requiring you to step in and fulfill the birth mother's needs, and his lifestyle is not compatible with parenthood, he is more likely to lose.

As a general rule, I think if you are *sure* there will be an objection from the birth father, it is safest to not even start the adoption. Sometimes, however, you may be unsure how a birth father will react, making your decision difficult. For example, the birth father's feelings may vacillate, or he may say things you believe he has no intent to follow through on. In those cases, you may wish to proceed, but you want to be sure the law will be on your side if litigation ends up being required. Many states give putative fathers a limited time to object, such as thirty days.

Not all states are "notice" states, however. Many are "registry" states. A registry is completely different in that it puts the burden on the birth father, not the adoptive parents. Men in these states typically must voluntarily register themselves as the possible father of an expected child in order to later seek to establish any rights. Their failure to do so will normally result in the termination of their rights when a designated period has passed, often thirty days. A court hearing will still be required to terminate his rights, but often all that must be established is his failure to register. Some registry states require that notice be given to putative fathers and use the registry as simply another way to help them be found.

Perhaps soon altering the above information is the "Proud Father" legislation. This pending congressional bill will, if passed, create a national birth father registry. It would likely supplement, not replace, state registries. At this time, the bill is still being amended, so its implications are presently unknown. It is believed, however, that even if it passes it would not markedly interfere with existing state law, but rather be an additional database to check for locating possible birth fathers.

Unknown "John Doe" birth fathers. What about if a birth mother has relations with more than one person and is not sure who the birth father is? Do you have to do blood tests? Normally, no. In most cases you give notice to each possible birth father, or see if they listed themselves in the state registry, and find out if any of them plan to object. If one or more does, then paternity testing will be required, as obviously only that father would have the right to object. If the father is unknown, your attorney or agency will simply terminate the rights of every possible father to eliminate any risk.

The state-by-state review provides information about birth fathers' rights in each state. In some states the laws in this area are either too complex or too vague, in which case they are not included.

Interstate Compact on the Placement of Children

It is becoming more and more common for adoptions to be interstate, meaning the child is born in one state, and you as adoptive parents live in a different state. Whenever a child is brought across state lines for purposes of adoption, a special law called the Interstate Compact on the Placement of Children (the ICPC) applies. Basically, it says that before a child can be brought across state lines, both the "sending state" (where the child was born) and the "receiving state" (where you live) must give their approval in writing. Violating the ICPC can put your adoption at risk. Some states even make violation a criminal offense.

The ICPC applies to both independent and agency adoptions. It normally does not apply to international adoptive placements, however. To obtain Interstate Compact approval, your attorney or agency will initially contact the sending state's Interstate Compact administrator. Each state has this special office, usually a division of the state's Department of Social Services. Each state has the right to make its own requirements, so for this reason there is no complete uniformity in satisfying the Interstate Compact, which adds to its complexity. Generally, however, you will be required to provide your preplacement home study, the birth mother's health history (and the birth father's, if it is available), and about half a dozen forms detailing the planned placement and outlining who will have financial and medical responsibility for the child.

Many states will also require the birth mother's consent to adoption and the hospital's discharge summary of the baby before giving final approval for you to leave the state. If you live in a state where independent adoptions do not require a preplacement home study, this is the one situation where you will be required to have one. Depending upon your state, you will obtain it through a private adoption agency, a social worker, or a state adoption office.

It commonly takes about one week postbirth for the sending state's Interstate Compact administrator to have what is needed to give its approval, at which point the documents are forwarded to the sending state for its approval. The receiving state's Interstate Compact administrator then needs to give its approval for you to transport the child across state lines and come home, and this is usually done within one to two days. In most cases, it is automatic that the required approval will be given, although the bureaucracy to obtain it can be daunting to anyone not an adoption professional.

The state-by-state review provides each state's Interstate Compact office address and telephone number.

The Indian Child Welfare Act

The Indian Child Welfare Act (ICWA), is a federal law taking precedent over state law. Passed into law by Congress in 1978, it was intended to protect Indian culture and keep Indian children from being removed from existing Indian families and placed into non-Indian foster or adoptive homes. The intent of the law is an honorable one, but sadly the language of the law is so vague and far-reaching it has become difficult to apply.

The ICWA provides that if a child is a member of an American Indian tribe, or is the biological child of a member and is eligible for membership, written notice of the planned adoption must be given to the tribe, granting the tribe the right to object and allow Indian adoptive parents to be considered. It also requires a court hearing to find "good cause" to place the child with a non-Indian family (such as the desires of the birth parents, lack of the "Indian" birth parent having a true cultural connection with the tribe, etc.), and for a judge to witness the birth parent's consent. Under the ICWA a birth parent normally has a longer time in which to withdraw their consent, as the ICWA grants them until the adoption is finalized, which might be six months or more after birth. Obviously, this scenario adds potential risk to you.

On the one hand, very few adoptions are actually affected by the Indian Child Welfare Act. On the other, many adoptions are impacted.

How can both those contradictory statements be true? Here's how. Many of the young women placing a child for adoption, when asked about their family background as part of a normal adoption health and social family history, will state they may have a small amount of Indian heritage. In this sense, many adoptions can be affected, as any possible tribe must be contacted to inquire about membership. To find the location of any named tribe, your attorney or agency will usually contact either the Bureau of Indian Affairs, and review the *Tribal Leaders Directory*. The Bureau of Indian Affairs is a federal government office with its headquarters in Washington, D.C., and regional offices all over the nation. It is then up to any contacted tribe to write back and state if membership exists and the ICWA applies.

Even if it is verified that the child you plan to adopt has some Indian blood, it does not mean the ICWA applies to your adoption. Every tribe has different rules regarding tribal eligibility. Many require a minimum of 25 percent Indian blood, while some use other factors and can accept less. Some tribes have closed membership, perhaps so as to not dilute their existing tribal benefits among a larger group, and will decline membership even for someone who otherwise might be eligible.

If it is determined that the ICWA applies to your adoption, the next inquiry is if the birth parent or child is living or domiciled on the tribal reservation. This increases the tribe's rights as clearly the child has a significant connection to the tribe, and their interest is understandably greater. In these cases, which are very rare, the tribe has the right to block the adoption and have a tribal court hear matters related to the child.

In the few cases where the ICWA does end up applying, normally the birth parent is not living or domiciled on a reservation. In these cases, the tribe has a less significant connection to the birth parent and child, and their rights are weaker as a result.

It should also be known that most tribes are supportive of adoption, even when the adoptive parents are non-Indian. The usual thinking is: "If this is what the birth parent wants, we will respect their decision about whom they've selected as adoptive parents." This is especially true in the many cases where the birth parent has had virtually no connection in her or his life to the tribe, never visiting the reservation or embracing tribal customs, etc. For this reason, only a small number of tribes actively seek to disrupt voluntary adoptions. In these cases, however, great caution must be used to do everything correctly. In some cases, such as where a tribe has indicated it will object and the birth parent was living on the tribal reservation, maximizing tribal rights, good judgment may dictate not even starting that adoption.

Birth Mother Financial Assistance

Many adoptions involve almost no financial assistance to the birth mother. Many birth mothers live at home or have a job and have insurance or Medicaid. They don't need, or are too proud to accept, financial help. Often the assistance might be limited to counseling and maternity clothes. However, some adoptions will involve financial assistance. Usually this is due to the birth mother being unemployed, just losing her job and not being employed long enough to qualify for benefits, or perhaps she and the birth father were living together and the pregnancy led to their breakup and now she needs some help. Regardless of the reason, some birth mothers will need your assistance.

Almost every state permits you to assist the birth mother with pregnancy-related assistance. Unlike surrogacy, where some states allow an actual payment for the service of being a surrogate, adoption laws forbids such remuneration. Most states will permit you to help with such basics as medical care, rent, food, utilities, maternity clothes, counseling, and transportation needs. (See your state's limits in the state-by-state review.) Some states will require a judge's approval prior to the payment, while others do not, perhaps requiring an accounting of all prior expenses to be submitted before granting the adoption.

Any assistance you provide is basically a gift. That means if she changes her mind and stops the adoption, you can't demand your money back. Neither can you write up a contract that says you will pay her rent in exchange for a baby. That's buying and selling a baby. It is usually wisest to make any pregnancy-related assistance through your agency or attorney. That way, not only does that give them a chance to confirm the payment is legal and appropriate but it establishes a degree of financial formality with the birth mother.

In most areas of adoption, the closer you are with the birth mother, the better. In financial areas, however, it can not only make both you and her feel uncomfortable, it leads to potential conflict. Let's say, for example, she requests assistance with a particular item and you know it falls outside of the permitted pregnancy-related assistance categories. It is much better for the birth mother to be told "no" by your agency or attorney (whom she will view as just doing their job), rather than by you (which she might interpret as being cheap or uncaring).

Some states have specific periods both before and after birth when assistance is allowed. Most, however, use general language like "the pregnancy-related period," which creates some flexibility. In most cases, living assistance starts, if needed at all, several months before the birth, and continues until about six weeks postbirth. As was discussed in Chapter 10, you should be cautious in working with a birth mother if her expenses seem inappropriately high, perhaps seeking to greatly escalate her lifestyle at your expense, even if the assistance is technically legal and falling into permitted pregnancy-related categories.

CHAPTER 13

Finalizing the Adoption and Postbirth Issues

Normally, going to court causes anxiety. It's rare we go there for a "good" reason. In the case of adoptions, however, we go only with joy. This is because most adoptive parents only have to go to court one time, and it's when everything is done and the adoption is ready to be finalized.

The Court Finalization Hearing

When the birth mother's consent has become irrevocable, the birth father has consented (or waived his rights or otherwise had his rights terminated), and any other legal obstacles have been satisfied and your home study is complete, your attorney or agency will schedule a court hearing for you to finalize the adoption. (Even in agency adoptions an attorney is normally used for the final hearing.) In almost every state each adoptive parent must be present, as well as the child and the attorney. The hearing is closed to the general public, although you can invite guests who can be present. Unlike most court hearings, which are quite formal, adoption finalizations tend to be casual and relaxed. In fact, most judges spend more time posing for pictures with the adoptive family and the child than in conducting legal proceedings.

Usually the hearings start with you being "sworn in." Then you confirm your identity, your desire to adopt the child, and your willingness to raise the child as your own, with the duties and obligations that accompany that, including the right of inheritance. The judge will then confirm that he or she read the final report from your agency or social worker in which you are recommended as adoptive parents. He or she will then sign and issue what is called a Decree of Adoption or Order of Adoption, granting the adoption and making you, officially and permanently, parents.

The Amended Birth Certificate

The original birth certificate (naming the biological mother as the child's mother and with the child's name listed as she elected) will become sealed and technically no longer exist very soon after your adoption is finalized. A new, amended birth certificate will then be issued, listing you as the child's new and only parents. This new birth certificate will not name you as *adoptive* parents, rather just as parents, as if you gave birth yourselves. It will also name the child as you've elected, in the event the birth mother put another first or last name. This new birth certificate will usually take several months to arrive from your state's birth registrar or bureau of vital statistics. In the meantime, you can use the Decree of Adoption to show your legal status as parents. In the future, when you do the many things parents do, such as registering your child for your school, Little League, and so on, you will only need to show your child's amended birth certificate, as would any parent. The decree will not be needed, except in a few legal areas, as discussed in this chapter.

Social Security Cards and Passports

When your child's amended birth certificate arrives you can obtain such items as a Social Security card and passport. Some birth mothers will have started the Social Security card process in the hospital, or you might be adopting an older child where one already exists. In those cases, you show the Decree of Adoption and the new birth certificate and have the Social Security information changed.

In most newborn adoptions, however, the hospitals do not have the birth mothers complete Social Security card applications, leaving it to be done by you when the adoption is complete. The Social Security Administration has vacillated regarding how adoptive parents can get a new Social Security card. Previously they could issue one immediately after the finalization hearing, and require only the original birth certificate and the Decree of Adoption. It was not necessary to wait for your amended birth certificate. More recently, however, they have been requiring the Decree of Adoption and the amended birth certificate, although it is uncertain if they will continue this policy.

A passport can be applied for right after the adoption is granted by providing either the original birth certificate and the Decree of Adoption, or waiting for the amended birth certificate and using only that.

Taxes, Tax Credits, and Dependents

You have the right to name your child as a dependent on your tax forms as soon as you have lawful physical custody. You don't need to wait until the adoption is granted. You will not have a Social Security card number at this early point, however, so the Internal Revenue Service can issue a temporary tax identification number for your child, to be used in place of a Social Security number on your return.

You are additionally eligible for a federal adoption tax credit as an adoptive parent, and it's substantial. It may even pay for your entire adoption. Generally, if your modified adjusted gross income is less than $170,820 in the year in which you finalize your domestic adoption, you are eligible for a $11,390 tax credit per adopted child. (It's per child, so this means a $22,780 tax credit for twins.) Your modified adjusted gross income can actually go as high as $210,820, but the credit decreases as you exceed $170,820. Be aware that a *credit* is much better than a mere *deduction*. An example of a deduction would be the interest payment on your home mortgage. The interest is deducted from your gross income, reducing the net income on which you pay taxes. A credit is a dollar-for-dollar elimination of taxes owed, like giving you back up to $11,390. If you can't use the full credit in the year in which you adopt because you don't have that much tax liability, it can be carried over for several years until fully used.

If you are doing an international adoption, you are also eligible for the credit, but you take the credit not only when the adoption is finalized, but as your expenses arise, not just after the granting of your adoption. In both domestic and international adoptions, the credit is only for actual expenses you incurred. So if your adoption only cost $5,500, you could only claim a tax credit of that amount. If you adopted a single child and your expenses were $18,000, you could claim the full credit, but would not be able to claim it for the $6,610 in excess. Your adoption expenses are eligible as long as they were lawful expenses, so the traditional expenses we've discussed (medical, living, attorney or agency fees) all qualify. Tax issues are complicated, however, so every adoptive parent should consult a tax professional. You might find that your state even has an additional state tax credit or other tax benefit.

The tax credit also exists in special-needs adoptions. There is one huge difference, however. The $11,390 amount stays the same, but you don't need to show that you actually incurred any expenses. So if your special-needs adoption cost only $500 (since many services may have been provided to you for free or a discounted fee), you are still eligible for the full tax credit. You will want to make sure your child qualifies as "special needs" before you count on receiving the credit, so check with your agency or special-needs exchange. Also, remember that to receive the tax benefits of the credit, you have to owe taxes. In other words, if your federal tax liability is going to be $15,000, your tax professional can show you how to only pay $3,010, so you are indirectly being given $11,390. If your income for the year you adopt is so low that you owe no federal taxes, you have no taxes to credit, meaning the federal government won't be issuing you a credit.

Postbirth Agreements

As discussed in more detail earlier, some adoptions are open. Many states provide that the birth mother or father can put an agreement with the adoptive parents in writing and file the document with the court. These agreements might call for the annual sending of pictures or letters, phone calls, or personal contact. These contracts are generally binding, unless their enforcement would no longer serve the best interests of the child.

Even in states where the agreements are specifically permitted, it is interesting that many birth and adoptive parents elect not to use them. Many seem to feel, upon getting to know and trusting each other, that no such formal contract is required. They seem to view this as some might a premarital agreement, feeling it taints their relationship. In adoption, however, a birth parent is very dependent upon adoptive parents keeping their promises, so you should never feel insulted if a birth mother indicates she'd like your promises in writing. After all, she's given you her promise in writing (the consent to adoption) that the child is yours forever. Receiving a promise in return is not asking too much. Even in states that don't have laws specifically permitting postbirth adoption agreements, they may be deemed enforceable, so you want to make sure that you feel comfortable with any promises you are asked to make.

Last Will and Testament

Once your child is adopted, he or she is your heir, just as if born to you. Accordingly, completing your adoption is an excellent time to update your will, or to write one if you don't yet have one. Separate from financial issues, however, is the welfare of your child if you and your spouse were to both die before your child reaches legal age. You will want to consider who will be the child's guardian, and who would manage your estate to best provide for your child's future.

CHAPTER 14

Surrogacy

This is a book on adoption. To adequately discuss the issue of surrogacy would take a book in itself, and indeed, many books exist on the subject. Accordingly, this chapter is to just give you a basic primer of how surrogacy works, the different types available, and some basic pros and cons. This brief overview might help you compare it to adoption if you are considering it as one of your family-building options.

There are two types of surrogacy, traditional and gestational. In traditional surrogacy, the surrogate is artificially inseminated, and she carries the child to term. It is her own egg that is fertilized, so she is the biological mother of the child. The sperm is that of the intended father (let's think of him as the adoptive father) or a sperm donor. In most states, after she releases the child to the intended parents, a stepparent adoption occurs, as the intended/adoptive father is the biological father, and his wife is the adopting parent. At this point any parental rights of the surrogate would end. Although this method was initially popular, with the advancement of new medical procedures, few surrogacies are now of the traditional variety.

In gestational surrogacy, the surrogate is implanted with an embryo via in vitro fertilization. The embryo is composed of the fertilized egg of the intended mother or egg donor. The egg was fertilized by the sperm of the intended/adoptive father or a sperm donor. In a gestational surrogacy, the surrogate is not genetically related to the child she is carrying. In most states, her rights as the birthing mother (and her husband's if applicable) are usually terminated in the fifth to eighth month of the pregnancy via a court adjudication of parentage. This gives rights to the intended parents upon the birth of the child, based upon the contract terms and the decisions reached by the parties prior to the pregnancy taking place. The vast majority of surrogacies are gestational.

Just as attorneys are deemed advisable in adoption, it is the same in surrogacy. You will want someone to screen potential surrogates to confirm candidates appear emotionally able to fulfill the role as surrogate, and that health backgrounds are appropriate, particularly if you are planning a traditional surrogacy (since it is her egg). Contracts will be required to not only define her (and your) duties and fees, but prescribe what will happen if things don't go as planned, such as a miscarriage. If she is married, her husband will have rights in most states, and that issue must be addressed. Many members of the American Academy of Adoption Attorneys also practice in the field of assisted reproduction. Although their bios in Chapter 15 do not include information on surrogacy experience, the AAAA website (www.adoptionattorneys .org) lists which members offer services in this field.

Surrogacy is normally quite a bit more expensive than adoption. There are two reasons for this. One is the medical costs involved in the surrogacy. The other is the fees of the surrogate. Unlike adoption, where a birth mother can't receive any gain (other than her pregnancy-related costs like food and rent), a surrogate can legally be paid a fee in most states. In a traditional surrogacy, the medical fees involved in the insemination, program fees, and the fees of the surrogate herself will usually total from $35,000 to $60,000. A gestational surrogacy will usually cost an additional $6,000 to $22,000 for the medical fees involved in the in vitro fertilization.

Just as in adoption, surrogacy involves risks. A surrogate might fail to become pregnant, meaning the medical costs are for naught. Her contracted fee, and that of the program overseeing the surrogacy, will be reduced, but some compensation will be required. If the pregnancy is initially successful but there is a miscarriage, she might be owed a larger portion of her fee, or her full fee. The same is true regarding the program overseeing the surrogacy.

There are also legal risks. In a traditional surrogacy, since the surrogate is the biological mother, she may seek to void the contract and maintain her parental rights. Her rights will be particularly strong in states where there is no specific authorization for surrogacy contracts. Even in gestational surrogacy, where she has no biological connection with the child, she might seek to establish custody or visitation. In these cases the courts are most likely to uphold the initial intent of the parties as set down in the contract, usually benefiting the intended/adoptive parents. For this reason, gestational surrogacy is seen as having few legal risks.

There are some very troubling issues that can occur with surrogacy. One term you will see in surrogacy contracts is "selective reduction." This means if the pregnancy is seen to be multiple births (not uncommon in with fertility drugs and the in vitro process) the intended/adoptive parents may have the legal right in their contract to terminate the viability of the other births. "Selective termination" is another issue, faced when the expected baby is seen to have a serious medical problem, such as Down's syndrome, giving them the right to terminate the pregnancy. Conflicts over such issues keep many adoption attorneys and agencies from crossing into the field of surrogacy.

Of course, many surrogacies are successful. Diane Michelsen, a California surrogacy attorney, estimates that approximately 50 percent of traditional surrogates become pregnant within three inseminations. The majority of the 50 percent who do not become pregnant are either more than thirty-six years old or attempting to be impregnated with sperm from men over age fifty. Regarding gestational surrogacies, approximately 85 percent of the surrogates carry a pregnancy to term. Of these, approximately 50 percent are twins. The failing 15 percent usually involves either an egg from a woman (the intended mother or donor) over age thirty-six, the use of less-than-ideal-grade frozen embryos, or those who did only one cycle who had an unexplained failure to implant.

Although the cost is higher, and the risk is more than doubled in surrogacy (the difficulty in achieving the pregnancy to even start the surrogacy/adoption and risks of the surrogacy changing her mind), many people continue to pursue surrogacy. The typical reason is the intended parents want the child to be fully or half their biological child.

CHAPTER 15

State-by-State Review

Each state has different laws and procedures. You will want to review the laws for your home state and all states in which you are considering working. Included here is information about each state's adoption office and key branches, their unique adoption laws and procedures, and a listing of every licensed private agency (including if they handle domestic or international adoptions, and if the latter, from what countries), and each member of the American Academy of Adoption Attorneys (including their biographies describing their experience and services).

State Adoption Office Information

The following is listed for every state:

- The state office overseeing adoption within the state (including the address, telephone number, and website address). The primary source for adoption state office information presented is the U.S. Department of Health and Human Services.
- The Interstate Compact administrator.
- The state adoption exchange. (In most cases this will be a website, permitting online viewing of waiting and special-needs children within the state. Please see Appendix B for national and regional exchanges.)
- The state bar association (to inquire about an attorney's license and inquire about any past complaints and resulting disciplinary proceedings).

- The annual number of adoptions finalized within the state. The data is provided by a study released by the U.S. Department of Health and Human Services in 2004 regarding adoptions completed in 2001. The figure given is the total number of adoptions via independent, private agency, public agency, and intercountry. The median percentage of the adoptions completed via public agencies was 32 percent. The median percentage of the adoptions that were intercountry was 12 percent. This means in most states the remaining 56 percent were independent and private agency adoptions, meaning the vast majority of these were newborn placements.

Summary of State Laws and Procedures

Many key legal issues are explored individually for each state. The information was compiled via independent research of state statutes and data provided by attorneys practicing within each state. Be aware that laws can change without notice, be interpreted differently, or applied by individual judges or authorities in different ways. Consultation with an attorney or licensed agency is necessary before initiating an adoption. The following information is provided for each state and the District of Columbia, allowing you to see the pros and cons of each state and determine which states might be right for you:

- Are both independent and agency adoptions permitted (and what is the percentage of each within the state for newborn placements)?
- Is a preplacement home study required for an independent adoption? This question relates only to an adoption completed fully in one state. Interstate adoptions always require a preplacement home study, even if your home state does not usually require one.
- What are the typical costs of a home study? This sum includes the preplacement portion investigation and the postplacement evaluation and supervision. Agencies almost always charge an additional, and often quite large, "placement fee" if they located the child for adoption and created the adoptive match for you.
- Who can file a Petition for Adoption within the state? Is it only residents, or can nonresidents do so when the baby is born there, or the agency supervising the placement is located there?

- Are the adoptive parents permitted to help with the birth mother's pregnancy-related assistance, and if so, for what specific items?
- Can the baby be released directly from the hospital to the adoptive parents, and if so, what documents or procedures are required?
- How long does it take after the baby's placement before the final hearing is set to finalize the adoption?
- Can adoptive parents advertise for a birth mother?
- How soon after birth may the birth mother sign the consent?
- Does she have a set period in which to withdraw her consent, and if so, for how long and with what legal burden? (Virtually every state permits a legal challenge by the birth mother if fraud or duress was used to obtain her consent, so this is not repeated for every state. As a practical matter, such challenges are almost nonexistent due to the lack of fraud and duress employed in adoption.)
- If the birth mother is a minor, does she need the consent of a parent or a guardian ad litem? (This information will only be listed if it is required, so its absence means there is no such requirement.)
- Is there a registry for putative (usually meaning "nonmarital") fathers, or is notice to him required? What are his rights to object? Only putative are discussed as this is the most common type of birth father in adoption and their rights vary tremendously state by state. Sometimes a summary of these laws is so complex, or vary within a state by judicial interpretation, a brief outline is impossible. In these cases it will simply be noted if a registry exists or notice is required. Men who are married to the birth mother (or who have otherwise escalated their rights, perhaps if they were living with and supporting an existing child) generally have rights equal to the birth mother, meaning their consent is normally required in many states.

Adoption Attorneys

Only attorneys who are members of the American Academy of Adoption Attorneys (over 300 members nationwide, discussed in Chapter 3) are listed. Each member was sent a detailed questionnaire about their law practice, and the information provided is a summary of their replies. To find new AAAA members, or the most up-to-date contact information for members, as well as see members' photographs, you may wish to visit the American Academy of Adoption Attorneys' website at www.adoptionattorneys.org.

Each attorney was asked the following:

- Their name, law firm name if not sole practitioners, address, telephone number, website, and email address.
- Are they in good standing with their state bar? All members replied "yes," so this information was not repeated in each biography.
- What year did they start practicing law?
- What is the total number of adoptions they've done in their career?
- How many adoptions did they complete last year?
- Do they have an international adoption program, and if so, from what country?
- What percentage of their clients locate a birth mother through the attorney's networking efforts, as compared to the adoptive parents finding their birth mother on their own?
- What percentage of the children they help place are newborns, as compared to toddlers and older children?
- Are they an adoptive parent, birth parent, or adoptee?
- Have they authored adoption books, or held office in national adoption organizations? (Many AAAA members listed a large number of adoption organizations to which they belong, but space limitations made it impossible to list most of them.)

Some attorneys did not complete their entire questionnaire. When that occurred, only the information provided was listed. Some questionnaire replies were not received, and in those cases just the attorney's name and basic contact information is provided, or limited information previously provided by the attorney to the author.

Private Adoption Agencies

Every licensed private adoption agency is listed for each state. In most cases there is an indication whether the agency handles domestic or international adoptions. For those agencies with international adoption programs, the specific countries in which each agency works is listed, if the information was available. The agency's city, telephone number, and website is provided.

Public agencies are not listed, but to find the local agency serving you, either contact your state's adoption office (the first office listed for each state within this chapter), your local telephone directory under "adoption" in the "County Government" listings, or in the federal government's website, www.childwelfare.gov (which was a primary resource for the agency information in this chapter). Before you retain an agency, it is recommended that you verify its license is in good standing with the state adoption office in the state in which the agency is located.

ALABAMA

STATE ADOPTION OFFICE: Alabama Department of Human Resources; PO Box 30400; Montgomery, AL 36130; (334) 242-8112; www.dhr.state.al.us/page .asp?pageid=306

ICPC ADMINISTRATOR: Alabama Department of Human Resources; 50 N. Ripley St.; Montgomery, AL 36130; (334) 242-9500; www.dhr.state.al.us

STATE ADOPTION EXCHANGE: Families 4 Alabama's Kids; Toll-free: (866) 425-5437; www.dhr.state.al.us/page.asp?pageid=483; fwilson@dhr.state.al.us

ALABAMA STATE BAR: (334) 269-1515; www.alabar.org

ANNUAL NUMBER OF ADOPTIVE ADOPTIONS FINALIZED IN STATE: 1,857

STATE LAWS AND PROCEDURES—FAST FACTS
Types permitted? Independent and agency (60% of newborns via independent).
Who can adopt in state? Residents, and nonresidents when child born in state or the agency making the placement is located in state.
How long after the child's placement to finalize the adoption in court? 3 months.
Is adoptive parent advertising (to find a birth mother) permitted? Yes.
Is a preplacement home study required? Independent—no. Agency—yes.
Typical home study fee? $800–$1,500 (agency fees usually higher if agency located child).
Can adoptive parents help birth mother with expenses? Yes: legal, medical, living.
Can child leave hospital with adoptive parents? Yes, with signed form.
When can birth mother sign her Consent to Adoption? If before birth before a judge. If after birth before a judge, social worker, or notary. (If under age 19 a guardian ad litem must be appointed.)
Can the consent be revoked? Yes, an automatic right for 5 days after birth or signing whichever is later; thereafter up to 14 days she must prove revocation would serve the child's best interests. After 14 days it is irrevocable.

What are the putative father's rights? His consent is implied unless he lists with registry; some counties additionally require attempted notice.

AMERICAN ACADEMY OF ADOPTION ATTORNEYS MEMBERS

David P. Broome; 155 Monroe St.; Mobile, AL 36633; (251) 432-9933; d.broome@adoptionattorneys.org
David Broome began practicing law in 1977.

Bryant A. Whitmire Jr.; 215 Richard Arrington Jr. Blvd. N., #501; Birmingham, AL 35203; (205) 324-6631; dwhitm@bellsouth.net
Bryant Whitmire began practicing law in 1972. He completed 160 adoptions last year. 90% are newborn placements. His clients locate their own birth mother.

LICENSED PRIVATE AGENCIES

A Angel Adoptions; Helena, AL; (205) 621-0316; (205) 621-0379; angeladoptions@msn.com; (Dom) (Intl)

AGAPE of Central Alabama, Inc.; Montgomery, AL; (334) 272-9466; www.agapeforchildren.org/; (Dom)

AGAPE of North Alabama, Inc.; Huntsville, AL; (256) 859-4481; www.agapecares.org; (Dom) (Intl)

Al-Hajj, Inc.; Montgomery, AL; (334) 272-7027; (Dom)

Alabama Baptist Children's Homes and Family Ministries, Inc.; Birmingham, AL; (205) 982-1112; www.abchome.org/; (Dom) (Intl)

Camellia Therapeutic Foster Agency; Phoenix City, AL; (334) 448-2999; (Dom)

Catholic Family Services; Birmingham, AL; (205) 324-6561; www.bhmdiocese.org/social_services.php; (Dom) (Intl)

Catholic Family Services; Florence, AL; (256) 768-1550; www.bhmdiocese.org/social_services.php; (Dom) (Intl)

Catholic Family Services; Huntsville, AL; (256) 536-0073; www.bhmdiocese.org/social_services.php; (Dom) (Intl)

Catholic Family Services; Tuscaloosa, AL; (205) 553-9046; www.bhmdiocese.org/social_services.php; (Dom) (Intl)

Catholic Social Services of Mobile; Mobile, AL; (251) 434-1550; www.cssmobile.org; (Dom) (Intl) China, Russian Federation

Catholic Social Services of Montgomery; Montgomery, AL; (334) 288-8890; www.cssalabama.org; (Dom)

Children of the World; Fairhope, AL; (334) 990-3550; www.childrenoftheworld.com; (Intl)

Children's Aid Society; Homewood, AL; (205) 943-5343; www.childrensaid.org; (Dom) (Intl)

Family Adoption Services, Inc; Birmingham, AL; (205) 290-0077; www.familyadoptionservices.com; (Dom) (Intl)

Lifeline Children's Services; Birmingham, AL; (205) 967-0811; www.lifelineadoption.org; (Dom) (Intl)

Southern Social Works, Inc.; Anniston, AL; (256) 237-4990; www.southernsocialworks.com; (Dom) (Intl)

Special Beginnings, Inc; Mobile, AL; (251) 776-7158; www.alabamaspecialbegin nings.org; (Dom) (Intl)

Specialized Alternatives for Families Youth of America (SAFY); Montgomery, AL; (334) 270-3181; www.safy.org; (Dom)

United Methodist Children's Home (UMCH); Selma, AL; (334) 875-7283; www.umch.net; (Dom) (Intl)

Villa Hope International Adoption; Birmingham, AL; (205) 870-7359; www.villahope .org; (Intl) China, Ecuador, Guatemala, Kazakhstan, Peru, Russian Federation, Ukraine

ALASKA

STATE ADOPTION OFFICE: Alaska Department of Health and Social Services; Office of Children's Services; 350 Main St., 4th Floor; PO Box 110630; Juneau, AK 99811; (907) 465-2145; www.hss.state.ak.us/ocs/adoptions/default.htm

ICPC ADMINISTRATOR: Alaska Department of Health and Social Services; PO Box 110630; 130 Seward St., Room 4F; Juneau, AK 99811-0630; (907) 465-3191; www.hss.state.ak.us/ocs

STATE ADOPTION EXCHANGE: Alaska Adoption Exchange; (206) 441-6822; www.akae .org

ALASKA BAR ASSOCIATION: (907) 272-7469; www.alaskabar.org

ANNUAL NUMBER OF ADOPTIVE ADOPTIONS FINALIZED IN STATE: 616

STATE LAWS AND PROCEDURES—FAST FACTS

Types permitted? Independent and agency (50% of newborns via independent).

Who can adopt in state? Residents, and nonresidents when child born in state.

How long after child's placement to finalize adoption in court? 3–6 months.

Is adoptive parent advertising (to find a birth mother) permitted? Yes.

Is a preplacement home study required? Yes, for both independent and agency.

Typical home study fee? $750 (agency fees usually higher if agency located child).

Can adoptive parents help birth mother with expenses? Yes: legal, medical, living.

Can child leave hospital with adoptive parents? Yes, with signed form.

When can birth mother sign her Consent to Adoption? Anytime after birth.

Can the consent be revoked? Independent adoption—yes, automatic right for 10 days; after 10 days a court must find the child's best interests would be served by revocation. Agency adoption—yes, automatic right for 10 days, then irrevocable.

What are the putative father's rights? No registry exists. Notice (usually 20 days) must be attempted.

AMERICAN ACADEMY OF ADOPTION ATTORNEYS MEMBERS

Robert B. Flint; 717 K St.; Anchorage, AK; (907) 276-1592; r.flint@adoptionattor neys.org

Robert Flint began practicing law in 1963.

LICENSED PRIVATE AGENCIES

Adoption Advocates International; Fairbanks, AK; (907) 457-3832; www.adoption advocates.org/alaska; (Dom) (Intl)

Alaska International Adoption Agency; Anchorage, AK; (907) 677-2888; www.akadoptions.com; (Intl) Russian Federation

Catholic Social Services (CSS); Anchorage, AK 99508; (907) 276-5590; www.cssalaska.org; (Dom)

Fairbanks Counseling and Adoption; Fairbanks, AK; (907) 456-4729; (Dom)

World Association for Children and Parents (WACAP); Anchorage, AK; (907) 338-7253; www.wacap.org; (Dom) (Intl)

ARIZONA

STATE ADOPTION OFFICE: Arizona Department of Economic Security; Administration for Children, Youth and Families; PO Box 6123-940A; Phoenix, AZ 85007; (602) 542-5499; www.de.state.az.us/dcyf/adoption/default.asp

ICPC ADMINISTRATOR: Arizona Department of Economic Security; PO Box 6123-030C-1; Phoenix, AZ 85005; (602) 542-5499

STATE ADOPTION EXCHANGE: Arizona Department of Economic Security; PO Box 17951; Tucson, AZ 85731; (520) 327-3324; www.de.state.az.us/dcyf/adoption/meet.asp

STATE BAR OF ARIZONA: (602) 252-4804; www.azbar.org

ANNUAL NUMBER OF ADOPTIVE ADOPTIONS FINALIZED IN STATE: 1,642

STATE LAWS AND PROCEDURES—FAST FACTS

Types permitted? Independent and agency (65% of newborns via independent).

Who can adopt in state? Residents only.

How long after child's placement to finalize adoption in court? 3 months if child placed at under 6 months of age; otherwise 6 months.

Is adoptive parent advertising (to find a birth mother) permitted? Yes.

Is a preplacement home study required? Yes, all adoptive parents must be "certified."

Typical home study fee? $1,500–$3,000 (agency fees usually higher if agency located child).

Can adoptive parents help birth mother with expenses? Yes, but requires court approval when total received exceeds $1,000.

Can child leave hospital with adoptive parents? Yes, release often via attorney/agency.

When can birth mother sign her Consent to Adoption? 72 hours after birth.

Can the consent be revoked? No, it is irrevocable.

What are the putative father's rights? There is a registry. Putative fathers have 30 days to file paternity action after notice or risk losing right to object.

AMERICAN ACADEMY OF ADOPTION ATTORNEYS MEMBERS

Philip (Jay) McCarthy Jr.; McCarthy Weston, PLLC.; 508 N. Humphreys; Flagstaff, AZ 86001; (928) 779-4252; www.mccarthyweston.com; jay@mccarthyweston.com
Jay McCarthy began practicing law in 1980. He has completed 600 adoptions in his career and last year completed 80. 95% are newborn placements. He is the recipient of the American Bar Association's 2000 Child Advocacy Award.

Rita A. Meiser, PLC; 1440 E. Missouri Ave., #201; Phoenix, AZ 85014; (602) 650-2473; rmeiser@meiserlaw.com
Rita Meiser began practicing law in 1976. She has completed 1,000 adoptions in her career and last year completed 83. 98% are newborn placements, 2% are toddlers. 20% of her clients find a birth mother through her office. She is an adoptive parent.

Scott E. Myers; 3180 E. Grant Rd.; Tucson, AZ 85716; (520) 327-6041; scott@smyerslaw.com
Scott Myers began practicing law in 1975. He has completed 1,000 adoptions in his career and last year completed 145. 40% are newborn placements. 25% of his clients find a birth mother through his office.

Kathryn A. Pidgeon, PC; 3131 E. Camelback Rd., #200; Phoenix AZ 85016; (602) 522-8700; skp3@aol.com
Kathryn Pidgeon began practicing law in 1989. She has completed 1,000 adoptions in her career and last year completed 100. 80% are newborn placements. Many of her cases involve helping foster parents adopt.

Daniel I. Ziskin, PC; PO Box 7447; Phoenix, AZ 85011-7447; (602) 234-2280; dan@adoptz.com
Dan Ziskin began practicing law in 1975. He has completed 1,300 adoptions in his career and last year completed 45. 95% are newborn placements. 10% of his clients find a birth mother through his office. He is an adoptive parent.

A biography was not available for the following AAAA member:
Michael J. Herrod; 1221 E. Osborn, #105; Phoenix, AZ 85014; (602) 277-7000; m.herrod@adoptionatorneys.org

LICENSED PRIVATE AGENCIES

Adoption Journeys of Arizona, Inc.; Tucson, AZ; (520) 327-0899; www.adoptionjourneys.org; (Dom) (Intl) China, Guatemala, Ukraine

Aid to Adoption of Special Kids (AASK); Phoenix, AZ; (602) 254-2275; www.AASKAZ.org; (Dom)

Arizona Baptist Children's Services (ABCS); Glendale, AZ; (623) 349-2227; www.abcs.org; (Dom)

Arizona Family Adoption Services, Inc.; Phoenix, AZ; (602) 254-2271; www.azadoptions.com; (Dom)

Arizona's Children Association (AzCA); Tucson, AZ; (520) 622-7611; www.arizonaschildren.org; (Dom)

Birth Hope Adoption Agency, Inc.; Phoenix, AZ; (602) 277-2868; (Dom) (Intl)

Black Family and Children's Services, Inc.; Phoenix, AZ; (602) 256-2948; (Dom)

Building Arizona Families; Litchfield Park, AZ; (623) 936-4729; www.Building ArizonaFamilies.com; (Dom) (Intl) Guatemala, Lithuania, Poland, Russian Federation, Ukraine

Casey Family Programs; Phoenix, AZ; (602) 252-9449; www.casey.org; (Dom)

Catholic Community Services in Western Arizona; Yuma, AZ; (520) 341-9400; www.ccs- soaz.org/ccswa.htm; (Dom)

Catholic Community Services of Southeastern Arizona; Bisbee, AZ; (520) 432-2285; www.ccs-soaz.org/csssea.htm; (Dom) (Intl)

Catholic Community Services of Southern Arizona, Inc. (CCS); Tucson, AZ; (520) 623-0344; www.ccs-soaz.org/css.htm; (Dom) (Intl); India, Korea (South)

Catholic Social Services of Central and Northern Arizona; Flagstaff, AZ; (928) 774-9125; (Dom)

Catholic Social Services of Central and Northern Arizona; Mesa, AZ; (480) 964-8771; www.catholicsocialserviceaz.org; (Dom)

Catholic Social Services of Central and Northern Arizona; Phoenix, AZ; (602) 997-6105; www.diocesephoenix.org/css; (Dom)

Catholic Social Services of Central and Northern Arizona; Prescott, AZ; (928) 778-2531; (Dom)

Christian Family Care Agency (CFCA); Phoenix, AZ; (602) 234-1935; www.cfcare.org; (Dom)

Christian Family Care Agency (CFCA); Tucson, AZ; (520) 296-8255; www.cfcare.org; (Dom)

Commonwealth Adoptions International, Inc.; Tucson, AZ; (520) 327-7574; www.commonwealthadoption.org; (Dom) (Intl) China, Colombia, India, Kazakhstan, Panama, Russian Federation, Ukraine, Vietnam

Dillon Southwest; Scottsdale, AZ; (480) 945-2221; www.dillonsouthwest.org; (Dom) (Intl) Korea (South) ·

Family Service Agency; Phoenix, AZ; (602) 264-9891; www.fsaphoenix.org; (Dom)

Hand in Hand International Adoptions; Mesa, AZ; (480) 892-5550; www.hihiadopt.org; (Dom) (Intl) China, Guatemala, Haiti, Moldova, Philippines, Russian Federation

Home Builders for Children, Inc.; Scottsdale, AZ; (480) 429-5344; (Dom) (Intl)

International Child Foundation, Inc. (ICF); Tucson, AZ; (520) 531-9931; www.childfound.org; (Dom) (Intl) Bulgaria, China, Guatemala, Kazakhstan, Russian Federation

International Family Services (IFS); Mesa, AZ; (480) 924-1779; www.ifservices.org; (Dom) (Intl) China, Guatemala, India, Russian Federation

LDS Family Services of Mesa; Mesa, AZ; (480) 968-2995; (Dom)

LDS Family Services of Snowflake; Snowflake, AZ; (520) 536-4117; www.itsaboutlove.org; (Dom)

Oasis Adoption Services, Inc. (OAS); Tucson, AZ; (520) 579-5578; www.oasisadoption.com; (Dom) (Intl)

A Place to Call Home; Mesa, AZ; (480) 456-0549; www.tocallhome.com; (Dom)

ARKANSAS

STATE ADOPTION OFFICE: Arkansas Department of Human Services; PO Box 2620; Little Rock, AR 72203; (501) 682-9273; www.state.ar.us

ICPC ADMINISTRATOR: Arkansas Department of Human Services; PO Box 1437; Slot S567; Little Rock, AR 72203-1437; (501) 682-8556; www.state.ar.us/dhs/chilnfam

STATE ADOPTION EXCHANGE: Arkansas Adoption Resource Exchange; PO Box 1437; Slot S565; Little Rock, AR 72203-1437; (501) 682-8959; www.accessarkansas .org; linda.dismuke@arkansas.gov

ARKANSAS BAR ASSOCIATION: (501) 375-4606; www.arkbar.com

ANNUAL NUMBER OF ADOPTIVE ADOPTIONS FINALIZED IN STATE: 1,698

STATE LAWS AND PROCEDURES—FAST FACTS

Types permitted? Independent and agency (40% of newborns via independent).

Who can adopt in state? Residents, and nonresidents when birth parent resides in state.

How long after child's placement to finalize adoption in court? 2 weeks.

Is adoptive parent advertising (to find a birth mother) permitted? Yes, but some newspapers decline.

Is a preplacement home study required? Independent—no, but must have it before interlocutory decree issued. Agency—yes.

Typical home study fee? $500–$1,200 (agency fees usually higher if agency located child; (there is usually no postplacement home study).

Can adoptive parents help birth mother with expenses? Yes: legal, medical, living.

Can child leave hospital with adoptive parents? Yes, but a court order or copy of Consent to Adoption usually required.

When can birth mother sign her Consent to Adoption? Before or after birth. If she is under 18 she must be appointed a guardian ad litem.

Can the consent be revoked? Yes, an automatic right for 10 days after signing or birth, whichever is later. Thereafter only if a court finds the child's best interests served by revocation. Once adoption finalized (usually 2 weeks later) it is irrevocable.

What are the putative father's rights? There is a registry, and registering entitles him to notice. He must show he established a significant relationship to the child to block adoption.

AMERICAN ACADEMY OF ADOPTION ATTORNEYS MEMBERS

Sandra C. Bradshaw; 207½ Main St.; Crossett, AR 71635; (870) 364-4300; s.bradshaw @adoptionattorneys.org
Sandra Bradshaw began practicing law in 1992.

Eugene T. Kelley; Kelley Law Firm; 303 W. Walnut St.; Rogers, AR 72757; (479) 636-1051; www.newworldawaits.com; eugenekelley@mac.com

Eugene Kelley began practicing law in 1968. He has completed 750 adoptions in his career. 96% are newborn placements. 90% of his clients find a birth mother through his office.

Kaye H. McLeod; 210 Linwood Ct.; Little Rock, AR 72205; (501) 663-6224; k.mcleod @adoptionattorneys.org

Kaye McLeod began practicing law in 1979. She has completed more than 1,600 adoptions in her career and last year completed 60. 98% are newborn placements. 2% of her clients find a birth mother through her office. She received the Congressional Angel in Adoption Award in 2002.

A biography was not available for the following AAAA member:

Keith H. Morrison; 320 N. Rollston Ave., #102; Fayetteville, AR 72701; (479) 521-5820; h.morrison@adoptionattorneys.org

LICENSED PRIVATE AGENCIES

Adoption Advantage, Inc.; Little Rock, AR; (501) 376-7778; www.adoptionadvantage .com; (Dom)

Adoption Services, Inc.; Little Rock, AR; (501) 664-0340; (Dom) (Intl)

Bethany Christian Services; Little Rock, AR; (501) 664-5729; www.bethany.org/arkansas; (Dom) (Intl)

Children's Homes, Inc.; Paragould, AR; (870) 239-4031; www.childrenshomes.org; (Dom)

Dillon International, Inc.; North Little Rock, AR; (501) 791-9300; www.dillonadopt .com; dillonarkansas@dillonadopt.com; (Intl)

Families Are Special, Inc. (FASI); North Little Rock, AR; (501) 785-9184; www .arkansasadopttoday.org; (Dom) (Intl) China, Guatemala, Kazakhstan, Russian Federation

Family Life Connections; Russellville, AR; (479) 968-5400; (Dom)

Gladney Center for Adoption; North Little Rock, AR; (501) 791-3126; www.gladney .org; (Dom) (Intl)

Holt International Children's Services; Little Rock, AR; (501) 568-2827; www.holtintl .org; (Intl)

Integrity, Inc.; Little Rock, AR; (501) 614-7200; (Intl)

Searcy Children's Homes, Inc.; Searcy, AR; (501) 268-3243; www.searcychildrens homes.org; (Dom)

Southern Christian Home; Morrilton, AR; (501) 354-2428; www.cswnet.com/~sch; (Dom)

Ventures for Children International; Fayetteville, AR; (479) 582-0305; www.ventures forchildren.org; (Intl)

CALIFORNIA

STATE ADOPTION OFFICE: California Department of Social Services; Child and Youth Permanency Branch; 744 P St.—MS 19-69; Sacramento, CA 95814; (916) 651-7464; www.childsworld.ca.gov

ICPC ADMINISTRATOR: California Department of Social Services; (same address as above); (916) 651-8114; (916) 651-8144

STATE ADOPTION EXCHANGE: California Kids Connection; (510) 272-0204; www .cakidsconnection.com; kidsconnection@familybuilders.org

STATE BAR OF CALIFORNIA: (415) 538-2250; www.calbar.org

ANNUAL NUMBER OF ADOPTIVE ADOPTIONS FINALIZED IN STATE: 9,202

STATE LAWS AND PROCEDURES—FAST FACTS

Types permitted? Independent and agency (85% of newborns via independent).
Who can adopt in state? Residents, and nonresidents when child born in state or the agency making the placement is located in state.
How long after child's placement to finalize adoption in court? 6–11 months.
Is adoptive parent advertising (to find a birth mother) permitted? No.
Is a preplacement home study required? Independent—no. Agency—yes.
Typical home study fee? Independent (by state/county)—$2,950. Agency—$4,000–$11,000 (agency fees usually higher if agency located child).
Can adoptive parents help birth mother with expenses? Yes: legal, medical, living.
Can child leave hospital with adoptive parents? Yes, with signed AD-22 form.
When can birth mother sign her Consent to Adoption? Anytime after doctor's discharge.
Can the consent be revoked? Independent adoption—yes, automatic right for 30 days, then irrevocable, unless birth parent signs a Waiver of Right to Revoke Consent, making it irrevocable immediately. Agency adoption—irrevocable upon signing, but birth parent can set own revocation time (e.g., 10, 20, 30 days).
What are the putative father's rights? There is no registry. Notice must be attempted. To block adoption, he must normally prove to a court he acted promptly and responsibly to meet the birth mother's needs and also objected promptly to adoption, otherwise his rights are terminated if adoption would serve best interests of the child.

AMERICAN ACADEMY OF ADOPTION ATTORNEYS MEMBERS

G. Darlene Anderson; 127 E. 3rd Ave., #202; Escondido, CA 92025; (760) 743-4700; gdaadopt@cox.net
Darlene Anderson began practicing law in 1982. She has completed 900 adoptions in her career and last year completed 40. 95% are newborn placements. 50% of her clients find a birth mother through her office.

David H. Baum; 16255 Ventura Blvd., #704; Encino, CA 91436; (818) 501-8355; www .adoptlaw.com; adoptlaw@lx.netcom.com
David Baum began practicing law in 1978. He has completed 1,000 adoptions in his career and last year completed 35. 95% are newborn placements. 65% of his clients find a birth mother through his office. He is an adoptive parent.

Timothy J. Blied; Schmiesing, Blied, Stoddart & Mackey; 2260 N. State College Blvd.; Fullerton, CA 92831; (714) 990-5100; www.sbsmlaw.com; admin@sbsmlaw.com
Timothy Blied began practicing law in 1979. He has completed 2,200 adoptions in his career and last year completed 70. 95% are newborn placements. 50% of his clients find a birth mother through his office. He is an adoptive parent.

D. Durand Cook, Esq.; 8383 Wilshire Blvd., #1030; Beverly Hills, CA 90211; (323) 655-2601; www.adoption-option.com; durand@adoption-option.com
Durand Cook began practicing law in 1970. He has completed 5,000 adoptions in his career and last year completed 66. 98% are newborn placements. 98% of his clients find a birth mother through his office.

Douglas R. Donnelly; 427 E. Carrillo St.; Santa Barbara, CA 93101; (805) 962-0988; www.adoptionlawfirm.com; doug@adoptionlawfirm.com
Douglas Donnelly began practicing law in 1977. He has completed 2,000 adoptions in his career and last year completed 66. 99% are newborn placements. 66% of his clients find a birth mother through his office. He is an adoptive parent.

Alison A. Foster; Family Connections, Christian Adoptions; 1120 Tully Rd.; Modesto, CA 95350; (209) 524-8844; www.fcadoptions.org
Alison Foster began practicing law in 1992. She has completed 1,250 adoptions as an adoption agency director. Last year the agency completed 275 adoptions. 2% are newborn placements.

Jane A. Gorman; Law Office of Gradstein & Gorman; 80 Stone Pine Rd., #101; Half Moon Bay, CA 94019; (650) 560-0123; www.placebaby4adoption.com; jagorman@aol.com
Jane Gorman began practicing law in 1986. She limits her practice to contested adoption litigation and has been involved in more than 2,000 such cases. She is a past president of the American Academy of Adoption Attorneys.

Marc Gradstein; Law Office of Gradstein & Gorman; 80 Stone Pine Rd., #101; Half Moon Bay, CA 94019; (650) 560-0123; www.placebaby4adoption.com; mgradstein@aol.com
Marc Gradstein began practicing law in 1973. He has completed 6,000 adoptions in his career and last year completed 80. 95% are newborn placements. 50% of his clients find a birth mother through his office. He is an adoptive parent.

Randall B. Hicks; 7177 Brockton Ave., #218; Riverside, CA 92506; (951) 787-8300; www.randallhicks.com; randy@randallhicks.com
Randall Hicks began practicing law in 1986. He has completed 900 adoptions in his career and last year completed 55. 99% are newborn placements. 90% of his clients find a birth mother through his office. He is the author of Adoption:

The Essential Guide to Adopting Quickly and Safely, *and a mystery series featuring an adoption attorney (visit www.tobydillon.com).*

Allen Hultquist; 43980 Mahlon Vail Cir., #403; Temecula, CA 92592; (951) 302-7777; www.aadoption.net; a.hultquist@adoptionattorneys.org
Allen Hultquist began practicing law in 1981. He has completed 1,500 adoptions in his career.

Joy L. Kolender; 11348 Monticook Ct.; San Diego, CA 92127; (858) 485-9823; adoptionatty@aol.com
Joy Kolender began practicing law in 1984. She has completed 700 adoptions in her career and last year completed 60. 98% are newborn placements. 4% of her clients find a birth mother through her office. She is an adoptive parent.

Karen R. Lane; 100 Wilshire Blvd., #2075; Santa Monica, CA 90401; (310) 393-9802; www.klane-adopt.com; karenrlane@sbcglobal.net
Karen Lane began practicing law in 1979. She has completed 3,500 adoptions in her career and last year completed 50. 100% are newborn placements. 70% of her clients find a birth mother through her office. She is a past president of the American Academy of Adoption Attorneys.

Celeste E. Liversidge; Adoption Law Group; 55 W. Sierra Madre Blvd., #100; Sierra Madre, CA 91024; (626) 794-4445; www.adoptionlawgroup.com; cliversidge@adoptionlawgroup.com
Celeste Liversidge began practicing law in 1995. She has completed 250 adoptions in her career and last year completed 35. 90% are newborn placements. 90% of her clients find a birth mother through her office.

Diane Michelsen; 3190 Old Tunnel Rd.; Lafayette, CA 94549; (925) 945-1880; www.familyformation.com; diane@familyformation.com
Diane Michelsen began practicing law in 1980. She has completed 3,600 adoptions in her career and last year completed 24. 95% are newborn placements. 20% of her clients find a birth mother through her office. She is a past president of the American Academy of Adoption Attorneys.

Kristine Pogalies; Stocks & Fentin, LLP; 600 B St., #2050; San Diego, CA 92101; (619) 231-2025; kpogalies@stocksfentin.com
Kristine Pogalies began practicing law in 1993. She has completed 250 adoptions in her career and last year completed 21. 99% are newborn placements. 60% of her clients find a birth mother through her office.

David J. Radis; 1901 Ave. of the Stars, #1900; Los Angeles, CA 90067; (310) 552-0536; www.radis-adop.com; radis@radis-adopt.com
David Radis began practicing law in 1974. He has completed 3,000 adoptions in his career and last year completed 62. 99% are newborn placements. 90% of his clients find a birth mother through his office.

Susan Romer; Adams & Romer; 1191 Church St.; San Francisco, CA 94114; (415) 643-4523; www.1-800-U-ADOPT-US.com; adamsromer@aol.com
Susan Romer began practicing law in 1993. She has completed 800 adoptions in her career and last year completed 62. 99% are newborn placements. 80% of her clients find a birth mother through her office.

Janis K. Stocks; Stocks & Fentin; 600 B St., #2050; San Diego, CA 92101; (619) 231-2025; jstocks@stocksfentin.com
Janis Stocks began practicing law in 1974. She has completed 900 adoptions in her career and last year completed 20. 100% are newborn placements. 90% of her clients find a birth mother through her office.

Ronald L. Stoddart; Nightlight Christian Adoptions; 801 E. Chapman Ave., #106; Fullerton, CA 92831; (714) 278-1020; www.nightlight.org; ron@nightlight.org
Ronald Stoddart began practicing law in 1974. He has completed 2,500 adoptions in his career and last year completed approximately 100. He is the director of Nightlight Christian Adoptions agency. He is an adoptive parent.

Robert R. Walmsley; Van Deusen, Youmans & Walmsley; 615 Civic Center Dr. West, #300; Santa Ana, CA 92701; (714) 547-6226; robert@familybuilding.com
Robert Walmsley began practicing law in 1987. He has completed 150 adoptions in his career. Much of his practice is dedicated to contested adoption litigation.

Felice A. Webster; 4525 Wilshire Blvd., #201; Los Angeles, CA 90010; (323) 664-5600; www.felicewebster.com; f.webster@adoptionattorneys.org
Felice Webster began practicing law in 1974. Last year she completed 70 adoptions. 90% are newborn placements. 50% of her clients find a birth mother through her office.

M. D. Widelock; 1801 Oak St.; Bakersfield, CA 93390; (661) 398-1189; www.thestork.com; widelock@thestork.com
M. D. Widelock began practicing law in 1986. He has completed 1,000 adoptions in his career and last year completed 79. 98% are newborn placements. 98% of his clients find a birth mother through his office.

Nanci R. Worcester; Adoption Law Center of Northern California; 1253 High St.; Auburn, CA 95603; (530) 888-1311; www.adoption-center.com; adopt@adoption-center.com
Nanci Worcester began practicing law in 1981. She has completed 2,000 adoptions in her career and last year completed 105. 99% are newborn placements. 30% of her clients find a birth mother through her office. She is an adoptive parent.

Biographies were not available for the following AAAA members:

Shannon M. Matteson; 3190 Old Tunnel Rd.; Lafayette, CA 94549; (925) 945-1880; s.matteson@adoptionattorneys.org

Lawrence Siegel; 907 Sir Francis Drake Blvd.; Kentfield, CA 94904; (415) 256-8844; l.siegel@adoptionattorneys.org

Jed Somit; 1970 Broadway, #625; Oakland, CA 94612; (510) 839-3215; j.somit@ adoptionattorneys.org

Ted Youmans; 615 Civic Center Dr. West, #300; Santa Ana, CA 92701; (714) 547-6226; t.youmans@adoptionattorneys.org

LICENSED PRIVATE AGENCIES

ACCEPT (An Adoption and Counseling Center); Los Altos, CA; (650) 917-8090; www .acceptadoptions.org; (Intl)

Across the World Adoptions (ATWA); Pleasant Hill, CA; (925) 356-6260; www.atwakids .org; (Intl) China, Guatemala, Kazakhstan, Russian Federation

Adopt a Child; Inglewood, CA; (323) 750-5855; (Dom)

Adopt a Special Kid (AASK); Oakland, CA; (510) 553-1748; www.adoptaspecialkid .org; (Dom)

Adopt International; Oakland, CA; (510) 653-8600; www.adopt-intl.org; (Intl)

Adopt International; Petaluma, CA; (707) 570-2940; www.adoptinter.org/; (Dom) (Intl)

Adopt International; San Francisco, CA; (415) 934-0300; www.adopt-intl.org/; (Dom) (Intl)

Adoption Connection; San Francisco, CA; (415) 359-2494; www.adoptionconnection .org/; (Dom) (Intl)

Adoption Horizons; Eureka, CA; (707) 444-9909; www.adoption-horizons.org; (Dom) (Intl) China, Kazakhstan, Korea (South), Liberia, Vietnam

The Adoption Network Catholic Charities CYO; San Francisco, CA; (415) 406-2387; www .cccyo.org; (Dom) (Intl)

Adoption Options, Inc; San Diego, CA; (619) 542-7772; www.adoption-options.org; (Intl) Kazakhstan, Mexico, Republic of Georgia, Russian Federation

Adoptions Unlimited, Inc.; Chino, CA; (909) 902-1412; www.adopting.com/aui; (Dom) (Intl)

Alternative Family Services Adoption Agency (AFS); San Francisco, CA; (415) 626-2700; www.alternativefamilyservices.org; (Dom)

Angels' Haven Outreach; Santa Clarita, CA; (661) 259-2943; www.angels-haven.com; (Intl)

Aspira Foster & Family Services; Daly City, CA; (805) 654-6800; www.aspiranet.org or www.mossbeachhomes.com; (Dom)

Bal Jagat Children's World, Inc.; Chatsworth, CA; (818) 709-4737; www.baljagat .org; (Intl) China, Guatemala, India, Romania, Russian Federation, Thailand, Ukraine

Bay Area Adoption Services (BAAS); Mountain View, CA; (650) 964-3800; www.baas
.org; (Intl) Brazil, Chile, China, Colombia, Ecuador, El Salvador, Ethiopia, Guatemala, Honduras, India, Japan, Kazakhstan, Mexico, Nicaragua, Peru, Philippines, Russian Federation, Taiwan, Ukraine, Vietnam

Bethany Christian Services, Inc.; Chino, CA; (909) 465-0057; www.bethany.org/
lamirada; (Dom) (Intl)

Bethany Christian Services—North Region; Modesto, CA; (209) 522-5121; www.bethany
.org/modesto; (Dom) (Intl) Albania, China, Colombia, Ecuador, Guatemala, India,
Korea (South), Lithuania, Philippines, Russian Federation, Ukraine

Bethany Christian Services—South Region; La Mirada, CA; (714) 994-0500; www.beth
any.org/lamirada; (Dom)

Better Life Children Services; Sacramento, CA; (916) 641-0661; (Dom)

A Better Way, Inc.; Berkeley, CA; (510) 601-0203; www.abetterwayinc.net; (Dom)

Black Adoption Placement and Research Center; Oakland, CA; (510) 430-3600; www
.baprc.org; (Dom)

Catholic Charities Adoption Agency; San Diego, CA; (619) 231-2828; www.ccdsd.org;
(Dom)

**Catholic Youth Organization—Catholic Charities (St. Vincent's Foster Family and Adoption
Agency)**; San Rafael, CA; (415) 507-4387; (Dom)

Children's Bureau; Los Angeles, CA; (323) 953-7356; www.all4kids.org; (Dom)

Children's Bureau of Southern California (CBSC); North Hollywood, CA; (818) 985-8154;
www.all4kids.org; (Dom)

Children's Home Society of California; Los Angeles, CA; www.chs-ca.org; (Dom)

Chrysalis House, Inc. (CHI); Fresno, CA; (559) 229-9862; www.chrysalishouse.com;
(Dom) (Intl) China, Guatemala, Kazakhstan, Philippines, Russian Federation,
Ukraine

East West Adoptions, Inc.; Berkeley, CA; (510) 644-3996; http://users.lmi.net/ewadopt;
(Intl) Armenia, China, Estonia, Guatemala, Kazakhstan, Moldova, Russian
Federation, Ukraine

Ettie Lee Youth and Family Services; Baldwin Park, CA; (626) 960-4861; (Dom)

Families First; Campbell, CA; (408) 369-2220; www.familiesfirstinc.org; (Dom)

Families First; Davis, CA; (530) 753-0220; www.familiesfirstinc.org; (Dom)

Families First; Fresno, CA; (559) 248-8550; www.familiesfirstinc.org; (Dom)

Families First; Modesto, CA; (209) 523-3710; www.familiesfirstinc.org; (Dom)

Families First; Oakland, CA; (510) 636-2000; www.familiesfirstinc.org; (Dom)

Families First; Sacramento, CA; (916) 641-9595; www.familiesfirstinc.org; (Dom)

Families First; Stockton, CA; (209) 954-3000; www.familiesfirstinc.org; (Dom)

Families for Children; Oakland, CA; (510) 663-5250; www.families4children.com;
(Dom)

Families for Children; Roseville, CA; (916) 789-8688; www.families4children.com;
(Dom)

Families United, Inc.; Folsom, CA; (916) 863-5457; (Dom)

Families United, Inc.; Lakeport, CA; (707) 263-9553; (Dom)

Families United, Inc.; Oroville, CA; (530) 532-0321; (Dom)

Family Builders by Adoption; Oakland, CA; (510) 272-0204; www.familybuilders.org; (Dom)

Family Connections Adoptions; Fresno, CA; (559) 325-9388; www.fcadoptions.org; (Dom) (Intl)

Family Connections Adoptions; Sacramento, CA; (916) 568-5966; www.fcadoptions .org/; (Dom) (Intl)

Family Connections Adoptions; Ventura, CA; (805) 477-7400; www.fcadoptions.org; (Dom) (Intl)

Family Connections Christian Adoptions; Modesto, CA; (209) 524-8844; www.fcadop tions.org; (Dom) (Intl) Brazil, Chile, China, Colombia, Costa Rica, Ecuador, Guatemala, Haiti, India, Kazakhstan, Korea (South), Marshall Islands, Republic of Korea, Russian Federation, Samoa, Ukraine, Vietnam

Family Linkage Adoption; Gilroy, CA; (408) 846-2130; www.rcskids.org; (Dom)

The Family Network, Inc.; Capitola, CA; (831) 462-8954; www.adopt-familynetwork .com; (Dom) (Intl) China, Guatemala, Latvia, Sierra Leone, Ukraine

Five Acres; Altadena, CA; (626) 798-6793; www.5acres.org; (Dom)

Future Families Adoption and Foster Care and Family Services; San Jose, CA; (408) 298-8789; www.futurefamilies.org; (Dom) (Intl)

Genesis Adoption Agency; Fresno, CA; (559) 439-5437; www.genesisadoptions.org; (Intl)

God's Families International Adoption Services; Trabuco Canyon, CA; (949) 858-7621; www.godsfamilies.org; (Intl) Azerbaijan, Belarus, Bulgaria, China, Guatemala, Japan, Kazakhstan, Russian Federation, Ukraine

Hand in Hand Foundation; Santa Cruz, CA; (831) 476-1866; http://handinhandfounda tion.com; (Dom)

Hannah's Children's Homes; Orange, CA; (714) 516-1077; (Dom)

Heartsent Adoptions, Inc.; Fair Oaks, CA; (916) 965-8881; www.heartsent.org; (Intl) China, Taiwan

Heartsent Adoptions, Inc.; Orinda, CA; (925) 254-8883; www.heartsent.org; (Intl) China, Taiwan

Heartsent Adoptions, Inc.; Pasadena, CA; (626) 793-8333; www.heartsent.org; (Intl) China, Taiwan

Holt International Children's Services; Sacramento, CA; (916) 487-4658; www.holtintl .org; (Intl)

Holy Family Services—Counseling and Adoption; San Bernardino, CA; (909) 885-4882; www.hfs.org; (Dom)

Holy Family Services—Counseling and Adoption; Santa Ana, CA; (714) 835-5551; www .hfs.org; (Dom)

Holy Family Services—Counseling and Adoption; Thousand Oaks, CA; (805) 374-6797; www.hfs.org; (Dom)

Holy Family Services Adoption & Foster Care (HFS); Pasadena, CA; (626) 432-5680; www .holyfamilyservices.org; (Dom)

Hope 4 Kids Adoption; San Juan Capistrano, CA; (949) 496-9430; www.hope4kids .com; (Dom)

Independent Adoption Center (IAC); Los Angeles, CA; (310) 215-3180; www.adoption help.org; (Dom) (Intl)

Independent Adoption Center (IAC); Pleasant Hill, CA; (925) 827-2229; www.adop tionhelp.org; (Dom) (Intl)

Indian Child and Family Services; Redlands, CA; (909) 793-1709; (Dom)

Infant of Prague; Fresno, CA; (559) 447-3333; www.infantofprague.org; (Dom)

Inner Circle Foster Care and Adoption Services; Van Nuys, CA; (818) 988-6300; www .fosterfamily.org; (Dom)

Institute for Black Parenting (IBP); Carson, CA; (310) 900-0930; www.institute forblackparenting.org; (Dom)

Institute for Black Parenting (IBP); Riverside, CA; (951) 782-2800; www.institute forblackparenting.org; (Dom)

International Christian Adoptions (ICA); Temecula, CA; (951) 695-3336; www.4achild .com; (Dom) (Intl) Kazakhstan, Mexico, Peru, Russian Federation, Ukraine

Kern Bridges Youth Homes Adoption Agency (KBYH); Bakersfield, CA; (661) 396-2301; www.kernbridges.com; (Dom)

Kinship Center; Pasadena, CA; (626) 744-9814; www.kinshipcenter.org; info@kinship center.org; (Dom)

Kinship Center; Redlands, CA; (909) 798-9547; www.kinshipcenter.org; (Dom)

Kinship Center; Salinas, CA; (831) 455-4706; www.kinshipcenter.org; (Dom)

Kinship Center; Santa Ana, CA; (714) 979-2365; www.kinshipcenter.org; (Dom)

Latino Family Institute, Inc.; West Covina, CA; (626) 472-0123; (Dom)

LDS Family Services; Colton, CA; (909) 824-0480; (Dom)

LDS Family Services; Concord, CA; (510) 685-2941; (Dom)

LDS Family Services; Fresno, CA; (559) 255-1446; (Dom)

LDS Family Services; Fountain Valley, CA; (714) 444-3463; (Dom)

LDS Family Services; San Diego, CA; (858) 467-9170; (Dom)

LDS Family Services; San Jose, CA; (408) 361-0133; www.ldsfamilyservices.org; (Dom)

LDS Family Services; Van Nuys, CA; (818) 781-5511; www.ldssocal.org; (Dom)

Life Adoption Services; Tustin, CA; (714) 838-5433; www.lifeadoption.com; (Dom)

Lilliput Children's Services; Chico, CA; (530) 896-1920; www.lilliput.org; (Dom)

Lilliput Children's Services; Placerville, CA; (530) 295-6104; (Dom)

Lilliput Children's Services; Redding, CA; (530) 722-9092; www.lilliput.org; (Dom)

Lilliput Children's Services; Sacramento, CA; (916) 923-5444; www.lilliput.org; (Dom)

Lilliput Children's Services; San Leandro, CA; (510) 483-2030; www.lilliput.org; (Dom)

Lilliput Children's Services; Stockton, CA; (209) 943-0530; www.lilliput.org; (Dom)

McKinley Children's Center; San Dimas, CA; (909) 599-1227; www.mckinleycc.org; (Dom)

Nightlight Christian Adoptions; Fullerton, CA; (714) 278-1020; www.nightlight.org; (Dom) (Intl) Belarus, Bulgaria, China, Russian Federation

Olive Crest Adoption Services; Santa Ana, CA; (714) 543-5437; www.olivecrest.org; (Dom)

Optimist Community Services (OYHFS); Los Angeles, CA; (323) 341-5561; www.oyhfs .org; (Dom)

PACT, an Adoption Alliance; Oakland, CA; (510) 243-9460; www.pactadopt.org; (Dom)

Partners for Adoption; Walnut Creek, CA; (925) 946-9658; www.partnersfor adoption.org; (Dom) (Intl)

Share Homes; Lodi, CA; (209) 334-6376; www.sharehomes.org; (Dom)

Sierra Adoption Services; Auburn, CA; (530) 887-0082; www.sierraadoption.org; (Dom)

Sierra Adoption Services; Nevada City, CA; (530) 478-0900; www.sierraadoption.org; (Dom)

Sierra Adoption Services; Sacramento, CA; (916) 368-5114; www.sierraadoption.org; (Dom) (Intl)

Southern California Foster Family and Adoption Agency (SCFFAA); Los Angeles, CA; (213) 365-2900; www.scffaa.org; (Dom)

Special Families Foster Care and Adoptions; San Diego, CA; (858) 277-9550; (Dom)

St. Patrick's Home for Children; Sacramento, CA; (916) 386-1603; (Dom)

Sycamores Adoption Agency; South Pasadena, CA; (626) 395-7100; www.sycamores .org; (Dom)

True to Life Children's Services; Sebastopol, CA; (707) 823-7300; www.tlc4kids.org; (Dom)

Valley Teen Ranch Foster Family and Adoption Agency; Fresno, CA; (559) 437-1144; (Dom)

Vista Del Mar Child and Family Services; Los Angeles, CA; (310) 836-1223; www.vista delmar.org; (Dom) (Intl)

Westside Children's Center; Culver City, CA; (310) 390-0551; www.westsidechildrens .org; (Dom)

COLORADO

STATE ADOPTION OFFICE: Colorado Department of Human Services (CDHS); 1575 Sherman St., 2nd Floor; Denver, CO 80203-1714; (303) 866-3197; www.change alifeforever.org

ICPC ADMINISTRATOR: Adoption Alliance; 2121 S. Oneida St., Suite 420; Denver, CO 80224; (303) 584-9900; www.adoptall.com

STATE ADOPTION EXCHANGE: The Adoption Exchange; (303) 755-4756; www.adoptex .org; kids@adoptex.org

COLORADO BAR ASSOCIATION: (303) 860-1115; www.cobar.org

ANNUAL NUMBER OF ADOPTIVE ADOPTIONS FINALIZED IN STATE: 2,877

STATE LAWS AND PROCEDURES—FAST FACTS

Types permitted? Agency only.

Who can adopt in state? Residents, and nonresidents when the agency making the placement is located in state.

How long after child's placement to finalize adoption in court? 6 months.
Is adoptive parent advertising (to find a birth mother) permitted? Yes, but law is vague.
Is a preplacement home study required? Yes.
Typical home study fee? $2,500 (agency fees usually higher if agency located child).
Can adoptive parents help birth mother with expenses? Yes: legal, medical, living.
Can child leave hospital with adoptive parents? Yes, via agency.
When can birth mother sign her Consent to Adoption? Two methods. The "traditional" one is the birth mother files a Petition for Relinquishment after the birth. At a hearing several weeks later the court issues an Order of Relinquishment and it can be set aside thereafter for 90 days only upon proof of fraud or duress. Some courts allow an "expedited" Petition for Relinquishment. This can't be filed until 4 days after birth and only when the child is under 1 year old. The Order for Relinquishment is issued within 7 days. The order is irrevocable.
Can the consent be revoked? See explanation above.
What are the putative father's rights? There is no registry. Notice to putative father must be attempted. He usually has 30 days to object after notice/birth, and the court will examine his relationship with the child, showing responsibility, fitness, etc.

AMERICAN ACADEMY OF ADOPTION ATTORNEYS MEMBERS
W. Thomas Beltz; Beltz, Edwards, Sabo & West, LLP; 729 S. Cascade Ave.; Colorado Springs, CO 80903; (719) 473-4444; www.bestlawllp.com; wtbeltz@bestlawllp.com
Thomas Beltz began practicing law in 1973. He has completed 2,000 adoptions in his career and last year completed 59. 50% are newborn placements.

Seth A. Grob; 31425 Forestland Dr.; Evergreen, CO 80439; (303) 679-8266; s.grob@adoptionattorneys.org
Seth Grob began practicing law in 1991. He has completed 600 adoptions in his career and last year completed 57. 85% are newborn placements. 25% of his clients find a birth mother through his office.

Biographies were not available for the following AAAA members:
Virginia L. Frank; 35715 U.S. Hwy. 40, #105D; Evergreen, CO 80439; (303) 918-6707; v.frank@adoptionattorneys.org

Daniel A. West; 729 S. Cascade Ave.; Colorado Springs, CO 80903; (719) 473-4444; d.west@adoptionattorneys.org

LICENSED PRIVATE AGENCIES
AAC Adoption and Family Network; Berthoud, CO; (970) 532-3576; www.aacadoption.com; (Intl) China, Korea (South)
ABBA Family Services; Parker, CO; (303) 333-8652; (Dom)
Adopt a Miracle; Evergreen, CO; (303) 216-9009; www.adoptamiracle.com; (Intl) Bulgaria, Kazakhstan, Russian Federation, Ukraine

Adoption Alliance, Inc.; Denver, CO; (303) 584-9900; www.adoptall.com; (Dom) (Intl)

Adoption Choice Center; Colorado Springs, CO; (719) 444-0198; (Dom)

Adoption Homestudy Agency of Colorado (AHA/CO); Denver, CO; (720) 214-0606; www .adoptionhomestudy.org; (Dom) (Intl) ·

Adoption Journey; Lafayette, CO; (303) 530-9124; (Dom) (Intl) Guatemala, Nepal, Russian Federation, Samoa, Ukraine

Adoption Options; Aurora, CO; (303) 695-1601; www.myoptions.org; (Dom) (Intl) Belarus, Guatemala

Adoptions Advocacy and Alternatives; Fort Collins, CO; (970) 493-5868; (Dom)

Adoption Services, Inc.; Broomfield, CO; (719) 632-9941; (Dom)

Angeldance International; Denver, CO; (303) 433-6655; www.angeldance.org; (Intl)

Bethany Christian Services of Colorado; Denver, CO; (303) 221-0734; www.bethany .org/colorado; (Dom) (Intl)

Catholic Charities and Community Services; Denver, CO; (303) 742-0828; www .ccdenver.org; (Dom)

Catholic Charities of Colorado Springs, Inc; Colorado Springs, CO; (719) 866-6535; www.ccharitiescs.org; (Dom) (Intl) China, Russian Federation

Catholic Charities of the Diocese of Pueblo, Inc.; Pueblo, CO; (719) 544-4233; www .pueblocharities.org/adoption.html; (Dom)

Chinese Children Adoption International (CCAI); Centennial, CO; (303) 850-9998; www .chinesechildren.org; (Intl) China

Children's Haven of Hope; Aurora, CO; (303) 699-4710; (Dom)

Christian Family Services of Colorado; Aurora, CO; (303) 337-6747; (Dom)

Claar Foundation, Inc.; Boulder, CO; (303) 415-1001; www.claarfoundation.org; (Intl) Guatemala, Nepal, Russian Federation, Ukraine

Colorado Adoption Center; Fort Collins, CO; (970) 493-8816; (Dom) (Intl)

Colorado Christian Home; Denver, CO; (303) 433-2541; (Dom)

Colorado Christian Services; Littleton, CO; (303) 761-7236; www.christianservices .org; (Dom)

Commonwealth Adoptions International, Inc. (CAII); Littleton, CO; (303) 733-7170; www.commonwealthadoption.org; (Dom) (Intl) Brazil, China, Colombia, Guatemala, India, Kazakhstan, Russian Federation, Taiwan, Ukraine, Vietnam

Creative Adoptions, Inc.; Littleton, CO; (303) 730-7791; www.creativeadoptions .com; (Dom)

Family Ties Adoption Agency; Arvada, CO; (303) 420-3660; (Dom)

Friends of Children of Various Nations; Denver, CO; (303) 837-9438; www.fcvn.net; (Intl)

Hand in Hand International Adoptions; Estes Park, CO; (970) 586-6866; www.hihiadopt .org; (Dom) (Intl) China, Guatemala, Haiti, Moldova, Philippines, Russian Federation, Thailand, Ukraine

Hope and Home; Colorado Springs, CO; (719) 575-9887; (Dom)

Hope's Promise; Castle Rock, CO; (303) 660-0277; www.hopespromise.com; (Dom) (Intl) Nepal, Sierra Leone, Vietnam

International Adoption Net; Centennial, CO; (303) 691-0808; www.adoptioninterna
tional.net; (Dom) (Intl) Bulgaria, China, Guatemala, Kazakhstan, Russian Federation, Ukraine, Vietnam

Kid's Crossing, Inc.; Colorado Springs, CO; (719) 632-4569; (Dom)

Kid's Crossing, Inc.; Pueblo, CO; (719) 545-3882; (Dom)

LDS Social Services; Aurora, CO; (303) 371-1000; www.itsaboutlove.org; (Dom)

Littlest Angels International; Cedaredge, CO; (970) 856-6177; www.littlestangels
international.com; (Dom) (Intl) Cambodia, China, Colombia, Guatemala, Haiti,
Kazakhstan, Marshall Islands, Nepal, Russian Federation, Taiwan

Loving Homes; Aurora, CO; (303) 671-6884; www.lovinghomes.net; (Dom)

Loving Homes; Pueblo, CO; (719) 545-6181; www.lovinghomes.net; (Dom)

Lutheran Family Services of Colorado; Colorado Springs, CO; (719) 227-7571; www
.lfsco.org; (Dom)

Lutheran Family Services of Colorado; Denver, CO; (303) 922-3433; www.lfsco.org;
(Dom)

Lutheran Family Services of Colorado; Ft. Collins, CO; (970) 266-1788; www.lfsco.org;
(Dom)

Rainbow House International; Greeley, CO; (303) 830-2108; www.rhi.org; (Intl)

Top of the Trail; Montrose, CO; (970) 249-4131; (Dom)

Youth Oasis Uplifting Nurturing Guidance Services (Y.O.U.N.G.S.); Colorado Springs, CO;
(719) 634-7395; (Dom)

CONNECTICUT

STATE ADOPTION OFFICE: Connecticut Department of Children and Families; Bureau
of Adoption and Interstate Compact Services; 505 Hudson St.; Hartford, CT
06106; (860) 550-6467; www.state.ct.us

ICPC ADMINISTRATOR: Connecticut Department of Children and Families; (same
address as above); (860) 550-6469

STATE ADOPTION EXCHANGE: Connecticut Department of Children and Families; (860)
550-6578; www.adoptuskids.org/states/ct/index.aspx; vera.esdaile@po.state.ct.us

CONNECTICUT BAR ASSOCIATION: (860) 223-4400; www.ctbar.org

ANNUAL NUMBER OF ADOPTIVE ADOPTIONS FINALIZED IN STATE: 1,164

STATE LAWS AND PROCEDURES—FAST FACTS

Types permitted? Agency only.

Who can adopt in state? Residents only.

How long after child's placement to finalize adoption in court? 6–12 months.

Is adoptive parent advertising (to find a birth mother) permitted? Yes.

Is a preplacement home study required? Yes.

Typical home study fee? $3,000–$10,000, often a sliding scale by income.

Can adoptive parents help birth mother with expenses? Yes, up to $1,500; in excess
with court approval.

Can child leave hospital with adoptive parents? Yes, via agency.
When can birth mother sign her Consent to Adoption? 48 hours after birth, and after mandatory counseling. If mother is under age 18, a guardian ad litem must be appointed.
Can the consent be revoked? A judge approves the consent, usually about one month after signing, at which point it becomes irrevocable.
What are the putative father's rights? There is no registry. Notice must be attempted on the putative father. Grounds, such as abandonment, must be found to terminate his rights.

AMERICAN ACADEMY OF ADOPTION ATTORNEYS MEMBERS

Janet S. Stulting; Shipman & Goodwin LLP; 1 Constitution Plaza; Hartford, CT 06103; (860) 251-5000; jstulting@goodwin.com
Janet Stulting began practicing law in 1980.

Biographies were not available for the following AAAA members:
Pamela Nolan Dale; 55 The Knoll; Southport, CT 06890; (203) 319-1440; p.dale@adoptionattorneys.org

Donald B. Sherer; 111 Prospect St., #500; Stamford, CT 06901; (203) 327-2084; d.sherer@adoptionattorneys.org

LICENSED PRIVATE AGENCIES

Adoption Center at Jewish Family Service; West Hartford, CT; (860) 236-1927; www.jfshartford.org; (Dom) (Intl)
Boys Village Youth and Family Services, Inc.; Milford, CT; (203) 877-0300; www.boysvill.org; (Dom)
Casey Family Services; Bridgeport, CT; (203) 372-3722; www.caseyfamilyservices.org; (Dom)
Casey Family Services; Hartford, CT; (860) 727-1030; www.caseyfamilyservices.org; (Dom)
Catholic Charities, Hartford District Office; Hartford, CT; (860) 522-8241; (Dom)
Catholic Charities of Fairfield County; Bridgeport, CT; (203) 372-4301; www.ccfc-ct.org; (Dom) (Intl) China
Catholic Charities, Catholic Family Services Archdiocese of Hartford; Rocky Hill, CT; (860) 257-4335; www.ccaoh.org/our_services/adoption/adoption.htm; (Dom)
Catholic Charities of the Diocese of Norwich; Norwich, CT; (860) 889-8346; www.ccfsn.org/adoption.htm; (Dom)
Catholic Charities, New Haven District Office; New Haven, CT; (203) 787-2207; (Dom)
Catholic Charities, Waterbury District Office; Waterbury, CT; (203) 755-1196; www.cccfs.org; (Dom)
Child Adoption Resource Association, Inc. (CARA); New London, CT; (860) 444-0553; www.adoptacarakid.org; (Dom) (Intl) China, Guatemala, Haiti, Kazakhstan, Korea (South), Poland, Russian Federation
Children's Center; Hamden, CT; (203) 248-2116; www.childrenscenterhamden.org/contact.html; (Dom)

China Adoption with Love, Inc.; Old Saybrook, CT; (860) 510-0807; www.cawli.org; (Intl) China

Community Residences, Inc.; Plainville, CT; (860) 621-7600; www.criinc.org; (Dom)

Connection, Inc.; Middletown, CT; (860) 343-5500; www.theconnectioninc.org; (Dom)

DARE Family Services, Inc.; East Hartford, CT; (860) 291-8688; (Dom)

Devereux Foundation; Washington, CT; (860) 868-7377; www.theglenholmeschool .org; (Dom)

Downey Side; East Hartford, CT; (860) 289-0708; www.downeyside.org; (Dom)

Family and Children's Agency Inc. (FCA); Hartford, CT; (203) 855-8765; www.familyand childrensagency.org; (Dom) (Intl) China, Korea (South), Russian Federation, Taiwan, Ukraine

Family and Children's Agency, Inc. (FCA); Norwalk, CT; (203) 855-8765; www.family andchildrensagency.org; (Dom) (Intl) China, Korea (South), Russian Federation, Taiwan, Ukraine

Family Services of Central Connecticut, Inc.; New Britain, CT; (860) 223-9291; (Dom)

Franciscan Family Care Center, Inc.; Meriden, CT; (203) 237-8084; (Dom)

Healing the Children Northeast, Inc.; New Milford, CT; (860) 355-1828; www.htcne .org; (Dom) (Intl)

International Alliance for Children, Inc.; New Milford, CT; (860) 354-3417; (Intl)

Institute of Professional Practice, Inc. (IPP); Woodbridge, CT; (203) 389-6956; http:// ippi.org; (Dom) Puerto Rico

Jewish Family Service of New Haven; New Haven, CT; (203) 389-5599; www.jfsnh.org; (Dom)

Jewish Family Services, Inc.; Bridgeport, CT; (203) 366-5438; www.jfsnh.org; (Dom)

Klingberg Family Centers, Inc. (KFC); New Britain, CT; (860) 224-9113; www.kling berg.org; (Dom) (Intl) China

LDS Family Services; Bloomfield, CT; www.ldsfamilyservices.org; (Dom)

Lutheran Social Services of New England (LSSNE); Rocky Hill, CT; (860) 257-9899; http:// adoptlss.org; (Dom) (Intl) Bulgaria, China, Kazakhstan, Moldova, Ukraine, Vietnam

New Opportunities for Waterbury, Inc.; Waterbury, CT; (203) 575-9799; www.newop portunitiesinc.org; (Dom)

North American Family Institute; Farmington, CT; (860) 284-1177; www.nafi.com; (Dom)

Rainbow Adoptions International, Inc.; Avon, CT; (860) 677-0032; www.rainbow adoptions.org; (Intl) Guatemala

Thursday's Child, Inc.; Bloomfield, CT; (860) 242-5941; www.tcadoption.org; (Dom) (Intl) China, Guatemala, Kazakhstan, Taiwan, Ukraine

Village for Families and Children, Inc.; Hartford, CT; (860) 297-0555; www.villagefor children.org; (Dom)

Wheeler Clinic, Inc.; Plainville, CT; (888) 793-3500; www.wheelerclinic.org; (Dom)

Wide Horizons for Children; West Hartford, CT; (860) 570-1740; www.whfc.org; (Dom) (Intl) China, Colombia, Ethiopia, Guatemala, India, Kazakhstan, Korea (South), Philippines, Russian Federation

DELAWARE

STATE ADOPTION OFFICE: Delaware Department of Services for Children, Youth and Their Families (DSCYF); Division of Family Services; 1825 Faulkland Rd.; Wilmington, DE 19805-1195; (302) 633-2655; www.state.de.us

ICPC ADMINISTRATOR: Delaware Department of Services for Children, Youth and Their Families; (302) 633-2698; (302) 633-2652; www.state.de.us/kids/dfsocm.htm

STATE ADOPTION EXCHANGE: Adoption Center of Delaware Valley; (215) 735-9988; www.acdv.org/waiting_children.html; acdv@adopt.org

DELAWARE STATE BAR ASSOCIATION: (302) 658-5279; www.dsba.org

ANNUAL NUMBER OF ADOPTIVE ADOPTIONS FINALIZED IN STATE: 225

STATE LAWS AND PROCEDURES—FAST FACTS
Types permitted? Agency only.
Who can adopt in state? Residents, and nonresidents when child born in state or the agency making the placement is located in state.
How long after child's placement to finalize adoption in court? 6–12 months.
Is adoptive parent advertising (to find a birth mother) permitted? No.
Is a preplacement home study required? Yes.
Typical home study fee? $2,000–$15,000.
Can adoptive parents help birth mother with expenses? Yes: legal, medical, living, but must be paid through adoption agency.
Can child leave hospital with adoptive parents? Yes, with agency approval.
When can birth mother sign her Consent to Adoption? Anytime after birth.
Can the consent be revoked? Yes, for 14 days; thereafter it is irrevocable.
What are the putative father's rights? There is a registry. If putative father registers within 30 days of the birth, he is entitled to notice.

AMERICAN ACADEMY OF ADOPTION ATTORNEYS MEMBERS
Harlan S. Tenenbaum; 3411 Silverside Rd., #101; Wilmington, DE 19810; (302) 477-0914; tenenbaum@aol.com
> *Harlan Tenenbaum, a graduate of the Brooklyn Law School, has been practicing law since 1994. He is also licensed to practice in New Jersey and New York. He estimates he has completed 600 adoptions in his career and last year completed approximately 86 (21 agency; 65 intercountry). His practice is limited to adoptions (typically 90% agency; 10% intercountry), and of these 90% are newborn placements, 10% are toddlers or above. He has adoption programs in China, Guatemala, Russia, and Kazakhstan. He reports 80% of his clients find a birth mother through his office; 20% find their own birth mother. He is the chairperson of the American Bar Association Adoption Committee.*

A biography was not available for the following AAAA member:
Ellen S. Meyer; 521 West St.; Wilmington, DE 19801; (302) 429-0344; e.meyer@adoptionattorneys.org

LICENSED PRIVATE AGENCIES

Adoption House, Inc.; Wilmington, DE; (302) 477-0944; www.adoptionhouse.org; (Dom) (Intl) China, Guatemala, Kazakhstan, Russian Federation

Adoptions from the Heart; Wilmington, DE; (302) 658-8883; www.adoptionsfromthe heart.org; (Dom) (Intl) China, Guatemala, India, Kazakhstan, Lithuania, Russian Federation, Ukraine, Vietnam

Bethany Christian Services, Inc.; Newark, DE; (302) 369-3470; www.bethany.org; (Dom) (Intl) Albania, Bulgaria, China, Colombia, Ecuador, Ethiopia, Guatemala, India, Japan, Korea (South), Lithuania, Philippines, Romania, Russian Federation, Ukraine

Catholic Charities, Inc.; Dover, DE; (302) 674-1600; www.cdow.org; (Dom)

Catholic Charities, Inc.; Georgetown, DE; (302) 856-9578; (Dom)

Catholic Charities, Inc.; Wilmington, DE; (302) 655-9624; www.cdow.org/pregnancy .html; (Dom)

Children and Families First (C&FF); Wilmington, DE; (302) 658-5177; www.cffde.org; (Dom)

Children's Choice of Delaware, Inc.; Dover, DE; (302) 678-0404; www.childrenschoice .org; (Dom) (Intl) Brazil, Bulgaria, China, Guatemala, Lithuania, Mexico

LDS Family Services; Newark, DE; (302) 456-3782; (Dom)

DISTRICT OF COLUMBIA

STATE ADOPTION OFFICE: District of Columbia Child and Family Services Agency; 400 6th St. SW; Washington, DC 20024; (202) 727-4733; www.dhs.dc.gov

ICPC ADMINISTRATOR: District of Columbia Child and Family Services Agency; 400 6th St. SW, Room 3042; Washington, DC 20024; (202) 727-3655; (202) 727-7709; www.dhs.dc.gov

STATE ADOPTION EXCHANGE: District of Columbia Child and Family Services Agency; (202) 442-6188; sjackson@cfsa-dc.org

DISTRICT OF COLUMBIA BAR ASSOCIATION: (202) 737-4700; www.dcbar.org

ANNUAL NUMBER OF ADOPTIVE ADOPTIONS FINALIZED IN STATE: 548

STATE LAWS AND PROCEDURES—FAST FACTS

Types permitted? Independent and agency (75% of newborns via independent).

Who can adopt in state? Residents, or nonresidents when the agency making the placement is located in state.

How long after child's placement to finalize adoption in court? 6–8 months.

Is adoptive parent advertising (to find a birth mother) permitted? Yes.

Is a preplacement home study required? Independent—no. Agency—yes.

Typical home study fee? $1,300–$1,800 (up to $7,500 if agency locates child).

Can adoptive parents help birth mother with expenses? Yes: legal and medical; not living.

Can child leave hospital with adoptive parents? Yes, some require court order.
When can birth mother sign her Consent to Adoption? Independent—anytime after
birth. Agency—72 hours after birth.
Can the consent be revoked? Independent—no, irrevocable upon signing and place-
ment of child. Agency—yes, an automatic right for 10 days.
What are the putative father's rights? There is no registry. Notice must be attempted.

AMERICAN ACADEMY OF ADOPTION ATTORNEYS MEMBERS

Mark Eckman; 4545 42nd St., NW, #302; Washington, DC 20016; (703) 242-8801;
www.datzfoundation.org; markeckman@hotmail.com
*Mark Eckman began practicing law in 1984. He has completed 1,000 adoptions
in his career and last year completed 110. He has an intercountry adoption program in Guatemala, Russia, and China and his practice is largely dedicated to
intercountry adoption.*

Jody Marten; 3360 Tennyson St., NW; Washington, DC 20015; (202) 537-0496;
www.jodymarten.com; jmartennis@aol.com
*Jody Marten began practicing law in 1985. She has completed 200 adoptions in
her career and last year completed approximately 15.*

Mark T. McDermott; 910 17th St., NW, #800; Washington, DC 20006; (202) 331-1440;
mcdermott@mtm-law.com
*Mark McDermott began practicing law in 1974. He has completed 1,400 adop-
tions in his career and last year completed 80. 99% are newborn placements. He
is an adoptive parent and a past president of the American Academy of Adoption
Attorneys. He also actively practices law in Maryland and Virginia.*

Peter J. Wiernicki; Joseph, Reiner & Wiernicki, P.C.; 1025 Connecticut Ave., NW,
#712; Washington, DC 20036; (202) 331-1955; pjr@jrw-law.com
*Peter Wiernicki began practicing law in 1986. He has completed 1,100 adoptions
in his career and last year completed 85. 95% are newborn placements.*

Michele Zavos; 1604 Newton St., NE; Washington, DC 20018; (202) 832-4186; www
.michelezavos.com; michelezavos@aol.com
*Michele Zavos began practicing law in 1979. She has completed 400 adoptions
in her career, many for same-sex couples. 50% are newborn placements, 50%
are toddlers or above.*

Please be aware that some AAAA members located in neighboring states also practice in the District of Columbia, including: Sharon Gustafson (VA), Stanton Phillips
(VA), and Harvey Schweitzer (MD).

LICENSED PRIVATE AGENCIES

Adoption Center of Washington, Inc.; Washington, DC; (202) 452-8278; www.adoption
center.com; (Dom)
Adoption Service Information Agency, Inc. (ASIA); Washington, DC; (202) 726-7193;
www.asia-adopt.org; (Dom) (Intl)

Adoptions Together; Washington, DC; (202) 628-7420; www.adoptionstogether.org; (Dom) (Intl)

Barker Foundation, Inc.; Washington, DC; (202) 363-7511; www.barkerfoundation .org; (Dom) (Intl)

Catholic Charities Archdiocese of Washington, DC; Washington, DC; (202) 526-4100; www.catholiccharities.org; (Dom)

Family and Child Services, Inc.; Washington, DC; (202) 289-1510; www.familyand childservices.org; (Dom)

Family and Child Services of Washington, DC/Adoption Resource Center (ARC); Washington, DC; (202) 289-1057; adoptionresourcecenterdc.org; (Dom)

International Families, Inc.; Washington, DC; (202) 667-5779; www.ifichild.com; (Dom) (Intl)

Lutheran Social Services of the National Capital Area; Washington, DC; (202) 723-3000; www.lssnca.org; (Dom)

Progressive Life Center; Washington, DC; (202) 842-4040; www.ntuplc.org; (Dom) (Intl)

FLORIDA

STATE ADOPTION OFFICE: Florida Department of Children and Families; Office of Family Safety; 1317 Winewood Blvd., Bldg. 6; Tallahassee, FL 32399-0700; (850) 922-5055; www.dcf.state.fl.us/adoption

ICPC ADMINISTRATOR: Florida Department of Children and Families; (same address as above); (850) 922-6656; taffy_compain@dcf.state.fl.us

STATE ADOPTION EXCHANGE: Florida Department of Children and Families; (same address as above); (850) 921-8357; www.dcf.state.fl.us/adoption; Kathleen_ Waters@dcf.state.fl.us

FLORIDA STATE BAR: (850) 561-5844; www.flabar.org

ANNUAL NUMBER OF ADOPTIVE ADOPTIONS FINALIZED IN STATE: 8,435

STATE LAWS AND PROCEDURES—FAST FACTS
Types permitted? Independent and agency (60% of newborns via independent).
Who can adopt in state? Residents only.
How long after child's placement to finalize adoption in court? 3–4 months.
Is adoptive parent advertising (to find a birth mother) permitted? No.
Is a preplacement home study required? Yes.
Typical home study fee? $900–$3,000 (agency fees usually higher if agency located child).
Can adoptive parents help birth mother with expenses? Yes, legal, medical, living, but not past 6 weeks postbirth.
Can child leave hospital with adoptive parents? Yes, usually via attorney.
When can birth mother sign her Consent to Adoption? 48 hours after birth or medical discharge from hospital, whichever is first.

Can the consent be revoked? No, irrevocable upon signing, unless child is over 6 months of age, then there is a 3-day revocation period.

What are the putative father's rights? There is a registry and he must register pre-birth or prior to filing of action to terminate his rights. If he objects, the court will examine his intent to support the child.

AMERICAN ACADEMY OF ADOPTION ATTORNEYS MEMBERS

Ginger S. Allen; Advocates for Children & Families; 16831 NE 6th Ave. N; Miami Beach, FL 33162; (305) 653-2474; www.adoptionflorida.org; gingerallen@adoptionflorida.org

Ginger Allen began practicing law in 1995. Last year she completed 30 adoptions. 100% are newborn placements. 85% of her clients find a birth mother through her office. She is an adoptive parent.

Madonna M. Finney; PO Box 10728; Tallahassee, FL 32302; (850) 577-3077; www.madonnafinney.com; mmfinney@aol.com

Madonna Finney began practicing law in 1988. She has completed 300 adoptions in her career and last year completed 34. 95% are newborn placements. 90% of her clients find a birth mother through her office.

Robison R. Harrell; 3 Clifford Dr.; Shalimar, FL 32579; (850) 651-5225; www.adoptioncenter.org; adoptioncenter@aol.com

Rob Harrell began practicing law in 1970. He has completed 350 adoptions in his career and last year completed 30. 90% are newborn placements. 75% of his clients find a birth mother through his office.

Michelle M. Hausmann; Hausmann & Hickman, PA; 2423 Quantum Blvd.; Boynton Beach, FL 33426; (561) 732-7030; www.hausmann&hickman.com; 2adopt@bellsouth.net

Michelle Hausmann began practicing law in 1990. She has completed 500 adoptions in her career and last year completed 45. 98% are newborn placements. 85% of her clients find a birth mother through her office.

Amy U. Hickman; Hausmann & Hickman, PA; 2423 Quantum Blvd.; Boynton Beach, FL 33426; (561) 732-7030; www.hausmann&hickman.com; 2adopt@bellsouth.net

Amy Hickman began practicing law in 1989. She has completed 150 adoptions in her career and last year completed 35. 99% are newborn placements. 80% of her clients find a birth mother through her office. She is the chairperson of the Family Law Section Adoption/Juvenile of the Florida Bar Association.

Brian T. Kelly; PO Box 10007; Jacksonville, FL 32247; (904) 348-6400; b.kelly@adoptionattorneys.org

Brian Kelly began practicing law in 1983.

Linda McIntyre; 2 NE 5th Ave.; Delray Beach, FL 33483; (561) 272-1422; l.mcintyre@adoptionattorneys.org

Linda McIntyre began practicing law in 1984. She has completed 1,000 adoptions in her career. 100% are newborn placements.

Michael A. Shorstein; Shorstein & Kelly, PA; PO Box 10007; Jacksonville, FL 32247; (904) 348-6400; www.adoption-usa.com; adoption@shorsteinkelly.com
Michael Shorstein began practicing law in 1986. He has completed 1,200 adoptions in his career and last year completed 120. 99% are newborn placements. 90% of his clients find a birth mother through his office.

Susan L. Stockham; 1800 Sista Dr.; Sarasota, FL 34241; (941) 924-4949; www.stock hamlaw.com; susan@stockhamlaw.com
Susan Stockham began practicing law in 1981. She has completed 1,000 adoptions in her career and last year completed 75. 90% are newborn placements. 75% of her clients find a birth mother through her office. She is an adoptive parent.

Jeanne Trudeau Tate; 418 W. Platt St.; Tampa, FL 33606; (813) 258-3355; www .floridaadoptionattorney.com; jeanne@jtatelaw.com
Jeanne Tate began practicing law in 1982. She has completed 2,000 adoptions in her career and last year completed 150. 95% are newborn placements. 40% of her clients find a birth mother through her office; 60% find their own birth mother. She was a recipient of the 2006 Congressional Angel in Adoption award.

Biographies were not available for the following AAAA members:

Mikal W. Grass; 701 W. Cypress Creek Rd., Suite 302; Ft. Lauderdale, FL 33309; (954) 202-7889; m.grass@adoptionattorneys.org

Anthony B. Marchese; 4010 Boy Scout Blvd., Suite 590; Tampa, FL 33607; (813) 877-6643

Mary Ann Scherer; 2734 E. Oakland Park Blvd., Suite 102; Ft. Lauderdale, FL 33306; (954) 564-6900; m.scherer@adoptionattorneys.org

Laurie Slavin; 16631 NE 6th Ave.; N. Miami Beach, FL 33162; (305) 653-2474; l.slavin@adoptionattorneys.org

Patricia L. Strowbridge, Esq.; 1516 E. Colonial Dr., Suite 202; Orlando, FL 32803; (407) 894-1525; www.strowbridge.com; patricia@strowbridge.com

Cheryl R. E. Yeary; 202 N. Swinton Ave.; Delray Beach, FL 33444; (561) 330-9901; c.yeary@adoptionattorneys.org

LICENSED PRIVATE AGENCIES

Adoption Advocates, Inc.; Largo, FL; (727) 391-8096; http://adoptionadvocatesinc .com; (Dom)

Adoption by Shepherd Care, Inc.; Hollywood, FL; (954) 981-2060; www.adoption shepherdcare.com; (Dom) (Intl) China, Colombia, Guatemala, Russian Federation

Adoption Placement, Inc.; Plantation, FL; (954) 474-8494; www.adoptionplacement
.com; (Dom) (Intl)

Adoption Resource Center, Inc.; Coral Springs, FL; (954) 255-3226; www.adopt
resource.org; (Intl) China, Guatemala, Korea (South), Russian Federation,
Ukraine

Adoption Source, Inc.; Boca Raton, FL; (561) 912-9229; http://adoptionsource.org;
(Intl)

Advocates for Children and Families (ACF); North Miami Beach, FL; (305) 653-2474;
www.adoptionflorida.org; (Dom) (Intl)

All About Adoptions, Inc.; Melbourne, FL; (407) 723-0088; www.allaboutadoptions
.org; (Dom) (Intl)

Axis Adoption & Consulting Services Inc.; Kenneth City, FL; (727) 656-3022; www
.axisadoption.org; (Dom) (Intl)

Beacon House Adoption Services, Inc.; Pensacola, FL; (850) 430-4005; (850) 430-4004;
www.beaconhouseadoption.com; (Dom) (Intl) China, Guatemala, Kazakhstan,
Russian Federation, Ukraine

A Bond of Love Adoption Agency, Inc. (ABL); Sarasota, FL; (941) 957-0064; www.abond
oflove.net; (Dom)

Catholic Charities; Panama City, FL; (850) 763-0475; (Dom)

Catholic Charities; Tampa, FL; (813) 631-4393; www.catholiccharities.org; (Dom)

Catholic Charities; West Palm Beach, FL; (561) 842-2406; www.diocesepb.org/
charities; (Dom)

Catholic Charities Bureau; Gainesville, FL; (352) 372-0294; www.ccbgainesville.org;
(Dom)

Catholic Charities Bureau; Jacksonville, FL; (904) 354-4846; www.ccbjax.org; (Dom)

Catholic Charities Bureau—St. Augustine Regional Office (CCB St. Augustine); St. Augustine, FL 32084; (904) 829-6300; www.ccbstaug.org; (Dom)

Catholic Charities—Diocese of Orlando; Orlando, FL; (407) 658-1818; www.ccorlando
.org; (Dom)

Catholic Charities—Diocese of Orlando, Eastern Regional Office; Cocoa, FL; (321) 636-
6144; www.ccorlando.org; (Dom)

Catholic Charities of Northwest Florida, Inc.; Pensacola, FL; (850) 436-6410; (Dom)

Catholic Charities of the Diocese of Venice, Inc.; Sarasota, FL; (941) 379-5119; www
.catholiccharitiesdov.org; (Dom)

The Children's Home, Inc.; Tampa, FL; (813) 855-4435; www.thechildrenshomeinc
.com; (Dom)

Children's Home Society of Florida; Fort Lauderdale, FL; (954) 453-6400; www.chsfl
.org; (Dom)

Children's Home Society of Florida; Fort Myers, FL; (239) 334-0222; www.chsfl.org;
(Dom)

Children's Home Society of Florida; Fort Pierce, FL; (772) 489-5601; www.chsfl.org;
(Dom)

Children's Home Society of Florida; Gainesville, FL; (352) 334-0955; www.helpflorida
children.org; (Dom)

Children's Home Society of Florida; Jacksonville, FL; (904) 493-7794; www.chsfl.org; (Dom) (Intl) China, Kazakhstan, Philippines, Russian Federation;

Children's Home Society of Florida; Melbourne, FL; (321) 752-3170; www.chsfl.org; (Dom)

Children's Home Society of Florida; Miami, FL; (305) 324-1262; www.chsfl.org; (Dom)

Children's Home Society of Florida; Orlando, FL; (407) 895-5800; www.chsfl.org; (Dom) (Intl)

Children's Home Society of Florida; Panama City, FL; (850) 747-5411; www.chsfl.org; (Dom)

Children's Home Society of Florida; Pensacola, FL; (850) 494-5990; www.chsfl.org; (Dom)

Children's Home Society of Florida; Tallahassee, FL; (850) 921-0772; www.chsfl.org; (Dom)

Children's Home Society of Florida; Tampa, FL; (813) 740-4266; www.chsfl.org; (Dom)

Children's Home Society of Florida; West Palm Beach, FL; (561) 868-4300; www.chsfl .org; (Dom)

China Adoption with Love, Inc.; North Naples, FL; www.cawli.org; (Intl) China

Christian Family Services; Gainesville, FL; (352) 378-6202; http://christianfamily services.com; (Dom)

A Chosen Child, Inc.; Orlando, FL; (407) 894-1599; www.achosenchild.com; (Dom)

Commonwealth Adoptions International, Inc. (CAII); Tampa, FL; (813) 269-4646; www .commonwealthadoption.org; (Dom) (Intl) Brazil, China, Colombia, Guatemala, India, Kazakhstan, Russian Federation, Taiwan, Ukraine

Cornerstone Adoption Services, Inc.; Tallahassee, FL; cori25@earthlink.net; (Dom) (Intl) China, Guatemala, Ukraine

Everyday Blessings (EB); Thonotosassa, FL; (813) 982-9226; www.everybless.org; (Dom)

Family Creations, Inc.; Bradenton, FL; (941) 727-9630; www.familycreations.org; (Dom) (Intl) China, Guatemala, Kazakhstan, Russian Federation, Ukraine

Family Support Services of North Florida; Jacksonville, FL; (904) 421-5800; www.fssjax .org; (Dom)

Florida Baptist Children's Homes; Cantonment, FL; (850) 968-1114; www.fbchomes .org; (Dom)

Florida Baptist Children's Homes; Lakeland, FL; (863) 688-4981; www.fbchomes.org; (Dom)

Florida Baptist Children's Homes; Miami, FL; (305) 271-4121; www.fbchomes.org; (Dom)

Florida Baptist Children's Homes; Tallahassee, FL; (850) 878-1458; www.fbchomes.org; (Dom)

Florida's Adoption Information Center and North American Council on Adoptable Children Representative; Jacksonville, FL; (904) 353-0679; www.adoptfl.org; (Dom) (Intl)

Florida Home Studies and Adoption, Inc. (FHSA); Sarasota, FL; (941) 342-8189; www .flhomestudies.com; (Intl) Bulgaria, Cambodia, China, Guatemala, Korea (South), Nepal, Taiwan, Thailand, Ukraine, Vietnam

Gift of Life, Inc.; Pinellas Park, FL; (727) 549-1416; www.giftoflifeinc.org; (Dom) (Intl)

Gorman Family Life Center, Inc. (Life for Kids); Winter Park, FL; (407) 629-5437; www .lifeforkids.com; (Dom) (Intl)

Heart of Adoptions, Inc.; Naples, FL; (239) 594-2830; www.floridaadoptionagency .com; (Dom)

Heart of Adoptions, Inc.; Orlando, FL; (407) 898-8280; www.floridaadoptionagency .com; (Dom)

Heart of Adoptions, Inc.; Tampa, FL; (813) 258-6505; www.floridaadoptionagency .com; (Dom) (Intl) Guatemala

Heart to Heart Adoption Service, Inc.; Royal Palm Beach, FL; (561) 383-8590; (Intl) China, Guatemala, Ukraine

Home at Last Adoption Agency; Coco Beach, FL; (321) 868-2229; www.home atlastadoption.com; (Dom) (Intl) Brazil, China, Colombia, El Salvador, Guatemala, Kazakhstan, Panama, Russian Federation, Ukraine

Homecoming Adoptions, Inc.; Orlando, FL; (407) 420-1900; www.homecoming adoptions.com; (Dom) (Intl) Brazil, China, Costa Rica, El Salvador, Guatemala, Ireland, Kazakhstan, Mexico, Nepal, Panama, Russian Federation, Tajikistan

Intercountry Adoption Center, Inc.; Bradenton, FL; (941) 761-1345; www.intercountry adopt.com; (Intl) China, Colombia, Ethiopia, Guatemala, Korea (South), Philippines, Poland, Russian Federation, Ukraine

Jewish Adoption and Foster Care Options (JAFCO); Sunrise, FL; (954) 749-7230; www .jafco.org; (Dom)

Jewish Community Services of South Florida, Inc.; Miami, FL; (305) 576-6550; www .jcsfl.org; (Dom)

Jewish Family and Community Services, Inc.; Jacksonville, FL; (904) 448-1933; www .jfcsjax.org; (Dom)

LDS Family Services; Orlando, FL; (407) 850-9141; (Dom)

Lifelink Child and Family Services; Sarasota, FL; (941) 957-1614; www.lifelink.org; (Intl) Bulgaria, China, India, Korea (South), Philippines, Thailand, Ukraine

A Loving Choice International, Inc. (ALCI); Wellington, FL; (561) 784-0041; www .alovingchoiceinternational.org; (Dom) (Intl) China, Guatemala, Latvia, Russian Federation

Mother Goose Adoptions of Florida, Inc.; Tavares, FL; (352) 552-5499; www.mother gooseadoptions.com; (Dom) (Intl)

New Beginnings Family and Children's Services; Largo, FL; (727) 584-5262; www .new-beginnings.org; (Intl) China, Korea (South), Peru, Russian Federation, Thailand, Vietnam

One World Adoption Services, Inc.; Deerfield Beach, FL; (954) 596-2222; www .oneworldadoption.com; (Dom)

Open Door Social Services; Orlando, FL; (407) 896-2323; www.opendoorss.com/en; (Dom)

Southwest Florida Children's Home; Fort Myers, FL; (239) 275-7151; www.royalpalm baptist.com; (Dom)

Universal Aid for Children; Pompano Beach, FL; (954) 785-0033; www.uacadoption
.org; (Intl) Colombia, Guatemala, Romania, Russian, Federation, Ukraine

GEORGIA

STATE ADOPTION OFFICE: Georgia Department of Human Resources; Division of Family and Children Services; 2 Peachtree St., NW; 85th Floor, Suite 460; Atlanta, GA 30311; (404) 657-3619; http://dfcs.dhr.georgia.gov

ICPC ADMINISTRATOR: (same address as above); (404) 463-2239; yadavenp@dhr.ga.us

STATE ADOPTION EXCHANGE: My Turn Now Photolisting; (404) 657-3479; http://167.193.144.179/mtnmenu2.asp

STATE BAR OF GEORGIA: (404) 527-8700; www.gabar.org

ANNUAL NUMBER OF ADOPTIVE ADOPTIONS FINALIZED IN STATE: 3,499

STATE LAWS AND PROCEDURES—FAST FACTS
Types permitted? Independent and agency (75% of newborns via independent).
Who can adopt in state? Residents only.
How long after child's placement to finalize adoption in court? 4 months.
Is adoptive parent advertising (to find a birth mother) permitted? No.
Is a preplacement home study required? Independent—no. Agency—yes.
Typical home study fee? $1,200–$1,600 (agency fees usually higher if agency located child). $300 if only independent postplacement.
Can adoptive parents help birth mother with expenses? Yes: medical only.
Can child leave hospital with adoptive parents? Yes, usually via attorney.
When can birth mother sign her Consent to Adoption? Independent—anytime after birth. Agency—24 hours after birth.
Can the consent be revoked? Yes, for 10 days, then irrevocable.
What are the putative father's rights? There is a registry. Notice must also be attempted even if he does not register. Upon notice, he has 30 days to file objection.
Note: Attorneys can't locate birth mothers to create an adoptive placement for a fee.

AMERICAN ACADEMY OF ADOPTION ATTORNEYS MEMBERS
Ruth F. Claiborne; Claiborne, Outman, & Surmay, PC; 60 Lenox Pointe, NE; Atlanta, GA 30324; (404) 442-6933; www.gababylaw.com; ruth@gababylaw.com
Ruth Claiborne began practicing law in 1976. She has completed 600 adoptions in her career and last year completed 60. 80% are newborn placements. 30% of her clients find a birth mother through her office. She was a recipient of the 2004 Congressional Angel in Adoption award.

Rhonda L. Fishbein; 2849 Paces Ferry Rd., #215; Atlanta, GA 30339; (770) 437-8582; www.rfishbeinadoption-law.com; rlfishbein@bellsouth.net
Rhonda Fishbein began practicing law in 1982. She has completed 1,300 adop-

tions in her career and last year completed 200. 90% are newborn placements. She is an adoptive parent and the founder and director of a licensed adoption agency.

Jerrold W. Hester; 3500 Parkway Ln., #230; Norcross, GA 30092; (770) 446-3645; j.hester@adoptionattorneys.org
Jerrold Hester began practicing law in 1975. He has completed 2,000 adoptions in his career and last year completed 60. He is a recipient of the 2002 Congressional Angel in Adoption award.

Sherriann H. Hicks; 368 South Perry St.; Lawrenceville, GA 30045; (678) 985-3011; shhicks@bellsouth.net
Sherriann Hicks began practicing law in 1993. She has completed 400 adoptions in her career and last year completed 42. 25% are newborn placements.

Richard A. Horder; Kilpatrick Stockton LLP; 1100 Peachtree St., Suite 2800; Atlanta, GA 30309; (404) 815-6538; www.kilpatrickstockton.com; rhorder@kilpatrick stockton.com
Richard Horder began practicing law in 1971. He has completed 600 adoptions in his career and last year completed 52. 80% are newborn placements. He is an adoptive parent.

James B. Outman; Claiborne, Outman, & Surmay, PC; 60 Lenox Pointe, NE; Atlanta, GA 30324; (404) 442-6933; www.gababylaw.com; jim@gababylaw.com
James Outman began practicing law in 1971. He has completed 200 adoptions in his career. 60% are newborn placements. He is an adoptive parent and a recipient of the 2003 Congressional Angel in Adoption award.

Josie Redwine; 2440 Sandy Plains Rd., #7; Marietta, GA 30066; (770) 579-6070; www.redwineattorney.com; redwinepc@aol.com
Josie Redwine began practicing law in 1996. She has completed 2,000 adoptions in her career and last year completed 270. 65% are newborn placements. She is a member of the Georgia Association of Licensed Adoption Agencies.

Lynn McNeese Swank; 118 North Ave., #6; Jonesboro, GA 30236; (770) 477-5318; www.swanklaw.com; swanklaw@mindspring.com
Lynn Swank began practicing law in 1975. Last year she completed 52 adoptions. 75% are newborn placements.

Biographies were unavailable for the following AAAA members:

Karlise Y. Grier; 811 Duffield Dr., NW; Atlanta, GA 30318; (404) 658-9999; k.grier@ adoptionattorneys.org

Irene Steffas; 4343 Shallowford Rd., Bldg. H-1; Marietta, GA 30062; (770) 642-6075; i.steffas@adoptionattorneys.org

Lori M. Surmay; 60 Lenox Pointe, NE; Atlanta, GA 30324; (404) 442-6933; l.surmay@ adoptionattorneys.org

Diane Woods; 707 Whitlock Ave., G-5; Marietta, GA 30064; (770) 429-1001; d.woods@adoptionattorneys.org

LICENSED PRIVATE AGENCIES

AAA Partners in Adoption; Alpharetta, GA; (770) 844-2080; (Dom) (Intl) Guatemala, Kazakhstan, Russian Federation, Ukraine

Adopt an Angel International; Hiawassee, GA; (706) 896-5094; www.adoptanangel .org; (Intl) Azerbaijan, Bulgaria, China, Guatemala, Kazakhstan, Peru, Romania, Russian Federation, Ukraine, Vietnam

Adoption Planning, Inc.; Atlanta, GA; (770) 437-1907; (Dom)

All God's Children, Inc; Bogart, GA; (706) 316-2421; (Dom)

Bethany Christian Services; Atlanta, GA; (770) 455-7111; www.bethany.org/atlanta; (Dom) (Intl)

Bethany Christian Services (BCS); Columbus, GA; (706) 576-5766; www.bethany.org/ columbus_ga; (Dom) (Intl)

Catholic Social Services, Inc.; Atlanta, GA; (404) 885-7275; www.cssatlanta.com; (Dom)

Christian Homes, Inc. (CHI); Pavo, GA; (229) 859-2654; (Dom)

Community Connections, Inc.; Stone Mountain, GA; (770) 465-9644; (Dom)

Covenant Care Services, Inc.; Macon, GA; (478) 475-4990; www.covenantcare adoptions.com; (Dom)

Elina International Adoption Services, Inc.; Roswell, GA; (770) 650-0730; www .elinaadoption.org; (Intl) Bulgaria, Kazakhstan, Russian Federation, Ukraine

Families First; Atlanta, GA; (404) 853-2867; www.familiesfirst.org; (Dom) (Intl)

Family Counseling Center/CSRA, Inc.; Augusta, GA; (706) 722-6512; (Dom)

Family Values Network, Inc.; Stone Mountain, GA; (Dom)

Forsyth County Child Advocacy Center, Inc.; Cumming, GA; (678) 208-1908; (Dom)

Genesis Adoptions; Alpharetta, GA; (678) 518-3911; www.genesisadoptions.org; (Intl)

Georgia Association for Guidance, Aid, Placement and Empathy (AGAPE), Inc.; Atlanta, GA; (404) 452-9995; (Dom)

Georgia Baptist Children's Home and Family Ministries, Inc.; Palmetto, GA; (770) 463-6240; www.gbchfm.org; (Dom)

Georgia Mentor, Inc.; Decatur, GA; (770) 496-5500; www.thementornetwork.com; (Dom) (Intl)

Georgia Youth Advocate Program, Inc.; Augusta, GA; (706) 722-3712; www.gyap.org; (Dom)

The Giving Tree, Inc.; Decatur, GA; (404) 633-3383; www.thegivingtree.org; (Dom)

GRN Community Service Board; Lawrenceville, GA; www.grncsb.com; (Dom)

Hope for Children, Inc.; Atlanta, GA; (770) 391-1511; www.hopeforchildren.org; (Dom) (Intl) China, Colombia, Russian Federation

Illien Adoptions International, Inc.; Atlanta, GA; (404) 815-1599; www.illienadopt.com; (Intl) Bulgaria, Haiti, India, Lithuania, Nepal, Russian Federation, Ukraine

Independent Adoption Center (IAC); Tucker, GA; (404) 321-6900; www.adoptionhelp .org; (Dom) (Intl)

Jewish Family Services, Inc.; Atlanta, GA; (770) 677-9300; (Dom)

LDS Family Services; Tucker, GA; (404) 939-2121; (Dom)

Lutheran Services of Georgia (LSG); Atlanta, GA; (404) 591-7068; www.lsga.org/ programs/adoption.htm; (Dom) (Intl)

One World Adoption Services; Buford, GA; (678) 714-6612; www.oneworldadoptions .org; (Dom) (Intl) Brazil, Bulgaria, China, Guatemala, Haiti, Kazakhstan, Russian Federation, Ukraine

The Open Door Adoption Agency, Inc. (TOD); Thomasville, GA; (229) 228-6339; www .opendooradoption.com; (Dom) (Intl)

Roots Adoption Agency, Inc.; Atlanta, GA; (770) 907-7770; www.rootsadopt.org; (Dom)

World Partners Adoption, Inc; Lawrenceville, GA; (770) 962-7860; www.world partnersadoption.org; (Intl) Bulgaria, China, Colombia, Guatemala, Kazakhstan, Russian Federation, Ukraine

HAWAII

STATE ADOPTION OFFICE: Hawaii Department of Human Services; 810 Richards St., Suite 400; Honolulu, HI 96813; (808) 586-5698; www.hawaii.gov

ICPC ADMINISTRATOR: Hawaii Department of Human Services; (same address as above); (808) 586-5699; kswink@dhs.hawaii.gov

STATE ADOPTION EXCHANGE: Central Adoption Exchange of Hawaii; (808) 586-5698; (808) 586-4806

HAWAII STATE BAR ASSOCIATION: (808) 537-1868; www.hsba.org

ANNUAL NUMBER OF ADOPTIVE ADOPTIONS FINALIZED IN STATE: 766

STATE LAWS AND PROCEDURES—FAST FACTS

Types permitted? Independent and agency (90% of newborns via independent).

Who can adopt in state? Residents, and nonresidents when child born in state or the agency making the placement is located in state.

How long after child's placement to finalize adoption in court? 2–6 months.

Is adoptive parent advertising (to find a birth mother) permitted? Yes, but many newspapers decline.

Is a preplacement home study required? No (court can even waive postplacement home study).

Typical home study fee? $1,500 (agency fees usually higher if agency located child).

Can adoptive parents help birth mother with expenses? Yes: legal, medical, living.

Can child leave hospital with adoptive parents? Yes, with form.

When can birth mother sign her Consent to Adoption? Anytime after the birth.

Can the consent be revoked? Yes, anytime prior to finalization of the adoption, only if a court finds the best interests of the child are served by revocation.

What are the putative father's rights? There is no registry. Notice must be attempted. If he objects, the court will consider the best interests of the child.

AMERICAN ACADEMY OF ADOPTION ATTORNEYS MEMBERS

Laurie A. Loomis; 1001 Bishop St., #2380; Honolulu, HI 96813; (808) 524-5066; l.loomis@adoptionattorneys.org

Laurie Loomis began practicing law in 1985.

LICENSED PRIVATE AGENCIES
Adopt International; Honolulu, HI; (808) 523-1400; www.adopt-intl.org; (Intl)
Catholic Charities Family Services; Honolulu, HI; (808) 536-1794; (Dom)
Child and Family Services (CFS); Honolulu, HI; (808) 543-8466; (Intl)
Crown Child Placement International, Inc.; Honolulu, HI; (808) 946-0443; (Intl)
Hawaii International Child Placement and Family Services, Inc.; Honolulu, HI ; (808) 589-2367; www.h-i-c.org; (Intl) China; Kazakhstan
Journeys of the Heart Adoption Services; Honolulu, HI; (808) 391-5493; http://hawaii-adoption.com; (Dom) (Intl) China, Guatemala, Haiti, India, Marshall Islands, Samoa, Ukraine, Vietnam
LDS Social Services; Honolulu, HI; (808) 945-3690; (Dom)

IDAHO

STATE ADOPTION OFFICE: Idaho Department of Health and Welfare; Division of Family and Community Services: 450 W. State St., 5th Floor, PO Box 83702; Boise, ID 83702; (208) 334-5697; www.healthandwelfare.idaho.gov

ICPC ADMINISTRATOR: Idaho Department of Health and Welfare; (same address as above); (208) 334-5697; (208) 334-6664; Mccarro2@idhw.state.id.us

STATE ADOPTION EXCHANGE: Idaho's Wednesday's Child; (208) 345-6646; www.idahowednesdayschild.org

IDAHO STATE BAR AND IDAHO LAW FOUNDATION, INC.: (208) 334-4500; www2.state.id.us/isb

ANNUAL NUMBER OF ADOPTIVE ADOPTIONS FINALIZED IN STATE: 1,048

STATE LAWS AND PROCEDURES—FAST FACTS
Types permitted? Independent and agency (60% of newborns via independent).
Who can adopt in state? Residents only.
How long after child's placement to finalize adoption in court? 3–7 months.
Is adoptive parent advertising (to find a birth mother) permitted? No.
Is a preplacement home study required? Yes.
Typical home study fee? $600–$1,200 (agency fees usually higher if agency located child).
Can adoptive parents help birth mother with expenses? Yes: legal and medical. Living assistance in excess of $2,000 requires judge's authorization.
Can child leave hospital with adoptive parents? Yes, some require attorney present.
When can birth mother sign her Consent to Adoption? Anytime after birth, but some judges require a 48-hour postbirth delay.
Can the consent be revoked? Irrevocable when witnessed by a judge.
What are the putative father's rights? There is a registry. He must register and file a paternity action prior to the birth mother signing her consent, or adoptive parents take custody, whichever occurs first.

AMERICAN ACADEMY OF ADOPTION ATTORNEYS MEMBERS

Alfred E. Barrus; Barrus Law Office; 1918 Overland Ave.; Burley, ID 83318; (208) 678-1155; a.barrus@adoptionattorneys.org
Alfred Barrus began practicing law in 1974. He has completed 600 adoptions in his career and last year completed 23. 80% are newborn placements. 10% of his clients find a birth mother through his office. He is an adoptive parent.

John T. Hawley Jr.; 420 W. Main St., #206; Boise, ID, 83702; (208) 336-6686; www.adoptionidaho.com; j.hawley@adoptionattorneys.org
John Hawley Jr. began practicing law in 1980. He has completed 500 adoptions in his career and last year completed 32. 80% are newborn placements. 30% of his clients find a birth mother through his office.

LICENSED PRIVATE AGENCIES

CASI Foundation for Children, Inc.; Boise, ID; (208) 376-0558; www.adoptcasi.org; (Dom) (Intl) Azerbaijan, China, Guatemala, Haiti, Mexico, Republic of Georgia, Russian Federation, Ukraine

Idaho Youth Ranch Adoption Services; Boise, ID; (208) 377-2613; www.youthranch.org; (Dom)

Idaho Youth Ranch Adoptions North; Coeur D'Alene, ID; (208) 667-1898; www.youthranch.org; (Dom)

LDS Family Services, Inc.; Burley, ID; (208) 678-8200; (Dom)

LDS Family Services, Inc.; Idaho Falls, ID; (208) 529-5276; (Dom)

LDS Family Services, Inc.; Pocatello, ID; (208) 232-7780; (Dom)

A New Beginning Adoption Agency, Inc.; Boise, ID; (208) 939-3865; www.adoptanewbeginning.org; (Dom) (Intl)

ILLINOIS

STATE ADOPTION OFFICE: Illinois Department of Children and Family Services: Service Intervention; 100 W. Randolph, Suite 6-100; Chicago, IL 60601; (312) 814-6858; www.state.il.us

ICPC ADMINISTRATOR: Illinois Department of Children and Family Services; (217) 785-2680; rdavidso@idcfs.state.il.us

STATE ADOPTION EXCHANGE: Adoption Information Center of Illinois (AICI); (312) 346-1516; www.adoptinfo-il.org; aici@adoptinfo-il.org

ILLINOIS STATE BAR ASSOCIATION: (217) 525-1760; www.illinoisbar.org

ANNUAL NUMBER OF ADOPTIVE ADOPTIONS FINALIZED IN STATE: 6,673

STATE LAWS AND PROCEDURES—FAST FACTS

Types permitted? Independent and agency.

Who can adopt in state? Residents, and nonresidents when agency making placement is in state.

How long after child's placement to finalize adoption in court? 6 months.

Is adoptive parent advertising (to find a birth mother) permitted? Yes.

Is a preplacement home study required? Independent—no, but some counties require (e.g., Cook). Agency—yes.

Typical home study fee? $3,000 (agency fees usually higher if agency located child). Fees less if only postplacement evaluation for independent is done.

Can adoptive parents help birth mother with expenses? Yes: legal, medical, living, but advance court approval required.

Can child leave hospital with adoptive parents? Yes, but usually a court order granting temporary legal custody is required.

When can birth mother sign her Consent to Adoption? 72 hours after birth.

Can the consent be revoked? No, it is irrevocable.

What are the putative father's rights? There is a registry. Notice must be given to any putative father who has registered within 30 days of the birth, or who can be identified by the birth mother.

AMERICAN ACADEMY OF ADOPTION ATTORNEYS MEMBERS

Shelley B. Ballard; Ballard Desai Bush-Joseph & Horwich; 221 N. LaSalle St., Suite 1136; Chicago, IL 60601; (312) 673-5312; www.infertility-law.com; sballard@infertility-law.com
Shelley Ballard began practicing law in 1987. She has completed 2,000 adoptions in her career. 80% are newborn placements. 1% of her clients find a birth mother through her office. She is an adoptive parent and past chairperson of the Chicago Bar Association Adoption Law Committee.

Kirsten Crouse Bays; Crouse, Cobb & Bays; 1513 University Dr.; Charleston, IL 61920; (217) 345-6099; www.iladoptlaw.com; kbays@charter.net
Kirsten Bays began practicing law in 1994. She has completed 1,000 adoptions in her career and last year completed 175. 80% are newborn placements. 50% of her clients find a birth mother through her office.

Deborah Crouse Cobb; Crouse, Cobb & Bays; 515 W. Main St.; Colinsville, IL 62234; (618) 344-6300; www.iladoptlaw.com; debcobb@sbcglobal.net
Deborah Cobb began practicing law in 1984. She has completed 1,000 adoptions in her career and last year completed 175. 80% are newborn placements. 50% of her clients find a birth mother through her office.

Joseph H. Gitlin; (815) 338-0021; 111 Dean St.; Woodstock, IL 60098
Joseph Gitlin began practicing law in 1959.

Susan F. Grammer; 2 Terminal Dr., Suite 17A/B; East Alton, IL 62024; (618) 259-2113; s.grammer@adoptionattorneys.org
Susan Grammer began practicing law in 1983.

Theresa Rahe Hardesty; 7513 N. Regent Pl.; Peoria, IL 61614; (309) 692-1087; trhadopt@insightbb.com
Theresa Hardesty began practicing law in 1977. She has completed 2,500 adop-

tions in her career and last year completed 150. 100% are newborn placements. 5% of her clients find a birth mother through her office.

Michelle M. Hughes; 221 N. LaSalle St., Suite 2020; Chicago, IL 60601; (312) 857-7287; m.hughes@adoptionattorney.org
Michelle Hughes began practicing law in 1989. She has completed 2,000 adoptions in her career and last year completed 181. 70% are newborn placements. 1% of her clients find a birth mother through her office.

Kimberly Kuhlengel-Jones; 255 E. St. Louis St.; PO Box 186; Nashville, IL 62263; (618) 327-3093; kuhlengel@earthlink.net
Kimberly Kuhlengel-Jones began practicing law in 1995. She has completed 300 adoptions in her career and last year completed 40. 99% are newborn placements. 10% of her clients find a birth mother through her office.

Richard Lifshitz; Mandel, Lipton and Stevenson, Ltd.; 203 N. LaSalle St., Suite 2210; Chicago, IL 60601; (312) 236-7080; www.mandellipton.com; rlifshitz@mandellipton.com
Richard Lifshitz began practicing law in 1976. He has completed 3,000 adoptions in his career and last year completed 80. 80% are newborn placements. His clients locate their own birth mother.

Sheila A. Maloney; 928 Warren Ave., Suite 3; Downers Grove, IL 60515; (630) 570-5050; www.iladoptionlawyer.com; stmesq@msn.com
Sheila Maloney began practicing law in 1986. She has completed 1,000 adoptions in her career and last year completed 140. 95% are newborn placements. She is an adoptive parent and is a past chairperson of the Chicago Bar Association Adoption Committee.

Kathleen Hogan Morrison; 70 W. Madison St., Suite 2100; Chicago, IL 60602; (312) 977-4477; www.chicagoadoptionattorney.com; k.morrison@adoptionattorneys.org
Kathleen Hogan Morrison began practicing law in 1976. She has completed 7,500 adoptions in her career and last year completed 325. 50% are newborn placements. All of her clients locate their own birth mother.

Sally Wildman; 200 N. LaSalle St., Suite 2750; Chicago, IL 60601; (312) 726-9214; www.swildmanlaw.com; s.wildman@adoptionattorneys.org
Sally Wildman began practicing law in 1985. She has completed 400 adoptions in her career and last year completed 47. 50% are newborn placements. All of her clients locate their own birth mother. She is a past chairperson of the American Bar Association Adoption Committee.

Biographies were not available for the following AAAA members:
Nidhi Desai; 221 N. LaSalle St., Suite 1136; Chicago, IL 60601; (312) 673-5312; n.desai@adoptionattorneys.org

Denise J. Patton; 4760 Fairfax Ave.; Palatine, IL 60067; (847) 925-9072; d.patton@
adoptionattorneys.org

Glenna J. Weith; 116 N. Chestnut St., Suite 230; Champaign, IL 61820; (217) 398-
1200; g.weigh@adoptionattorneys.org

LICENSED PRIVATE AGENCIES

Adoption Ark; Buffalo Grove, IL; (847) 279-0502; www.adoptionark.com; (Intl)

Adoption-Link, Inc.; Oak Park, IL; (708) 524-1433; www.adoptionlinkillinois.com;
(Dom) (Intl)

Adoption World; Chicago, IL; (312) 664-8933; (Dom)

Aunt Martha's Youth Services; Chicago Heights, IL; (708) 754-1044; (Dom)

Aurora Catholic Charities; Aurora, IL; (630) 820-3220; www.ccrfd.org; (Dom) (Intl)

The Baby Fold (TBF); Normal, IL; (309) 454-1770; http://thebabyfold.org; (Dom) (Intl)

Bethany Christian Services of Illinois; Chicago, IL; (773) 264-0200; www.bethany.org/
chicago; (Dom) (Intl)

Catholic Charities, Chicago Archdiocese; Chicago, IL; (312) 655-7071; www.catholic
charities.net; (Dom) (Intl)

Catholic Charities, Joliet Diocese; Joliet, IL; (815) 723-3053; www.cc-doj.org; (Dom)
(Intl)

Catholic Charities, Peoria Diocese; Peoria, IL; (309) 671-5720; www.ccdop.org; (Dom)
(Intl)

Catholic Charities, Springfield Diocese; Springfield, IL; (217) 523-9201; www.cc.dio
.org; (Dom)

Catholic Social Services of Southern Illinois; Belleville, IL; (618) 394-5900; http://cssil
.org; (Dom) (Intl)

Center for Family Building, Inc. (CFB); Skokie, IL; (847) 869-1518; www.centerfor
family.com; (Dom) (Intl)

Chicago Child Care Society; Chicago, IL; (773) 643-0452; www.cccsociety.org; (Dom)

Children's Home and Aid Society of Illinois (CHASI); Chicago, IL; (312) 424-0200; www
.chasi.org; (Dom) (Intl) Guatemala

Children's Home and Aid Society of Illinois (CHASI); Granite City, IL; (618) 452-8900;
www.chasi.org; (Dom) (Intl)

Children's Home and Aid Society of Illinois (CHASI); Rockford, IL; (815) 962-1043; www
.chasi.org; (Dom) (Intl)

Children's Hope International (CHI); Des Plaines, IL; (847) 297-5504; www.childrenshope
.com; (Dom) (Intl) China, Colombia, Kazakhstan, Russian Federation, Vietnam

Cornerstone: Foundations for Families; Quincy, IL; (217) 222-8254; www.cornerstone
quincy.org; (Dom)

Counseling and Family Service; Peoria, IL; (309) 676-2400; (Dom) (Intl)

The Cradle; Evanston, IL; (847) 475-5800; www.cradle.org; (Dom) (Intl) Russian
Federation

Evangelical Child and Family Agency (ECFA); Wheaton, IL; (630) 653-6400; www
.evancfa.org; (Dom) (Intl) China, Guatemala, Russian Federation

Family Choices; Collinsville, IL; (618) 344-6600; (Dom) (Intl)

Family Counseling Clinic, Inc.; Mundelein, IL; (847) 566-7121; www.familycounseling clinic.com; (Dom) (Intl) Azerbaijan, China, Nepal, Panama, Poland

Family Resource Center (FRC); Chicago, IL; (773) 334-2300; www.adoptillinois.org; (Dom) (Intl) China, Ukraine

Glenkirk; Northbrook, IL; (847) 272-5111; www.glenkirk.org; (Dom) (Intl)

Hobby Horse House; Jacksonville, IL; (217) 243-7708; (Dom) (Intl) China, Colombia, Ethiopia, Guatemala, Hungary. India, Mexico, Romania, Russian Federation, Ukraine

Hope for the Children; Rantoul, IL; (217) 893-4673; www.hope4children.org; (Dom)

Illini Christian Ministries (ICM); St. Joseph, IL; (217) 469-7566; www.icchm.org; (Dom)

Illinois Baptist Children's Home & Family Services; Mt. Vernon, IL; (618) 242-4944; www .bchfs.com/mtvernon.html; (Dom) (Intl)

Jewish Children's Bureau of Chicago; Chicago, IL; (773) 467-3747; www.jcbchicago .org; (Dom) (Intl)

Journeys of the Heart Adoption Services; Glen Ellyn, IL; (630) 469-4367; www .journeysoftheheart.net; (Dom)

Lifelink/Bensenville Home Society; Bensenville, IL; (630) 521-8281; www.lifelink adoption.org; (Intl)

Lifelink International Adoption; Rockford, IL; (815) 639-0967; www.lifelinkadoption .org; (Intl) Bulgaria, China, Korea (South), Philippines, Ukraine

Lutheran Child and Family Services; Belleville, IL; (618) 234-8904; (Dom)

Lutheran Child and Family Services; Mt. Vernon, IL; (618) 242-3284; www.lcfs.org; (Dom)

Lutheran Child and Family Services; Oak Park, IL; (708) 763-0700; www.lcfs.org; (Dom) (Intl)

Lutheran Child and Family Services; Springfield, IL; (217) 544-4631; www.lcfs.org; (Dom)

Lutheran Social Services of Illinois; Chicago, IL; (773) 371-2700; www.lssi.org; (Dom)

Lutheran Social Services of Illinois (LSSI); Des Plaines, IL; (847) 635-4600; www.lssi .org; (Dom) (Intl)

Lutheran Social Services of Illinois (LSSI); West Peoria, IL; (309) 671-0300; www.lssi .org; (Dom) (Intl)

New Life Social Services; Chicago, IL; (773) 478-4773; www.nlss.org; (Dom) (Intl)

Project Oz Adoptions, Inc.; Ottawa, IL; (815) 433-0377; www.projectoz.com; (Dom) (Intl) Bulgaria, Guatemala, Haiti, Russian Federation, Ukraine

St. Mary's Services; Arlington Heights, IL; (847) 870-8181; www.stmaryservices .com; (Dom)

Sunny Ridge Family Center, Inc.; Wheaton, IL; (630) 668-5117; www.sunnyridge.org; (Dom) (Intl) China, Ethiopia, Guatemala, India, Kazakhstan, Korea (South), Philippines, Poland, Russian Federation, Ukraine

Uniting Families Foundation; Lake Villa, IL; (847) 356-1452; http://members.aol.com/ unitingfam/index.html; (Dom)

Volunteers of America of Illinois; Belleville, IL; (618) 271-9833; www.voaillinois.com; (Dom)

Volunteers of America of Illinois; Chicago, IL; (312) 707-9477; www.voaillinois.com; (Dom)

INDIANA

STATE ADOPTION OFFICE: Indiana Department of Child Services; 402 W. Washington St., Room W364; Indianapolis, IN 46204; (317) 234-4211; www.in.gov/fssa/adoption/

ICPC ADMINISTRATOR: Indiana Department of Child Services; (same as above); (317) 232-4769; (317) 232-4436; www.state.in.us/dcs

STATE ADOPTION EXCHANGE: Indiana's Adoption Program; Toll-free: (888) 252-3678; www.adoptachild.in.gov; adoption@iquest.net

INDIANA STATE BAR ASSOCIATION: (317) 639-5465; www.state.in.us/isba

ANNUAL NUMBER OF ADOPTIVE ADOPTIONS FINALIZED IN STATE: 3,588

STATE LAWS AND PROCEDURES—FAST FACTS
Types permitted? Independent and agency (65% of newborns via independent).
Who can adopt in state? Residents, or if the agency making the placement is located in state.
How long after child's placement to finalize adoption in court? 3–12 months.
Is adoptive parent advertising (to find a birth mother) permitted? Yes.
Is a preplacement home study required? Independent—no. Agency—yes.
Typical home study fee? $1,500–$2,000 (agency fees usually higher if agency located child).
Can adoptive parents help birth mother with expenses? Yes: legal, medical, living, but can't exceed $3,000.
Can child leave hospital with adoptive parents? Yes, usually a court order is required.
When can birth mother sign her Consent to Adoption? Anytime after birth.
Can the consent be revoked? Yes, within 30 days if proved to a court the child's best interests would be served by revocation. However, if the birth mother appears in court to confirm her consent, it is irrevocable upon signing.
What are the putative father's rights? There is a registry. Failure to register within 30 days of the birth is an implied consent to adoption.

AMERICAN ACADEMY OF ADOPTION ATTORNEYS MEMBERS
Lisa M. Bowen-Slaven; 108 W. Michigan; LaGrange, IN 46761; (260) 463-4949; www.beersmallers.com; l.slavin@adoptionattorneys.org
Lisa M. Bowen-Slaven began practicing law in 1993. She has completed several hundred adoptions in her career. 50% are newborn placements. All of her clients find their own birth mother.

Joel D. Kirsh; Kirsh & Kirsh, PC; 2930 E. 96th St.; Indianapolis, IN 46240; (800) 333-5736; www.kirsh.com; jkirsh@kirsh.com
Joel Kirsh began practicing law in 1984. He has completed 3,000 adoptions

in his career and last year completed approximately 130. 100% are newborn placements. 50% of his clients find a birth mother through his office.

Steven M. Kirsh; Kirsh & Kirsh PC; 2930 E. 96th St.; Indianapolis, IN 46240; (800) 333-5736; www.kirsh.com; skirsh@kirsh.com
Steven Kirsh began practicing law in 1979. He has completed 3,000 adoptions in his career and last year completed 130. 100% are newborn placements. 50% of his clients locate their own birth mother through his office. He is a past president of the American Academy of Adoption Attorneys and a recipient of the 2005 Congressional Angel in Adoption award.

Sally A. Thomas; Lorch & Naville, LLC; 506 State St.; New Albany, IN 47150; (812) 949-1000; www.lorchnaville.com; sthomas@lorchnaville.com
Sally Thomas began practicing law in 1984. She has completed several hundred adoptions in her career. 70% are newborn placements.

Keith M. Wallace; Bowers Harrison; 25 NW Riverside Dr., 2nd Floor; Evansville, IN 47708; (812) 426-1231; www.bowersharrison.com; kwallace@ftia.org
Keith Wallace began practicing law in 1983. He has completed 3,000 adoptions in his career and last year completed 417. He operates international adoption programs in India, Russia, China, Vietnam, and Guatemala.

Biographies were not available for the following AAAA members:
Michael P. Bishop; 8888 Keystone Crossing, Suite 1200; Indianapolis, IN 46240; (317) 580-4848; m.bishop@adoptionattorneys.org

John Q. Herrin; 2417 East 65th St.; Indianapolis, IN 46220; (317) 610-4145; j.herrin@adoptionattorneys.org

Timothy J. Hubert; 20 NW 1st St., 9th Floor; PO Box 916; Evansville, IN 47708; (812) 424-7575; t.hubert@adoptionattorneys.org

Franklin I. Miroff; 500 E. 96th St., Suite 100; Indianapolis, IN 46240; (317) 582-1040; f.miroff@adoptionattorneys.org

Michael G. Naville; 506 State St.; PO Box 1343; New Albany, IN 47151; (812) 949-1000; m.naville@adoptionattorneys.org

LICENSED PRIVATE AGENCIES
Adoption Resource Services, Inc.; Elkhart, IN; (574) 293-0229; (Dom) (Intl)
Adoption Support Center, Inc.; Indianapolis, IN; (317) 255-5916; www.adoptionsupportcenter.com; (Dom)
Adoptions of Indiana, Inc. (AD-IN, Inc.); Carmel, IN; (317) 574-8950; www.ad-in.org; (Dom) (Intl) Bulgaria, China, Guatemala, Russian Federation, South Africa, Ukraine
Baptist Children's Home and Family Ministries, Inc. (BCH); Valparaiso, IN; (219) 462-4111; www.baptistchildrenshome.org; (Dom)
Bethany Christian Services (BCS); Indianapolis, IN; (317) 568-1000; www.bethany.org/indiana; (Dom) (Intl) Albania, China, Colombia, Guatemala, India, Korea (South), Lithuania, Philippines, Russian Federation, Ukraine

Catholic Charities; Fort Wayne, IN; (260) 422-5625; www.diocesefwsb.org/charity/adoption.htm; (Dom)

Catholic Charities; South Bend, IN; (574) 234-3111; www.diocesefwsb.org/charity/adoption.htm; (Dom)

Catholic Charities—Diocese of Gary; Gary, IN; (219) 886-3565; www.catholic-charities.org; (Dom) (Intl)

Catholic Charities—Diocese of Gary; Michigan City, IN; (219) 879-9312; http://catholic-charities.org; (Dom)(Intl)

Catholic Charities of Evansville; Evansville, IN; (812) 423-5456; www.charitiesevv.org; (Dom) (Intl)

Center for Family Building, Inc. (CFB); Munster, IN; (219) 836-0163; www.centerforfamily.com; (Dom)

Childplace, Inc.; Jeffersonville, IN; (812) 282-8248; www.childplace.org; (Dom)

Children Are the Future; Gary, IN; (219) 881-0750; (Dom) (Intl)

Children's Bureau/Family Place; Indianapolis, IN; (317) 545-5281; www.childrensbureau.org; (Dom)

Children's Bureau of Indianapolis, Inc.; Indianapolis, IN; (317) 264-2700; www.childrensbureau.org; (Dom)

Compassionate Care General Baptist Family & Childrens Ministries, Inc.; Oakland City, IN; (812) 749-4152; www.compassionatecareadopt.org; (Dom) (Intl) China, Estonia, Guatemala, Haiti, Kazakhstan, Moldova, Romania, Russian Federation, Ukraine

Families Thru International Adoption, Inc.; Evansville, IN; (812) 479-9900; www.ftia.org; (Intl) Brazil, China, Guatemala, India, Russian Federation, Vietnam

Greater Love Adoption Decision, Inc. (GLAD, Inc.); Evansville, IN; (812) 424-4523; http://the-cathedral.org/modules.php?name=glad; (Dom) (Intl) China, Haiti, Romania, Russian Federation

Hand in Hand International Adoptions; Albion, IN; (260) 636-3566; www.hihiadopt.org; (Intl) China, Guatemala, Haiti, Moldova, Philippines, Russian Federation

Independent Adoption Center (IAC); Indianapolis, IN; (317) 887-2015; www.adoptionhelp.org; (Dom) (Intl)

LDS Family Services, Inc.; Indianapolis, IN; (317) 872-1749; www.itsaboutlove.org; (Dom)

Loving Option, Inc.; Bluffton, IN; (260) 824-9077; www.lovingoption.org; (Dom)

Lutheran Child and Family Services; Indianapolis, IN; (317) 359-5467; www.lutheranfamily.org; (Dom)

Specialized Alternatives for Families and Youth of America (SAFY); Muncie, IN; (765) 287-8477; www.safy.org; (Dom)

St. Elizabeth/Coleman Pregnancy and Adoption Services; Indianapolis, IN; (317) 787-3412; www.stelizabeths.org; (Dom)

St. Elizabeth's Regional Maternity Center; New Albany, IN; (812) 949-7305; www.stelizabeths1.org; (Dom)

Sunny Ridge Family Center, Inc.; Munster, IN; (219) 836-2117; www.sunnyridge.org; (Dom) (Intl)

The Villages, Inc. (The Villages); Bloomington, IN; (317) 273-7575; www.villages.org; (Dom)

IOWA

STATE ADOPTION OFFICE: Iowa Department of Human Services (DHS); Hoover State Office Bldg., 5th Floor; 1305 E. Walnut Ave.; Des Moines, IA 50319-0114; (515) 281-5358; www.dhs.state.ia.us

ICPC ADMINISTRATOR: Iowa Department of Human Services; (same address as above); (515) 281-5730; (515) 281-4597; www.dhs.state.ia.us/ACFS/ACFS.asp

STATE ADOPTION EXCHANGE: KidSake Foster/Adopt Iowa; (515) 289-4649; www.iakids.org; kidsake@iakids.org

IOWA STATE BAR ASSOCIATION: (515) 280-7429; www.iowabar.org

ANNUAL NUMBER OF ADOPTIVE ADOPTIONS FINALIZED IN STATE: 1,116

STATE LAWS AND PROCEDURES—FAST FACTS

Types permitted? Independent and agency (60% of newborns via independent).

Who can adopt in state? Residents, and nonresidents when child born in state or the agency making the placement is located in state.

How long after child's placement to finalize adoption in court? 7 months.

Is adoptive parent advertising (to find a birth mother) permitted? Yes.

Is a preplacement home study required? Yes.

Typical home study fee? $1,100–$3,500 (agency fees usually higher if agency located child).

Can adoptive parents help birth mother with expenses? Yes: legal, medical and living.

Can child leave hospital with adoptive parents? Yes, but often a court order required.

When can birth mother sign her Consent to Adoption? 72 hours after birth.

Can the consent be revoked? Yes, automatic right to revoke for 96 hours. Soon thereafter there is a court order terminating parental rights, making it irrevocable.

What are the putative father's rights? There is a registry. Notice must be given to those registered, or otherwise known to the birth mother.

AMERICAN ACADEMY OF ADOPTION ATTORNEYS MEMBERS

Lori L. Klockau; Law Offices of Bray and Klockau PLC; 402 S. Linn St.; Iowa City, IA 52240; (319) 338-7968; brayklockau@bkfamilylaw.com

Lori Klockau began practicing law in 1991. She has completed 600 adoptions in her career and last year completed 22. 95% are newborn placements. 20% of her clients locate a birth mother through her office. She is the cochairperson of the Adoption Committee, Family Law Section, American Bar Association.

A biography was not available for the following AAAA member:

Maxine M. Buckmeier; 600 4th St., Suite 304; Sioux City, IA 51102; (712) 233-3660; m.buckmeier@adoptionattorneys.org

LICENSED PRIVATE AGENCIES

4 R Kids; Sioux City, IA; (712) 258-8033; teresa@longlines.com; (Dom)

Abby's One True Gift Adoptions; Waukee, IA; (515) 987-0565; www.onetruegift.com; (Dom)

Adoption Connection: The Iowa Center for Adoption; Ankeny, IA; (515) 965-8029; www.adoptioniowa.com; (Dom)

Adoption International, Inc.; Clive, IA; (515) 727-5840; (Intl) Russian Federation

American Home Finding Association (AHFA); Ottumwa, IA; (515) 682-3449; www.ahfa.org; (Dom)

Avalon Center Adoption Agency; Mason City, IA; (641) 422-0070; www.avaloncenter.us; (Dom) (Intl)

Bethany Christian Services of Northwest Iowa; Orange City, IA; (712) 737-4831; www.bethany.org/nwiowa; (Dom) (Intl)

Bethany Christian Services of South Central Iowa; Cedar Rapids, IA; (319) 832-2321; www.bethany.org/desmoines; (Dom) (Intl)

Bethany Christian Services of South Central Iowa; Urbandale, IA 50322; (515) 270-0824; www.bethany.org/desmoines; (Dom) (Intl)

Catholic Charities Diocese of Des Moines; Des Moines, IA; (515) 244-3761; www.dmdiocese.org; (Dom)

Catholic Charities of the Archdiocese of Dubuque; Dubuque, IA; (563) 588-0558; www.arch.pvt.k12.ia.us/Charities/charitieshome.html; (Dom)

Catholic Charities of the Archdiocese of Dubuque; Mason City, IA; (641) 424-9683; www.arch.pvt.k12.ia.us/Charities/charitieshome.html; (Dom)

Catholic Charities of the Diocese of Sioux City, Iowa, Inc.; Carroll, IA; (712) 792-9597; www.scdiocese.org/deptindex.html; (Dom)

Catholic Charities of the Diocese of Sioux City, Iowa, Inc.; Fort Dodge, IA; (515) 576-4156; www.scdiocese.org/deptindex.html; (Dom)

Children and Families of Iowa; Ankeny, IA; (515) 289-2272; www.cfiowa.org; (Dom)

Children and Families of Iowa; Centerville, IA; (641) 856-3852; www.cfiowa.org; (Dom)

Children and Families of Iowa; Des Moines, IA; (515) 288-1981; www.cfiowa.org; (Dom)

Children and Families of Iowa; Fort Dodge, IA; (515) 573-2193; www.cfiowa.org; (Dom)

Children and Families of Iowa; Osceola, IA; (641) 342-3444; www.cfiowa.org; (Dom)

Children's Square USA—Child Connect; Council Bluffs, IA; (712) 322-3700; (Dom) (Intl)

Children's Square USA—Child Connect; Sioux City, IA; (712) 255-9061; (Dom) (Intl)

Coleman Counseling; Bode, IA; (515) 379-2101; (Dom) (Intl)

Crittenton Center; Sioux City, IA; (712) 255-4321; www.crittentoncenter.org; (Dom)

Faithful Charities Foundation—Faithful Adoption (FCF); Council Bluffs, IA; (712) 256-7705; www.faithfuladoption.org; (Dom) (Intl) Guatemala, Kazakhstan, Panama, Russian Federation, Taiwan, Ukraine

Families, Inc.; West Branch, IA; (319) 643-2532; (Dom)

Family Connections; McCallsburg, IA; (641) 487-7832; www.family-connections-services.com/home.html; (Dom)

Family Connections; Schleswig, IA; (712) 676-2288; www.family-connections-services.com; (Dom)

Family Resources Adoption Network; New Hampton, IA; (641) 394-5800; www .familyres.net; (Intl) Armenia, China, Guatemala, Lithuania, Mexico, Russian Federation

Family Resources, Inc.; Davenport, IA; (563) 326-6431; www.famres.org; (Dom)

First Resources Corporation; Centerville, IA; (641) 856-5382; (Dom) (Intl)

First Resources Corporation; Knoxville, IA; (641) 842-7462; (Dom) (Intl)

First Resources Corporation; Oskaloosa, IA; (641) 673-1421; (Dom) (Intl)

First Resources Corporation; Ottumwa, IA; (515) 856-5382; (Dom) (Intl)

First Resources Corporation; Sigourney, IA; (641) 622-2543; (Dom) (Intl)

Four Oaks, Inc. of Iowa; Cedar Rapids, IA; (319) 364-0259; www.fouroaks.org; (Dom)

Gift of Love International Adoptions, Inc.; Des Moines, IA; (515) 255-3388; www .giftoflove.org; (Intl) Cambodia, China, Guatemala, Kazakhstan, Philippines, Russian Federation, Ukraine, Vietnam

Hillcrest Family Services; Cedar Rapids, IA; (319) 362-3149; www.hillcrest-fs.org; (Dom)

Hillcrest Family Services; Maquoketa, IA; (563) 652-4958; www.hillcrest-fs.org; (Dom)

Holt International Children's Services; LeGrand, IA; (641) 479-2054; www.holtintl.org; (Intl)

Integrative Health Services, Inc.; Williamsburg, IA; (319) 668-2050; (Dom) (Intl)

LDS Family Services; West Des Moines, IA; (515) 226-0484; www.itsaboutlove.org; (Dom) (Intl)

Lutheran Family Service of Iowa (LFS); Fort Dodge, IA; (515) 573-3138; www.lfsiowa .org; (Dom) (Intl)

Lutheran Family Services of Nebraska, Inc.; Council Bluffs, IA; (712) 242-1040; www .lfsneb.org; (Dom) (Intl) China, Guatemala, Hong Kong—China, Kazakhstan, Philippines, Poland, Russian Federation

Lutheran Services in Iowa (LSI); Clinton, IA; (563) 243-8200; www.lsiowa.org; (Dom) (Intl)

Lutheran Services in Iowa (LSI); Denison, IA; (712) 263-9341; www.lsiowa.org; (Dom) (Intl)

New Horizons Adoption Agency, Inc.; Mason City, IA; (641) 421-7332; www.nhadoption agency.com; (Dom) (Intl) China, Russian Federation

Stork Adoption Agency; Norwalk, IA; www.storkadopt.com; (Intl) Bulgaria, El Salvador, Russian Federation

Tanager Place; Ottumwa, IA; (641) 684-5381; www.tanagerplace.org; (Dom) (Intl)

Tanager Place—Cedar Rapids; Cedar Rapids, IA; (319) 365-9164; www.tanagerplace .org; (Dom) (Intl)

West Iowa Family Services; Denison, IA; (712) 263-8445; www.family-connections-services.com; (Dom) (Intl)

Young House Family Services, Inc.; Burlington, IA; (319) 752-4000; www.younghouse
.org; (Dom)
Youth and Shelter Services, Inc.; Ames, IA; (515) 233-3141; www.yss.ames.ia.us; (Dom)

KANSAS

STATE ADOPTION OFFICE: Kansas Department of Social and Rehabilitation Services,
Children and Family Policy Division; Docking State Office Bldg.—5th Floor
South; 915 SW Harrison, Room 551-S; Topeka, KS 66612-1870; (785) 296-
0918; www.srskansas.org

ICPC ADMINISTRATOR: Kansas Department of Social and Rehabilitation Services, Children and Family Policy Division; (same address as above); (785) 296-0918; (785)
368-8159; www.srskansas.org; pal@srskansas.org

STATE ADOPTION EXCHANGE: Coming Home Kansas; (785) 274-3100; (785) 274-3188;
www.cominghomekansas.org

KANSAS BAR ASSOCIATION: (785) 234-5696; www.ksbar.org

ANNUAL NUMBER OF ADOPTIVE ADOPTIONS FINALIZED IN STATE: 1,880

STATE LAWS AND PROCEDURES—FAST FACTS:
Types permitted? Independent and agency (85% of newborns via independent).
Who can adopt in state? Residents, and nonresidents when child born in state or the
agency making the placement is located in state.
How long after child's placement to finalize adoption in court? 1–6 months.
Is adoptive parent advertising (to find a birth mother) permitted? No.
Is a preplacement home study required? Yes.
Typical home study fee? $500–$1,500 (agency fees usually higher if agency located
child).
Can adoptive parents help birth mother with expenses? Yes: legal, medical, living.
Can child leave hospital with adoptive parents? Yes, but court order required.
When can birth mother sign her Consent to Adoption? 12 hours after birth. If she is
under age 18 she must have an attorney.
Can the consent be revoked? No, it is irrevocable.
What are the putative father's rights? There is no registry. Notice must be attempted
and he has 30 days thereafter to object. It must be proved he is unfit, abandoned
the child, raped, or failed to support the birth mother for the last 6 months of
the pregnancy.

AMERICAN ACADEMY OF ADOPTION ATTORNEYS MEMBERS
Jill Bremyer-Archer; Bremyer & Wise, LLC; 120 W. Kansas; PO Box 1146; McPher-
son, KS 67460; (620) 241-0554; www.bwisecounsel.com; jbarcher@bwisecoun
sel.com
   *Jill Bremyer-Archer began practicing law in 1980. Of her adoptions, 75% are
   newborn placements. She reports all of her clients locate their own birth mother.*

Allan A. Hazlett; 1622 Washburn; Topeka, KS 66604; (785) 232-2011; ksadoptlaw@aol.com
Allan Hazlett began practicing law in 1967. He has completed 600 adoptions in his career and last year completed 40. 90% are newborn placements. 55% of his clients find a birth mother through his office. He is a past president of the American Academy of Adoption Attorneys.

Douglas J. Keeling; 200 E. 1st St., Suite 202; Wichita, KS 67202; (316) 265-2210; d.keeling@adoptionattorneys.org
Douglas Keeling began practicing law in 1984. He has completed 1,000 adoptions in his career and last year completed 59. 30% are newborn placements. 30% of his clients find a birth mother through his office. He is an adoptive parent.

Joseph N. Vader; 108 E. Poplar; PO Box 1185; Olathe, KS 66051; (913) 764-5010; jvader@sbcglobal.net
Joseph Vader began practicing law in 1964. He has completed 500 adoptions in his career and last year completed 14. 90% are newborn placements. 10% of his clients find a birth mother through his office.

Biographies were not available for the following AAAA members:
Martin W. Bauer; 100 N. Broadway, Suite 500; Wichita, KS 67202; (316) 265-9311; m.bauer@adoptionattorneys.org

Richard A. Macias; 901 N. Broadway; Witchita, KS 67214-3531; (316) 265-5245

LICENSED PRIVATE AGENCIES
Adoption and Beyond, Inc.; Overland Park, KS; (913) 381-6919; www.adoption-beyond.org; (Dom)
Adoption and Counseling Services for Families, Inc.; Overland Park, KS; (913) 339-6776; http://adoptionandcounselingservices.com; (Dom) (Intl)
Adoption and Fertility Resources; Overland Park, KS; (816) 781-8550; (Dom)
Adoption Centre of Kansas, Inc.; Wichita, KS; (316) 265-5289; www.adoptioncentre.com; (Dom)
Adoption of Babies and Children, Inc. (ABC Adoption); Lenexa, KS; (913) 894-2223; www.abcadoption.com; (Dom) (Intl) China, Guatemala, Korea (South), Russian Federation
Adoption Option, Inc.; Overland Park, KS; (913) 642-7900; (Dom)
American Adoptions; Overland Park, KS; www.americanadoptions.com; (Dom) (Intl) Australia, Belgium, Canada, Denmark, Dominican Republic, Germany, Guam, Ireland, Italy, Japan, Mexico, Netherlands, Poland, Puerto Rico, Sweden, Switzerland, United Kingdom, Virgin Islands (U.S.)
Catholic Charities, Diocese of Dodge City; Great Bend, KS; (620) 792-1393; (Dom)
Catholic Charities, Diocese of Salina; Salina, KS; (785) 825-0208; www.catholiccharities salina.org/adoption.htm; (Dom)
Catholic Charities Pregnancy & Adoption Services; Wichita, KS; (316) 263-0507; www.wkscatholiccharities.org/home1.html; (Dom)

Catholic Community Services; Kansas City, KS; (913) 621-1504; www.catholic charitiesks.org; (Dom)

Children's Hope International; Overland Park, KS; (913) 338-4673; www.childrenshope .com; (Intl) China, Colombia, Kazakhstan, Russian Federation, Vietnam

Christian Family Services of the Midwest, Inc.; Overland Park, KS; (913) 383-3337; www .cfskc.org; (Dom)

Family Life Services of Southern Kansas; Arkansas City, KS; (316) 442-1688; (Dom)

Heartland International Adoptions; Wichita, KS; (316) 265-5289; (Intl)

Inserco, Inc.; Wichita, KS; (316) 681-3840; (Dom)

KVC Behavioral HealthCare, Inc. (KVC); Olathe, KS; (913) 322-4900; www.kvc.org; (Dom)

Special Editions Adoption Agency; Olathe, KS; (913) 681-9604; (Dom)

Sunflower Family Services; Hays, KS; (913) 625-4600; www.sunflowerfamily.org; (Dom)

The Villages, Inc.; Topeka, KS; (785) 267-5900; (Dom)

KENTUCKY

STATE ADOPTION OFFICE: Kentucky Cabinet for Families and Children; 275 E. Main St., 3CE; Frankfort, KY 40621; (502) 564-2147; http://chfs.ky.gov

ICPC ADMINISTRATOR: Kentucky Cabinet for Families and Children; (same address as above); (502) 564-2147; (502) 564-9554

STATE ADOPTION EXCHANGE: Special Needs Adoption Program (SNAP); (502) 564-2147; https://apps.chfs.ky.gov; deborah.green@ky.gov

KENTUCKY BAR ASSOCIATION: (502) 564-3795; www.kybar.org

ANNUAL NUMBER OF ADOPTIVE ADOPTIONS FINALIZED IN STATE: 2,086

STATE LAWS AND PROCEDURES—FAST FACTS

Types permitted? Independent and agency (80% of newborns via independent).

Who can adopt in state? Residents only.

How long after child's placement to finalize adoption in court? 3–4 months.

Is adoptive parent advertising (to find a birth mother) permitted? No.

Is a preplacement home study required? Yes.

Typical home study fee? $1,700–$2,500 (agency fees usually higher if agency located child).

Can adoptive parents help birth mother with expenses? Yes: legal, medical, living.

Can child leave hospital with adoptive parents? Yes, with proof of home study.

When can birth mother sign her Consent to Adoption? 72 hours after birth. If she is under age 18, a guardian ad litem must be appointed for her.

Can the consent be revoked? There are two options. If a Voluntary and Informed Consent is signed, it can be revoked for 20 days. If a Voluntary Petition to Terminate Parental Rights is filed and granted by the court, it is irrevocable upon the court order. Both are available in independent adoption; in agency only the latter.

What are the putative father's rights? There is no registry. There is no requirement for birth mothers to identify birth father unless married to him or cohabited during the pregnancy. Those men get 20 days' notice to file an objection.

AMERICAN ACADEMY OF ADOPTION ATTORNEYS MEMBERS

Carolyn S. Arnett; 401 W. Main St., Suite 1704; Louisville, KY 40202; (502) 585-4368; c.arnett@adoptionattorneys.org
Carolyn Arnett began practicing law in 1984.

Mitchell A. Charney; Goldberg & Simpson; 9300 Shelbyville Rd., Suite 600; Louisville, KY 40222; (502) 589-4440; www.gsatty.com; mcharney@gsatty.com
Mitchell Charney began practicing law in 1970. He has completed 500 adoptions in his career and last year completed 11. 90% are newborn placements. 50% of his clients find a birth mother through his office.

Ellie Goldman; 333 W. Vine St., Suite 1201; Lexington, KY 40507; (859) 381-1145; e.goldman@adoptionattorneys.org
Ellie Goldman began practicing law in 1976. She has completed 400 adoptions in her career, and last year completed 30. 100% are newborn placements. 33% of her clients find a birth mother through her office.

A biography was not available for the following AAAA member:
Waverley W. Townes; 401 W. Main St., Suite 1900; Louisville, KY 40202; (502) 589-4404; w.townes@adoptionattorneys.org

LICENSED PRIVATE AGENCIES

Access Adoptions, Inc.; Lexington, KY; (859) 271-9078; (Dom) (Intl)
Adopt! Inc.; Lexington, KY; (859) 276-6249; www.adoptinc.org; (Dom) (Intl)
Adoption and Home Study Specialists, Inc. (AHSS); Louisville, KY; (502) 423-7713; (Dom) (Intl)
Adoption Assistance, Inc.; Danville, KY; (859) 236-2761; www.adoptionassistance.com; (Dom)
Adoptions of Kentucky; Louisville, KY; (502) 585-3005; www.adoptionsofkentucky.com; (Dom)
Bluegrass Christian Adoption Services; Lexington, KY 40503; (859) 276-2222; www.bluegrassadoption.org; (Dom) (Intl)
Catholic Charities; Owensboro, KY; (270) 683-1545 ext. 128; www.kycatholiccharitiesadoption.org; (Dom)
Catholic Charities of Louisville, Inc.; Louisville, KY; (502) 637-9786; www.catholiccharitieslouisville.org; (Dom)
Catholic Social Service Bureau; Lexington, KY; (859) 253-1993; http://cssb.cdlex.org; (Dom)
Catholic Social Services of Northern Kentucky; Covington, KY; (859) 581-8974; http://cssnky.org; (Dom) (Intl)
Childplace, Inc.; Louisville, KY; (502) 363-1633; www.childplace.org; (Dom)
Children's Home of Northern Kentucky; Covington, KY; (859) 261-8768; www.chnk.org; (Dom) (Intl)

Diocesan Catholic Children's Home; Ft. Thomas, KY; (859) 331-2040; www.dcchome
.org; (Dom)

Ed Necco and Associates, Inc.; Ashland, KY; (606) 324-9775; www.necco.org; (Dom)

Ed Necco and Associates, Inc.; Bowling Green, KY; (270) 781-8112; www.necco.org;
(Dom)

Ed Necco and Associates, Inc.; Lexington, KY; (859) 264-8976; www.necco.org;
(Dom)

Ed Necco and Associates, Inc.; Owensboro, KY; (270) 685-5500; www.necco.org;
(Dom)

Ed Necco and Associates, Inc.; Paducah, KY; (270) 898-1293; www.necco.org; (Dom)

A Helping Hand Adoption Agency; Lexington, KY; (859) 263-9964; www.world
adoptions.org; (Intl) China, Guatemala

Holly Hill Children's Home; California, KY; (859) 635-0500; (Dom) (Intl)

Home of the Innocents; Louisville, KY; (502) 995-4402; www.homeoftheinnocents
.org; (Dom)

Jewish Family and Vocational Service; Louisville, KY; (502) 452-6341; www.jfvs.com;
(Dom) (Intl)

Kentucky Adoption Services, Inc. (KAS); Owensboro, KY; (270) 684-2598; www
.kentuckyadoptionservices.org; (Dom) (Intl) China, Guatemala, Korea (South)

Kentucky Baptist Homes for Children (KBHC); Louisville, KY; (502) 568-9117; www
.kbhc.org; (Dom)

Kentucky United Methodist Homes for Children and Youth; Owensboro, KY; (270) 684-
3554; www.kyumh.org; (Dom) (Intl)

New Beginnings Family Services, Inc.; Louisville, KY; (502) 485-0722; www.new
beginningsinc.com; (Dom) (Intl)

SAFY of Kentucky; Edgewood, KY; (859) 341-9333; www.safy.org; (Dom)

SAFY of Kentucky; Lexington, KY; (859) 971-2585; www.safy.org; (Dom)

St. Elizabeth's Regional Maternity Center; Louisville, KY; (502) 412-0990; www.steliza
beths.org; (Dom)

St. Joseph Children's Home; Louisville, KY; (502) 893-0241; www.sjkids.org; (Dom)

Treatment Foster Care and Adoption Services; Hazard, KY; (606) 398-7245; (Dom) (Intl)

Villages; Louisville, KY; (502) 361-7010; (Dom) (Intl)

Western Kentucky United Methodist Family Services; Paducah, KY; (270) 443-9004;
www.memphis-umc.org/familyservices/familyservices.htm; (Dom) (Intl)

LOUISIANA

STATE ADOPTION OFFICE: Louisiana Department of Social Services; Office of Community Services; 333 Laurel St.—PO Box 3318; Baton Rouge, LA 70821; (225)
342-4086; www.dss.state.la.us

ICPC ADMINISTRATOR: Louisiana Department of Social Services; (same address as
above); (225) 342-4013; (225) 342-0965

STATE ADOPTION EXCHANGE: Louisiana Adoption Resource Exchange (LARE); Toll-
free: (800) 259-3428; www.adoptuskids.org; cbilliod@dss.state.la.su

LOUISIANA STATE BAR ASSOCIATION: (504) 566-1600; www.lsba.org

ANNUAL NUMBER OF ADOPTIVE ADOPTIONS FINALIZED IN STATE: 1,391

STATE LAWS AND PROCEDURES—FAST FACTS

Types permitted? Independent and agency (50% of newborns via independent).

Who can adopt in state? Residents, and nonresidents when birth parent lives and relinquishes in state or the agency making the placement is located in state.

How long after child's placement to finalize adoption in court? 8–14 months.

Is adoptive parent advertising (to find a birth mother) permitted? No.

Is a preplacement home study required? Yes.

Typical home study fee? $1,000–$1,500 (agency fees usually higher if agency located child).

Can adoptive parents help birth mother with expenses? Yes: legal, medical, living.

Can child leave hospital with adoptive parents? Yes, often via attorney/agency.

When can birth mother sign her Consent to Adoption? No sooner than 5 days after birth. She must have her own attorney (if independent) and if under 18, a parent or guardian ad litem's consent.

Can the consent be revoked? No, irrevocable upon signing.

What are the putative father's rights? There is a registry. Notice must be attempted on those registered, or identified by birth mother. Usually he is given 15 days to object after notice.

AMERICAN ACADEMY OF ADOPTION ATTORNEYS MEMBERS

Terri Hoover Debnam; 500 N. 7th St.; West Monroe, LA 71291; (318) 387-8811; www
.centerforadoption.com; terridebnam@jam.rr.com
Terri Debnam began practicing law in 1986. She has completed 250 adoptions in her career and last year completed 45. 98% are newborn placements. 60% of her clients find a birth mother through her office.

Edith H. Morris; 1515 Poydras St., Suite 1870; New Orleans, LA 70112; (504) 524-3781; e.morris@adoptionattorneys.org
Edith Morris began practicing law in 1985.

A biography was not available for the following AAAA member:
Noel E. Vargas II; 146 N. Telemachus St.; New Orleans, LA 70119; (504) 488-0200; n.vargas@adoptionattorneys.org

LICENSED PRIVATE AGENCIES

Acorn Adoption, Inc.; Mandeville, LA; (985) 626-3800; www.acornadoption.org; (Dom)

Beacon House Adoption Services, Inc. (BHAS); Baton Rouge, LA; (225) 272-3221; www
.beaconhouseadoption.com; (Dom) (Intl) China, Guatemala, Kazakhstan, Russian Federation, Ukraine

Catholic Charities Archdiocese of New Orleans (CCANO); Metairie, LA; (504) 885-1141; www.adoptnola.com; (Dom) (Intl)

Catholic Community Services of Baton Rouge, Inc. (CCS/CM&A); Baton Rouge, LA; (225) 336-8708; www.ccsbr.org; (Dom) (Intl)

Catholic Social Services of Houma—Thibodaux; Houma, LA; (985) 876-0490; www .htdiocese.org; (Dom) (Intl)

Catholic Social Services of Lafayette; Lafayette, LA; (337) 261-5654; www.dol-louisiana .org; (Dom) (Intl) China, Russian Federation

Children's Bureau of New Orleans; New Orleans, LA; (504) 525-2366; (Dom) (Intl)

DeColores Adoptions International; Lake Charles, LA; (337) 855-7398; www.decolores adoptions.com; (Intl) China, Guatemala, Russian Federation, Ukraine

Holy Cross Child Placement Agency, Inc.; Shreveport, LA; (318) 865-3199; (Dom) (Intl)

Institute for Black Parenting (IBP); New Orleans, LA; (504) 245-9386; www.institute forblackparenting.org; (Dom)

Jewish Family Service of Greater New Orleans (JFS); Metairie, LA; (504) 831-8475; www .jfsneworleans.org; (Dom) (Intl)

LDS Social Services; Slidell, LA; (985) 649-2774; www.itsaboutlove.org; (Dom)

Louisiana Baptist Children's Home (LBCH); Monroe, LA; (318) 343-2244; www.lbch.org; (Dom)

Mercy Ministries of America, Inc.; Monroe, LA; (318) 388-2040; www.mercyministries .com; (Dom)

Open Arms Adoption Services, Inc.; Shreveport, LA; (318) 798-7664; www.adoptinla .com; (Dom) (Intl)

St. Elizabeth Foundation (SEF); Baton Rouge, LA; (225) 769-8888; www.stelizabeth foundation.org; (Dom)

St. Gerard's Adoption Network, Inc.; Eunice, LA; (504) 457-1111; (Dom) (Intl)

Volunteers of America of Greater New Orleans, Inc.; Adoption and Maternity Services; Metairie, LA; (504) 836-8702; www.voagno.org; (Dom)

Volunteers of America of North Louisiana; Monroe, LA; (318) 322-2272; www.voa northla.com; (Dom) (Intl)

Volunteers of America of North Louisiana (VOA); Shreveport, LA; (318) 221-5000; www .voanorthla.org; (Dom) (Intl)

MAINE

STATE ADOPTION OFFICE: Maine Department of Health and Human Services (DHHS-BCFS); Bureau of Child and Family Services; 221 State St.; Augusta, ME 04333-0011; (207) 287-2976; www.afamilyforme.org

ICPC ADMINISTRATOR: Maine Department of Health and Human Services; (same address as above); (207) 287-5060; www.afamilyforme.org

STATE ADOPTION EXCHANGE: A Family for ME; Toll-Free: (877) 505-0545; www .afamilyforme.org; info@afamilyforme.org

MAINE STATE BAR ASSOCIATION: (207) 622-7523; www.mainebar.org

ANNUAL NUMBER OF ADOPTIVE ADOPTIONS FINALIZED IN STATE: 957

STATE LAWS AND PROCEDURES—FAST FACTS
Types permitted? Independent and agency.

Who can adopt in state? Residents, and nonresidents when birth parent lives and relinquishes in state or the agency making the placement is located in state.

How long after child's placement to finalize adoption in court? Two months in independent adoption; 6 months in agency adoption.

Is adoptive parent advertising (to find a birth mother) permitted? No.

Is a preplacement home study required? Independent—no. Agency—yes.

Typical agency home study fee? $1,600 (agency fees usually higher if agency located child).

Can adoptive parents help birth mother with expenses? Yes: legal, medical, living.

Can child leave hospital with adoptive parents? Yes, with correct forms.

When can birth mother sign her Consent to Adoption? Anytime after birth.

Can the consent be revoked? Yes, for 3 days.

What are the putative father's rights? There is no registry. Notice to him must be attempted, usually giving him 20 days in which to file any objection.

AMERICAN ACADEMY OF ADOPTION ATTORNEYS MEMBERS

Judith M. Berry; 28 State St.; Gorham, ME 04038; (207) 839-7004; judithberryme@aol.com

Judith Berry began practicing law in 1991. She has completed 500 adoptions in her career and last year completed 40. 90% are newborn placements. 40% of her clients find a birth mother through her office. She is an adoptive parent.

LICENSED PRIVATE AGENCIES

Adopt Cambodia; Woolwich, ME; (207) 442-7612; nhendrie@roteang.org; (Intl)

China Adoption with Love, Inc.; Portland, ME; Toll-free: (800) 888-9812; www.cawli.org; (Intl) China

Families and Children Together (FACT); Bangor, ME; (207) 941-2347; www.familiesandchildren.org; (Dom)

Good Samaritan Agency; Bangor, ME; (207) 942-7211; http://good_samaritan1.tripod.com; (Dom) (Intl)

International Adoption Services Centre, Inc. (IASC); Gardiner, ME; (207) 582-8842; www.adoptioninternational.org; (Dom) (Intl) China, Nepal

Maine Adoption Placement Service (MAPS); Bangor, ME; (207) 941-9500; www.mapsadopt.org; (Dom) (Intl) Cambodia, China, Guatemala, India, Kazakhstan, Russian Federation, Sierra Leone

Maine Adoption Placement Service (MAPS); Houlton, ME; (207) 532-9358; www.mapsadopt.org; (Dom) (Intl) Cambodia, China, Guatemala, India, Kazakhstan, Russian Federation, Sierra Leone, Vietnam

Maine Adoption Placement Services (MAPS); Portland, ME; (207) 772-3678; http://mapsadopt.org; (Dom) (Intl) China, Guatemala, India, Kazakhstan, Nepal, Peru, Russian Federation, Ukraine

Maine Children's Home for Little Wanderers; Waterville, ME; (207) 873-6350; www.mainechildrenshome.org; (Dom) (Intl)

SMART Child and Family Services; Windham, ME; (207) 893-0386; www.smartcfs.org; (Dom)

St. Andre's Home, Inc.; Biddeford, ME; (207) 282-3351; (Dom) (Intl)

MARYLAND

STATE ADOPTION OFFICE: Maryland Department of Human Resources; 311 W. Saratoga St.; Baltimore, MD 21201; (410) 767-7506; www.dhr.state.md.us

ICPC ADMINISTRATOR: Maryland Department of Human Resources; (same address as above); (410) 767-7506; (410) 333-0922; www.dhr.state.md.us

STATE ADOPTION EXCHANGE: Maryland Adoption Resource Exchange (MARE); (same address as above); (410) 767-7359; (410) 767-7737; www.adoptuskids.org; mare @dhr.state.md.us

MARYLAND STATE BAR ASSOCIATION: (410) 685-7878; www.msba.org

ANNUAL NUMBER OF ADOPTIVE ADOPTIONS FINALIZED IN STATE: 4,384

STATE LAWS AND PROCEDURES—FAST FACTS
Types permitted? Independent and agency (60% of newborns via independent).
Who can adopt in state? Residents, and nonresidents when child born in state or the agency making the placement is located in state.
How long after child's placement to finalize adoption in court? 3–6 months.
Is adoptive parent advertising (to find a birth mother) permitted? Yes.
Is a preplacement home study required? Independent—no. Agency—yes.
Typical agency home study fee? $1,300–$1,800 (up to $18,000 if agency locating child).
Can adoptive parents help birth mother with expenses? Yes: legal, medical, but not living.
Can child leave hospital with adoptive parents? Yes, but court order required.
When can birth mother sign her Consent to Adoption? Anytime after birth.
Can the consent be revoked? Yes, for 30 days, then irrevocable.
What are the putative father's rights? There is no registry. Notice must be attempted. His rights are usually terminated if he files no objection within 30 days after notice.

AMERICAN ACADEMY OF ADOPTION ATTORNEYS MEMBERS
Jeffrey E. Badger; Long & Badger, PA; 124 E. Main St.; Salisbury, MD 21801; (410) 749-2356; www.longbadger.com; jbadger@longbadger.com
Jeffrey Badger began practicing law in 1980. He has completed 300 adoptions in his career and last year completed 28. 50% are newborn placements. He is an adoptive parent.

John R. Greene; Cohen & Greene PA; 156 South St.; Annapolis, MD 21401; (410) 268-4500; www.familiesthruadoption.com; jrgreenelaw@comcast.net
John Greene began practicing law in 1976. He has completed 600 adoptions in his career and last year completed 95. 65% are newborn placements.

Margaret E. Swain; 301 W. Pennsylvania Ave.; Towson, MD 21204; (410) 583-0688; artlawmes@aol.com;
Margaret Swain began practicing law in 1987. She has completed 300 adoptions in her career and last year completed 26. 85% are newborn placements.

Carolyn H. Thaler; 29 W. Susquehanna Ave., Suite 205; Towson, MD 21204; (410) 828-6627; c.thaler@adoptionattorneys.org
Carolyn Thaler began practicing law in 1983. She has completed 1,000 adoptions in her career.

Peter J. Wiernicki; Joseph, Reiner & Wiernicki, PC; 11140 Rockville Pike, Suite 620; Rockville, MD 20852; (301) 230-2446; pjr@jrw-law.com
Peter Wiernicki began practicing law in 1986. He has completed 1,100 adoptions in his career and last year completed 85. 95% are newborn placements. He is a board member of Resolve.

Biographies were not available for the following AAAA members:
Jeffrey Berman; 5830 Hubbard Dr.; Rockville, MD 20852; (301) 468-1818; j.berman@ adoptionattorneys.org

Ellen Ann Callahan; 12600 War Admiral Way; Gaithersburg, MD 20878; (301) 258-2664; e.callahan@adoptionattorneys.org

Harvey Schweitzer; 7315 Wisconsin Ave., Suite 601; Bethesda, MD 20814; (301) 469-3382; h.schweitzer@adoptionattorneys.org

Please be aware that some AAAA attorneys located in neighboring states also practice in Maryland, including Mark McDermott (DC).

LICENSED PRIVATE AGENCIES
Adoption Options/JSSA; Rockville, MD; (301) 816-2700; www.jssa.org; (Dom) (Intl)
Adoption Resource Center, Inc.; Baltimore, MD; (410) 744-6393; www.adoptresource .org; (Intl) China, Guatemala, Korea (South), Russian Federation, Ukraine
Adoption Service Information Agency, Inc.; Silver Spring, MD; (301) 587-7068; (Intl)
Adoptions Forever, Inc.; Rockville, MD; (301) 468-1818; www.adoptionsforever.com; (Dom) (Intl) Bulgaria, China, El Salvador, Ukraine
Adoptions Together; Silver Spring, MD; (301) 439-2900; www.adoptionstogether.org; (Dom) (Intl)
Adoptions Together, Inc.—Center for Adoptive Families; Baltimore, MD; (410) 869-0620; www.centerforadoptivefamilies.org; (Dom) (Intl) Azerbaijan, China, Guatemala, Latvia, Lithuania, Russian Federation, Ukraine, Vietnam
The Barker Foundation; Bethesda, MD; (301) 664-9664; www.barkerfoundation.org; (Dom) (Intl) China, Colombia, El Salvador, Guatemala, India, Korea (South), Taiwan
Bethany Christian Services; Crofton, MD; (410) 721-2835; www.bethany.org/ maryland; (Dom) (Intl) Albania, Bulgaria, China, Colombia, India, Kazakhstan, Korea (South), Lithuania, Philippines, Russian Federation, Ukraine
Board of Child Care; Baltimore, MD; (410) 922-2100; www.boardofchildcare.org; (Dom) (Intl)
Burlington United Methodist Family Services, Inc.; Oakland, MD; (301) 334-1285; www .bumfs.org; (Dom)

CASI Foundation for Children; Olney, MD; (301) 570-9600; www.adoptcasi.org; (Dom) (Intl) Azerbaijan, China, Guatemala, Haiti, Mexico, Republic of Georgia, Russian Federation, Ukraine

Catholic Charities; Baltimore, MD; (410) 659-4050; www.catholiccharities-md.org; (Dom) (Intl) Korea (South), Philippines, Thailand

Catholic Charities Archdiocese of Washington, DC; Wheaton, MD; (301) 942-1856; www .catholiccharitiesdc.org; (Dom)

Catholic Charities, Inc.; Salisbury, MD; (410) 749-1121; www.cdow.org; (Dom)

Children's Choice; Stevensville, MD; (410) 643-9290; www.childrenschoice.org; (Dom) (Intl) Lithuania, Mexico

Cradle of Hope Adoption Center, Inc.; Silver Spring, MD; (301) 587-4400; www.cradle hope.org; (Intl)

Creative Adoptions, Inc.; Columbia, MD; (301) 596-1521; www.creativeadoptions .org; (Intl) China, Jamaica, Russian Federation

Datz Foundation; Gaithersburg, MD; (301) 258-0629; www.datzfound.com; (Dom) (Intl)

Diakon Lutheran Social Ministries; Baltimore, MD; (410) 633-6990; www.diakon.org; (Dom) (Intl)

Family and Children's Society; Baltimore, MD; (410) 669-9000; www.fcsmd.org; (Dom)

Family Building Center; Towson, MD; (410) 296-5126; www.familybuild.com; (Dom)

Frank Adoption Center Maryland; Frederick, MD; (301) 682-5025; www.fortheloveofa child.org; (Intl) Kazakhstan, Russian Federation

Holy Cross Child Placement Agency, Inc.; Chevy Chase, MD; (301) 907-6887; (Dom) (Intl)

International Children's Alliance (ICA); Silver Spring, MD; (301) 495-9710; www .adoptica.org; (Dom) (Intl)

International Families, Inc.; Silver Spring, MD; (301) 622-2406; (Intl)

International Social Service; Baltimore, MD; (443) 451-1200; www.iss-usa.org; (Intl)

Jewish Family Services—Adoption Alliances; Owings Mills, MD; (410) 581-1031; www .jfs.org; (Dom) (Intl) Belarus, Bulgaria, Guatemala, Ukraine

LDS Family Services; Frederick, MD; (301) 694-5896; www.lds.org; (Dom) (Intl)

Lutheran Social Services of the National Capital Area; Takoma Park, MD; (301) 434-0080; www.lssnca.org; (Dom) (Intl)

The Mentor Network; Baltimore, MD; (410) 944-5055; (Dom)

Project Oz Adoptions, Inc. (Project Oz); Dunkirk, MD; (410) 286-5454; www.project oz.com; (Dom) (Intl) Bulgaria, China, Guatemala, Haiti, Russian Federation, Ukraine

World Child, Inc.; Silver Spring, MD; (301) 588-3000; www.worldchild.org; (Intl) Bolivia, Bulgaria, China, Colombia, Guatemala, Kazakhstan, Peru, Russian Federation, Ukraine, Vietnam

MASSACHUSETTS

STATE ADOPTION OFFICE: Massachusetts Department of Social Services; 24 Farnsworth St.; Boston, MA 02210; (617) 748-2267; www.mass.gov

ICPC ADMINISTRATOR: Massachusetts Department of Social Services; Central Office, 24 Farnsworth St.; Boston, MA 02110; (617) 748-2345

STATE ADOPTION EXCHANGE: Massachusetts Adoption Resource Exchange, Inc. (MARE); (617) 542-3678; www.mareinc.org

MASSACHUSETTS BAR ASSOCIATION: (617) 338-0500; www.massbar.org

ANNUAL NUMBER OF ADOPTIVE ADOPTIONS FINALIZED IN STATE: 3,259

STATE LAWS AND PROCEDURES—FAST FACTS
Types permitted? Agency only.
Who can adopt in state? Residents, and nonresidents when child born in state or the agency making the placement is located in state.
How long after child's placement to finalize adoption in court? 7–12 months.
Is adoptive parent advertising (to find a birth mother) permitted? No.
Is a preplacement home study required? Yes.
Typical agency home study fee? $2,500–$12,000.
Can adoptive parents help birth mother with expenses? Yes: legal, medical, living.
Can child leave hospital with adoptive parents? Yes, via agency.
When can birth mother sign her Consent to Adoption? No sooner than 4 days after birth.
Can the consent be revoked? No, it is irrevocable upon signing.
What are the putative father's rights? There is a registry. Notice must be attempted if he is registered or known to birth mother. If he objects, his fitness, and the child's best interests, are considered.

AMERICAN ACADEMY OF ADOPTION ATTORNEYS MEMBERS
Elizabeth Bartholet; Harvard Law School; 1575 Massachusetts Ave.; Cambridge, MA 02138; (617) 495-3128; www.law.harvard.edu/faculty/bartholet; ebarthol@law.harvard.edu
Elizabeth Bartholet began practicing law in 1965. She estimates she has completed 40 adoptions in her career and last year completed 2. She is a Harvard professor and is the author of Family Bonds: Adoption, Infertility and the New World of Child Production *and* Nobody's Children.

Karen K. Greenberg; Konowite & Greenberg, PC; 220 Cedar St.; Wellesley Hills, MA 02481; (781) 237-0033; www.kongreen.com; kkg@kongreen.com
Karen Greenberg began practicing law in 1983. Last year she completed 44 adoptions. 95% are newborn placements. She is an adoptive parent.

Paula Mackin; 18 Westview Terr.; W. Newton, MA 02465; (617) 332-0781; www.adoptionmassachusetts.com; mackinpb@aol.com
Paula Mackin began practicing law in 1975. She has completed several hundred adoptions in her career. 75% are newborns. She is an adoptive parent.

Biographies were not available for the following AAAA members:
Susan L. Crockin; 29 Crafts St., #500; Newton, MA 02460; (617) 332-7070; s.crockin@adoptionattorneys.org

Herbert D. Friedman; 92 State St., 7th Floor; Boston, MA 02109; (617) 723-7700; h.friedman@adoptionattorneys.org

Jeffrey M. Kaye; 302 Broadway; Methuen, MA 01844; (617) 720-0028; j.kaye@ adoptionattorneys.org

LICENSED PRIVATE AGENCIES

Act of Love Adoptions; Boston, MA; (617) 587-1583; www.mspcc.org; (Dom)

Adoption Choices/Jewish Family Service of Metrowest; Framingham, MA; (508) 875-3100; www.adoptionchoices.info; (Dom) (Intl) China, Guatemala, Russian Federation

AdoptionLink; Springfield, MA; (413) 737-2601; www.jfslink.org; (Dom) (Intl)

Adoption Resource Associates, Inc.; Cambridge, MA; (617) 492-8888; (Dom)

Adoption Resource Center at Brightside for Families and Children; West Springfield, MA; (413) 827-4258; www.brightsideadoption.org; (Dom) (Intl) China

Adoption Resources; Newton, MA; (617) 332-2218; www.adoptionresources.org; (Dom) (Intl) Russian Federation

Adoption with Love, Inc. (AWL); Newton, MA; (617) 964-4357; www.adoptionswith love.org; (Dom)

Alliance for Children, Inc.; Wellesley, MA; (781) 431-7148; www.allforchildren.org; (Dom) (Intl) China, Colombia, Ecuador, Guatemala, India, Russian Federation, Ukraine, Vietnam

Angel Adoptions, Inc.; Waltham, MA; (781) 899-9222; www.angel-adoptions.org; (Dom) (Intl)

Beacon Adoption Center, Inc.; Great Barrington, MA; (413) 528-2749; www.mich aelmccurdy.com/beacon.htm; (Dom) (Intl)

Bethany Christian Services; North Andover, MA; (978) 794-9800; www.bethany.org/ newengland; (Dom) (Intl)

Boston Adoption Bureau, Inc.; Boston, MA; (617) 277-1336; (Dom)

Bright Futures Adoption Center, Inc.; Acton, MA; (978) 263-5400; www.bright-futures .org; (Dom)

Brightside, Inc.; Pittsfield, MA; (413) 496-9491; (Dom)

Cambridge Family and Children's Services; Cambridge, MA; (617) 876-4210; www.help families.org; (Dom) (Intl)

Catholic Charities of Somerville; Somerville, MA; (617) 625-1920; www.ccab.org/ default.htm; (Dom)

Catholic Charities of Worcester; Leominster, MA; (508) 798-0191; (Dom)

Catholic Charities, Merrimack Valley; Lawrence, MA; (978) 685-5930; (Dom)

Catholic Social Services of Fall River, Inc.; Fall River, MA; (508) 674-4681; www.cssdioc .org; (Dom) (Intl)

Child and Family Service; New Bedford, MA; (508) 996-8572; www.child-family services.org; (Dom)

Children's Aid and Family Service of Hampshire County, Inc. (CAFS); Northampton, MA; (413) 584-5690; (413) 586-9436; www.cafshc.org; (Dom)

Children's Friend, Inc.; Worcester, MA; (508) 753-5425; www.childrensfriend.org/ index.html; (Dom) (Intl) Korea (South)

Children's Legal Services, Inc.; Brookline, MA; (617) 264-7333; www.childlaw.org; (Dom)

Children's Services of Roxbury, Inc.; Roxbury, MA; (617) 445-6655; www.csrox.org; (Dom)

China Adoption with Love, Inc. (CAWLI); Brookline, MA; (617) 731-0798; www.cawli.org; (Intl) China

Communities for People, Inc.; Boston, MA; (617) 572-3678; http://communities-for-people.org; (Dom)

DARE Family Services; Danvers, MA 01923; www.volunteersolutions.org; (Dom)

Florence Crittenton League; Lowell, MA; (978) 452-9671; www.fcleague.org; (Intl)

A Full Circle Adoptions; Northampton, MA; (413) 587-0007; www.fullcircleadoptions.org; (Dom)

Gift of Life Adoption Services, Inc.; Seekonk, MA; (508) 761-5661; www.giftoflife.cc; (Intl) China, Russian Federation

Home for Little Wanderers; Boston, MA; (617) 267-3700; www.thehome.org; (Dom) (Intl) China, Colombia, Ethiopia, Guatemala, India, Nepal, Russian Federation, Vietnam

Love the Children of Massachusetts; Duxbury, MA; (781) 934-0063; (Dom) (Intl)

Lutheran Social Services of New England, Inc.; Worcester, MA; (508) 791-4488; www.adoptlss.org; (Dom) (Intl)

A Red Thread Adoption Services, Inc.; Norwood, MA; (781) 762-2428; www.redthread adopt.org; (Dom) (Intl)

United Homes for Children; Dorchester, MA; (617) 825-3300; (Dom)

United Homes for Children; Tewksbury, MA; (978) 640-0089; (Dom)

Wide Horizons for Children, Inc. (WHFC); Waltham, MA; (781) 894-5330; www.whfc.org; (Dom) (Intl) China, Colombia, Ethiopia, Guatemala, India, Kazakhstan, Korea (South), Philippines, Russian Federation

MICHIGAN

STATE ADOPTION OFFICE: Michigan Department of Human Services; Child and Family Services Administration; PO Box 30037—Suite 413; Lansing, MI 48909; (517) 373-3513; www.michigan.gov

ICPC ADMINISTRATOR: Michigan Department of Human Services; (same address as above); (517) 373-6918; www.michigan.gov

STATE ADOPTION EXCHANGE: Michigan Adoption Resource Exchange (MARE); (517) 783-6273; www.mare.org

STATE BAR OF MICHIGAN: (517) 346-6300; www.michbar.org

ANNUAL NUMBER OF ADOPTIVE ADOPTIONS FINALIZED IN STATE: 6,274

STATE LAWS AND PROCEDURES—FAST FACTS

Types permitted? Independent and agency (25% of newborns via independent).

Who can adopt in state? Residents, and nonresidents when child present in state or the agency making the placement is located in state.

How long after child's placement to finalize adoption in court? 6 months.

Is adoptive parent advertising (to find a birth mother) permitted? Yes.

Is a preplacement home study required? Yes.

Typical agency home study fee? $1,000–$1,500 (agency fees usually higher if agency located child).

Can adoptive parents help birth mother with expenses? Yes: legal, medical, but not living.

Can child leave hospital with adoptive parents? Yes, with Temporary Placement Agreement.

When can birth mother sign her Consent to Adoption? Anytime after birth.

Can the consent be revoked? No, irrevocable once signed before a judge.

What are the putative father's rights? There is no registry. Notice must be attempted if he is known to birth mother or files a Notice of Intent to Claim Paternity. If he seeks to block adoption, his rights can be terminated if the child's bests interests are served by adoption.

AMERICAN ACADEMY OF ADOPTION ATTORNEYS MEMBERS

Herbert A. Brail; The Keane Law Firm; 930 Mason St.; Dearborn, MI 48124; (313) 278-8775; www.keanelaw.com; h.brail@adoptionattorneys.org
Herbert Brail began practicing law in 1982. He has completed 700 adoptions in his career and last year completed 35. 95% are newborn placements. All of his clients find their own birth mother.

Kenneth A. Rathert; Rathert Law Offices, PC; 137 N. Park St.; Kalamazoo, MI 49007; (269) 349-6808; www.rathertlaw.com; kenrathert@rathertlaw.com
Kenneth Rathert began practicing law in 1976. He has completed 400 adoptions in his career and last year completed 50. 50% are newborn placements. 5% of his clients find a birth mother through his office.

Biographies were not available for the following AAAA members:

Lauran F. Howard; 1200 N. Telegraph Rd., #452; Pontiac, MI 48341; (248) 858-0038; l.howard@adoptionattorneys.org

Monica Farris Linkner; 121 W. Washington St., #300; Ann Arbor, MI 48104; (734) 214-0200; m.linkner@adoptionattorneys.org

LICENSED PRIVATE AGENCIES

Adoptaid of Greater Hopes, formerly known as Adoptions of the Heart, Inc.; Grand Rapids, MI; (616) 365-3166; www.greaterhopes.org; (Dom) (Intl) China

Adoption Associates, Inc.; Farmington Hills, MI; (248) 474-0990; www.adoptassoc.com; (Dom) (Intl)

Adoption Associates, Inc.; Jenison; MI; (616) 667-0677; www.adoptassoc.com; (Dom) (Intl) China, Guatemala, Moldova, Russian Federation

Adoption Associates, Inc.; Lansing, MI; (517) 327-1388; www.adoptassoc.com; (Dom) (Intl) China, Guatemala, Russian Federation

Adoption Associates, Inc.; Saginaw, MI; (989) 497-5437; www.adoptassoc.com; (Dom) (Intl)

Adoption Consultants, Inc. (ACI); Farmington, MI; (248) 737-0336; www.aciadoption .com; (Dom) (Intl) Azerbaijan, Bulgaria, Guatemala, Kazakhstan, Lithuania, Russian Federation, Ukraine

Adoption Options Worldwide; West Bloomfield, MI; (248) 855-2813; (Dom) (Intl) Guatemala, Russian Federation, Ukraine, Vietnam

AdoptionPros; Jenison, MI; (616) 457-6537; www.adoptionpros.com; (Dom) (Intl) China, Guatemala, Kazakhstan, Republic of Georgia, Russian Federation, Ukraine

Alternatives for Children and Families; Flint, MI; (810) 235-0683; (Dom)

Americans for International Aid and Adoption (AIAA); Troy, MI; (248) 362-1207; www .aiaaadopt.org; (Intl) Guatemala, India, Korea (South)

Baptist Children's Home and Family Ministries, Inc.; St. Louis, MI; (989) 681-2171; www .baptistchildrenshome.org; (Dom)

Bethany Christian Services; Fremont, MI; (231) 924-3390; www.bethany.org/ fremont_mi; (Dom) (Intl) Albania, Bulgaria, China, Colombia, Guatemala, India, Kazakhstan, Korea (South), Lithuania, Philippines, Russian Federation

Bethany Christian Services; Grand Rapids, MI; (612) 224-7617; www.bethany.org/ grandrapids; (Dom)

Bethany Christian Services; Madison Heights, MI; (248) 414-4080; www.bethany.org/ madisonhts_mi; (Dom) (Intl) Albania, Bulgaria, China, Colombia, Guatemala, India, Korea (South), Kosova, Lithuania, Philippines, Romania, Russian Federation, Ukraine

Bethany Christian Services; Traverse City, MI; (231) 995-0870; www.bethany.org/ traverse; (Dom) (Intl)

Bethany Christian Services of Holland (BCS); Holland, MI; (616) 396-0623; www .bethany.org/holland; (Dom) (Intl)

Bethany Christian Services of Southwest Michigan (BCS); Kalamazoo, MI; (269) 372-8800; www.bethany.org/southwestmi; (Dom) (Intl)

Bethany Christian Services of Southwest Michigan (BCS); Three Rivers, MI; (269) 279-8003; www.bethany.org/southwestmi; (Dom) (Intl)

Catholic Charities of Shiawassee and Genessee Counties; Flint, MI; (810) 232-9950; www .catholiccharitiessg.org; (Dom)

Catholic Charities of Shiawassee and Genessee Counties; Owosso, MI; (989) 723-8239; www.catholiccharitiessg.org; (Dom)

Catholic Family Service of the Diocese of Saginaw; Bay City, MI; (989) 892-2504; www .saginaw.org/cfs.htm; (Dom)

Catholic Family Service of the Diocese of Saginaw; Saginaw, MI; (989) 753-8446; www .saginaw.org/cfs.htm; (Dom)

Catholic Family Services; Kalamazoo, MI; (269) 381-9800; www.catholicfamily services.org; (Dom)

Catholic Human Services, Inc.; Alpena, MI; (989) 356-6385; http://catholichuman
services.com; (Dom)

Catholic Human Services, Inc.; Gaylord, MI; (989) 732-6761; www.catholichuman
services.com; (Dom)

Catholic Human Services, Inc.; Traverse City, MI; (231) 947-8110; www.catholic
humanservices.com; (Dom) (Intl)

Catholic Services of Macomb; Clinton Township, MI; (586) 416-2300; www.csma
comb.org/adoption.htm; (Dom)

Catholic Social Services of Kent County; Grand Rapids, MI; (616) 456-1443; www.cssgr
.org; (Dom)

Catholic Social Services of Muskegon; Muskegon, MI; (231) 726-4735; (Dom)

Catholic Social Services of Oakland County; Pontiac, MI; (248) 333-3700; www.cssoc
.org; (Dom)

Catholic Social Services of Oakland County; Southfield, MI; (248) 552-0750; www.cssoc
.org; (Dom)

Catholic Social Services of St. Clair County; Port Huron, MI; (810) 987-9100; www.cssst
clair.org; (Dom)

Catholic Social Services of the Upper Peninsula, Inc. (CSSUP); Escanaba, MI; (906) 786-
7212; www.dioceseofmarquette.org; (Dom)

Catholic Social Services of the Upper Peninsula, Inc. (CSSUP); Houghton, MI; (906) 482-
1624; www.dioceseofmarquette.org; (Dom)

Catholic Social Services of the Upper Peninsula, Inc. (CSSUP); Iron Mountain, MI; (906)
724-3323; www.dioceseofmarquette.org; (Dom)

Catholic Social Services of the Upper Peninsula, Inc. (CSSUP); Ironwood, MI; (906) 932-
0138; www.dioceseofmarquette.org; (Dom)

Catholic Social Services of the Upper Peninsula, Inc. (CSSUP); Marquette, MI; (906) 227-
9121; (906) 227-9119; www.dioceseofmarquette.org; (Dom)

Catholic Social Services of the Upper Peninsula, Inc. (CSSUP); Sault Ste. Marie, MI; (906)
635-1508; www.dioceseofmarquette.org; (Dom)

Catholic Social Services of Washtenaw County (CSS); Ann Arbor, MI; (734) 971-9781;
www.csswashtenaw.org/adoption; (Dom)

Catholic Social Services of Wayne County (CSSWC); Detroit, MI; (313) 883-2100; www
.csswayne.org; (Dom)

Child and Family Services, Capital Area; Lansing, MI; (517) 882-4000; www
.childandfamily.org; (Dom)

Child and Family Services of Northeast Michigan, Inc.; Alpena, MI; (989) 356-4567; www
.cfsnemi.org; (Dom)

Child and Family Services of Northwestern Michigan, Inc.; Traverse City, MI; (231) 946-
8975; www.cfsnwmi.org; (Dom)

Child and Family Services of Southwest Michigan; Benton Harbor, MI; (269) 925-7355;
www.cfsswmi.org; (Dom)

Child and Family Services of Western Michigan, Inc. (CFSWM); Grand Haven, MI; (616)
846-5880; www.cfswm.org; (Dom)

Child and Family Services of Western Michigan, Inc. (CFSWM); Holland, MI; (616) 396-
2301; www.cfswm.org; (Dom)

Child and Family Services of the Upper Peninsula, Inc.; Marquette, MI; (906) 228-4025; www.cfsup.org; (Dom)

Child and Parent Services, Inc.; Bingham Farms, MI; (248) 646-7790; www.childand parentservices.com; (Dom) (Intl)

Children's Center of Wayne County; Detroit, MI; (313) 832-3555; www.thechildrens center.org; (Dom)

Children's Hope Adoption Services; Mt. Pleasant, MI; (989) 775-8229; (Dom) (Intl)

Christ Child House; Detroit, MI; (313) 584-6077; www.christchildhouse.org; (Dom) (Intl)

Christian Family Services; Southfield, MI; (248) 557-8390; www.cfspyo.org; (Dom)

D. A. Blodgett for Children; Grand Rapids, MI; (616) 451-2021; www.dablodgett.org; (Dom) (Intl) Belgium, China, Guatemala, India, Indonesia, Pacific Islands

Eagle Village, Inc.; Hersey, MI; (231) 832-7270; www.eaglevillage.org; (Dom)

Eastern European Adoption Services; Dearborn, MI; (313) 561-5563; (Intl)

Ennis Center for Children, Inc.; Detroit, MI; (313) 342-2699; www.enniscenter.org; (Dom)

Ennis Center for Children, Inc.; Detroit, MI; (810) 233-4031; www.enniscenter.org; (Dom)

Ennis Center for Children, Inc.; Flint, MI; (810) 233-4031; www.enniscenter.org; (Dom)

Ennis Center for Children, Inc.; Waterford, MI; (248) 618-1260; www.enniscenter.org; (Dom)

Evergreen Children's Services; Detroit, MI; (313) 862-1000; www.evergreenserv.org; (Dom)

Family Adoption Consultants (FAC); Kalamazoo, MI; (269) 343-3316; www.facadopt .org; (Dom) (Intl) China, Guatemala, Korea (South), Philippines

Family Adoption Consultants (FAC); Utica, MI; (586) 726-2988; www.facadopt.org; (Dom) (Intl) China, Guatemala, Korea (South), Philippines

Family Counseling and Children's Services of Lenewee County; Adrian, MI; (517) 265-5352; www.fccservices.org; (Dom)

Family Matchmakers, Inc.; Grand Rapids, MI; (616) 243-1803; www.familymatch makers.org; (Dom)

Family Service and Children's Aid (FSCA); Jackson, MI; (517) 787-7920; www .strong-families.org; (Dom) (Intl)

Family and Children Services; Battle Creek, MI; (269) 965-3247; www.fcsource.org; (Dom)

Family and Children Services; Kalamazoo, MI; (269) 344-0202; www.fcsource.org; (Dom)

Family and Children's Services of Midland; Midland, MI; (989) 631-5390; www .fcsmidland.org; (Dom)

Family and Children's Services, Inc.; Hastings, MI; (269) 948-8465; www.fcsource.org; (Dom)

Forever Families, Inc.; Novi, MI; (248) 344-9606; www.forever-families.org; (Dom)

Hands Across the Water (HATW); Ann Arbor, MI; (734) 477-0135; www.hatw.org; (Dom) (Intl) Brazil, Bulgaria, Guatemala, Kazakhstan, Lithuania, Poland, Russian Federation

HelpSource, Inc.; Wayne, MI; (734) 973-1900; www.helpsourceagency.com; (Dom)

Homes for Black Children (HBC); Detroit, MI; (313) 961-4777; www.homesforblackchil dren.org; (Dom)

Jewish Family Service Alliance for Adoption; West Bloomfield, MI; (248) 592-2345; www.jfsdetroit.org; (Dom)

Judson Center; Ann Arbor, MI; (734) 528-1692; www.judsoncenter.org; (Dom)

Judson Center; Redford, MI; (313) 794-5653; www.judsoncenter.org; (Dom)

Keane Center for Adoption; Dearborn, MI; (313) 277-4664; www.keaneadoption.org; (Dom)

LDS Family Services—Farmington Hills; Farmington Hills, MI; (248) 553-0902; www .providentliving.org; (Dom)

Lula Belle Stewart Center; Detroit, MI; (313) 867-2372; www.lulabellestewart.org; (Dom)

Lutheran Adoption Service (LAS); Ann Arbor, MI; (734) 971-1944; www.lssm.org/ service/adoption; (Dom) (Intl)

Lutheran Adoption Service (LAS); Bay City, MI; (989) 686-3170; www.lssm.org/service/ adoption; (Dom) (Intl)

Lutheran Adoption Service (LAS); Kalamazoo, MI; (269) 345-5776; jcare@lssm.org; www.lssm.org; (Dom) (Intl)

Lutheran Adoption Service (LAS); Lansing, MI; (517) 886-1380; www.lssm.org/service/ adoption; (Dom) (Intl)

Methodist Children's Home Society; Detroit, MI; (313) 531-4060; (313) 531-3372; www.resa.net; (Dom)

Michigan Indian Child Welfare Agency; Baraga, MI; (906) 353-4204; (Dom)

Michigan Indian Child Welfare Agency; Grand Rapids, MI; (616) 454-9221; (Dom)

Michigan Indian Child Welfare Agency; Lansing, MI; (517) 393-3256; (Dom)

Michigan Indian Child Welfare Agency; Southfield, MI; (248) 552-1142; (Dom)

Michigan Indian Child Welfare Agency; Wilson, MI; (906) 466-9221; (Dom)

Michigan Indian Child Welfare Agency—Anishnabek Community Family Services (ACFS); Sault Ste. Marie, MI; (906) 632-5250; www.saulttribe.org; (Dom)

Morning Star Adoption Center (MSAC); Southfield, MI; (248) 483-5484; www.morning staradoption.org; (Dom)

Oakland Family Services (OFS); Pontiac, MI; (248) 858-7766; www.oaklandfamily services.com; (Dom)

Orchards Children's Services; Detroit, MI; (313) 387-1801; www.orchards.org; (Dom)

Orchards Children's Services; Southfield, MI; (248) 258-0440; www.orchards.org; (Dom)

Orchards Children's Services; Sterling Heights, MI; (586) 997-3886; www.orchards .org; (Dom)

Spaulding for Children; Southfield, MI; (248) 443-7080; www.spaulding.org; (Dom)

Spectrum Human Services, Inc.; Southfield, MI; (248) 552-8020; www.spectrum human.org; (Dom)

Spectrum Human Services, Inc.; Westland, MI; (734) 458-8736; www.spectrumhuman .org; (Dom)

St. Vincent Catholic Charities; Lansing, MI; (517) 323-4734; www.stvcc.org; (Dom)

St. Vincent and Sarah Fisher Center; Farmington Hills, MI; (248) 626-7527; www.svsf center.org; (Dom) (Intl)

Teen Ranch, Inc.; Clifford, MI; (989) 635-7511; www.teenranch.com; (Dom)

MINNESOTA

STATE ADOPTION OFFICE: Minnesota Department of Human Services; Human Services Bldg.; 444 Lafayette Road; St. Paul, MN 55155-3831; (651) 282-3793; www .dhs.state.mn.us

ICPC ADMINISTRATOR: Minnesota Department of Human Services; Children and Family Services; (same address as above); (651) 296-2210; (651) 297-1949; www.dhs .state.mn.us

STATE ADOPTION EXCHANGE: Minnesota Adoption Resource Network, Inc.; (612) 861-7115; www.mnadopt.org; info@mnadopt.org

MINNESOTA STATE BAR ASSOCIATION: (612) 333-1183; www.mnbar.org

ANNUAL NUMBER OF ADOPTIVE ADOPTIONS FINALIZED IN STATE: 2,094

STATE LAWS AND PROCEDURES—FAST FACTS

Types permitted? Independent ("direct placement") and agency (80% of newborns via direct placement).

Who can adopt in state? Residents only.

How long after child's placement to finalize adoption in court? 3–6 months.

Is adoptive parent advertising (to find a birth mother) permitted? Yes.

Is a preplacement home study required? Yes.

Typical agency home study fee? $2,200–$6,000 (agency fees usually higher if agency located child).

Can adoptive parents help birth mother with expenses? Yes: legal, medical, but not living.

Can child leave hospital with adoptive parents? Yes, but usually court order required.

When can birth mother sign her Consent to Adoption? 72 hours after birth. If she is a minor, a parent or guardian ad litem must also consent.

Can the consent be revoked? Yes, for 10 days, then irrevocable.

What are the putative father's rights? There is a registry. He can file up to 30 days after birth. He gets notice only if registered and has 30 days to file objection, or his rights waived.

Note: Attorneys are not permitted to locate birth mothers to create adoptive matches.

AMERICAN ACADEMY OF ADOPTION ATTORNEYS MEMBERS

Gary A. Debele; Walling, Berg & Debele, PA; 121 S. 8th St., #1100; Minneapolis, MN 55402; (612) 335-4288; www.wbdlaw.com; gary.debele@wbdlaw.com

Gary Debele began practicing law in 1987. He has completed 250 adoptions in his career and last year completed 23. 80% are newborn placements. He is an adoptive parent. He authored a chapter in Adoption Law: Practice and Procedure in the 21st Century.

Jody Ollyver DeSmidt; Walling, Berg & Debele, PA; 121 S. 8th St., #1100; Minneapolis, MN 55402; (612) 340-1150; www.wbdlaw.com; jody.desmidt@wbdlaw.com
Jody DeSmidt began practicing law in 1982. She has completed 800 adoptions in her career and last year completed 56. 85% are newborn placements.

Judith D. Vincent; 111 3rd Ave. S., Suite 360; Minneapolis, MN 55401; (612) 332-7772; www.adoptionlaw-mn.com; jvincent@adoptionlaw.mn.com
Judith Vincent began practicing law in 1978. She has completed 2,500 adoptions in her career and last year completed 110. 90% are newborn placements, 10% are toddlers or above. She is an adoptive parent.

Biographies were not available for the following AAAA members:

Jessica J. W. Maher; 121 S. 8th St., #1100; Minneapolis, MN 55402; (612) 340-1150; www.wbdlaw.com; jessica.maher@wbdlaw.com

Wright S. Walling; 121 S. 8th St., #1100; Minneapolis, MN 55402; (612) 340-1150; www.wbdlaw.com; w.walling@adoptionattorneys.org

LICENSED PRIVATE AGENCIES

African American Adoption Agency; St. Paul, MN; (651) 659-0460; www.afadopt.org; (Dom)

Bethany Christian Services; Plymouth, MN; (763) 553-0344; www.bethany.org/plymouth; (Dom) (Intl) Bulgaria, China, Colombia, Guatemala, India, Japan, Kazakhstan, Korea (South), Lithuania, Philippines, Russian Federation, Ukraine

Bethany Christian Services; Wilmar, MN; (320) 214-0601; www.bethany.org/plymouth; (Dom) (Intl) Albania, Bulgaria, China, Colombia, Guatemala, India, Japan, Kazakhstan, Korea (South), Lithuania, Philippines, Russian Federation, Ukraine

Caritas Family Services; St. Cloud, MN; (320) 650-1660; www.ccstcloud.org; (Dom) (Intl)

Catholic Charities of the Diocese of Winona; Winona, MN; (507) 454-2270; www.ccwinona.org; (Dom)

Catholic Charities/Seton Services; St. Paul, MN; (651) 641-1180; www.ccspm.org; (Dom)

Child Link International (CLI); Richfield, MN; (612) 861-9048; www.child-link.com; (Intl) Russian Federation

Children's Home Society & Family Services (CHSFS); St. Paul, MN; (651) 646-6393; www.childrenshomeadopt.org; (Dom) (Intl) China, Colombia, Ecuador, Ethiopia, Guatemala, Honduras, India, Kazakhstan, Korea (South), Moldova, Peru, Russian Federation, Ukraine, Vietnam

Chosen Ones Adoption Agency; Maplewood, MN; (651) 770-5508; www.chosen1s.org; (Dom) (Intl) China

Crossroads Adoption Services; Minneapolis, MN; (952) 831-5707; www.crossroads adoption.com; (Dom) (Intl) China, Colombia, Guatemala, India, Nepal, Peru, Philippines, Russian Federation, Thailand, Ukraine

Downey Side; Owatonna, MN; (507) 446-8503; www.downeyside.org; (Dom)

Downey Side; St. Cloud, MN; (320) 240-1433; (Dom)

Downey Side; St. Paul, MN; (651) 228-0117; www.downeyside.org; (Dom)

European Children's Adoption Services; Plymouth, MN; (763) 694-6131; www.ecasus .org; (Intl) Bulgaria, China, Guatemala, Kazakhstan, Lithuania, Mongolia, Philippines, Russian Federation, Ukraine

Family Alternatives; Minneapolis, MN; (612) 379-5341; www.familyalternatives.org; (Dom)

Family Resources; Anoka, MN; (763) 422-8590; www.familyres.net; (Intl) China, Guatemala, Russian Federation, Ukraine

HOPE Adoption and Family Services International, Inc.; Oak Park Heights, MN; (651) 439-2446; www.hopeadoptionservices.org; (Dom) (Intl)

International Adoption Services (IAS); Edina, MN; (952) 893-1343; www.ias-ww.com; (Intl) China, Guatemala, Russian Federation, Ukraine

LDS Social Services; Brooklyn Center, MN; (763) 560-0900; www.providentliving .org; (Dom) (Intl)

Love Basket, Inc.; Duluth, MN; (218) 720-3097; www.lovebasket.org; (Dom) (Intl)

Lutheran Social Services of Minnesota (LSS); Duluth, MN; (218) 726-4888; www .minnesotaadoption.org; (Dom) (Intl)

Lutheran Social Services of Minnesota (LSS); South Minneapolis, MN; (612) 879-5230; www.minnesotaadoption.org; (Dom) (Intl) Colombia, Guatemala, Ukraine

Lutheran Social Services of Minnesota (LSS); St. Cloud, MN; (320) 251-7700; www .minnesotaadoption.org; (Dom) (Intl)

Lutheran Social Services of Minnesota (LSS); Moorhead, MN; (218) 236-1494 ext. 207; www.minnesotaadoption.org; (Dom) (Intl)

New Horizons Adoption Agency, Inc. (NHAA); Frost, MN (507) 878-3200; www .nhadoptionagency.com; (Dom) (Intl)

New Life Family Services (NLFS); Richfield, MN; (612) 866-7643; www.newlifefamily services.com; (Dom)

North Homes, Inc.; Grand Rapids, MN; (218) 327-3000; www.northhomesinc.org; (Dom)

PATH (Professional Association of Treatment Homes); Bemidji, MN; (218) 751-7515; http:// pathinc.org; (Dom)

PATH (Professional Association of Treatment Homes); Fergus Falls, MN; (218) 739-3074; www.pathinc.org; (Dom)

PATH (Professional Association of Treatment Homes); Marshall, MN; (507) 532-4635; www.pathinc.org; (Dom)

PATH (Professional Association of Treatment Homes); St. Cloud, MN; (320) 529-0862; www.pathinc.org; (Dom)

PATH (Professional Association of Treatment Homes) (PATH, Inc.); St. Paul, MN; (651) 641-0455; www.pathinc.org; (Dom)

Permanent Family Resource Center (PFRC); Fergus Falls, MN; (218) 998-3400; www.permanentfamily.org; (Dom)

Reaching Arms International, Inc.; New Hope, MN; (763) 591-0791; http://reaching arms.org; (Intl) Armenia, Guatemala, Poland, Russian Federation, Ukraine

Summit Adoption Home Studies, Inc.; St. Paul, MN; (651) 645-6657; www.summit adoption.com; (Dom) (Intl) Armenia, Brazil, Bulgaria, Cambodia, Chile, China, Ecuador, Estonia, Ethiopia, Guatemala, Haiti, Israel, Kazakhstan, Lao People's Democratic Republic, Liberia, Marshall Islands, Mexico, Mongolia, Nepal, Poland, Romania, Russian Federation, Rwanda

Upper Midwest American Indian Center; Minneapolis, MN; (612) 522-4436 (Dom)

Wellspring Adoption Agency; Minneapolis, MN; (612) 379-0980; (Dom) (Intl)

MISSISSIPPI

STATE ADOPTION OFFICE: Mississippi Department of Human Services; Division of Family and Child Services; 750 N. State St.; Jackson, MS 39202; (601) 359-4981; www.mdhs.state.ms.us

ICPC ADMINISTRATOR: Mississippi Department of Human Services; (same address as above); (601) 359-4986; phickman@mdhs.state.ms.us

STATE ADOPTION EXCHANGE: Mississippi Adoption Resource Exchange; (601) 359-4407; www.mdhs.state.ms.us

MISSISSIPPI BAR ASSOCIATION: (601) 948-4471; www.msbar.org

ANNUAL NUMBER OF ADOPTIVE ADOPTIONS FINALIZED IN STATE: 866

STATE LAWS AND PROCEDURES—FAST FACTS

Types permitted? Independent and agency.

Who can adopt in state? Residents, and nonresidents if agency making placement is in state.

How long after child's placement to finalize adoption in court? 6 months.

Is adoptive parent advertising (to find a birth mother) permitted? Yes.

Is a preplacement home study required? Independent—no (court can even waive the postplacement home study). Agency—yes.

Typical agency home study fee? $750–$1,300 (agency fees usually higher if agency located child).

Can adoptive parents help birth mother with expenses? Yes: legal, medical, but not living.

Can child leave hospital with adoptive parents? Yes, usually via attorney/agency.

When can birth mother sign her Consent to Adoption? 72 hours after birth.

Can the consent be revoked? No statutory law, but courts usually state irrevocable upon signing.

What are the putative father's rights? There is no registry. Notice must be attempted.

AMERICAN ACADEMY OF ADOPTION ATTORNEYS MEMBERS

Wes Daughdrill; Young Williams, PA; 210 E. Capitol St., #2000; Jackson, MS 39225; (601) 360-9030; www.youngwilliams.com; wes.daughdrill@young williams.com

Wes Daughdrill began practicing law in 1993. He has completed 60 adoptions in his career and last year completed approximately 6. 95% are newborn placements.

A biography was not available for the following AAAA member:

Dan J. Davis; 352 Spring St.; Tupelo, MS 38802; (662) 841-1090; d.davis@adoption attorneys.org

Please be aware some AAAA attorneys located in neighboring states also practice in Mississippi, including Sandra C. Bradshaw (AR).

LICENSED PRIVATE AGENCIES

Acorn Adoption, Inc.; St. Louis, MS; Toll-free: (888) 221-1370; www.acornadoption .org; (Dom)

Beacon House Adoption Services, Inc.; Gulfport, MS; (228) 863-8383; www.beacon houseadoption.com; (Dom)

Bethany Christian Services (BCS); Columbus, MS; (662) 327-6740; www.bethany.org/ mississippi; (Dom) (Intl)

Bethany Christian Services (BCS); Hattiesburg, MS; (601) 264-4984; www.bethany .org/mississippi; (Dom) (Intl)

Bethany Christian Services (BCS); Jackson, MS; (601) 366-4282; www.bethany.org/ mississippi; (Dom) (Intl)

Catholic Charities, Inc.; Jackson, MS; (601) 355-8634; http://catholiccharitiesjackson .org; (Dom)

Catholic Social and Community Services; Biloxi, MS; (228) 702-2137; www.biloxidiocese .org; (Dom) (Intl)

Mississippi Children's Home Society; Jackson, MS; (601) 352-7784; www.mchscares .org/adoption.htm; (Dom) (Intl)

New Beginnings of Tupelo; Tupelo, MS; (662) 842-6752; www.nbi.cc; (Dom) (Intl)

Southern Christian Services for Children and Youth, Inc.—Harden House Adoption Program (HHAP); Fulton, MS; (662) 862-7318; www.hardenhouse.org; (Dom) (Intl) China, Ethiopia, Guatemala, Haiti, Russian Federation

World Child, Inc.; Gulfport, MS; www.worldchild.org; (Dom)

MISSOURI

STATE ADOPTION OFFICE: Missouri Department of Social Services; 615 Howerton Ct.; PO Box 88; Jefferson City, MO 65103-0088; (573) 751-3171; www.dss .mo.gov

ICPC ADMINISTRATOR: Missouri Department of Social Services; (same address as above); (573) 751-2981; www.dss.mo.gov

STATE ADOPTION EXCHANGE: Missouri Adoption Photolisting; www.adoptuskids.org;

MISSOURI BAR: (573) 635-4128; www.mobar.org

ANNUAL NUMBER OF ADOPTIVE ADOPTIONS FINALIZED IN STATE: 2,554

STATE LAWS AND PROCEDURES—FAST FACTS

Types permitted? Independent and agency (60% of newborns via independent).

Who can adopt in state? Residents, and nonresidents when child born in state or the agency making the placement is located in state.

How long after child's placement to finalize adoption in court? 6 months.

Is adoptive parent advertising (to find a birth mother) permitted? Yes.

Is a preplacement home study required? Yes.

Typical agency home study fee? $1,000–$5,000 (agency fees usually higher if agency located child).

Can adoptive parents help birth mother with expenses? Yes: legal, medical, living.

Can child leave hospital with adoptive parents? Yes, but sometimes court order or Power of Attorney required.

When can birth mother sign her Consent to Adoption? 48 hours after birth.

Can the consent be revoked? Yes, until a judge confirms the consent, thereafter irrevocable.

What are the putative father's rights? There is a registry. He must register within 15 days of the birth. If he does not do so or file paternity action, he waives his rights.

AMERICAN ACADEMY OF ADOPTION ATTORNEYS MEMBERS

Mary Beck; 2775 Shag Bark; Columbia, MO 65203; (573) 446-7554; beckm@missouri.edu

Mary Beck began practicing law in 1988. Last year she completed 26 adoptions. 90% are newborn placements. 1% of her clients find a birth mother through her office.

Catherine W. Keefe; Keefe & Brodie; 130 S. Bemiston, #602; Clayton, MO 63105; (314) 726-6242; ckeefe@keefebrodie.com

Catherine Keefe began practicing law in 1986. She has completed 500 adoptions in her career and last year completed 37. 75% are newborn placements.

Sanford P. Krigel; 4550 Belleview; Kansas City, MO 64111; (816) 756-5800; s.krigel@adoptionattorneys.org

Sanford Krigel began practicing law in 1976.

Allan F. Stewart; Stewart, Mittleman, Heggie & Henry LLC; 222 S. Central St., #501; St. Louis, MO 63105; (314) 863-8484; vdrm22825@sbclgobal.net

Allan Stewart began practicing law in 1973. He has completed 3,000 adoptions in his career and last year completed 25. 90% are newborn placements. 5% of his clients find a birth mother through his office.

F. Richard Van Pelt; Van Pelt & Van Pelt, PC; 1524 E. Primrose, Suite A; Springfield, MO 65804; (417) 886-9080; www.vanpeltlaw.com
Richard Van Pelt began practicing law in 1983. 80% of his adoptions are newborn placements.

Kay A. Van Pelt; Van Pelt & Van Pelt PC; 1524 E. Primrose, Suite A; Springfield, MO 65804; (417) 886-9080; www.vanpeltlaw.com;
Kay Van Pelt began practicing law in 1983. 80% of his adoptions are newborn placements.

Betty K. Wilson; Oliver Walker Wilson, LLC; 401 Locust St., #406; Columbia, MO 65205; (573) 443-3134; www.owwlaw.com; bwilson@owwlaw.com;
Betty Wilson began practicing law in 1975. She has completed 920 adoptions in her career and last year completed 35. 8% are newborn placements. 3% of her clients find a birth mother through her office.

A biography was not available for the following AAAA member:
Michael J. Belfonte; 1125 Grand Blvd., #1301; Kansas City, MO 64106; (816) 842-3580; m.belfonte@adoptionattorneys.org

Please be aware that some AAAA members located in neighboring states also practice in Missouri, including: Susan Grammer (IL) and Joseph Vader (KS).

LICENSED PRIVATE AGENCIES
Action for Adoption; St. Louis, MO; (816) 490-0198; (Dom) (Intl)
Adopt Kids, Inc.; Kirkwood, MO; (314) 965-2203; www.adoptkidsinc.com; (Dom) (Intl)
Adoption Advocates; Kansas City, MO; (816) 753-1881; (Dom) (Intl)
Adoption and Beyond, Inc.; Lee's Summit, MO; (816) 822-2800; www.adoptionbeyond.org; (Dom)
Adoption and Fertility Resources; Liberty, MO; (816) 781-8550; (Dom) (Intl)
Adoption Counseling, Inc.; Independence, MO; (816) 507-0822; (Dom) (Intl)
Adoption for Families, Inc.; Springfield, MO; (417) 882-7700; www.adoptionforfamilies.com; (Dom) (Intl) Azerbaijan, China, Guatemala, Kazakhstan, Russian Federation
Adoption Haven; St. Louis, MO; (314) 822-5708; www.adoptionhaven.com; (Dom)
Adoption Option; Liberty, MO; (816) 224-1525; (Dom) (Intl)
Adoption Solutions, LLC; Jefferson City, MO; (573) 632-6646; (Dom) (Intl)
BFT Holding Corporation dba Bringing Families Together, LLC (BFT); Hazelwood, MO; (314) 731-3969; (314) 731-3906; www.bringingfamiliestogether.com; (Dom)
Bethany Christian Services; Chesterfield, MO; (636) 536-6363; www.bethany.org/missouri; (Dom) (Intl)
Boys and Girls Town of Missouri; St. James, MO; (573) 265-3251; www.bgtm.org; (Dom)
Butterfield Youth Services (BYS); Marshall, MO; (660) 886-2253; www.bys-kids.org; (Dom)

Catholic Charities of Kansas City/St. Joseph, Inc; Kansas City, MO; (816) 221-4377; www.catholiccharities-kcsj.org; (Dom) (Intl)

Catholic Services for Children and Youth; St. Louis, MO; (314) 792-7400; www.ccstl.org; (Dom) (Intl)

Central Baptist Family Services; St. Louis, MO; (314) 241-4345; (Dom) (Intl)

Children of the World, Inc.; Clayton, MO; (314) 721-4070; www.childrenoftheworld net.com; (Intl) Azerbaijan, Brazil, Guatemala, Republic of Georgia, Ukraine

Children's Home Society of Missouri (CHS); Brentwood, MO; (314) 968-2350; www.chsmo.com; (Dom) (Intl) China, India, Puerto Rico, Russian Federation

Children's Hope International; St. Louis, MO; (314) 890-0086; www.childrens hopeint.org; (Intl) China, Colombia, Guatemala, India, Kazakhstan, Nepal, Russian Federation, Vietnam

Christian Family Life Center (CFLC); St. Louis, MO; (314) 432-4400; www.cflcenter.org; (Dom) (Intl) Bulgaria, Guatemala, Kazakhstan, Russian Federation, Ukraine

Christian Family Services; Webster Groves, MO; (314) 968-2216; www.cfserve.org; (Dom)

Christian Family Services of the Midwest, Inc.; Kansas City, MO; (816) 457-6900; cfskc.org; (Dom) (Intl)

Christian Salvation Services; St. Louis, MO; (314) 535-5919; www.csstpe.org.tw; (Dom) (Intl)

Crittenton Children's Center—St. Luke's Health Care System; Kansas City, MO; (816) 765-6600; www.saintlukeshealthsystem.org; (Dom)

Dillon International, Inc.; St. Louis, MO; (314) 576-4100; www.dillonadopt.com; (Intl) China, Guatemala, Haiti, India, Kazakhstan, Korea (South), Ukraine, Vietnam

Faith House; St. Louis, MO; (314) 367-5400; www.faithvillage.org; (Dom)

Family Care Center; Chesterfield, MO; (314) 576-6493; (Dom) (Intl)

The Family Conservancy; Kansas City, MO; (816) 436-0486; www.thefamilycon servancy.org; (Dom) (Intl)

Friends of African-American Families and Children Service Center; St. Louis, MO; (314) 535-2453; (Dom)

Future, Inc.; St. Louis, MO; (636) 391-8868; (Dom) (Intl)

A Gift of Hope Adoptions; Columbia, MO; (573) 886-8977; www.agiftofhope adoptions.com; (Dom)

Holt International Children's Services; Kansas City, MO; (816) 822-2169; www.holtintl.org; (Intl) Bulgaria, China, Ecuador, Guatemala, Haiti, India, Korea (South), Mongolia, Philippines, Thailand, Vietnam

Hope N. Heller, Ph.D. Adoption Services, Inc.; St. Louis, MO; (314) 567-7500; www.hopenhellerphd.com; (Dom) (Intl)

James A. Roberts Agency; Kansas City, MO; (816) 753-3333; (Dom) (Intl)

LDS Family Services; Independence, MO; (816) 461-5512; www.ldsfamilyservices.org; (Dom) (Intl)

LIGHT House, Inc.; Kansas City, MO; (816) 361-2233; www.lighthouse-inc.org; (Dom)

Love Basket, Inc.; Hillsboro, MO; (636) 797-4100; www.lovebasket.org; (Dom) (Intl) Ethiopia, Guatemala, India, Ukraine

Lutheran Family and Children's Services of Missouri (LFCS); University City, MO; (314) 787-5100; www.lfcsmo.org; (Dom) (Intl)

Missouri Alliance for Children and Families LLC (MACF); Jefferson City, MO; (573) 556-8090; www.ma-cf.org; (Dom)

Missouri Baptist Children's Home/MBCH Children and Family Ministries; Bridgeton, MO; (314) 739-6811; www.mbch.org; (Dom)

New Family Connection; St. Charles, MO; (636) 949-0577; (Dom) (Intl)

Our Little Haven; St. Louis, MO; (314) 531-3183 ext. 238; www.ourlittlehaven.org/foster.htm; (Dom)

Presbyterian Children's Services, Inc. dba Farmington Children's Home (A); Farmington, MO; (573) 756-6744; www.presbyterianchildren.org; (Dom)

Reaching Out Thru International Adoption, Inc.; St. Charles, MO; (314) 606-9529; www.adoptachild.us; (Intl) Azerbaijan, Brazil, Cambodia, China, Guatemala, Kazakhstan, Russian Federation, Taiwan, Vietnam

Respond, Inc.; St. Louis, MO; (314) 383-4243; (Dom)

Safe Cradle Adoption Agency; Creve Coeur, MO; (314) 306-6647; (Dom) (Intl)

Salvation Army Foster Care Case Management; Kansas City, MO; (816) 756-2769; (Dom)

Seek International Adoption Agency; St. Louis, MO; (314) 293-0242; www.seekadoption.org; China, Guatemala, Kazakhstan, Russian Federation, Ukraine

Small World Adoption Foundation, Inc. (SWAF); Ballwin, MO; (636) 207-9229; www.swaf.com; (Intl)

Special Additions, Inc.; Lees Summit, MO; (816) 421-3737; (Dom)

Spofford—Cornerstone; Kansas City, MO; (816) 508-3400; (Dom) (Intl)

Universal Adoption Services (UAS); Jefferson City, MO; (573) 634-3733; www.uas-adoption.blogspot.com; (Dom)

Urban Behavioral Healthcare Institute (UBH); St. Louis, MO; (314) 577-5000; www.urbanbehav.com; (Dom)

MONTANA

STATE ADOPTION OFFICE: Montana Department of Public Health and Human Services (DPHHS); PO Box 8005; Helena, MT 59604-8005; (406) 444-5975; www.dphhs.mt.gov; ltaffs@mt.gov

ICPC ADMINISTRATOR: Montana Department of Public Health and Human Services; (same address as above); (406) 444-5917; kmorse@mt.gov

STATE ADOPTION EXCHANGE: Montana Waiting Children Photolistings; (same address as above); (406) 444-5900; www.adoptuskids.org; askaboutadoption@mt.gov

STATE BAR OF MONTANA: (406) 442-7660; www.montanabar.org

ANNUAL NUMBER OF ADOPTIVE ADOPTIONS FINALIZED IN STATE: 600

STATE LAWS AND PROCEDURES—FAST FACTS

Types permitted? Independent and agency (50% of newborns via independent).

Who can adopt in state? Residents.
How long after child's placement to finalize adoption in court? 6 months.
Is adoptive parent advertising (to find a birth mother) permitted? No.
Is a preplacement home study required? Yes.
Typical agency home study fee? $1,000–$2,000 (agency fees usually higher if agency located child).
Can adoptive parents help birth mother with expenses? Yes: legal, medical, living.
Can child leave hospital with adoptive parents? Yes.
When can birth mother sign her Consent to Adoption? 72 hours after birth.
Can the consent be revoked? Yes, only if fraud is proved. When the consent is approved by a court, then irrevocable.
What are the putative father's rights? There is a registry.

AMERICAN ACADEMY OF ADOPTION ATTORNEYS MEMBERS:
Dennis E. Lind; 201 W. Main St., #201; Missoula, MT 59802; (406) 728-0810; d.lind@adoptionattorneys.org

LICENSED PRIVATE AGENCIES
An Act of Love; Lewistown, MT; (406) 538-5990; (Dom)
Heritage Adoption Services; Bozeman, MT; (406) 599-1041; www.heritageadoption.org; (Intl)
Catholic Social Services of Montana (CSSM); Helena, MT; (406) 442-4130; www.catholicsocialservicesofmontana.org; (Dom)
LDS Family Services; Helena, MT; (406) 443-1660; www.ldsfamilyservices.org; (Dom)
Lifeline of Hope Adoptions; Kalispell, MT; (406) 257-0868; http://lifelineofhope.org/lifelineofhope/intadopt.html; (Intl) Bulgaria, Kazakhstan, Russian Federation
Lutheran Family Services; Great Falls, MT; (406) 761-4341; www.lssmt.org; (Dom)
A New Arrival; Twin Bridges, MT; (406) 684-5312; www.anewarrival.com; (Intl)
Path Program/Intermountain Children's Home; Helena, MT; (406) 442-7920; www.intermountain.org; (Dom)
Sacred Portion Children's Outreach; Bozeman, MT; (406) 586-5773; www.sacredportion.org/Intervention.htm; (Intl)
Youth Homes (DFHFK); Missoula, MT; (406) 721-2754; http://youthhomes.com; (Dom)

NEBRASKA

STATE ADOPTION OFFICE: Nebraska Department of Health and Human Services; PO Box 95044; 301 Centennial Mall South—Child and Family Services Division; Lincoln, NE 68509-5044; (402) 471-9331; www.hhs.state.ne.us

ICPC ADMINISTRATOR: Nebraska Department of Health and Human Services: PO Box 95044; Lincoln, NE 68509-5044; (402) 471-9254

STATE ADOPTION EXCHANGE: Nebraska Adoption Exchange; (402) 471-9331; www.hhs.state.ne.us; mary.dyer@hhss.state.ne.us

NEBRASKA STATE BAR ASSOCIATION: (402) 475-7091; www.nebar.com

ANNUAL NUMBER OF ADOPTIVE ADOPTIONS FINALIZED IN STATE: 939

STATE LAWS AND PROCEDURES—FAST FACTS
Types permitted? Independent and agency.
Who can adopt in state? Residents.
How long after child's placement to finalize adoption in court? 7 months.
Is adoptive parent advertising (to find a birth mother) permitted? Yes.
Is a preplacement home study required? Yes.
Typical agency home study fee? $1,500–$2,500 (agency fees usually higher if agency located child).
Can adoptive parents help birth mother with expenses? Yes: legal, medical, but not living unless proved her safety requires it.
Can child leave hospital with adoptive parents? Yes, usually via attorney/agency.
When can birth mother sign her Consent to Adoption? 48 hours after birth.
Can the consent be revoked? No statutory law on the subject, but usually only if best interests of child served by denying adoption.
What are the putative father's rights? There is a registry. He is given notice of the registry and he has 5 days from notice/birth to file. If he does, he has 30 more days to file paternity action. If not, his rights terminated.

AMERICAN ACADEMY OF ADOPTION ATTORNEYS MEMBERS
Kelly N. Tollefsen; Morrow, Poppe, Otte, Watermeler, & Phillips, PC; 201 N. 8th St., #300; Lincoln, NE 68508; (402) 474-1731; www.morrowpoppelaw.com; knt@morrowpoppelaw.com
Kelly Tollefson began practicing law in 2000. She has completed 125 adoptions in her career and last year completed 62. 100% are newborn placements. 10% of her clients find a birth mother through her office.

Please be aware than some AAAA members in neighboring states also practice in Nebraska, including: John Hughes (SD) and Maxine Buckmeier (IA).

LICENSED PRIVATE AGENCIES
Adoption Links Worldwide (ALW); Omaha, NE; (402) 556-2367; www.alww.org; (Dom)
Catholic Charities; Omaha, NE; (402) 554-0520; http://mockingbird.creighton.edu/cc; (Dom)
Child Saving Institute; Omaha, NE (402) 553-6000; www.childsaving.org; (Dom)
Holt International Children's Services; Omaha, NE; (402) 934-5031; www.holtintl.org; (Intl)
Jewish Family Services; Omaha, NE; (402) 330-2024; (Dom)
Lutheran Family Services of Nebraska, Inc. (LFS of NE); Omaha, NE; (402) 661-7100; www.lfsneb.org; (Dom) (Intl) Bulgaria, China, Colombia, Guatemala, Moldova, Nepal, Philippines, Poland, Russian Federation

Nebraska Children's Home Society (NCHS); Omaha, NE; (402) 451-0787; www.nchs.org; (Dom)

Nebraska Christian Services, Inc.; Omaha, NE; (402) 334-3278; (Dom)

NEVADA

STATE ADOPTION OFFICE: Nevada Department of Human Resources; Division of Child and Family Services; 4220 S. Maryland Pkwy.—Bldg. B, Suite 300; Las Vegas, NV 89119; (702) 486-7633; www.dcfs.state.nv.us

ICPC ADMINISTRATOR: Nevada Department of Human Resources; 711 E. 5th St.; Carson City, NV 89701; (775) 684-4418; http://dcfs.state.nv.us

STATE ADOPTION EXCHANGE: Nevada Photolisting Service; Toll-free: (888) 423-2659; http://dcfs.state.nv.us

STATE BAR OF NEVADA: (702) 382-0504; www.nvbar.org

ANNUAL NUMBER OF ADOPTIVE ADOPTIONS FINALIZED IN STATE: 764

STATE LAWS AND PROCEDURES—FAST FACTS
Types permitted? Independent and agency.
Who can adopt in state? Residents only.
How long after child's placement to finalize adoption in court? 7 months.
Is adoptive parent advertising (to find a birth mother) permitted? No.
Is a preplacement home study required? Yes.
Typical agency home study fee? $8,500.
Can adoptive parents help birth mother with expenses? Yes: legal, medical, living.
Can child leave hospital with adoptive parents? Yes, if consent signed.
When can birth mother sign her Consent to Adoption? 72 hours after birth.
Can the consent be revoked? No statutory law on subject, but judges usually require finding the child's best interests served by denying adoption.
What are the putative father's rights? There is no registry. Notice to him must be attempted. If he objects the court will usually require proof the child's best interests served by denying adoption.

AMERICAN ACADEMY OF ADOPTION ATTORNEYS MEMBERS
Israel "Ishi" Kunin; 3551 E. Bonanza Rd., #110; Las Vegas, NV 89110; (702) 438-8060; ishiadoptatty@aol.com
Ishi Kunin began practicing law in 1980. She has completed 500 adoptions in her career and last year completed 21. 99% are newborn placements. 70% of her clients find a birth mother through her office.

Eric A. Stovall; 200 Ridge St., #222; Reno, NV 89501; (775) 337-1444; eric@ericstovalllaw.com
Eric Stovall began practicing law in 1987. He has completed 250 adoptions in his career and last year completed 56. 90% are newborn placements. All of his clients find their own birth mother.

LICENSED PRIVATE AGENCIES

The Adoption Alliance; Las Vegas, NV; (702) 968-1986; www.adoption-alliance.com; (Dom)

Catholic Charities of Southern Nevada (CCSN Adoption); Las Vegas, NV; (702) 385-3351; www.catholiccharities.com; (Dom) (Intl)

Catholic Community Services of Northern Nevada; Reno, NV; (775) 322-7073; www.ccsnn.org; (Dom)

LDS Family Services; Las Vegas, NV; (702) 385-1072; http://ldsfamilyservices.org; (Dom)

Premier Adoption Agency; Mesquite, NV; (702) 346-4922; www.premieradoption.org; (Dom) (Intl)

NEW HAMPSHIRE

STATE ADOPTION OFFICE: New Hampshire Department of Health and Human Services; Division for Children, Youth and Families; 129 Pleasant St.—Brown Bldg.; Concord, NH 03301; (603) 271-4707; www.dhhs.state.nh.us

ICPC ADMINISTRATOR: New Hampshire Department of Health and Human Services; (same address as above); (603) 271-4708; lbombaci@dhhs.state.nh.us

STATE ADOPTION EXCHANGE: New Hampshire Department of Health and Human Services; (same address as above); (603) 271-4707; www.dhhs.state.nh.us

NEW HAMPSHIRE BAR ASSOCIATION: (603) 224-6942; www.nhbar.org

ANNUAL NUMBER OF ADOPTIVE ADOPTIONS FINALIZED IN STATE: 630

STATE LAWS AND PROCEDURES—FAST FACTS

Types permitted? Independent and agency (60% of newborns via independent).

Who can adopt in state? Residents, and nonresidents when child born in state or the agency making the placement is located in state.

How long after child's placement to finalize adoption in court? 6 months.

Is adoptive parent advertising (to find a birth mother) permitted? Yes.

Is a preplacement home study required? Yes.

Typical agency home study fee? $800–$4,000 (agency fees usually higher if agency located child).

Can adoptive parents help birth mother with expenses? Yes: legal, medical, living.

Can child leave hospital with adoptive parents? Yes, but form required.

When can birth mother sign her Consent to Adoption? 72 hours after birth. If she is under 18, a parent must usually consent as well.

Can the consent be revoked? No, irrevocable upon signing.

What are the putative father's rights? There is a registry. His failure to register prior to birth mother consenting to adoption ends his rights.

AMERICAN ACADEMY OF ADOPTION ATTORNEYS MEMBERS

James J. Bianco Jr.; 18 Center St.; Concord, NH 03301; (603) 225-7170; www.biancopa.com; adoption@biancopa.com

James Bianco began practicing law in 1973. He has completed 500 adoptions in his career, and last year completed 20. 100% are newborn placements. 99% of his clients find a birth mother through his office.

Margaret Cunnane Hall; 37 High St.; Milford, NH 03055; (603) 673-8323; www .margaretcunnanehall.com; mchall@mchallesq.com
Margaret Hall began practicing law in 1979. She has completed 1,000 adoptions in her career and last year completed 40. 100% are newborn placements. 95% of her clients find a birth mother through her office. She is an adoptive parent.

Ann McLane Kuster; Rath, Young, and Pignatelli; 1 Capital Plaza; Concord, NH 03302; (603) 226-2600; www.rathlaw.com; amk@rathlaw.com
Ann Kuster began practicing law in 1984. She has completed 200 adoptions in her career and last year completed 12. 100% are newborn placements. 50% of her clients find a birth mother through her office.

Patricia B. Quigley; 67 Central St.; Manchester, NH 03101; (603) 644-8300; www .adoptionnh.com; patquigley@adoptionnh.com
Patricia Quigley began practicing law in 1982. She has completed 200 adoptions in her career and last year completed 25.

LICENSED PRIVATE AGENCIES
Adoptive Families for Children, Inc. (AFFC); Keene, NH; (603) 357-4456; (Dom) (Intl) Ukraine
Bethany Christian Services of New England; Candia, NH; (603) 483-2886; www .bethany.org/newengland; (Dom) (Intl) Albania, China, Colombia, Guatemala, India, Japan, Kazakhstan, Korea (South), Lithuania, Philippines, Russian Federation, Ukraine
Casey Family Services; Concord, NH; (603) 224-8909; www.caseyfamilyservices.org; (Dom)
Child and Family Services of New Hampshire; Manchester, NH; (603) 668-1920; www .cfsnh.org; (Dom)
China Adoption with Love, Inc.; Nashua, NH; Toll-free: (800) 888-9812; www .cawli.org; (Intl)
Creative Advocates for Children and Families; Manchester, NH; (603) 623-5006; (Dom)
LDS Family Services (LDSFS); Nashua, NH; (603) 889-0148; www.ldsfamilyservices .org; (Dom)
Lutheran Social Services of New England (LSS); Concord, NH; (603) 224-8111; www .adoptlss.org; (Intl) China, Russian Federation
New Hampshire Catholic Charities, Inc.; Manchester, NH; (603) 669-3030; www .catholiccharitiesnh.org; (Dom)
New Hope Christian Services; Rumney, NH; (603) 225-0992; www.christianadoptions .net/index.html; (Intl) Romania, Russian Federation, Ukraine

Wide Horizons for Children; Bedford, NH; (603) 792-2030; www.whfc.org; (Dom) (Intl) China, Colombia, Ethiopia, Guatemala, India, Korea (South), Philippines, Russian Federation

NEW JERSEY

STATE ADOPTION OFFICE: New Jersey Department of Human Services; Office of Resource Families and Adoption Support; 50 E. State St.; PO Box 717; Trenton, NJ 08625; (609) 984-6080; www.state.nj.us

ICPC ADMINISTRATOR: New Jersey Department of Human Services; Interstate Services Unit; 225 S. Warren St.; PO Box 700; Trenton, NJ 08625; (609) 292-3188; www.state.nj.us

STATE ADOPTION EXCHANGE: New Jersey Division of Youth and Family Services Adoption Exchange; (609) 984-5453; www.state.nj.us

NEW JERSEY STATE BAR ASSOCIATION: (732) 249-5000; www.njsba.com

ANNUAL NUMBER OF ADOPTIVE ADOPTIONS FINALIZED IN STATE: 2,384

STATE LAWS AND PROCEDURES—FAST FACTS
Types permitted? Independent and agency.
Who can adopt in state? Residents, and nonresidents when child born in state or the agency making the placement is located in state.
How long after the child's placement to finalize the adoption in court? 6–9 months.
Is adoptive parent advertising (to find a birth mother) permitted? Yes.
Is a preplacement home study required? Yes.
Typical home study fee? $1,500–$2,500 (agency fees usually higher if agency located child).
Can adoptive parents help birth mother with expenses? Yes: legal, medical, living.
Can child leave hospital with adoptive parents? Many placements made directly outside of hospital in independent adoption.
When can birth mother sign her Consent to Adoption? Independent—anytime after the birth. Agency—72 hours after birth.
Can the consent be revoked? Independent—yes, until either birth parent appears before a judge and agrees to termination of rights, usually about 2 weeks postbirth; or not appear and have rights terminated at a preliminary hearing, usually about 2 months postbirth. Agency—no, it is irrevocable upon signing.
What are the putative father's rights? There is no registry. Notice must be attempted on him and he has 120 days to object or get named on birth certificate. He can stop adoption if he proves his fitness and that adoption not in best interests of child.
Note: Attorneys cannot charge a fee to find birth mothers to create adoptive matches.

AMERICAN ACADEMY OF ADOPTION ATTORNEYS MEMBERS:

Donald C. Cofsky; Cofsky & Zeidman, LLC; 209 Haddon Ave.; Haddonfield, NJ 08033; (856) 429-5005; www.209law.com; dcc@209law.com
Donald Cofsky began practicing law in 1973. He has completed 1,500 adoptions in his career and last year completed 90. 80% are newborn placements. All of his clients find their own birth mother. He was a recipient of 2005 Congressional Angel in Adoption award.

Robin Fleischner; 374 Millburn Ave., #303E; Millburn, NJ 07041; (973) 376-6623; www.adoptlawyer.com; robin@adoptlawyer.com
Robin Fleischner began practicing law in 1980. She has completed 1,000 adoptions in her career and last year completed 50. 100% are newborn placements. 50% of her clients find a birth mother through her office. She is an adoptive parent.

Elizabeth A. Hopkins; Peter J. Liska, LLC; 766 Shrewsbury Ave.; Tinton Falls, NJ 07724; (732) 933-7777; www.peterliska.com; liz@peterliska.com
Elizabeth Hopkins began practicing law in 1984. 60% of her adoptions are newborn placements. All of her clients find their own birth mother.

James W. Miskowski; 45 N. Broad St.; Ridgewood, NJ 07450; (800) 213-7441; jwm4600@aol.com
James Miskowski began practicing law in 1974. He has completed 2,000 adoptions in his career and last year completed 65. 95% are newborn placements. 50% of his clients find a birth mother through his office. He is an adoptive parent.

Toby Solomon; 5 Becker Farm Rd.; Roseland, NJ 07068; (973) 533-0078; www.tobysolomon.com; tsolomon@tobysolomon.com
Toby Solomon began practicing law in 1983. She is a past chairperson of the Adoption Subcommittee of the New Jersey Family Law State Bar.

Deborah Steincolor; 295 Montgomery St.; Bloomfield, NJ 07003; (973) 743-7500; dsteincolor@aol.com
Deborah Steincolor began practicing law in 1987. She has completed 1,800 adoptions in her career and last year completed 73. 100% are newborn placements.

Harlan S. Tenenbaum; 55 Spruce St.; Princeton, NJ 08542; (609) 497-9393; tenenbaum@aol.com
Harlan Tenenbaum began practicing law in 1994. He has completed 600 adoptions in his career and last year completed 86. He has adoption programs in China, Guatemala, Russia, and Kazakhstan. He is the chairperson of the American Bar Association Adoption Committee.

Biographies were not available for the following AAAA members:

Craig B. Bluestein; 1 Greentree Ctr., #201; Marlton, NJ 08053; (609) 988-5513; c.bluestein@adoptionattorneys.org

Steven B. Sacharow; 1810 Chapel Ave. West; Cherry Hill, NJ 08002; (856) 661-1919; s.sacharow@adoptionattorneys.org

LICENSED PRIVATE AGENCIES

Adoption Services, Inc.; Westmont, NJ; (717) 737-3960; http://adoptionservices.org; (Dom) (Intl) China, Guatemala, Russian Federation

Adoptions from the Heart; Cherry Hill, NJ; (856) 665-5655; www.adoptionsfromthe heart.org; (Dom) (Intl) China, Ecuador, Guatemala, India, Kazakhstan, Mongolia, Ukraine, Vietnam

Adoptions from the Heart; Hazlet, NJ; (732) 335-8883; www.adoptionsfromtheheart .org; (Dom) (Intl) China, Ecuador, Guatemala, India, Kazakhstan, Mongolia, Ukraine, Vietnam

Bethany Christian Services; Midland Park, NJ; (201) 444-7775; www.bethany.org/ newjersey; (Dom) (Intl)

Better Living Services; Westfield, NJ; (908) 654-0277; (Dom)

Catholic Charities; Burlington, NJ; (609) 386-6221; www.catholiccharitiestrenton .org; (Dom) (Intl)

Catholic Charities; Perth Amboy, NJ; (732) 324-8200; www.ccdom.org; (Dom) (Intl)

Catholic Charities; Vineland, NJ; (856) 691-1841; (Dom)

Catholic Community Services of Newark; Kearny, NJ; (201)246-7378; www.ccsnewark .org; (Dom) (Intl)

Catholic Family and Community Services (Adoption & Counseling Services); Paterson, NJ; (973) 523-9595; www.cfcsadoptions.org; (Dom) (Intl) China, Colombia, Ecuador, Guatemala, India, Kazakhstan, Korea (South), Moldova, Peru, Philippines, Republic of Georgia, Romania, Russian Federation, Sierra Leone, Ukraine

Children's Aid and Family Services, Inc.; Cedar Knolls, NJ; (973) 285-0165; www.cafsnj .org; (Dom)

Children's Aid and Family Services, Inc.; Paramus, NJ; (201) 226-0300; www.cafsnj.org; (Dom) (Intl) Bulgaria

Children's Home Society of New Jersey; Trenton, NJ; (609) 695-6274; www.chsofnj.org; (Dom) (Intl)

Children of the World; Verona, NJ; (973) 239-0100; (Intl)

Downey Side, Inc.; Point Pleasant Beach, NJ; (609) 538-8200; www.downeyside.org; (Dom)

Family and Children's Services; Elizabeth, NJ; (908) 352-7474; (Dom)

Family Options; Red Bank, NJ; (732) 936-0770; www.adoptionsbyfamilyoptions.org; (Dom) (Intl) China, Korea (South), Russian Federation

Golden Cradle Adoption Services, Inc.; Cherry Hill, NJ; (856) 667-2229; www.golden cradle.org; (Dom) (Intl) China, Georgia, Guatemala, Russian Federation

Growing Families Worldwide Adoption Agency, Inc.; Parlin, NJ; (732) 525-2067; www .gfwaa.org; (Dom) (Intl)

Holt International Children's Services; Trenton, NJ; (609) 882-4972; www.holtintl.org; (Intl)

Homestudies & Adoption Placement Services, Inc. (HAPS); Teaneck, NJ; (201) 836-5554; www.haps.org; (Dom) (Intl) China, Guatemala, Kazakhstan, Russian Federation

Jewish Family and Children's Services of Southern New Jersey (JFCS); Mount Laurel, NJ; (856) 778-7775; www.jfcssnj.org; (Dom) (Intl)

Jewish Family Service of Metro West; Florham Park, NJ; (973) 765-9050; www.jfs-metronj.org;

Jewish Family Services of Monmouth County; Asbury Park, NJ; (732) 774-6886; www.jfcsmonmouth.org; (Dom)

A Loving Choice Adoption Associates; Shrewsbury, NJ; (732) 224-0924; (Dom)

Lutheran Social Ministries of New Jersey; Burlington, NJ; (609) 386-7171; www.lsmnj.org; (Dom)

Reaching Out Thru International Adoption (ROTIA); Somerdale, NJ; (856) 435-2222; www.adoptachild.us; (Intl) Azerbaijan, China, Guatemala, Japan, Kazakhstan, Lesotho, Nepal, Taiwan, Ukraine, Vietnam

Seedlings, Inc.; Whippany, NJ; (973) 884-7488; www.seedlings-inc.org; (Intl)

Small World Agency; Palmyra, NJ; (856) 829-2769; www.swa.net; (Dom) (Intl)

Spence-Chapin Services to Families and Children; Summit, NJ; (908) 522-0043; www.spence-chapin.org; (Dom) (Intl)

Welcome House Adoption Program (of Pearl S. Buck International) (PSBI); Sicklerville, NJ; (856) 952-6268; (Intl)

Wide Horizons for Children (WHFC); Plainfield, NJ; (908) 756-3000; www.whfc.org; (Dom) (Intl) China, Colombia, Ethiopia, Guatemala, India, Lithuania, Moldova, Republic of Korea, Republic of Moldova, Russian Federation, Ukraine

Youth Consultation Services (YCS); East Orange, NJ; (973) 395-0801; www.ycs.org; (Dom)

NEW MEXICO

STATE ADOPTION OFFICE: New Mexico Department of Children, Youth and Families (DCYF); PERA Bldg., Room 254; PO Drawer 5160; Santa Fe, NM 87502-5160; (505) 827-8455; www.cyfd.org

ICPC ADMINISTRATOR: New Mexico Department of Children, Youth and Families; (same address as above); (505) 827-8457; (505) 827-8480

STATE ADOPTION EXCHANGE: New Mexico Department of Children, Youth and Families; (same address as above); www.cyfd.org; mjruttkay@cyfd.state.nm.us

STATE BAR OF NEW MEXICO: (505) 797-6066; www.nmbar.org

ANNUAL NUMBER OF ADOPTIVE ADOPTIONS FINALIZED IN STATE: 680

STATE LAWS AND PROCEDURES—FAST FACTS

Types permitted? Independent and agency (65% of newborns via independent).

Who can adopt in state? Residents, and nonresidents when child born in state or the agency making the placement is located in state.

How long after the child's placement to finalize the adoption in court? 4 months.

Is adoptive parent advertising (to find a birth mother) permitted? Yes.

Is a preplacement home study required? Yes.

Typical home study fee? $1,500–$2,500 (agency fees usually higher if agency located child).

Can adoptive parents help birth mother with expenses? Yes: legal, medical, living, but must be paid directly to provider of services, not to birth mother.

Can child leave hospital with adoptive parents? Yes, with signed form.

When can birth mother sign her Consent to Adoption? 48 hours after birth.

Can the consent be revoked? No, it is irrevocable upon signing.

What are the putative father's rights? There is a registry. Notice must be attempted if he registered within 10 days of birth or was named by birth mother. If he filed paternity action or listed with registry within 10 days, his consent is required. If not, his rights can be severed by showing adoption is in best interests of child.

AMERICAN ACADEMY OF ADOPTION ATTORNEYS MEMBERS

Harold O. Atencio; Atencio Law Office, PC; PO Box 66468; Albuquerque, NM 87193; (505) 839-9111; adopt@atenciolawpc.com
Harold Atencio began practicing law in 1988. He has completed 500 adoptions in his career and last year completed 52. 99% are newborn placements. All of his clients find their own birth mothers.

Lisa H. Olewine; 4801 Lang, #110; Albuquerque, NM 87199; (505) 858-3316; adoptionlaw@msn.com
Lisa Olewine began practicing law in 2001. She is an adoptive parent.

Ross S. Randall; 2416 Camino De Vida; Santa Fe, NM 87505; (505) 424-0322; randallawnm@msn.com
Ross Randall began practicing law in 1968. 90% of his adoptions are newborn placements. He is an adoptive and foster parent.

LICENSED PRIVATE AGENCIES

AAA Adoption Assistance Agency; Albuquerque, NM; (505) 821-7779; www.adoption assistanceagency.org; (Dom)

Adoptions Plus; Albuquerque, NM; (505) 323-6002; www.adoptionsplus.org; (Dom) (Intl)

Catholic Charities; Albuquerque, NM; (505) 724-4670; http://ccasfnm.org; (Dom)

Catholic Charities; Santa Fe, NM; (505) 424-9789; www.catholiccharitiesasf.org/santafe/adoption.htm; (Dom) (Intl)

Catholic Charities; Santa Rosa, NM; (505) 472-5938; http://catholiccharitiesasf.org; (Dom) (Intl) China, Guatemala

Child-Rite, Inc.; Taos, NM; (505) 758-0343; www.childrite.org; (Dom)

Families for Children; Albuquerque, NM; (505) 881-4200; (Dom)

Family Matters: Adoption Resources; Albuquerque, NM; (505) 344-8811; (Dom) (Intl)
Brazil, China, Ethiopia, Guatemala, Korea (South), Ukraine

LDS Family Services; Albuquerque, NM; (505) 345-3046; (Dom)

LDS Family Services; Farmington, NM; (505) 327-6123; http://ldsfamilyservices.org;
(Dom)

La Familia, Inc.; Albuquerque, NM; (505) 766-9361; www.la-familia-inc.org; (Dom)
(Intl)

New Mexico Christian Children's Home; Portales, NM; (505) 356-4232; www.nmcch
.org; (Dom)

New Mexico Parent and Child Resources, Inc.; Albuquerque, NM; (505) 858-3028; www
.nmpcr.org; (Dom)

Rainbow House International; Belen, NM; (505) 861-1234; www.rhi.org; (Intl)

NEW YORK

STATE ADOPTION OFFICE: New York State Office of Children and Family Services (OCFS);
New York State Adoption Service; 52 Washington St., Room 323; Rensselaer,
NY 12144; (518) 473-5754; www.ocfs.state.ny.us

ICPC ADMINISTRATOR: New York State Office of Children and Family Services; (same
address as above); (518) 473-1591; (518) 486-6326; www.ocfs.state.ny.us/
adopt

STATE ADOPTION EXCHANGE: New York State Office of Children and Family Services;
(same address as above); (518) 473-5754; www.ocfs.state.ny.us; carol.mccarthy
@dfa.state.ny.us

NEW YORK STATE BAR ASSOCIATION: (518) 463-3200; www.nysba.org

STATE LAWS AND PROCEDURES—FAST FACTS

Types permitted? Independent and agency (70% of newborns via independent).

Who can adopt in state? Residents, and nonresidents when child born in state or the
agency making the placement is located in state.

How long after the child's placement to finalize the adoption in court? 3–12
months.

Is adoptive parent advertising (to find a birth mother) permitted? Yes.

Is a preplacement home study required? Yes.

Typical home study fee? $850–$2,000 (agency fees usually higher if agency located
child).

Can adoptive parents help birth mother with expenses? Yes: legal, medical. Living
assistance can only be for 2 months prebirth and 1 month postbirth unless court
approves more.

Can child leave hospital with adoptive parents? Yes, with signed form.

When can birth mother sign her Consent to Adoption? Anytime after birth.

Can the consent be revoked? No, if consent witnessed by judge it is irrevocable.

Other options: If witnessed by a notary (independent adoption) it is revocable for 45 days if a judge finds the child's best interests served by stopping adoption. If witnessed by an agency social worker (agency adoption), the revocation period is 30 days rather than 45.

What are the putative father's rights? There is a registry. Notice must be attempted if he registers, or is named by birth mother. To stop adoption he must prove adoption is not in best interests of child.

AMERICAN ACADEMY OF ADOPTION ATTORNEYS MEMBERS

Anne Reynolds Copps; 126 State St.; Albany, NY 12207; (518) 436-4170; www .arcopps.net; arcopps@nycap.rr.com
Anne Copps began practicing law in 1982. She has completed 1,000 adoptions in her career and last year completed 200. 50% are newborn placements.

Robin Fleischner; 11 Riverside Dr., #14NW; New York, NY 10023; (212) 362-6945; www.adoptlawyer.com; robin@adoptlawyer.com
Robin Fleischner began practicing law in 1980. She has completed 1,000 adoptions in her career and last year completed 50. 100% are newborn placements. She is an adoptive parent.

Gregory A. Franklin; Ashcraft, Franklin & Young, LLP; 95 Allens Creek Rd., Bldg. 1, #202; Rochester, NY 14618; (585) 442-0540; www.adoptionny.com; gfranklin@ afylaw.com
Gregory Franklin began practicing law in 1984. He has completed 1,200 adoptions in his career and last year completed 50. 80% are newborn placements. He is an adoptive parent.

Laurie B. Goldheim; 20 Old Nyack Tpke., #300; Nanuet, NY 10954; (845) 624-2727; www.adoptionrights.com; lgoldheim@adoptionrights.com
Laurie Goldheim began practicing law in 1990. She has completed 1,200 adoptions in her career and last year completed 80. 100% are newborn placements. She is an adoptee.

Michael S. Goldstein; 262 W. End Ave., Suite 1A; New York, NY 10023; (914) 939-1111; www.adoptgold.com; info@adoptgold.com
Michael Goldstein began practicing law in 1982. He has completed 2,200 adoptions in his career and last year completed 100. 95% are newborn placements. He is an adoptive parent and a recipient of the Congressional Angel in Adoption award in 2006.

Kevin P. Harrigan; Harrigan & Dolan; 2 Clinton Sq., #215; Syracuse, NY 13202; (315) 478-3138; kevharr@twcny.rr.com
Kevin Harrigan began practicing law in 1978. He has completed 1,100 adoptions in his career and last year completed 91. 80% are newborn placements.

Flory G. Herman; 47 Plaza Dr.; Williamsville, NY 14221; (716) 639-3900; www .adoptionstar.com; f.herman@adoptionattorneys.org
Flory Herman began practicing law in 1989. She has completed 125 adoptions

in her career and is counsel to Adoption STAR. She produced and directed the documentary film "I Have Roots and Branches": Personal Reflections on Adoption.

Frederick J. Magovern; Magovern & Sclafani; 111 John St.; New York, NY 10038; (212) 962-1450; f.magovern@adoptionattorneys.org
Frederick Magovern began practicing law in 1972. He has completed 500 adoptions in his career.

Cynthia Perla Meckler; 8081 Floss Ln.; East Amherst, NY 14051; (716) 741-4164; c.meckler@adoptionattorneys.org
Cynthia Meckler began practicing law in 1980. She has completed 600 adoptions in her career and last year completed 30. 90% are newborn placements.

Suzanne B. Nichols; Rosenstock Lowe & Nichols; 70 W. Red Oak Ln.; White Plains, NY 10604; (914) 697-4870; adoptnpro@aol.com
Suzanne Nichols began practicing law in 1985. She has completed 1,000 adoptions in her career and last year completed 40. 70% are newborn placements.

Brendan C. O'Shea; Gleason, Dunn, Walsh, & O'Shea; 40 Beaver St.; Albany, NY 12207; (518) 432-7511; boshea@gdwo.net
Brendan O'Shea began practicing law in 1980. He has completed 1,000 adoptions in his career and last year completed 85, domestic and intercountry.

Douglas H. Reiniger; 630 3rd Ave.; New York, NY 10017; (212) 972-5430; d.reiniger @adoptionattorneys.org
Douglas Reiniger began practicing law in 1981. He has completed 1,000 adoptions in his career and last year completed 18. 90% are newborn placements. He is a past president of the American Academy of Adoption Attorneys.

Benjamin J. Rosin; Rosin, Steinhagen, & Mendal; 630 3rd Ave.; New York, NY 10017; (212) 972-5430; brosin@lawrsm.com
Benjamin Rosin began practicing law in 1966. He has completed 1,000 adoptions in his career and last year completed 30. 85% are newborn placements, 15% are toddlers or above. He is an adoptive parent.

Nina E. Rumbold; Rumbold & Seidelman; 1145 Baldwin Rd.; Yorktown Heights, NY 10598; (914) 962-3001; www.adoptionlawny.com
Nina Rumbold began practicing law in 1978. Last year she completed approximately 50 adoptions. 95% are newborn placements.

Denise Seidelman; Rumbold & Seidelman; 1145 Baldwin Rd.; Yorktown Heights, NY 10598; (914) 962-3001; www.adoptionlawny.com; dseidelman@adoption lawny.com
Denise Seidelman began practicing law in 1980. She has completed 500 adoptions in her career and last year completed 50. 95% are newborn placements.

Deborah Steincolor; 845 3rd Ave., #1400; New York, NY 10022; (212) 421-7807; dsteincolor@aol.com

Deborah Steincolor began practicing law in 1987. She has completed 1,800 adoptions in her career and last year completed 73. 100% are newborn placements.

Golda Zimmerman; 711 E. Genesee St., #200; Syracuse, NY 13210; (315) 475-3322; g.zimmerman@adoptionattorneys.org
Golda Zimmerman began practicing law in 1980. She is an adoptive parent.

Biographies were not available for the following AAAA members:
Stephen Lewin; 845 3rd Ave., #1400; New York, NY 10022; (212) 759-2600; s.lewin @adoptionattorneys.org

Rebecca L. Mendel; 630 3rd Ave.; New York, NY 10017; (212) 972-5430; r.mendel @adoptionattorneys.org

LICENSED PRIVATE AGENCIES

ABSW Child Adoption, Counseling and Referral Service; New York, NY; (212) 831-5181; (Dom)

Adoption and Counseling Services, Inc.; Syracuse, NY; (315) 471-0109; (Dom)

Advocates for Adoption, Inc.; New York, NY; (212) 957-3938; www.advocatesfor adoption.com; (Dom)

Adoptions from the Heart; Clifton Park, NY; (518) 371-4782; www.adoptionsfromthe heart.org; (Dom) (Intl) China, Ecuador, Guatemala, India, Kazakhstan, Mongolia, Ukraine, Vietnam

Adoption House, Inc.; Lindenhurst, NY; (516) 921-1102; www.adoptionhouse.org; (Dom) (Intl)

Adoption Services, Inc.; Vestal, NY; (717) 737-3960; http://adoptionservices.org; (Dom) (Intl) China, Guatemala, Russian Federation

Adoption STAR (Support, Training, Advocacy and Resources), Inc.; Williamsville, NY; (716) 639-3900; www.adoptionstar.com; (Dom)

ARISE Child and Family Services; Syracuse, NY; (315) 472-3171; www.ariseinc.org/ default.tpl; (Dom)

Association to Benefit Children (ABC); New York, NY; (212) 831-1322; www.a-b-c.org; (Dom)

Baker Victory Services; Lackawanna, NY; (716) 828-9510; www.bakervictoryservices .org; (Dom) (Intl)

Berkshire Farms Center and Family Services for Youth; Canaan, NY; (518) 781-4567; www.berkshirefarm.org; (Dom)

Bethany Christian Services; Warwick, NY; (845) 987-1453; www.bethany.org/war wick_ny; (Dom) (Intl) Albania, Bulgaria, China, Colombia, Ecuador, Guatemala, India, Japan, Korea (South), Lithuania, Philippines, Romania, Russian Federation, Ukraine,

Buffalo Urban League, Inc.; Buffalo, NY; (716) 854-7625; www.buffalourbanleague .org; (Dom)

Cardinal McCloskey Services; White Plains, NY; (914) 997-8000; www.cardinalmc closkeyservices.org; (Dom)

Catholic Charities of Buffalo; Buffalo, NY; (716) 856-4494; www.ccwny.org; (Dom)

Catholic Charities of Cortland; Cortland, NY; (607) 756-5992; (Dom)
Catholic Charities of Ogdensburg; Ogdensburg, NY; (315) 393-2255; (Dom)
Catholic Charities of Oneida and Madison Counties; Utica, NY; (315) 724-2158; (Dom)
Catholic Charities of Plattsburgh; Plattsburgh, NY; (518) 561-0470; (Dom)
Catholic Charities of Rome; Rome, NY; (315) 337-8600; (Dom)
Catholic Charities of Syracuse; Syracuse, NY; (315) 424-1840; (Dom)
Catholic Family Center; Rochester, NY; (585) 546-7220; www.cfcrochester.org; (Dom)
    (Intl)
Catholic Guardian Society of New York; Bronx, NY; (718) 828-0300; (Dom) (Intl)
Catholic Home Bureau for Dependent Children (CHB); New York, NY; (212) 371-1000;
    http://chbmaternity.org; (Dom)
Catholic Social Services of Broome County; Binghamton, NY; (607) 729-9166; www
    .catholiccharitiesbc.org;
Child and Family Adoption, Inc.; Highland, NY; (845) 691-4520; (Dom)
Child and Family Services of Erie; Buffalo, NY; (716) 882-0555; www.childfamilybny
    .org; (Dom)
Child Development Support Corporation; Brooklyn, NY; (718) 230-0056; (Dom)
Children at Heart Adoption Services, Inc.; Mechanicville, NY; (518) 664-5988; www
    .childrenatheart.com; (Intl) Brazil, Kazakhstan
Children of the World Adoption Agency, Inc. (CWAANY); Syosset, NY; (516) 935-1235;
    http://cwaany.org; (Intl) Romania, Russian Federation
Children's Aid Society (CAS); New York, NY; (212) 949-4961; www.childrensaid
    society.org; (Dom)
Children's Home of Poughkeepsie; Poughkeepsie, NY; (845) 452-1420; www.childrens
    home.us; (Dom)
Children's Hope International (CHI); New York City, NY; (212) 244-2062; www
    .childrenshope.com; (Intl) China, Colombia, Kazakhstan, Russian Federation,
    Vietnam
Children's Village (CV); New York, NY; (212) 932-9009; www.childrensvillage.org;
    (Dom)
Coalition for Hispanic Family Services; Brooklyn, NY; (718) 497-6090; (Dom)
Community Counseling and Mediation (CCM-FCAP); Brooklyn, NY; (718) 875-7751;
    http://ccmnyc.org; (Dom)
Community Maternity Services; Albany, NY; (518) 482-8836; www.cccms.com; (Dom)
Concord Family Services, Inc.; Brooklyn, NY; (718) 398-3499; (Dom)
Downey Side Families for Youth; New York, NY; (212) 714-2200; www.downeyside
    .org; (Dom)
Dunbar Association, Inc.; Syracuse, NY; (315) 476-4269; (Dom)
Edwin Gould Services for Children and Families; New York, NY; (212) 598-0050; www
    .egscf.org; (Dom)
Episcopal Social Service (ESS); New York, NY; (212) 886-5649; www.episcopal
    socialservices.org; (Dom)
Family Connections; Cortland, NY; (607) 756-6574; (Dom)
Family Focus Adoption Services; Little Neck, NY; (718) 224-1919; http://familyfocus
    adoption.org; (Dom)

Family Services of Westchester, Inc.; Port Chester, NY; (914) 937-2320; www.fsw.org; (Dom) (Intl)

Family and Children's Agency, Inc. (FCA); Larchmont, NY; (914) 834-5806; www.family andchildrensagency.org; (Dom) (Intl) China, Korea (South), Russian Federation, Taiwan, Ukraine

Family and Children's Services of Broome County; Binghamton, NY; (607) 729-6206; www.familyandchildrenssociety.org; (Dom) (Intl)

Family and Children's Services of Ithaca; Ithaca, NY; (607) 273-7494; www.fcsith.org; (Dom)

Family Tree Adoption Agency; Clifton Park, NY; (518) 371-1336; www.familytree adoption.org/international.htm; (Dom) (Intl) China, Guatemala, Kazakhstan, Russian Federation, Ukraine

Forestdale, Inc.; Forest Hills, NY; (718) 263-0740; www.forestdaleinc.org; (Dom)

Gateway-Longview; Buffalo, NY; (716) 882-8468; www.gateway-longview.org; (Dom)

Good Shepherd Services; Bronx, NY; (212) 243-7070; www.goodshepherds.org; (Dom)

Graham's Gift; Grand Island, NY; (716) 775-6715; (Dom)

Graham-Windham Child Care; Bronx, NY; (212) 529-6445; www.graham-windham .org/index.html; (Dom)

Hale House Center, Inc.; New York, NY; (212) 663-0700; www.halehouse.org; (Dom)

Happy Families International Center, Inc.; Cold Spring, NY; (845) 265-9272; www .happyfamilies.org; (Intl) Armenia, Azerbaijan, Guatemala, Kazakhstan, Russian Federation, Ukraine

Harlem-Dowling Children Services; New York, NY; (212) 749-3656; (Dom)

Heartshare Human Services; Brooklyn, NY; (718) 422-4200; www.heartshare.org; (Dom)

Hillside Children's Center (HCC); Rochester, NY; (585) 654-4528; www.hillside.com/ who/hcc.htm; (Dom) (Intl)

Hillside Children's Center; West Seneca, NY; (716) 848-6405; (Dom) (Intl)

Ibero American Action League, Inc.; Rochester, NY; (585) 256-8900; www.iaal.org/en/ index.htm; (Dom)

Jewish Board of Family and Children's Services, Inc.; New York, NY; (212) 582-9100; www.jbfcs.org; (Dom)

Jewish Child Care Association; New York, NY; (212) 558-9949; www.jccany.org/ adoption/adoption.asp; (Dom)

Jewish Family Services of Erie County; Buffalo, NY; (716) 883-1914; www.jfsbuffalo .org; (Dom)

Jewish Family Services of Rochester (JFS); Rochester, NY; (585) 461-0110; www.jfs rochester.org; (Dom) (Intl)

Karing Angels International Adoptions, Inc.; Oceanside, NY; (516) 764-9563; www .KaringAngelsIntl.org; (Intl) Guatemala, Kazakhstan

Lakeside Family and Children's Services; Brooklyn, NY; (718) 237-9700; www.lakeside family.org; (Dom)

LDS Family Services of New York; Poughkeepsie, NY; (914) 462-1288; (Dom)

Leake and Watts Children's Home; Yonkers, NY; (914) 375-8700; (Dom)
Little Flower Children's Services; Brooklyn, NY; Toll-free: (800) 323-0316; www.little
  flowerny.org; (Dom)
Lutheran Service Society of New York (LSS of NY); Williamsville, NY; (716) 631-9212;
  www.lssofny.org; (Dom) (Intl) Poland
Lutheran Social Services, Inc.; New York, NY; (212) 784-8935; (Dom)
MercyFirst; Brooklyn, NY; (718) 232-1500; www.mercyfirst.org; (Dom)
Miracle Makers, Inc.; Brooklyn, NY; (718) 483-3000; (Dom)
New Alternatives for Children (NAC); New York, NY; (212) 696-1550; www.nac-inc
  .org; (Dom)
New Beginnings Family and Children's Services, Inc.; Mineola, NY; (516) 747-2204;
  www.new-beginnings.org; (Intl) China, Korea (South), Peru, Russian Federa-
  tion, Thailand, Vietnam
New Hope Family Services; Syracuse, NY; (315) 437-8300; www.newhopefamily
  services.com; (Dom)
New Life Adoption Agency; Syracuse, NY; (315) 422-7300; www.newlifeadoption.org;
  (Dom) (Intl) China
New Life International, Inc.; Brooklyn, NY; (718) 787-1284; (Intl)
New York Council on Adoptable Children (COAC); New York, NY; (212) 475-0222; www
  .coac.org; (Dom)
New York Foundling Hospital; New York, NY; (212) 727-6810; www.nyfoundling.org;
  (Dom)
Ohel Children's Home and Family Services; Brooklyn, NY; (718) 851-6300; www.ohel
  family.org; (Dom)
Parsons Child and Family Center; Albany, NY; (518) 426-2600; www.parsonscenter
  .org; (Dom)
Pius XII Youth/Family Services; Bronx, NY; (718) 562-7855; (Dom)
Protestant Board of Guardians; Brooklyn, NY; (718) 636-8103; (Dom)
Salvation Army Foster Home; New York, NY; (212) 807-6100; www.salvationarmy-
  newyork.org/index.htm; (Dom)
SCO Family of Services; Glenn Cove, NY; (516) 759-1844; (Dom)
Seamen's Society for Children and Families; Staten Island, NY; www.roots-wings.org;
  (Dom)
Sheltering Arms Children's Services; New York, NY; (646) 442-0313; (Dom)
Small World Charity, Inc.; New York, NY; (212) 629-4008; www.smallworldcharity
  .org; (Intl)
Spence-Chapin Services to Families and Children; New York, NY; (212) 369-0300;
  www.spence-chapin.org; (Dom) (Intl) Bulgaria, China, Colombia, Ecuador,
  Guatemala, India, Kazakhstan, Korea (South), Moldova, Russian Federation,
  Vietnam
St. Augustine Center; Buffalo, NY; (716) 881-3700; www.sac-inc.org; (Dom)
St. Christopher Ottilie; Glen Cove, NY; (516) 671-1253; www.stchristopher-ottilie
  .org; (Dom)
St. Christopher's—Jennie Clarkson Child Care Services, Inc.; Dobbs Ferry, NY; (914) 693-
  3030; www.watpa.org/sc/sc.html; (Dom)

St. Dominic's Home; Bronx, NY; (718) 993-5765; www.stdominicshome.org; (Dom)
St. Vincent's Services; Brooklyn, NY; (718) 522-2318; www.svs.org/default.shtm;
(Dom)
Urban League of Rochester, Inc.; Rochester, NY; (585) 325-6530; (Dom)
Voice for International Development and Adoption (VIDA); Hudson, NY; (518) 828-4527;
www.vidaadopt.org; (Intl) Bolivia, Bulgaria, China, Colombia, Guatemala,
Honduras, Japan, Peru, Philippines
Wide Horizons for Children (WHFC); Oyster Bay, NY; (516) 922-0751; www.whfc.org;
(Dom) (Intl) China, Colombia, Ethiopia, Guatemala, India, Kazakhstan, Korea
(South), Philippines, Russian Federation
You Gotta Believe!; Brooklyn, NY; (718) 372-3003; www.yougottabelieve.org; (Dom)

NORTH CAROLINA

STATE ADOPTION OFFICE: North Carolina Division of Social Services; Division of
Social Services; 325 North Salisbury St., Suite 715–2409 Mail Service Center;
Raleigh, NC 27699-2409; (919) 733-9464; www.dhhs.state.nc.us/dss/adopt

ICPC ADMINISTRATOR: North Carolina Division of Social Services; (same address as
above); (919) 733-9464; (919) 733-3052; www.dhhs.state.nc.us/dss/adopt

STATE ADOPTION EXCHANGE: North Carolina Kids Adoption and Foster Care Network;
330 S. Greene St., Suite 200; Greensboro, NC 27401; (336) 217-9770; www
.adoptuskids.org; nckids@uncg.edu

NORTH CAROLINA BAR ASSOCIATION: (919) 677-8574; www.ncbar.org

ANNUAL NUMBER OF ADOPTIVE ADOPTIONS FINALIZED IN STATE: 2,328

STATE LAWS AND PROCEDURES—FAST FACTS
Types permitted? Independent and agency (80% of newborns via independent).
Who can adopt in state? Residents only.
How long after the child's placement to finalize the adoption in court? 6 months.
Is adoptive parent advertising (to find a birth mother) permitted? Yes.
Is a preplacement home study required? Yes.
Typical home study fee? $2,000–$3,400 or sliding scale via state (agency fees usu-
ally higher if agency located child).
Can adoptive parents help birth mother with expenses? Yes: legal, medical, living.
Can child leave hospital with adoptive parents? Yes.
When can birth mother sign her Consent to Adoption? Anytime after birth.
Can the consent be revoked? Yes, for 7 days, plus an extra 5 days in indepen-
dent adoption if the home study is not delivered to birth mother before the
placement.
What are the putative father's rights? There is no registry. Notice must be attempted
and he usually has 30 days to object. To stop adoption he must prove he acknowl-
eged paternity, communicated with the birth mother, and provided support,
before Petition for Adoption was filed.

AMERICAN ACADEMY OF ADOPTION ATTORNEYS MEMBERS

Bobby D. Mills; Herring McBennet; 2 Hannover Sq., #1860; Raleigh, NC 27601; (919) 821-1860; www.hermcb.com; bmills@hermcb.com
Bobby Mills began practicing law in 1985. He completed 80 adoptions last year. 95% are newborn placements. 50% of his clients find a birth mother through his office.

W. David Thurman; Thurman, Wilson, & Boutwell, PA; 301 S. McDowell St., #608; Charlotte, NC 28204; (704) 377-4164; www.thurmanwilsonboutwell.com; w.thurman@adoptionattorneys.org
David Thurman began practicing law in 1983. He has completed 2,500 in his career and last year completed 108. 85% are newborn placements. His clients find their own birth mother.

Brinton D. Wright; Brinton & Cone; 324 W. Wendover Ave., #107; Greensboro, NC 27408; (336) 373-1500; b.wright@adoptionattorneys.com
Brinton Wright began practicing law in 1976. He has completed 1,000 adoptions in his career and last year completed 80. 95% are newborn placements, His clients find their own birth mother. He is an adoptive parent.

LICENSED PRIVATE AGENCIES

Adoption Resource Center, Inc.; Raleigh, NC; (910) 872-0031; www.adoptresource .org; (Intl) China, Guatemala, Korea (South), Russian Federation, Ukraine

ADOPTIONS by Julia Childers, Ph.D, LCSW; Newton, NC; (828) 465-7005; www .adoptionsagency.com; (Dom)

AGAPE of NC, Inc.; Greensboro, NC; (336) 855-7107; (Dom) (Intl)

Amazing Grace Adoptions; Raleigh, NC; (919) 858-8998; www.agadoptions.org; (Dom) (Intl) Ukraine

Another Choice for Black Children; Charlotte, NC; (704) 394-1124; www.acfbc.org; (Dom)

Bethany Christian Services; Asheville, NC; (828) 274-7146; www.bethany.org/ northcarolina; (Dom) (Intl)

Bethany Christian Services; Charlotte, NC; (704) 541-1833; www.bethany.org/ northcarolina; (Dom) (Intl)

Bethany Christian Services; Raleigh, NC; (919) 510-9511; www.bethany.org/northcar olina; (Dom) (Intl)

Carolina Adoption Services, Inc.; Greensboro, NC; (336) 275-9660; www.carolina adoption.org; (Intl) Armenia Azerbaijan, China, Guatemala, Korea (South), Moldova, Peru, Republic of Georgia, Russian Federation, Ukraine, Vietnam

Catholic Social Ministries; Raleigh, NC; (919) 790-8533; www.dioceseofraleigh.org/ how/social; (Dom) (Intl)

Catholic Social Services; Charlotte, NC; (704) 370-6155; www.cssnc.org; (Dom) (Intl) Belarus, China, Russian Federation

A Child's Hope; Raleigh, NC; (919) 839-8800; www.achildshope.com; (Dom)

Christian Adoption Services; Matthews, NC; (704) 847-0038; www.christianadopt .org; (Dom) (Intl)

Christian World Adoption (CWA); Flat Rock, NC; (828) 693-7007; www.cwa.org; (Intl) China, Ethiopia, Guatemala, Honduras, Kazakhstan, Russian Federation, Ukraine

The Datz Foundation, Inc.; Concord, NC; (919) 839-8800; www.datzfound.com; (Dom) (Intl)

Family Services, Inc.; Winston-Salem, NC; (336) 722-8173; http://familyserv.org; (Dom)

Frank Adoption Center; Raleigh, NC; (919) 510-9135; www.frankadopt.org; (Intl)

Gladney Center for Adoption; Greenville, NC; (252) 355-6267; www.adoptionsby gladney.com; (Dom) (Intl) China, Guatemala, Kazakhstan, Russian Federation, Thailand, Ukraine

Grandfather Home; Banner Elk, NC; (828) 898-5465; www.grandfatherhome.org; (Dom)

Home Study Services of North Carolina; Raleigh, NC; (919) 272-6953; www.personal computerwizards.com/homestudy; (Dom) (Intl)

Independent Adoption Center (IAC); Raleigh, NC; (919) 676-6288; www.adoptionhelp .org;

International Adoption Guides (IAG); Belmont, NC; (704) 829-7880; www.adoption guides.org; (Dom) (Intl) China, Guatemala, Haiti, Russian Federation

LDS Family Services; Charlotte, NC; (704) 535-2436; www.ldsfamilyservices.org; (Dom)

Lutheran Family Services in the Carolinas, Inc. (LFS); Raleigh, NC; (919) 832-2620; www .lfscarolinas.org; (Dom) (Intl)

Mandala Adoption Services; Chapel Hill, NC; (919) 942-5500; www.mandalaadoption .org; (Dom) (Intl) Azerbaijan, Bulgaria, Cambodia, China, Guatemala, Kazakhstan, Panama, Ukraine, Vietnam

Methodist Home for Children (MHC); Raleigh, NC; (919) 833-5428; www.mhfc.org; (Dom)

Nathanson Adoption Services, Inc.; Charlotte, NC; (704) 553-9506; www.nathanson adopt.com; (Dom) (Intl)

Nazareth Children's Home; Rockwell, NC; (704) 279-5556; www.nazch.com; (Dom)

Newlife Christian Adoptions (NLCA); Garner, NC; (919) 779-1004; www.newlifechristian adoptions.org; (Dom)

Omni Community Services; Raleigh, NC; www.omnivisions.com; (Dom) (Intl)

Saint Mary International Adoptions (Nonprofit international adoption agency); Charlotte, NC; (704) 527-7673; www.smiaadopt.com; (Intl) Bulgaria, Poland, Russian Federation, Ukraine

A Way for Children; Charlotte, NC; (704) 576-6033; awayforchildren@earthlink.net; (Dom) (Intl)

Yahweh Center, Inc.; Wilmington, NC; (910) 675-3533; http://yahwehcenter.org; (Dom)

NORTH DAKOTA

STATE ADOPTION OFFICE: North Dakota Department of Human Services (NDDHS); Children and Family Services Division; State Capitol, Department 325; Bismarck, ND 58505; (701) 328-4805; www.state.nd.us

ICPC ADMINISTRATOR: North Dakota Department of Human Services; (same address as above); (701) 328-4152; (701) 328-3538; sofrid@state.nd.us

STATE ADOPTION EXCHANGE: North Dakota Department of Human Services (NDDHS); (same address as above); (701) 328-2316; www.state.nd.us; dhseo@state.nd.us

STATE BAR ASSOCIATION OF NORTH DAKOTA: (701) 255-1404; www.sband.org

ANNUAL NUMBER OF ADOPTIVE ADOPTIONS FINALIZED IN STATE: 368

STATE LAWS AND PROCEDURES—FAST FACTS
Types permitted? Agency only.
Who can adopt in state? Residents, and nonresidents when agency making placement is located in state.
How long after the child's placement to finalize the adoption in court? 7 months.
Is adoptive parent advertising (to find a birth mother) permitted? Yes.
Is a preplacement home study required? Yes.
Typical home study fee? $4,000–$8,000.
Can adoptive parents help birth mother with expenses? Yes: legal, medical, living, but must be paid directly to provider of services, not to birth mother.
Can child leave hospital with adoptive parents? Yes, if licensed foster parents, or with court order.
When can birth mother sign her Consent to Adoption? There is no consent. She files a Petition for Relinquishment with the court, heard no sooner than 48 hours after birth or signing of the petition, whichever occurs later.
Can the consent be revoked? No, it is irrevocable upon the court hearing.
What are the putative father's rights? There is no registry. Notice must be attempted. He can block the adoption unless he is proved unfit.

AMERICAN ACADEMY OF ADOPTION ATTORNEYS MEMBERS
William P. Harrie; 201 N. 5th St., #1800; Fargo, ND 58102; (701) 237-5544; w.harrie@adoptionattorneys.org

LICENSED PRIVATE AGENCIES
The Adoption Option (The Village Family Service Center/Lutheran Social Services of North Dakota); Bismarck, ND; (701) 255-1165; www.thevillagefamily.org; (Dom)
The Adoption Option (The Village Family Service Center/Lutheran Social Services of North Dakota); Fargo, ND; (701) 451-4900; www.thevillagefamily.org; (Dom) (Intl)
The Adoption Option (The Village Family Service Center/Lutheran Social Services of North Dakota); Grand Forks, ND; (701) 746-4584; www.thevillagefamily.org; (Dom) (Intl)
The Adoption Option (The Village Family Service Center/Lutheran Social Services of North Dakota); Minot, ND; (701) 852-3328; www.thevillagefamily.org; (Dom)
Adults Adopting Special Kids (AASK); Fargo, ND; (701) 356-7993; www.catholiccharitiesnd.org/AASK.htm; (Dom)
Catholic Charities North Dakota (CCND); Fargo, ND; (701) 235-4457; www.catholiccharitiesnd.org; (Dom) (Intl) China, Colombia, Guatemala, Kazakhstan, Philippines, Russian Federation, Taiwan

Catholic Charities North Dakota (CCND); Grand Forks, ND; (701) 775-4196; www
.catholiccharitiesnd.org; (Dom) (Intl)
Christian Family Life Services; Fargo, ND; (701) 237-4473; www.cflsadoption.org;
(Dom)
LDS Family Services; Bismarck, ND; (612) 560-0900; (Dom)

OHIO

STATE ADOPTION OFFICE: Ohio Department of Job and Family Services; Office of Children and Families; 255 E. Main St., 3rd Floor; Columbus, OH 43215; (614) 466-9274; http://jfs.ohio.gov/oapl/index.htm

ICPC ADMINISTRATOR: Ohio Department of Job and Family Services; (same address as above); (614) 752-6248; (614) 728-9682; http://jfs.ohio.gov

STATE ADOPTION EXCHANGE: AdoptOHIO; (same address as above); (614) 466-9274; www.odjfs.state.oh.us; pattep01@odjfs.state.oh.us

OHIO STATE BAR ASSOCIATION: Toll-free: (800) 282-6556; www.ohiobar.org

ANNUAL NUMBER OF ADOPTIVE ADOPTIONS FINALIZED IN STATE: 5,564

STATE LAWS AND PROCEDURES—FAST FACTS
Types permitted? Independent and agency (70% of newborns via independent).
Who can adopt in state? Residents, and nonresidents when child born in state or the
agency making the placement is located in state.
How long after the child's placement to finalize the adoption in court? 6–12
months.
Is adoptive parent advertising (to find a birth mother) permitted? No.
Is a preplacement home study required? Yes.
Typical home study fee? $3,500 (agency fees usually higher if agency located child).
Can adoptive parents help birth mother with expenses? Yes: legal, medical, but living usually not permitted.
Can child leave hospital with adoptive parents? Yes, sometimes a court order required.
When can birth mother sign her Consent to Adoption? 72 hours after birth.
Can the consent be revoked? Independent—yes, until court enters final or interlocutory order (1–6 months), but only if proved adoption not in child's best interests.
Agency—no, it is irrevocable upon signing.
What are the putative father's rights? There is a registry. He must register within
30 days of birth. If so, he can seek to block adoption by proving he provided
birth mother support during pregnancy.

AMERICAN ACADEMY OF ADOPTION ATTORNEYS MEMBERS
Susan Garner Eisenman; 3363 Tremont Rd., #304; Columbus, OH 43221; (614) 326-
1200; adoptohio@aol.com
Susan Eisenman began practicing law in 1974. She has completed 2,000 adoptions in her career. 40% are newborn placements. 15% of her clients find a birth mother through her office. She is an adoptive parent.

Ellen Essig; Katz, Greenberger, & Norton, LLP; 105 E. 4th St., #400; Cincinnati, OH 45202; (513) 721-5151; www.kgnlaw.com; ee@kgnlaw.com
Ellen Essig began practicing law in 1986. She has completed 100 adoptions in her career and last year completed 10. 95% are newborn placements. Her clients find their own birth mother.

Jerry M. Johnson; Hunt & Johnson, LLC; 400 W. North St.; Lima, OH 45801; (419) 222-1040; www.hjlaw.biz; hj@hjlaw.biz
Jerry Johnson began practicing law in 1975. He has completed 600 adoptions in his career and last year completed 40. 85% are newborn placements. 60% of his clients find a birth mother through his office.

Lori S. Nehrer; 111 Stow Ave., #100; Cuyahoga Falls, OH 44221; (330) 928-3373; nehkas@aol.com
Lori Nehrer began practicing law in 1985. She has completed 500 adoptions in her career and last year completed 70. 90% are newborn placements. 5% of her clients find a birth mother through her office. She is an adoptee and a birth parent.

Rosemary Ebner Pomeroy; 500 W. Wilson Bridge Rd., #110; Worthington, OH 43085; (614) 885-2101; ebnerpom@netwalk.com
Rosemary Pomeroy began practicing law in 1988. She has completed 200 adoptions in her career and last year completed 40. 60% are newborn placements.

Michael R. Voorhees; Voorhees & Levy, LLC; 11159 Kenwood Rd.; Cincinnati, OH 45242; (513) 489-2555; mike@ohioadoptionlawyer.com
Michael Voorhees began practicing law in 1987. He has completed 800 adoptions in his career and last year completed 100. 90% are newborn placements. 10% of his clients find a birth mother through his office.

Biographies were not available for the following AAAA members:
James S. Albers; 88 N. 5th St.; Columbus, OH 43215; (614) 464-4414; j.albers@adoptionattorneys.org

Margaret L. Blackmore; 536 S. High St.; Columbus, OH 43215; (614) 221-1341; p.hamilton@adoptionattorneys.org

Patrick A. Hamilton; 400 S. 5th St., #103; Columbus, OH 43215; (614) 464-4532

Carolyn Mussio; 3411 Michigan Ave.; Cincinnati, OH 45208; (513) 871-8855; c.mussio@adoptionattorneys.org

James Swain; 318 W. 4th St.; Dayton, OH 45402; (937) 223-5200

LICENSED PRIVATE AGENCIES
Adolescent Oasis, Inc.; Dayton, OH; (937) 228-2810; (Dom) (Intl)
Adopting Children Today Information/Option Network (ACTION Adoption, Inc.); Dayton, OH 45415; (937) 277-6101; www.action-adoption.org; (Dom)
Adoption by Gentle Care; Columbus, OH; (614) 469-0007; www.adoptionbygentlecare.org; (Dom)

Adoption Center, Inc.; North Jackson, OH; (330) 547-8225; (Dom) (Intl)

Adoption Circle; Columbus, OH; (614) 237-7222; www.adoptioncircle.org; (Dom) (Intl)

Adoption Home Study Services of Ohio; Alliance, OH; (330) 829-9400; www.home studyohio.com; (Dom) (Intl)

Adoption Link, Inc.; Yellow Springs, OH; (937) 767-2466; www.adoptionlink.org; (Dom) (Intl)

Adriel, Inc.; West Liberty, OH; (937) 465-0010; www.adriel.org; (Dom)

Advantage Adoption and Foster Care, Inc. (AAFC); Mansfield, OH; (419) 528-4411; http://advantageadoption.org; (Dom)

Agape for Youth, Inc.; Centerville, OH; (937) 439-4406; www.agapeforyouth.com; (Dom)

Alliance Human Services; Akron, OH; (330) 434-3790; (Dom) (Intl)

American International Adoption Agency, Inc. (AIAA); Williamsfield, OH; (330) 876-5656; http://aiaagency.com; (Intl) China, Russian Federation

Applewood Centers, Inc.; Cleveland, OH; (216) 741-2241 ext. 1252; www.applewood centers.org; (Dom)

The Bair Foundation; Kent, OH; (330) 673-6339; www.bair.org; (Dom)

Beech Acres; Cincinnati, OH; (513) 231-6630; www.beechacres.org; (Dom)

Beech Brook; Cleveland, OH; (216) 831-2255; www.beechbrook.org; (Dom)

Bellefaire JCB; Shaker Heights, OH; (216) 932-2800; www.bellefairejcb.org; (Dom) (Intl)

Berea Children's Home and Family Services (BCHFS); Berea, OH; (440) 260-8309; www.bchfs.org; (Dom)

The Buckeye Ranch; Grove City, OH; (614) 875-2371; www.buckeyeranch.org; (Dom)

Building Blocks Adoption Service, Inc.; Medina, OH; (330) 725-5521; www.bbas.org; (Intl) Bulgaria, Guatemala, Haiti, Kazakhstan, Russian Federation, Ukraine

Care to Adopt; Cincinnati, OH; (513) 793-1885; www.caretoadopt.com/index.php; (Dom) (Intl) Bulgaria, China, Guatemala, Haiti, Kazakhstan, Lithuania, Panama, Russian Federation, Ukraine

Caring for Kids, Inc.; Munroe Falls, OH; (330) 688-0044; (Dom) (Intl)

Caring Hearts Adoption Agency, Inc.; Greenville, OH; (937) 316-6168; www.caring heartsadoption.org; (Dom)

Catholic Charities, Diocese of Toledo; Toledo, OH; (419) 244-6711; www.catholic charitiesnwo.org; (Dom)

Catholic Charities Family Center of Elyria; Elyria, OH; (440) 366-1106; www.cleveland catholiccharities.org; (Dom)

Catholic Charities of Ashtabula County; Ashtabula, OH; (440) 992-2121; www.catholic charitiesashtabula.org; (Dom)

Catholic Charities Regional Agency; Warren, OH; (216) 393-4254; (Dom) (Intl)

Catholic Charities Services Corporation of Cleveland (CCS/Parmadale); Parma, OH; (440) 845-7700; www.clevelandcatholiccharities.org; (Dom)

Catholic Social Services, Inc. (CSS); Columbus, OH; (614) 221-5891; www.colscss .org; (Dom) (Intl) Bulgaria, Cambodia, China, Colombia, Guatemala, Honduras,

India, Kazakhstan, Republic of Georgia, Russian Federation, Thailand, Ukraine, Vietnam

Catholic Social Services of Southwestern Ohio; Cincinnati, OH; (513) 241-7745; http://cssdoorway.org; (Dom)

Catholic Social Services of the Miami Valley (CSSMV); Dayton, OH; (937) 223-7217; www.cssmv.org; (Dom) (Intl)

Cherub International Adoption Services, Inc.; Springboro, OH; (937) 748-4812; (Intl)

Children of India, Inc. (COI); Macedonia, OH; (216) 533-5284; www.childrenofindia.org; (Intl) India

Children's Home of Cincinnati, Ohio (CHOC); Cincinnati, OH; (513) 272-2800; www.thechildrenshomecinti.org; (Dom)

A Child's Waiting Adoption Program; Akron, OH; (330) 665-1811; www.achildswaiting.com; (Dom)

Christian Children's Home of Ohio (CCHO); Wooster, OH; (330) 345-7949; http://ccho.org; (Dom)

Cleveland Christian Home, Inc. (CCH); Cleveland, OH; (216) 416-4266; www.cchome.org; (Dom)

Community Services of Stark County, Inc.; North Canton, OH; (330) 305-9696; www.communityservicesofstark.org; (Dom)

Directions for Youth and Families; Columbus, OH; (614) 251-0130; www.directionsforyouth.org; (Dom)

Diversion Adolescent Foster Care of Ohio, Inc.; Findlay, OH; (419) 422-4770; www.diversionfostercare.org; (Dom)

European Adoption Consultants; Strongsville, OH; (440) 846-9300; www.eaci.com; (Intl) China, Guatemala, Kazakhstan, Russian Federation, Ukraine

Families Thru International Adoption (FTIA); Cincinnati, OH; (513) 794-1515; www.ftia.org; (Intl) Brazil, China, Guatemala, India, Russian Federation, Ukraine, Vietnam

Family Adoption Consultants (FAC); Macedonia, OH; (216) 468-0673; www.facadopt.org; (Dom) (Intl) China, Guatemala, Korea (South), Philippines

Focus on Youth, Inc.; 8904 Brookside Ave.; West Chester, OH 45069; (513) 644-1030; www.focusonyouth.com; (Dom)

Graceworks Lutheran Services; Cincinnati, OH; (513) 326-5430; http://graceworks.org; (Dom) (Intl) Brazil, Bulgaria, Burundi, China, Colombia, El Salvador, Ethiopia, Guatemala, Haiti, Honduras, Hong Kong—China, India, Kazakhstan, Korea (South), Mexico, Paraguay, Peru, Philippines, Republic of Georgia, Romania, Russian Federation, Taiwan, Thailand, Ukraine, Venezuela, Vietnam

Greenleaf Family Center; 212 E. Exchange St.; Akron, OH 44304; (330) 376-9494; www.greenleafctr.org; (Dom)

Hannah's Hope Adoption Cathedral Ministries, Inc.; Sylvania, OH; (419) 882-8463; www.toledoclc.com; (Dom)

House of Samuel, Inc.; Cambridge, OH; (740) 439-5634; (Dom) (Intl)

Inner Peace Homes, Inc.; Bowling Green, OH; (419) 354-6525; (Dom)

Jewish Family Services—Adoption Connection; Cincinnati, OH; (513) 489-1616; www.adoptioncincinnati.org; (Dom) (Intl)

LDS Family Services, Inc.; Groveport, OH; (614) 836-2466; www.ldsfamilyservices .org; (Dom) (Intl)

Lighthouse Youth Services, Inc. (LYS); Cincinnati, OH; (513) 221-3350; www.lys.org; (Dom) (Intl)

Lutheran Children's Aid and Family Services (LCAFS); .Cleveland, OH; (216) 281-2500; www.bright.net/~lcafs; (Dom) (Intl)

Lutheran Social Services of Central Ohio; Columbus, OH; (614) 421-3611; www.lssco .org; (Dom) (Intl)

Lutheran Social Services of Mid-America; Dayton, OH; (937) 643-0020; www.lssma .org/adoption; (Dom)

Lutheran Social Services of Mid-America; Springfield, OH; (937) 325-3441; www.lssma .org/adoption; (Dom) (Intl)

Lutheran Social Services of Northwest Ohio (LSSNWO); Fremont, OH; (419) 334-3431; www.lssnwo.org; (Dom) (Intl)

Lutheran Social Services of Northwest Ohio (LSSNWO); Perrysburg, OH; (419) 872-9111; www.lssnwo.org; (Dom) (Intl)

Mid-Western Children's Home; Pleasant Plain, OH; (513) 877-2141; www.mid-western .org; (Dom)

Northeast Ohio Adoption Services; Warren, OH; (330) 856-5582; (Dom)

Ohio Youth Advocate Program, Inc.; Cleveland, OH; (614) 777-8777; www.nyap.org/ OH/home_f.aspx; (Dom)

Options for Families and Youth (OFY); Brook Park, OH; (216) 267-7070; www.ofycares .org; (Dom)

A Place to Call Home, Inc.; Johnstown, OH; (740) 967-2167; (Dom) (Intl)

Private Adoption Services, Inc.; Cincinnati, OH; (513) 871-5777; www.private adoptionservice.com; (Dom) (Intl) China, Guatemala, Russian Federation

Specialized Alternatives for Families and Youth (SAFY); Delphos, OH; (419) 532-7239; www.safy.org; (Dom)

United Methodist Children's Home (UMCH); Worthington, OH; (614) 885-5020; www .umchohio.org; (Dom)

V. Beacon, Inc.; Maumee, OH; (419) 887-1629; (Dom) (Intl)

Westark Family Services, Inc.; Massillon, OH; (330) 832-5043; (Dom) (Intl)

World Family Adoption Studies, Inc.; Columbus, OH; (614) 459-8406; (Dom) (Intl)

Worlds Together, Inc.; Cincinnati, OH; (513) 631-6590; www.worldstogether.org; (Dom) (Intl) China, Guatemala, India, Russian Federation, Ukraine, Vietnam

Youth Engaged for Success; Dayton, OH; (937) 837-4200; (Dom)

Youth Services Network of Southwest Ohio, Inc. (YSN); Kettering, OH; (937) 294-4400; www.ysn.org; (Dom)

OKLAHOMA

STATE ADOPTION OFFICE: Oklahoma Department of Human Services; 907 S. Detroit, Suite 750; Tulsa, OK 74120; (918) 588-1735; www.okdhs.org/adopt

ICPC ADMINISTRATOR: Oklahoma Department of Human Services; PO Box 25352;

2400 N. Lincoln Blvd.; Oklahoma City, OK 73125; (918) 592-3471; (405) 522-2433

STATE ADOPTION EXCHANGE: Oklahoma Adoption Exchange; (405) 521-2475; www .okdhs.org; linda.foster@okdhs.org

OKLAHOMA BAR ASSOCIATION: (405) 416-7000; www.okbar.org

ANNUAL NUMBER OF ADOPTIVE ADOPTIONS FINALIZED IN STATE: 1,533

STATE LAWS AND PROCEDURES—FAST FACTS

Types permitted? Independent and agency (60% of newborns via independent).

Who can adopt in state? Residents, and nonresidents when child has "significant contacts" in state, such as 6 months of residency.

How long after the child's placement to finalize the adoption in court? 7 months.

Is adoptive parent advertising (to find a birth mother) permitted? Yes.

Is a preplacement home study required? Yes.

Typical home study fee? $750–$2,000 (agency fees usually higher if agency located child).

Can adoptive parents help birth mother with expenses? Yes: legal, medical, living, but must be paid directly to provider of services, not to birth mother. Court approval required for living assistance over $500.

Can child leave hospital with adoptive parents? Yes, with signed form or court order.

When can birth mother sign her Consent to Adoption? Anytime after birth. If she is under age 16, a parent's consent is required as well.

Can the consent be revoked? No, it is irrevocable upon signing.

What are the putative father's rights? There is a registry. Notice must be attempted if he is registered or named by birth mother. If he objects, the court will examine his financial support to birth mother during the pregnancy.

AMERICAN ACADEMY OF ADOPTION ATTORNEYS MEMBERS

Barbara K. Bado; Bado & Bado; 1800 Canyon Park Cir., #301; Edmond, OK 73013; (405) 340-1500; b.bado@adoptionattorneys.org
Barbara Bado began practicing law in 1978. She has completed 600 adoptions in her career, and last year completed 30. 97% are newborn placements. 95% of her clients find a birth mother through her office.

John Terry Bado; Bado & Bado; 1800 Canyon Park Cir., #301; Edmond, OK 73013; (405) 340-1500; j.bado@adoptionattorneys.org
John Bado began practicing law in 1971. He has completed 600 adoptions in his career and last year completed 30. 97% are newborn placements. 95% of his clients find a birth mother through his office.

John M. O'Connor; Newton, O'Connor, Turner & Ketchum, PC; 15 W. 6th St., #2700; Tulsa, OK 74119; (918) 587-0101; www.newtonoconnor.com; joconnor@ newtonoconnor.com
John O'Connor began practicing law in 1981. He has completed 350 adoptions

in his career and last year completed 21. 85% are newborn placements. 5% of his clients find a birth mother through his office.

Jack H. Petty; Petty and Associates; 6666 NW 39 Expy.; Bethany, OK 73008; (405) 787-6911; jack.petty@coxinet.net
Jack Petty began practicing law in 1967. He has completed 1,000 adoptions in his career and last year completed 50. 100% are newborn placements. 20% of his clients find a birth mother through his office.

Peter K. Schaffer; 204 N. Robinson Ave., #2305; Oklahoma City, OK 73102; (405) 239-7707; p.schaffer@adoptionattorneys.org
Peter Schaffer began practicing law in 1974. He has completed 350 adoptions in his career.

Phyllis L. Zimmerman; 15 W. 6th St., #1220; Tulsa, OK 74119; (918) 582-6151; p.zimmerman@adoptionattorneys.org
Phyllis Zimmerman began practicing law in 1963.

Biographies were not available for the following AAAA members:
Virginia Frank; 5350 S. Western Ave., #218; Oklahoma City, OK 73109; (405) 632-7999; v.frank@adoptionattorneys.org

Mark A. Morrison; 524 W. Evergreen St.; Durant, OK 74702; (580) 924-1661; m.morrison@adoptionattorneys.org

Mike Yeksavich; 1107 S. Peoria; Tulsa, OK 74120; (918) 592-6050; m.yeksavich@adoptionattorneys.org

LICENSED PRIVATE AGENCIES
Adoption Affiliates; Tulsa, OK; (918) 664-2275; www.connectinghearts.org; (Dom)
Adoption Center of Northeastern Oklahoma; Tulsa, OK; (918) 748-9200; (Dom) (Intl)
Adoption Choices of Oklahoma; Oklahoma City, OK; (405) 632-7999; www.adoption choices.org; (Dom)
Baptist Children's Home; Oklahoma City, OK; (405) 691-7781; www.obhc.org; (Dom)
Bethany Adoption Service; Bethany, OK; (405) 789-5423; (Dom)
Bless This Child, Inc.; Checotah, OK; (918) 473-7045; www.blessthischild.com; (Intl) Costa Rica, Russian Federation
Catholic Social Services; Tulsa, OK; 918-585-8167 Ext. 116; (Dom)
Cherokee Nation; Tahlequah, OK; (Dom)
Chosen Child Adoption Agency; Tulsa, OK; (918) 298-0082; www.chosenchild adoption.com; (Dom)
Christian Homes; Duncan, OK; (405) 252-5131; www.christianhomes.com; (Dom)
Christian Services of Oklahoma (CSO); Edmond, OK; (405) 478-3362; www.christian-adoption.org; (Dom)
Crisis Pregnancy Outreach (CPO); Jenks, OK; (918) 296-3377; www.crisispregnancy outreach.org; (Dom)
Deaconess Home Pregnancy and Adoption Services; Oklahoma City, OK; (405) 949-4200; www.deaconesshome.com; (Dom)

Dillon International, Inc.; Tulsa, OK; (918) 749-4600; www.dillonadopt.com; (Intl) China, Guatemala, Haiti, India, Kazakhstan, Korea (South)

Fresh Start; Tulsa, OK; (918) 592-0539; (Dom)

Heritage Family Services; Tulsa, OK; (918) 491-6767; www.heritagefamilyservices.org; (Dom) (Intl)

LDS Family Services of Oklahoma; Tulsa, OK; (918) 665-3090; www.ldsfamilyservices.org; (Dom)

Natasha's Story, Inc.; Tulsa, OK; (918) 747-3617; (Dom)

Oklahoma Home Study (OHS); Edmond, OK; (405) 341-0045; http://oklahomahomestudy.com; (Dom) (Intl)

SAFY of America; Oklahoma City, OK; (405) 942-5570; www.safy.org; (Dom)

Small Miracles International (SMI); Midwest City, OK; (405) 732-7295; www.smiint.org; (Dom) (Intl) Guatemala

OREGON

STATE ADOPTION OFFICE: Oregon Department of Human Services; Human Services Bldg., Adoption Unit, 2nd Floor; 500 Summer St. NE, E-71; Salem, OR 97310-1068; (503) 947-5358; www.dhs.state.or.us/children/adoption

ICPC ADMINISTRATOR: Oregon Department of Human Services; (same address as above); (503) 945-6685; www/dhs.state.or.us

STATE ADOPTION EXCHANGE: Oregon's Waiting Children; www.nwae.org

OREGON STATE BAR: (503) 620-0222; www.osbar.org

ANNUAL NUMBER OF ADOPTIVE ADOPTIONS FINALIZED IN STATE: 2,029

STATE LAWS AND PROCEDURES—FAST FACTS

Types permitted? Independent and agency (70% of newborns via independent).

Who can adopt in state? Residents, and nonresidents when child born in state or the agency making the placement is located in state.

How long after the child's placement to finalize the adoption in court? 4–7 months.

Is adoptive parent advertising (to find a birth mother) permitted? Yes, if adoptive parents are certified via an agency home study.

Is a preplacement home study required? Yes.

Typical home study fee? $1,500 (agency fees usually higher if agency located child).

Can adoptive parents help birth mother with expenses? Yes: legal, medical, living.

Can child leave hospital with adoptive parents? Yes, with signed form.

When can birth mother sign her Consent to Adoption? Anytime after birth.

Can the consent be revoked? If birth mother has an attorney and signs a Certificate of Irrevocability (commonly done), it is irrevocable upon signing. If she does not, she can withdraw it until the adoption is final.

What are the putative father's rights? There is no registry, but he must notify state if he files a filiation (paternity) action. Only those who register, or whom the birth mother states supported her, or offered to do so, are entitled to notice.

AMERICAN ACADEMY OF ADOPTION ATTORNEYS MEMBERS

Timothy F. Brewer; 590 W. 13th Ave.; Eugene, OR 97401; (541) 683-1814; www .adoption.tfbrewer.com; tim@tfbrewer.com
Timothy Brewer began practicing law in 1985. He has completed 200 adoptions in his career and last year completed 35. 65% are newborn placements. His clients find their own birth mother.

Catherine M. Dexter; Dexter & Moffet; 25260 SW Parkway Ave., Suite C; Wilsonville, OR 97070; (503) 582-9010; www.oregonadopt.com
Catherine Dexter began practicing law in 1982. She has completed 1,800 adoptions in her career and last year completed 60. 95% are newborn placements. 60% of her clients find a birth mother through her office.

J. Eric Gustafson; Lyon, Weigand & Gustafson, PS; 154 Treasure Cove Ln.; Manzanita, OR 97130; (509) 248-7220; www.northwestadoptions.com; egustafson @lyon-law.com
Eric Gustafson began practicing law in 1973. He has completed 800 adoptions in his career and last year completed 52. 90% are newborn placements. 90% of his clients find a birth mother through his office. He is an adoptive parent.

John R. Hassen; Hornecker, Cowling, Hassen & Heysell, LLP; 717 Murphy Rd.; Medford, OR 97504; (541) 779-8900; www.roguelaw.com; jrh@roguelaw.com
John Hassen began practicing law in 1965. He has completed 600 adoptions in his career. 80% of these are newborn placements.

Susan C. Moffet; Dexter & Moffet; 25260 SW Parkway Ave., Suite C; Wilsonville, OR 97070; (503) 582-9010; www.oregonadopt.com; smoffett@oregonadopt.com
Susan Moffet began practicing law in 1987. She has completed 1,200 adoptions in her career and last year completed 76. 95% are newborn placements. 70% of her clients find a birth mother through her office.

Laurence H. Spiegel; 4040 Douglas Way; Lake Oswego, OR 97035; (503) 635-7773; www.adoption-oregon.com; lhspiegel@msn.com
Laurence Spiegel began practicing law in 1981. He has completed 2,000 adoptions in his career and last year completed 100. 85% are newborn placements. 35% of his clients find a birth mother through his office. He is an adoptive parent.

Biographies were not available for the following AAAA members:

John Chally; 825 NE Multnomah, #1125; Portland, OR 97232; (503) 238-9720; j.chally@adoptionattorneys.org

Sandra L. Hodgson; 825 NE Multnomah, #1125; Portland, OR 97232; (503) 238-9720; s.hodgson@adoptionattorneys.org

Robin E. Pope; 12125 SW 2nd St.; Beaverton, OR 97005; (503) 352-3524

LICENSED PRIVATE AGENCIES

Adoption Avenues Agency; Portland, OR; (503) 977-2870; www.adoptionavenues
.org; (Intl) Bulgaria, Chile, China, Ecuador, Ethiopia, Guatemala, Kazakhstan,
Romania, Russian Federation

Adoptions of Southern Oregon; Klamath Falls, OR; (541) 273-9326; (Dom)

All God's Children International; Portland, OR; (503) 282-7652; www.allgodschildren
.org; (Intl)

Associated Services for International Adoption (ASIA); Lake Oswego, OR; (503) 697-
6863; www.asiadopt.org; (Intl) China

Boys and Girls Aid Society of Oregon; Portland, OR; (503) 222-9661; www.boysand
girlsaid.org; (Dom)

Catholic Charities, Inc.; Portland, OR; (503) 238-5196; www.catholiccharitiesoregon
.org; (Dom)

Children's Hope International Oregon Regional Office (CHI); Troutdale, OR; (503) 665-
1589; www.childrenshope.com/oregon/index.htm; (Intl)

Christian Community Placement Center; Salem, OR; (503) 588-5647; (Dom)

Christian Family Adoptions; Portland, OR; (503) 232-1211; www.christianfamily
adoptions.org; (Dom)

CRISTA Ministries, New Hope Child and Family Agency; Portland, OR; (503) 282-6726;
www.newhopewa.org; (Dom) (Intl)

Dove Adoptions International, Inc.; Banks, OR; (503) 324-9010; www.adoptions.net;
(Intl) Ethiopia, Guatemala, Mexico, Russian Federation, Ukraine

Holt International Children's Services; Eugene, OR; (541) 687-2202; www.holtintl.org;
(Intl) Bulgaria, China, Ecuador, Guatemala, Haiti, India, Korea (South), Mongolia, Philippines, Romania, Thailand, Uganda, Vietnam

International Family Services (IFS); Newberg, OR; (503) 538-3665; www.ifservices.org;
(Intl) China, Guatemala, India, Kazakhstan, Russian Federation, Tajikistan,
Ukraine

Journeys of the Heart Adoption Services; Hillsboro, OR; (503) 681-3075; www
.journeysoftheheart.net; (Dom) (Intl)

LDS Family Services; Tigard, OR; (503) 620-1191; (Dom)

Northwest Adoptions and Family Services; Salem, OR; (503) 581-6652; (Dom) (Intl)

Open Adoption & Family Services, Inc. (OA&FS); Portland, OR; (503) 226-4870; www
.openadopt.org; (Dom)

Orphans Overseas; Portland, OR; (503) 297-2006; www.orphansoverseas.org; (Dom)

PLAN Loving Adoptions Now, Inc. (PLAN); McMinnville, OR; (503) 472-8452; www
.planlovingadoptions.org; (Dom) (Intl) China, Colombia, Guatemala, Haiti,
India, Liberia, Russian Federation, Ukraine, Vietnam

Tree of Life Adoption Center; Portland, OR; (503) 244-7374; www.toladopt.org; (Dom)
(Intl) Bulgaria, China, Guatemala, Haiti, Kazakhstan, Lithuania, Republic of
Moldova, Romania, Russian Federation, Ukraine

PENNSYLVANIA

STATE ADOPTION OFFICE: Pennsylvania Department of Public Welfare; Office of Children, Youth, and Families; 7th & Foster Sts., PO Box 2675; Harrisburg, PA 17105-2675; (717) 705-4401; www.dpw.state.pa.us

ICPC ADMINISTRATOR: Pennsylvania Department of Public Welfare; PO Box 2675; Harrisburg, PA 17105; (717) 772-7016; www.dpw.state.pa.us

STATE ADOPTION EXCHANGE: Pennsylvania Adoption Exchange (PAE); (717) 772-7011; www.adoptpakids.org; klollo@state.pa.us

PENNSYLVANIA BAR ASSOCIATION: (717) 238-6715; www.pa-bar.org

ANNUAL NUMBER OF ADOPTIVE ADOPTIONS FINALIZED IN STATE: 4,748

STATE LAWS AND PROCEDURES—FAST FACTS
Types permitted? Independent and agency (50% of newborns via independent).
Who can adopt in state? Residents, and nonresidents when child born in state or the agency making the placement is located in state.
How long after the child's placement to finalize the adoption in court? 3–12 months.
Is adoptive parent advertising (to find a birth mother) permitted? Yes.
Is a preplacement home study required? Yes.
Typical home study fee? $1,600–$2,100 (agency fees usually higher if agency located child).
Can adoptive parents help birth mother with expenses? Yes: legal, medical, but not living.
Can child leave hospital with adoptive parents? Yes, with signed form.
When can birth mother sign her Consent to Adoption? 72 hours after birth.
Can the consent be revoked? Yes, for 30 days.
What are the putative father's rights? There is a registry. If he objects, his rights can be terminated upon proof of 4 months of abandonment if child is a newborn, rape, or his inability to parent.

AMERICAN ACADEMY OF ADOPTION ATTORNEYS MEMBERS
Denise M. Bierly; Dilafiled, McGer, Jones & Kauffman; 300 S. Allen St., #300; State College, PA 16801; (814) 237-6278; d.bierly@adoptionattorneys.org
Denise Bierly began practicing law in 1990. She has completed 350 adoptions in her career and last year completed 32. 80% are newborn placements. 5% of her clients find a birth mother through her office. She is an adoptive parent.

Craig B. Bluestein; 7237 Hollywood Rd.; Ft. Washington, PA 19034; (215) 576-1030; c.bluestein@adoptionattorneys.org
Craig Bluestein began practicing law in 1979.

Harry L. Bricker Jr.; 407 N. Front St.; Harrisburg, PA 17101; (717) 233-2555; hlblaw@verizon.net
Harry Bricker began practicing law in 1958. He has completed 800 adoptions

in his career and last year completed 17. 90% are newborn placements. His clients find their own birth mother. He is an adoptive parent.

Barbara L. Binder Casey; 527 Elm St.; Reading, PA 19601; (610) 376-9742; www .aaaaadoptababy.com; bcasey@infantadoptions.com
Barbara Casey began practicing law in 1978. She has completed 500 adoptions in her career and last year completed 60. 80% are newborn placements. 80% of her clients find a birth mother through her office.

Steven G. Dubin; 80 2nd Street Pike, #7; Southampton, PA 18966; (215) 322-4100; www.myownchild.com; sgdubin@comcast.net
Steven Dubin began practicing law in 1979. He has completed 600 adoptions in his career and last year completed 35. 95% are newborn placements. 90% of his clients find a birth mother through his office.

Debra M. Fox; 355 W. Lancaster Ave.; Haverford, PA 19041; (610) 896-9972; www .transitionsadoption.com; mail@transitionsadoption.com
Debra Fox began practicing law in 1985. She has completed 1,000 adoptions in her career and last year completed 50. 100% are newborn placements. 90% of her clients find a birth mother through her office.

Tara E. Gutterman; Adoption Resource Center; 4701 Pine St., Suite J-7; Philadelphia, PA 19143; (215) 748-1441; www.adoptionarc.com; taralaw@aol.com
Tara Gutterman began practicing law in 1991. She has completed 800 adoptions in her career and last year completed 100. 100% are newborn placements. 99% of her clients find a birth mother through her office. She is the director of an adoption agency.

Deborah L. Lesko; Shields & Lesko, PC; 5055 Buttermilk Hollow Rd.; Pittsburgh, PA 15122; (412) 469-3500; www.shieldsandlesko.com; dlesko@shieldsandlesko.com
Deborah Lesko began practicing law in 1983. She has completed 3,000 adoptions in her career and last year completed approximately 200. 90% are newborn placements. 5% of her clients find a birth mother through her office.

Martin S. Leventon; 1011 Cedargrove Rd.; Wynnewood, PA 19096; (610) 642-7182; martinleventon49@yahoo.com
Martin Leventon began practicing law in 1981. He has completed 750 adoptions in his career and last year completed 32. 100% are newborn placements. 90% of his clients find a birth mother through his office.

Mary Ann Petrillo; 412 Main St.; Irwin, PA 15642; (724) 861-8333; www.mary annpetrillo.com; mapster1@aol.com
Mary Ann Petrillo began practicing law in 1983. She has completed 1,000 adoptions in her career and last year completed 52. 85% are newborn placements. 20% of her clients find a birth mother through her office. She is an adoptive parent.

William Rosen; 150 S. Warner Rd., #144; King of Prussia, PA 19406; (610) 688-8600; wpr@lavida.org

William Rosen began practicing law in 1988. He has completed 3,500 adoptions in his career, much of which is dedicated to international adoption. He is a member of the American Immigration Lawyers Association.

Stuart S. Sacks; Smigel, Anderson & Sacks; 4431 N. Front St.; Harrisburg, PA 17110; (717) 234-2401; www.sasllp.com; ssacks@sasllp.com
Stuart Sacks began practicing law in 1973. He has completed 1,100 adoptions in his career and last year completed 29. 99% are newborn placements. 5% of his clients find a birth mother through his office. He is an adoptive parent.

Samuel C. Totaro Jr.; Mellon, Webster & Shelly, PC; 87 N. Broad St.; Doylestown, PA 18901; (215) 348-7700; www.mellonwebster.com; stotaro@mellonwebster .com
Samuel Totaro began practicing law in 1975. He has completed 3,000 adoptions in his career and last year completed 70. 99% are newborn placements. 90% of his clients find a birth mother through his office. He is a past president of the American Academy of Adoption Attorneys.

A biography was not available for the following AAAA member:
Jay H. Ginsburg; 527 Swede St.; Norristown, PA 19401; (610) 277-1999; j.ginsburg@ adoptionattorneys.org

LICENSED PRIVATE AGENCIES
AAA Transitions Adoption Agency, Inc; Haverford, PA; (610) 642-4155; (Dom) (Intl)
Absolute Love Adoptions (ALA); Irwin, PA; (724) 861-8300; www.absolutelove adoptions.org; (Dom)
Adelphoi Village, Inc.; Latrobe, PA; (724) 520-1111; www.adelphoivillage.org/ newfiles/fstrprnt.html; (Dom)
Adopt Abroad, Inc.; Langhorne, PA; (215) 702-0561; www.adopt-abroad.com; (Dom) (Intl) Bulgaria, Kazakhstan, Poland, Russian Federation, Ukraine
Adopt-a-Child, Inc.; Pittsburgh, PA; (412) 421-1911; www.adopt-a-child.org; (Intl) Russian Federation
Adoption by Choice; Erie, PA; (814) 836-9887; (Dom)
Adoption Connection, Inc.; New Brighton, PA; (724) 846-2615; (Dom) (Intl) Guatemala
Adoption Home Study Associates of Chester County, Inc. (AHSA); West Chester, PA; (610) 429-1001; (Dom) (Intl)
Adoption Horizons; Carlisle, PA; (717) 249-8850; www.adoptionhorizonspa.com/ index.html; (Dom) (Intl) Bulgaria, China, Guatemala, India, Korea (South), Philippines, Russian Federation, Vietnam
Adoption House, Inc.; Norristown, PA; (215) 523-9234; www.adoptionhouse.org; (Dom) (Intl) China, Guatemala, Kazakhstan, Russian Federation
Adoption International Program, Inc.; Havertown, PA; Toll-free: (866) 969-8445; www .adoptioninternationalprogram.com; (Dom) (Intl) Azerbaijan, Guatemala, Kazakhstan, Nepal, Ukraine
Adoption Resource Center, Inc.; Philadelphia, PA; (215) 844-1082; www.adoptionarc .com; (Dom)

Adoption Services, Inc.; Camp Hill, PA; (717) 737-3960; www.adoptionservices.org; (Intl) China, Guatemala, Russian Federation

Adoptions from the Heart; Allentown, PA; (610) 432-2384; www.adoptionsfromthe heart.org; (Dom) (Intl) China, Ecuador, Guatemala, India, Kazakhstan, Mongolia, Ukraine, Vietnam

Adoptions from the Heart; Greensburg, PA; (724) 853-6533; www.adoptionsfromthe heart.org; (Dom) (Intl) China, Ecuador, Guatemala, India, Kazakhstan, Mongolia, Ukraine, Vietnam

Adoptions from the Heart; Harrisburg, PA; (717) 232-1787; www.adoptionsfromthe heart.org; (Dom) (Intl) China, Ecuador, Guatemala, India, Kazakhstan, Mongolia, Ukraine, Vietnam

Adoptions from the Heart; Lancaster, PA; (717) 399-7766; www.adoptionsfromthe heart.org; (Dom) (Intl) China, Ecuador, Guatemala, India, Kazakhstan, Mongolia, Ukraine, Vietnam

Adoptions from the Heart; Wynnewood, PA; (610) 642-7200; www.adoptionsfromthe heart.org; (Dom) (Intl) China, Ecuador, Guatemala, India, Kazakhstan, Mongolia, Ukraine, Vietnam

Adoptions Forever, Inc.; Havertown, PA; (610) 853-2635; www.adoptionsforever.org; (Dom) (Intl) Bulgaria, Guatemala, Ukraine

Adoption Home Studies and Services, Inc.; Shrewsbury, PA; (717) 227-9560; www .adopthomestudyserv.com; (Intl) Brazil, Guatemala, Hungary, Mexico, Russian Federation

Adoptions International, Inc.; Philadelphia, PA; (215) 238-9057; www.adoptionsintl .org; (Intl) Azerbaijan, China, El Salvador, Guatemala, Nepal, Ukraine

Adoption Unlimited, Inc.; Lancaster, PA; (717) 431-2021; www.adoptionunlimited .org; Russian Federation

Asociacion Puertorriquenos en Marcha; Philadelphia, PA; (215) 235-6788; (Dom)

Association of Puerto Ricans on the March (APM); Philadelphia, PA; (215) 329-9580; http://apmphila.org; (Dom) (Intl) Dominica, Mexico, Puerto Rico

Bair Foundation of Pennsylvania, Inc.; Middletown, PA; (717) 985-6450; (Dom)

Bair Foundation of Pennsylvania, Inc.; Pittsburgh, PA; (412) 341-6850; (Dom)

Best Nest, Inc.; Philadelphia, PA; (215) 546-8060; www.bestnest.org; (Dom)

Best Nest, Inc.; Williamsport, PA; (570) 321-1969; www.bestnest.org; (Dom)

Bethanna, Inc.; Southampton, PA; (215) 355-6500; www.bethanna.org; (Dom)

Bethany Christian Services; Fort Washington, PA; (215) 628-0202; www.bethany.org; (Dom) (Intl)

Bethany Christian Services, Inc.; Lancaster, PA; (717) 299-1926; www.bethany.org; (Dom)

Bethany Christian Services of Western Pennsylvania, Inc.; Wexford, PA; (724) 940-2900; www.bethany.org; (Dom) (Intl) Albania, China, Colombia, Ecuador, Guatemala, India, Japan, Korea (South), Lithuania, Philippines, Russian Federation, Ukraine

Black Adoption Services; Pittsburgh, PA; (412) 471-8722; www.3riversadopt.org; (Dom)

A Brave Choice; Wynnewood, PA; (610) 642-7182; (Dom)

Carson Valley School; Philadelphia, PA; (215) 849-5505; mharris@carsonvalley.org; (Dom)

Catholic Charities; Pittsburgh, PA; (412) 456-6960; www.ccpgh.org/website/adoption.htm; (Dom)

Catholic Charities Counseling and Adoption Services, Inc.; Dubois, PA; (814) 371-4717; (Dom)

Catholic Charities Counseling and Adoption Services, Inc.; Erie, PA; (814) 456-2091; (Dom)

Catholic Charities Counseling and Adoption Services, Inc.; Sharon, PA; (724) 346-4142; (Dom)

Catholic Charities Diocese of Allentown; Reading, PA; (610) 376-7144; www.allentown diocese.org/csa/unitedway.html; (Dom) (Intl) Guatemala, Korea (South)

Catholic Charities, Inc.; Harrisburg, PA; (717) 564-7115; www.hbgdiocese.org; (Dom) (Intl) China, Guatemala, Kazakhstan, Russian Federation

Catholic Charities of Greensburg; Greensburg, PA; (724) 837-1840; (Dom) (Intl)

Catholic Charities of the Diocese of Pittsburgh, Inc.; Pittsburgh, PA; (412) 456-6960; www.ccpgh.org/website/home.htm; (Dom) (Intl)

Catholic Social Services; Philadelphia, PA; (215) 854-7050; www.adoption-phl.org; (Dom) (Intl)

Catholic Social Services; Stroudsburg, PA; (570) 476-6460; (Dom)

Catholic Social Services Diocese of Scranton; Hazleton, PA; (570) 455-1521; (Dom)

Catholic Social Services Diocese of Scranton; Tunkhannock, PA; (570) 836-1101; (Dom)

Catholic Social Services of Luzerne County; Wilkes-Barre, PA; (570) 822-7118; (Dom)

Catholic Social Services of Lycoming County, Inc.; Williamsport, PA; (570) 322-4220; (Dom)

Catholic Social Services of Philadelphia (CSS); Philadelphia, PA; (215) 854-7050; www .adoption-phl.org; (Dom) China, Korea (South), Philippines, Poland, Taiwan, Vietnam

Catholic Social Services of the Diocese of Altoona-Johnstown; Altoona, PA; (814) 944-9388; (Dom)

Cherubs for Us; Collegeville, PA; (610) 489-8590; (Dom)

Child and Home Study Associates; Media, PA; (610) 565-1544; www.chsadoptions.org; (Dom) (Intl)

Child to Family Connections, Inc.; Meadville, PA; (814) 336-3007; (Dom)

Children of the Light Mission, Inc.; Philadelphia, PA; (215) 473-5300; (Dom)

Children's Aid Home Programs of Somerset County, Inc.; Somerset, PA; (814) 443-1637; www.cahprogram.org; (Dom)

Children's Aid Society; Mercer, PA; (724) 662-4730; (Dom) (Intl)

Children's Aid Society; Norristown, PA; (610) 279-2755; www.childrensaid.net; (Dom) (Intl)

Children's Aid Society in Clearfield County; Clearfield, PA; (814) 765-2686; (814) 765-6530; www.childaid.org; (Dom)

Children's Aid Society of Franklin County; Chambersburg, PA; (717) 263-4159; (Dom)

Children's Choice, Inc.; Harrisburg, PA; (717) 230-9980; www.childrenschoice.org; (Dom) (Intl) Bulgaria, China, Guatemala, Lithuania, Mexico

Children's Choice, Inc.; Lewisburg, PA; (570) 522-1030; www.childrenschoice.org; (Dom) (Intl) Brazil, Bulgaria, China, Guatemala, Lithuania, Mexico

Children's Choice, Inc.; Philadelphia, PA; (610) 521-6270; www.childrenschoice.org; (Dom) (Intl) Brazil, Bulgaria, China, Kazakhstan, Lithuania, Mexico, Ukraine

The Children's Home of Pittsburgh; Pittsburgh, PA; (412) 441-4884; www.childrens homepgh.org; (Dom)

Children's Home of York, Inc.; York, PA; (717) 755-1033; www.choyork.org; (Dom)

Children's Service Center of Wyoming Valley, Inc.; Wilkes-Barre, PA; (570) 825-6425; www.cscwv.org; (Dom) (Intl)

Children's Services, Inc.; Philadelphia, PA; (215) 546-3503; (Dom)

COBYS Family Services; Leola, PA; (717) 656-6580; www.cobys.net; (Dom)

Common Sense Adoption Services; Mechanicsburg, PA; (717) 766-6449; www .csas-swan.org; (Dom) (Intl)

Commonwealth Adoptions International, Inc. (CAI); Cranberry Township, PA; (724) 772-8190; www.commonwealthadoption.org; (Intl)

CONCERN—Professional Services for Children, Youth and Families; Fleetwood, PA; (610) 944-0445; www.concern4kids.org; (Dom)

Council of Spanish Speaking Organizations, Inc. (CONCILIO); Philadelphia, PA; (215) 627-3100; www.elconcilio.net; (Dom)

Covenant Family Resources; King of Prussia, PA; (610) 354-0555; (Dom)

Delta Community Supports, Inc.; Glenside, PA; (215) 887-6300; (Dom)

Diakon Adoption and Foster Care; Mechanicsburg, PA; (717) 795-0320; www.diakon .org/adoption; (Dom) (Intl)

Diakon Adoption & Foster Care Services; Topton, PA; (610) 682-1504; www.diakon.org/ adoption; (Dom) (Intl)

Diakon Adoption Services; York, PA; (717) 845-9113; www.diakon.org/adoption; (Dom) (Intl)

Eckels Adoption Agency, Inc.; Williamsport, PA; (570) 323-2520; (Dom) (Intl)

Every Child, Inc.; Pittsburgh, PA; (412) 665-0600; www.everychildinc.org; (Dom)

Families Caring for Children, Inc.; Nanticoke, PA; (570) 735-9082; (Dom)

Families International Adoption Agency, Inc.; Pittsburgh, PA; (412) 362-6630; (Intl)

Families United Network, Inc.; Dillsburg, PA; (717) 502-1576; www.families4kids.org; (Dom)

Families United Network, Inc.; Mount Joy, PA; (717) 492-9338; www.families4kids .org/foster/foster.htm; (Dom)

Families United Network, Inc.; Muncy, PA; (717) 492-9338; www.families4kids.org; (Dom)

Families United Network, Inc.; Trafford, PA; (412) 373-2355; www.families4kids.org/ default.htm; (Dom)

Family Adoption Center; Pittsburgh, PA; (412) 288-2138; www.fhcinc.org; (Dom) (Intl)

Family Care Services, Inc.; Chambersburg, PA; (717) 263-2285; (Dom)

Family Pathways; Butler, PA; (724) 284-9440; (Dom)

Family Service; Lancaster, PA; (717) 397-5241; www.fslancaster.org; (Dom) (Intl)

Family Services and Children's Aid Society of Venango County; Oil City, PA; (814) 677-4005; (Dom)

Family Services of Northwestern Pennsylvania; Erie, PA; (814) 866-4500; www.family serviceserie.org; (Dom)

Family Services of Western Pennsylvania; Pittsburgh, PA; (412) 820-2050; www.fswp .org; (Dom)

A Field of Dreams Adoption Services, Inc.; Bellefonte, PA; (814) 355-4310; http:// afieldofdreams.com; (Dom) (Intl) China, Guatemala, Haiti, India, Ukraine

Friends Association for the Care and Protection of Children; West Chester, PA; (610) 431-3598; www.friendsassoc.org; (Dom)

Friendship House-Adoption, Inc.; Pottstown, PA; (610) 327-2200; www.friendship housepa.org; (Dom)

Genesis of Pittsburgh, Inc.; Pittsburgh, PA; (412) 766-2693; http://trfn.clpgh.org/ genesis; (Dom)

Hempfield Behavioral Health; Harrisburg, PA; (717) 221-8004; (Dom)

ILB Adoption Agency, Inc.; Pittsburgh, PA; (412) 521-2413; (Dom)

Institute for Human Resources & Services, Inc; Kingston, PA; (570) 288-9386; (Dom)

International Adoption Center (IAC); Philadelphia, PA; (610) 521-2667; www.inter nationaladoptioncenter.net; (Intl) Brazil, Bulgaria, China, Colombia, Guate-mala, Kazakhstan, Lithuania, Mexico

International Assistance Group, Inc.; Oakmont, PA; (412) 781-6470; www.iagadop tions.org; (Intl)

International Families Adoption Agency; Philadelphia, PA; (215) 735-7171; www .4adoption.com; (Intl) Guatemala, Romania

International Family Services (IFS); Irwin, PA; (724) 864-9522; www.ifservices.org; (Dom) (Intl) China, Guatemala, India, Russian Federation

Jewish Family & Children's Service; Philadelphia, PA; (215) 698-9950; (Dom) (Intl)

Jewish Family and Children's Service, Inc. (Family Hope Connection); Pittsburgh, PA; (412) 422-7200; www.fhcadopt.org; (Dom) (Intl)

Juvenile Justice Center, Inc.; Philadelphia, PA; (215) 849-2112; www.juvenilejustice .org; (Dom)

KidsPeace National Centers, Inc.; Bethlehem, PA; (610) 799-8350; www.kidspeace.org; (Dom)

KidsPeace National Centers, Inc.; Doylestown, PA; (215) 348-3400; www.kidspeace .org; (Dom)

KidsPeace National Centers, Inc.; Duncansville, PA; (814) 693-7708; www.kidspeace .org; (Dom)

KidsPeace National Centers, Inc.; Honesdale, PA; (570) 253-7910; www.kidspeace.org; (Dom)

KidsPeace National Centers, Inc.; New Cumberland, PA; (717) 770-7364; (Dom)

KidsPeace National Centers, Inc.; Reading, PA; (610) 374-0946; www.kidspeace.org; (Dom)

KidsPeace National Centers, Inc.; Schuylkill Haven, PA; (570) 385-6821; www .kidspeace.org; (Dom)

KidsPeace National Centers, Inc.; Williamsport, PA; (570) 326-7811; www.kidspeace .org; (Dom)

La Vida International Adoption Agency, Inc.; Malvern, PA; (610) 647-8008; (Dom)

La Vida International, Inc.; King of Prussia, PA; (610) 688-8008; www.lavida.org; (Dom) (Intl)

Life Adoption Services; Paoli, PA; (610) 644-1107; www.lifeadoptions.com; (Dom) (Intl)

Living Hope Adoption Agency, Inc.; Telford, PA; (215) 721-8880; www.livinghope adoption.org; (Intl) China

Love the Children, Inc.; Quakertown, PA; (215) 536-4180; www.lovethechildren.com; (Intl) Korea (South)

Lutheran Children and Family Service of Eastern Pennsylvania; Roslyn, PA; (215) 456-5700; (215) 881-6800; www.lcfsinpa.org; (Dom) (Intl) Cambodia

Lutheran Home at Topton; One South Home Avenue; Topton, PA 19562; (610) 682-1504; www.diakon.org; (Dom)

Lutheran Service Society of Western Pennsylvania (LSS); Greensburg, PA; (724) 837-9385; www.lsswpa.org; (Dom) (Intl)

Madison Adoption Associates; Boothwyn, PA; (610) 459-0454; www.madison adoption.com; (Dom) (Intl) Bulgaria, China, Guatemala, Kazakhstan, Ukraine

Main Street Adoption Service, Inc.; Lancaster, PA; (925) 228-9401; www.main streetadoption.com; (Intl) Bulgaria, Guatemala, Hungary, Kazakhstan, Lithuania, Russian Federation, Ukraine

Methodist Family Services of Philadelphia (MFSP); Philadelphia, PA; (215) 877-1927; (Dom)

New Beginnings Family and Children's Services; Matamoras, PA; (516) 747-2204; www.new-beginnings.org; (Intl) China, Korea (South), Peru, Russian Federation, Thailand

New Foundations, Inc.; Philadelphia, PA; (215) 203-8733; www.nfi4kids.org; (Dom)

Northeast Treatment Center (NET); Philadelphia, PA; (215) 451-7000; www.net-centers.org; (Dom)

Northern Home for Children and Family Services (NHCFS); Philadelphia, PA; (215) 482-1423; (Dom)

Northwestern Human Services of PA, Inc. (NHS); Chambersburg, PA; (717) 263-7295; http://nhsonline.org; (Dom)

Open Door Children and Youth Services, Inc.; Reading, PA; (610) 372-2200; www.open doorcys.com; (Dom)

PAACT; Liverpool, PA; (717) 444-3629; (Dom)

PERL, Inc., for Families and Children; Philadelphia, PA; (215) 247-8843; www.perlinc.org; (Dom) (Intl)

Pinebrook Services for Children & Youth, Inc.; Allentown, PA; (610) 432-3919; www.pine brookservices.org; (Dom)

Plan-It for Kids PC, Inc.; Berlin, PA; (814) 267-3182; www.plan-itforkids.org; (Dom) (Intl) Guatemala, Slovakia, Ukraine

Presbyterian Children's Village Services (PCVS); Philadelphia, PA; (215) 878-2480; www.pcv.org; (Dom) (Intl)

Presbyterian Children's Village Services (PCVS); Rosemont, PA; (610) 525-5400; www.pcv.org; (Dom)

Pressley Ridge Adoption Services; Pittsburgh, PA; (412) 321-6995; www.pressleyridge.org; (Dom)

Professional Family Care Services, Inc.; Johnstown, PA; (814) 255-9559; www.pfcs.org; (Dom)

Project Oz Adoptions, Inc.; Meadville, PA; (814) 333-4201; www.projectoz.com; (Dom) (Intl) Bulgaria, China, Guatemala, Haiti, Russian Federation, Ukraine

Project STAR/Beaver County; Monaca, PA; (724) 775-0209; www.amazingkids.org/ps_01.asp; (Dom)

Project STAR/The Children's Institute; Pittsburgh, PA; (412) 244-3066; www.amazingkids.org; (Dom)

PSI Services II, Inc.; Philadelphia, PA; (215) 238-5008; (Dom)

Rainbow Adoption and Family Tree Foster Care; Pittsburgh, PA; (412) 782-4457; www.angelfire.com/pa/cotraicadopt; (Dom)

Rejoice! Inc.; Allentown, PA; (610) 439-1990; www.rejoice-inc.org; (Dom)

Rejoice! Inc, Foster Care and Adoption Agency; Harrisburg, PA; (717) 221-0722; www.rejoice-inc.org; (Dom)

The Salvation Army Children's Services (SACS); Allentown, PA; (610) 821-7706; (Dom)

Sanctuary House of Chambersburg, Inc.; Chambersburg, PA; (717) 267-2744; (Dom)

A Second Chance; Pittsburgh, PA; (412) 665-2300; www.asecondchance-kinship.com; (Dom)

Southern Latitudes Adoption Services (SoLats); Warminster, PA; (215) 343-8500; www.southernlatitudesadoptions.com; (Dom) (Intl)

Spectrum Family Network Adoption Services; Pittsburgh, PA; (412) 362-3600; (Dom)

St. Joseph's Center; Scranton, PA; (570) 342-8379; www.stjosephscenter.org; (Dom)

Tabor Children's Services, Inc.; Doylestown, PA; (215) 348-4071; www.tabor.org; (Dom)

Tabor Children's Services, Inc.; Philadelphia, PA; (215) 842-4800; www.tabor.org; (Dom)

Three Rivers Adoption Council/Black Adoption Services (TRAC); Pittsburgh, PA; (412) 471-8722; www.3riversadopt.org; (Dom)

Try-Again Homes, Inc.; Washington, PA; (724) 225-0510; www.try-againhomes.org; (Dom)

Volunteers of America of Pennsylvania, Inc.; Philadelphia, PA; (215) 925-2620; www.voapa.org; (Dom)

Volunteers of America of Pennsylvania, Inc.; Wilkes-Barre, PA; (570) 825-5261; www.voapa.org; (Dom)

Women's Christian Alliance; Philadelphia, PA; (215) 236-9911; www.wcafamily.org; (Dom)

World Links International Adoption Agency (WLIAA); Scranton, PA; (570) 344-8890; www.wliaa.org; (Intl) Armenia, Bulgaria, Kazakhstan, Moldova, Poland, Russian Federation, Ukraine

Youth Service, Inc. (YSI); Philadelphia, PA; (215) 222-3262; www.ysiphila.org; (Dom)

RHODE ISLAND

STATE ADOPTION OFFICE: Rhode Island Department of Children, Youth and Families (RIDCYF); Adoption & Foster Care Preparation & Support; 101 Friendship St.; Providence, RI 02903; (401) 528-3799; www.dcyf.ri.gov/adoption.htm

ICPC ADMINISTRATOR: Rhode Island Department of Children, Youth and Families; 530 Wood St.; Bristol, RI 02809; (401) 254-7077; (401) 254-7099; www.dcyf.ri.gov

STATE ADOPTION EXCHANGE: Adoption Rhode Island; (401) 724-1910; www.adoptionri.org; adoptionri@ids.net

RHODE ISLAND BAR ASSOCIATION: (401) 421-5740; ribar.com

ANNUAL NUMBER OF ADOPTIVE ADOPTIONS FINALIZED IN STATE: 617

STATE LAWS AND PROCEDURES—FAST FACTS

Types permitted? Independent and agency.

Who can adopt in state? Residents, and nonresidents when agency making placement is located in state.

How long after the child's placement to finalize the adoption in court? 6–8 months.

Is adoptive parent advertising (to find a birth mother) permitted? No.

Is a preplacement home study required? Independent—no, but commonly done. Agency—yes.

Typical home study fee? $1,200–$1,300 (agency fees usually higher if agency located child).

Can adoptive parents help birth mother with expenses? Yes: legal, medical, but not living.

Can child leave hospital with adoptive parents? Yes, usually directly via birth mother.

When can birth mother sign her Consent to Adoption? Anytime after birth.

Can the consent be revoked? Independent—yes, until the consent is affirmed before a judge (usually 3 months postbirth), then irrevocable. Agency—a voluntary Petition to Terminate Parental Rights can be filed no sooner than the 15th day after birth and is irrevocable with the court's order.

What are the putative father's rights? There is no registry. Notice must be attempted.

AMERICAN ACADEMY OF ADOPTION ATTORNEYS MEMBERS

William J. Gallogly; 1220 Kingstown Rd.; Wakefield, RI 02879; (401) 789-8810; w.gallogly@adoptionattorneys.org

LICENSED PRIVATE AGENCIES

Adoption Network, Ltd.; Wakefield, RI; (401) 788-9118; www.adoptionnetworklimited.com; (Dom)

Adoption Options/Jewish Family Services; Providence, RI; (401) 331-5437; www.adoptionoptions.org; (Dom)

Children's Friend and Service; Providence, RI; (401) 331-2900; www.cfsri.org; (Dom)

China Adoption with Love, Inc.; Providence, RI; Toll-free: (800) 888-9812; www.cawli.org; (Intl) China

Communities for People, Inc.; Providence, RI; (401) 273-7103; www.communities-for-people.org; (Dom)

Gift of Life, Inc.; Cranston, RI; (401) 943-6484; www.giftoflife.cc; (Intl) China, Russian Federation

International Adoptions, Inc.; Woonsocket, RI; (401) 767-2300; (Intl)

Little Treasures Adoption Services; Warwick, RI; (401) 828-7747; www.littletreasures adopt.org; (Intl) Guatemala

Lutheran Social Services; Cranston, RI; (401) 785-0015; www.adoptlss.org/ri.html; (Dom) (Intl) Bulgaria, China, Kazakhstan, Moldova, Ukraine, Vietnam

A Red Thread Adoption Services, Inc.; Providence, RI; Toll-free: (888) 871-9699; www.redthreadadopt.org; (Dom) (Intl)

Urban League of Rhode Island, Inc. (Minority Recruitment & Child Placement Program); Providence, RI; (401) 351-5000; (Dom)

Wide Horizons for Children (WHFC); Providence, RI; (401) 421-4752; www.whfc.org; (Dom) (Intl) China, Colombia, Ethiopia, Guatemala, India, Korea, Lithuania, Moldova, Russian Federation, Ukraine

SOUTH CAROLINA

STATE ADOPTION OFFICE: South Carolina Department of Social Services; Division of Human Services; PO Box 1520; Columbia, SC 29202-1520; (803) 898-7707; www.state.sc.us

ICPC ADMINISTRATOR: South Carolina Department of Social Services; 1535 Confederate Ave.; PO Box 1520; Columbia, SC 29202-1520; (803) 898-7637; www.state.sc.us

STATE ADOPTION EXCHANGE: South Carolina Council on Adoptable Children; (803) 256-2622; www.sc-adopt.org; gail-coac@sc.rr.com

SOUTH CAROLINA BAR: (803) 799-6653; www.scbar.org

ANNUAL NUMBER OF ADOPTIVE ADOPTIONS FINALIZED IN STATE: 1,648

STATE LAWS AND PROCEDURES—FAST FACTS

Types permitted? Independent and agency (70% of newborns via independent).

Who can adopt in state? Residents, and nonresidents when child born in state or the agency making the placement is located in state.

How long after the child's placement to finalize the adoption in court? 3–12 months.

Is adoptive parent advertising (to find a birth mother) permitted? Yes.

Is a preplacement home study required? Yes.

Typical home study fee? $700–$900 (agency fees usually higher if agency located child).

Can adoptive parents help birth mother with expenses? Yes: legal, medical, living.

Can child leave hospital with adoptive parents? Yes, with signed form.
When can birth mother sign her Consent to Adoption? Anytime after birth.
Can the consent be revoked? No, it is irrevocable upon signing.
What are the putative father's rights? There is no registry. Notice must be attempted and he has 30 days to object. The court will consider his financial support to the child.

AMERICAN ACADEMY OF ADOPTION ATTORNEYS MEMBERS

Rick Corley; 1214 King St.; Beaufort, SC 22901; (843) 524-3232; rcorley@islc.net
Rick Corley began practicing law in 1976. He has completed 400 adoptions in his career and last year completed 55. 50% are newborn placements. 10% of his clients find a birth mother through his office.

L. Dale Dove; 235 E. Main St., #110; Rock Hill, SC 29731; (803) 327-1910; lddove@rhtc.net
Dale Dove began practicing law in 1983. He has completed 600 adoptions in his career and last year completed 50. 90% are newborn placements, 10% are toddlers or above. His clients find their own birth mother. He is an adoptive parent.

Thomas P. Lowndes; 128 Meeting St.; Charleston, SC 29401; (843) 723-1688; t.lowndes@adoptionattorneys.org
Thomas Lowndes began practicing law in 1966.

James Fletcher Thompson; PO Box 1853; Spartanburg, SC 29304; (864) 573-5533; www.adoptionsc.com; jfthompson@thompsonlawfirm.net
James Thompson began practicing law in 1989. He has completed 1,000 adoptions in his career and last year completed 75. 95% are newborn placements. 75% of his clients find a birth mother through his office.

Stephen Yacobi; 408 N. Church St.; Greenville, SC 29601; (864) 242-3271; www.scadoptlaw.com; syacobi@bellsouth.net
Stephen Yacobi began practicing law in 1980. He has completed 500 adoptions in his career and last year completed 56. 95% are newborn placements. 40% of his clients find a birth mother through his office; 60% find their own birth mother.

LICENSED PRIVATE AGENCIES

Adoption Advocacy, Inc.; Spartanburg, SC; (864) 590-8851; (Dom) (Intl)
Bethany Christian Services; Florence, SC; (843) 629-1177; www.bethany.org/south carolina; (Dom) (Intl)
Bethany Christian Services; Greenville, SC; (864) 235-2273; www.bethany.org/south carolina; (Dom) (Intl) Albania, Bulgaria, China, Colombia, India, Korea (South), Lithuania, Philippines, Russian Federation, Ukraine
Bethany Christian Services; Myrtle Beach, SC; (843) 839-5433; www.bethany.org/southcarolina; (Dom) (Intl)
Bethany Christian Services; West Columbia, SC; (803) 796-9332; www.bethany.org/southcarolina; (Dom) (Intl) Albania, China, Colombia, Ecuador, Guatemala, Haiti, Hong Kong—China, Kazakhstan, Kosova, Lithuania, Philippines, Ukraine

Carolina Adoption Services (CAS); Charleston, SC; (843) 852-9104; www.carolina adoption.org; (Intl) Armenia, Azerbaijan, China, Guatemala, Korea (South), Moldova, Peru, Republic of Georgia, Russian Federation, Ukraine, Vietnam

Carolina Hope Christian Adoption, Inc.; Greenville, SC; (864) 268-0570; www.carolina hopeadoption.org; (Dom) (Intl) Brazil, China, Guatemala, Kazakhstan, Korea (South), Lithuania, Nepal

Catholic Charities Diocese of Charleston; Charleston, SC; (843) 402-9115; www .catholiccharities.org; (Dom)

Cherished Children International Adoption Agency (CCIAA); Greenville, SC; (864) 261-7500; www.homestead.com/prosites-rommom; (Intl) Cambodia, China, Colombia, Guatemala, Kazakhstan, Moldova, Romania, Russian Federation

Child of the Heart; Mount Pleasant, SC; (843) 881-2973; www.childoftheheart.org; (Intl) Russian Federation, Ukraine

Children Unlimited of Family Service Center (Children Unlimited); Columbia, SC; (803) 799-8311; www.children-unlimited.org; (Dom)

A Chosen Child Adoption Services (ACCAS); Summerville, SC; (843) 851-4004; www .accadoptionservices.com; (Dom) (Intl) China, Colombia, El Salvador, Guatemala, Russian Federation

Christian Family Services, Inc. (CFS); Fort Mill, SC; (803) 548-6030; www.christian familyservices.org; (Dom)

Lutheran Family Services in the Carolinas (LFS); Columbia, SC; (803) 750-9917; www .lfscarolinas.org; (Dom) (Intl)

Small World Ministries, Inc.; Belton, SC; (864) 338-4673; (Dom) (Intl)

Southeastern Children's Home, Inc.; Duncan, SC; (864) 439-0259; www.sech.org; (Dom)

Special Link; Greenville, SC; (864) 233-4872; www.special-link.org; (Dom)

A Vision of Hope Adoption Agency; Seneca, SC; (864) 882-8835; (Dom) (Intl)

Worldwide Adoption Services, Inc.; Spartanburg, SC; (864) 814-1336; www.worldwide adoption.org; (Intl) Bulgaria, Cambodia, China, El Salvador, Guatemala, Haiti, Kazakhstan, Romania, Russian Federation, Vietnam

SOUTH DAKOTA

STATE ADOPTION OFFICE: South Dakota Department of Social Services; Department of Child Protective Services; 700 Governor's Dr.; Pierre, SD 57501-2291; (605) 773-3227; www.state.sd.us

ICPC ADMINISTRATOR: South Dakota Department of Social Services; (same address as above); Patricia Reiss, (605) 773-3227

STATE ADOPTION EXCHANGE: South Dakota Department of Social Services; www.dss .sd.gov/adoption/childrenwaiting

STATE BAR OF SOUTH DAKOTA: (605) 224-7554; www.sdbar.org

ANNUAL NUMBER OF ADOPTIVE ADOPTIONS FINALIZED IN STATE: 399

STATE LAWS AND PROCEDURES—FAST FACTS

Types permitted? Independent and agency (40% of newborns via independent).

Who can adopt in state? Residents only.

How long after the child's placement to finalize the adoption in court? 6 months.

Is adoptive parent advertising (to find a birth mother) permitted? Yes.

Is a preplacement home study required? Yes.

Typical home study fee? $800–$1,500 (agency fees usually higher if agency located child).

Can adoptive parents help birth mother with expenses? Yes: legal, medical, and living, but prior court approval required.

Can child leave hospital with adoptive parents? Yes, with signed form.

When can birth mother sign her Consent to Adoption? Petition for Voluntary Termination of Parental Rights can't be filed sooner than 5th day after birth. Court hearing scheduled to grant order usually 1–25 days later.

Can the consent be revoked? Yes, prior to court order. After order, consent is irrevocable.

What are the putative father's rights? There is no registry. Notice must be attempted, usually giving him 30 days notice to object.

AMERICAN ACADEMY OF ADOPTION ATTORNEYS MEMBERS

John R. Hughes; 431 N. Phillips Ave., #330; Sioux Falls, SD 57104; (605) 339-3939; j.hughes@adoptionattorneys.org

The following AAAA member additionally practices in South Dakota from a neighboring state:

Maxine M. Buckmeier; 600 4th St., #304; Sioux City, IA 51102; (712) 233-3660; m.buckmeier@adoptionattorneys.org

LICENSED PRIVATE AGENCIES

All About U Adoptions, Inc. (AAU); Milbank, SD; (605) 949-2507; www.allaboutu adoptions.org; (Dom)

Bethany Christian Services, Inc.; Rapid City, SD; (605) 343-7196; www.bethany .org/southdakota; (Dom) (Intl) Albania, Bulgaria, China, Colombia, India, Japan, Kazakhstan, Korea (South), Lithuania, Philippines, Russian Federation, Ukraine

Bethany Christian Services, Inc.; Sioux Falls, SD; (605) 336-6999; www.bethany.org; (Dom) (Intl)

Catholic Family Services, Inc.; Aberdeen, SD; (605) 226-1304; www.sfcatholic.org/cfs; (Dom)

Catholic Family Services, Inc.; Sioux Falls, SD; (605) 988-3775; www.sfcatholic.org/cfs/adoptions.html; (Dom)

Catholic Social Services (CSS); Rapid City, SD; (605) 348-6086; www.catholic-social-services.net; (Dom)

Children's Home Society (CHS); Sioux Falls, SD; (605) 334-6004; www.chssd.org; (Dom) (Intl)

LDS Family Services, Inc.; Rapid City, SD; (605) 342-3500; (Dom)
Lutheran Social Services of South Dakota; Aberdeen, SD; (605) 229-1500; www.lsssd
.org; (Dom) (Intl)
Lutheran Social Services of South Dakota; Rapid City, SD; (605) 348-0477; www.lsssd
.org; (Dom) (Intl)
Lutheran Social Services of South Dakota; Sioux Falls, SD; (605) 336-3347; www.lsssd
.org; (Dom) (Intl)
New Horizons Adoption Agency, Inc.; Sioux Falls, SD; (605) 332-0310; www.nhadoption
agency.com; (Dom) (Intl)
Sisseton Wahpeton Sioux Tribe; Agency Village, SD; (605) 698-3992; (Dom)

TENNESSEE

STATE ADOPTION OFFICE: Tennessee Department of Children's Services; Cordell Hull
Bldg., 8th Floor; 436 6th Ave. North; Nashville, TN 37243-1290; (615) 253-
6351; www.state.tn.us; http://w4.systranlinks.com

ICPC ADMINISTRATOR: Tennessee Department of Children's Services; (same address as
above); (615) 532-5618; (615) 253-5422

STATE ADOPTION EXCHANGE: Tennessee Department of Children's Services; www.state
.tn.us

TENNESSEE BAR ASSOCIATION: (615) 383-7421; www.tba.org

ANNUAL NUMBER OF ADOPTIVE ADOPTIONS FINALIZED IN STATE: 2,633

STATE LAWS AND PROCEDURES—FAST FACTS
Types permitted? Independent and agency (60% of newborns via independent).
Who can adopt in state? Residents only.
How long after the child's placement to finalize the adoption in court? 6 months.
Is adoptive parent advertising (to find a birth mother) permitted? Yes.
Is a preplacement home study required? Yes.
Typical home study fee? $1,200 (agency fees usually higher if agency located child).
Can adoptive parents help birth mother with expenses? Yes: legal, medical, and liv-
ing, but living assistance limited to 90 days prior to, and 45 days after, birth.
Can child leave hospital with adoptive parents? Yes, with signed form.
When can birth mother sign her Consent to Adoption? No sooner than 4 days after
birth.
Can the consent be revoked? Yes, for 10 days, then irrevocable.
What are the putative father's rights? There is a registry. Notice must be attempted
if he is registered or named by birth mother. His rights often severed if he did not
file a paternity action within 30 days.

AMERICAN ACADEMY OF ADOPTION ATTORNEYS MEMBERS
Lisa L. Collins; 1 American Ctr.; 3100 W. End Ave., #1210; Nashville, TN 37203;
(615) 269-5540; www.tnadopt.com

Lisa Collins began practicing law in 1993. She has completed 1,500 adoptions in her career.

Dawn Coppock; PO Box 388; Strawberry Plains, TN 37871; (865) 933-8173; d.coppock@adoptionattorneys.org
Dawn Coppock began practicing law in 1987. Last year she completed 106 adoptions. 99% are newborn placements. 7% of her clients find a birth mother through her office.

Michael S. Jennings; Samples, Jennings, Ray and Clem, PLLC; 130 Jordan Dr.; Chattanooga, TN 37421; (423) 892-2006; m.jennings@adoptionattorneys.org
Michael Jennings began practicing law in 1984. Last year he completed 120 adoptions. 98% are newborn placements. 15% of his clients find a birth mother through his office.

Robert D. Tuke; Trauger & Tuke; 222 4th Ave. North; Nashville, TN 37219; (615) 256-8585; www.tntlaw.net; rtuke@tntlaw.net
Robert Tuke began practicing law in 1976. He has completed 400 adoptions in his career. 100% of his adoptions are newborn placements. His clients find their own birth mother. He is a past president of the American Academy of Adoption Attorneys.

A biography was not available for the following AAAA member:
Paul M. Buchanan; PO Box 198985; Nashville, TN 37219; (615) 256-9999; p.buchanan @adoptionattorneys.org

LICENSED PRIVATE AGENCIES
Adoption Consultants in Tennessee, Inc.; Knoxville, TN; (865) 769-9441; (Dom) (Intl)
Adoption Counseling Services (ACS); Germantown, TN; (901) 753-9089; www.adoption andyou.com; (Dom) (Intl)
Adoption Home Studies and Social Services; Chattanooga, TN; (423) 802-6367; (Dom) (Intl)
Adoption Place, Inc.; Nashville, TN; (615) 365-7020; (Dom) (Intl)
Adoption Promises; Huntingdon, TN; (731) 986-2001; www.adoptionpromises.com; (Dom)
Associated Catholic Charities, Inc./St. Peter Maternity and Adoption Services; Memphis, TN; (901) 722-4700; www.cathchar.org; (Dom) (Intl)
Association for Guidance, Aid, Placement and Empathy (AGAPE); Memphis, TN; (901) 323-3600; www.agapemeanslove.org; (Dom)
Association for Guidance, Aid, Placement and Empathy (AGAPE); Nashville, TN; (615) 781-3000; http://agapenashville.org; (Dom)
Bethany Christian Services; Chattanooga, TN; (423) 622-7360; www.bethany.org/ easttennessee; (Dom) (Intl)
Bethany Christian Services of Middle Tennessee; Nashville, TN; (615) 242-0909; www .bethany.org/nashville; (Dom) (Intl)
Catholic Charities of East Tennessee, Inc.; Knoxville, TN; (865) 524-9896; www .etcatholiccharities.com; (Dom)

Catholic Charities of Tennessee, Inc.; Nashville, TN; (615) 352-3087; http://cctenn.org; (Dom) (Intl)

The Center for Family Development; Shelbyville, TN; (931) 684-4676; www.thecenter forfamilydevelopment.org; (Dom) (Intl)

Child and Family Tennessee; Knoxville, TN; (865) 524-7483; www.child-family.org; (Dom)

Children's Hope International; Brentwood, TN; (615) 309-8109; www.childrens hopeint.org; (Intl) China, Colombia, Guatemala, India, Russian Federation, Vietnam

Christian Children's Homes of Tennessee—Elizabethton (CCHTN); Elizabethton, TN; (423) 542-4245; 4369; http://cch-tn.org; (Dom) (Intl) Bulgaria, China, Guatemala, Russian Federation

Christian Children's Homes of Tennessee—Knoxville (CCHTN—Knox); Knoxville, TN; (865) 357-7949; http://cch-tn.org; (Dom) (Intl)

Crossroads Counseling Center; Morristown, TN; (423) 581-5342; (Dom)

Exceptional Needs Care Management Agency, Inc.; Memphis, TN; (901) 360-0194; (Dom) (Intl)

Frontier Health/Traces; Kingsport, TN; (423) 224-1067; www.frontier.org; (Dom)

Global Village International Adoptions; Murfreesboro, TN; (615) 890-3507; www .globalvillageadopt.org; (Intl)

Greater Chattanooga Christian Services, Inc.; Chattanooga, TN; (423) 499-9535; www .chattanoogachristianservices.org; (Dom)

Harmony Adoptions of Tennessee, Inc.; Maryville, TN; (865) 982-5225; http://harmony.cc; (Dom)

Heaven Sent Children, Inc.; Murfreesboro, TN; (615) 898-0803; www.heavensent children.com; (Dom) (Intl) Azerbaijan, China, Guatemala

Holston United Methodist Home for Children, Inc.; Chattanooga, TN; (423) 855-4682; www.holstonhome.org; (Dom) (Intl) Philippines

Holston United Methodist Home for Children, Inc.; Greeneville, TN; (423) 638-4171; www.holstonhome.org; (Dom) (Intl)

Holston United Methodist Home for Children, Inc.; Johnson City, TN; (423) 952-2290; www.holstonhome.org; (Dom) (Intl)

Holston United Methodist Home for Children, Inc.; Knoxville, TN; (865) 633-9844; www .holstonhome.org; (Dom) (Intl)

International Assistance and Adoption Project (IAAP); Signal Mountain, TN; (423) 886-6986; www.iaapadoption.com; (Intl)

Jewish Family Service, Inc.; Memphis, TN; (901) 767-2525; http://jewishfamilyservice memphis.org; (Dom) (Intl)

Jewish Family Service of Nashville and Middle Tennessee, Inc.; Nashville, TN; (615) 354-1664; www.jfsnashville.org; (Dom) (Intl)

Life Choices, Inc.; Memphis, TN; (901) 388-1172; www.life-choices.org; (Dom)

Mercy Ministries of America; Nashville, TN; (615) 831-6987; www.mercyministries .com; (Dom)

Mid-Cumberland Children's Services, Inc.; Smithville, TN; (615) 597-7134; (Dom) (Intl)

Mid-South Christian Services; Memphis, TN; (901) 818-9996; www.bethany.org/memphis; (Dom) (Intl) Albania, China, Colombia, Ecuador, Guatemala, India, Korea (South), Lithuania, Philippines, Russian Federation, Ukraine

Miriam's Promise; Nashville, TN; (615) 292-3500; www.miriamspromise.org; (Dom) Philippines

Omni Visions; Nashville, TN; (615) 460-7051; www.omnivisions.com; (Dom)

Partnership for Families, Children and Adults; Chattanooga, TN; (423) 755-2822; www.partnershipfca.com; (Dom)

Porter-Leath Children's Center (PLCC); Memphis, TN; (901) 577-2500; www.porter-leath.org; (Dom) (Intl)

Small World, Inc.; Hermitage, TN; (615) 883-4372; www.swa.net; (Dom) (Intl) China, Guatemala, Mongolia, Russian Federation

Smoky Mountain Children's Home; Sevierville, TN; (865) 453-4644; www.smch.cc; (Dom)

Tennessee Baptist Children's Homes, Inc.; Brentwood, TN; (615) 376-3140; www.tbch4kids.org; (Dom)

Tennessee Children's Home; Ashland City, TN; (615) 307-3205; http://smithdray.tripod.com/tch; (Dom)

Tennessee Children's Home—East; Knoxville, TN; (865) 584-0841; http://smithdray.tripod.com/tch; (Dom)

Williams International Adoptions, Inc. (WIAI); Memphis, TN; (901) 373-6003; www.williamsinternational.org; (Intl) Guatemala, India, Kazakhstan, Romania, Russian Federation, Thailand, Ukraine

TEXAS

STATE ADOPTION OFFICE: Texas Department of Family and Protective Services; 701 W. 51st St., MC E-558; PO Box 149030; Austin, TX 78714-9030; (512) 438-4760; www.tdprs.state.tx.us

ICPC ADMINISTRATOR: Texas Department of Family and Protective Services; (512) 438-5141; (512) 339-5815; www.dfps.state.tx.us

STATE ADOPTION EXCHANGE: Texas Adoption Resource Exchange (TARE); Toll-free: (800) 233-3405; www.adoptchildren.org

STATE BAR OF TEXAS: (512) 463-1463; www.texasbar.com

ANNUAL NUMBER OF ADOPTIVE ADOPTIONS FINALIZED IN STATE: 7,957

STATE LAWS AND PROCEDURES—FAST FACTS

Types permitted? Independent and agency (40% of newborns via independent).

Who can adopt in state? Residents, and nonresidents when child born in state or the agency making the placement is located in state.

How long after the child's placement to finalize the adoption in court? 5–6 months.

Is adoptive parent advertising (to find a birth mother) permitted? No.

Is a preplacement home study required? Yes.

Typical home study fee? $2,000 (agency fees usually higher if agency located child).

Can adoptive parents help birth mother with expenses? Yes: legal, medical, and living, but nonmedical expenses must be paid through an agency.

Can child leave hospital with adoptive parents? Yes, with signed form.

When can birth mother sign her Consent to Adoption? 48 hours after birth.

Can the consent be revoked? Two consent options. One method makes the consent irrevocable upon signing, on the condition a court accepts her consent and terminates her rights within 60 days. The other is to make it revocable for 10 days, then irrevocable thereafter.

What are the putative father's rights? There is a registry. Notice must be attempted if he registers or is named by the birth mother. Usually he is given about 20 days in which to object.

AMERICAN ACADEMY OF ADOPTION ATTORNEYS MEMBERS

Vika Andrel; 1220 Deer Creek Cir.; Dripping Springs, TX 78620; (512) 448-4605; www.andreladoptionlawyer.com; vikaa49@aol.com
Vika Andrel began practicing law in 1985. She has completed 1,000 adoptions in her career and last year completed 67. 100% are newborn placements.

Harold C. Brown; 201 Main St., Suite 801; Fort Worth, TX 76102; (817) 338-4888; c.brown@adoptionattorneys.org
Harold Brown began practicing law in 1960.

Lester R. Buzbee III; 116 S. Ave. C; Humble, TX 77338; (281) 540-8060; www.buzbeelaw.com; l.buzbee@adoptionattorneys.org
Lester Buzbee began practicing law in 1977. He has completed 700 adoptions in his career and last year completed 59. 80% are newborn placements.

Carla M. Calabrese; Calabrese Associates, PC; 5944 Luther Ln., Suite 875; Dallas, TX 75225; (214) 939-3000; www.calabreselaw.com; carla@calabreselaw.com
Carla Calabrese began practicing law in 1986. She has completed 500 adoptions in her career and last year completed 27. 99% are newborn placements. She is an adoptive parent and is the founder of an adoption agency.

David Charles Cole; 3631 Fairmont St., #201; Dallas, TX 75219; (214) 363-5117; d.cole@adoptionattorneys.org
David Cole began practicing law in 1987.

Heidi Bruegel Cox; 6300 John Ryan Dr.; Fort Worth, TX 76132; (817) 922-6043; adoptionsbyglandney.org; heidi.cox@gladney.org
Heidi Cox began practicing law in 1986. She has completed 3,000 adoptions in her career and last year completed 150. She is general counsel for the Gladney Center for Adoption, as they have many international adoption programs.

Michael R. Lackmeyer; 1201 S. W. S. Young Dr.; Killeen, TX 76543; (254) 690-2223; m.lackmeyer@adoptionattorneys.org
Michael Lachmeyer began practicing law in 1970.

Mel W. Shelander; 245 N. 4th St.; Beaumont, TX 77701; (409) 833-2165; mws@she landerlaw.com
Mel Shelander began practicing law in 1976. He has completed 500 adoptions in his career and last year completed 25. 100% are newborn placements. He is an adoptive parent.

Steve Watkins; Watkins & Perkins; 5602 Wesley St.; Greenville, TX 75403; (903) 454-6688; www.watkins-perkins.com; steve@watkins-perkins.com
Steve Watkins began practicing law in 1980. He has completed 100 adoptions in his career and last year completed 18. 80% are newborn placements.

Jenny L. Womack; Palmer & Manuel, LLP; 8350 N. Central Expy., #1111; Dallas, TX 75206; (214) 242-6449; jwomack@pamlaw.com
Jenny Womack began practicing law in 1998. She has completed 140 adoptions in her career and last year completed 26. 80% are newborn placements. She serves as general counsel of an adoption agency.

Ellen A. Yarrell; 1900 S. James Pl., #850; Houston, TX 77056; (713) 621-3332; ellen@ eayatty.com
Ellen Yarrell began practicing law in 1979. She has completed 1,000 adoptions in her career and last year completed 80. 80% are newborn placements. She is a past president of the American Academy of Adoption Attorneys.

Linda M. Zuflacht; 5370 Prue Rd.; San Antonio, TX 78240; (210) 699-6088; www .adoptionservicesassociates.org; l.zuflacht@adoptionattorneys.org
Linda Zuflacht began practicing law in 1978. She founded Adoption Services Associates, an adoption agency. They do approximately 70 adoptions per year.

Biographies were not available for the following AAAA members:
Gerald A. Bates; 3200 River Front Dr., #204; Fort Worth, TX 76107; (817) 338-2840; g.bates@adoptionattorneys.org

Dale R. Johnson; 7303 Blanco Rd.; San Antonio, TX 78216; (210) 349-3761; d.johnson@adoptionattorneys.org

Charles E. Myers; 4400 Buffalo Gap Rd., #2500; Abilene, TX 79606; (325) 692-2708; c.myers@adoptionattorneys.org

Susan I. Paquet; 601 Bailey Ave.; Fort Worth, TX 76107; (817) 596-3337; s.paquet@ adoptionattorneys.org

Irv W. Queal; 8117 Preston Rd., #800; Dallas, TX 75225; (214) 696-3200; i.queal@ adoptionattorneys.org

Donald R. Royall; 4500 Post Oak Pl., #341; Houston, TX 77027; (713) 462-6500; d.royall@adoptionattorneys.org

Melody Brooks Royall; 4500 Post Oak Pl., #341; Houston, TX 77027; (713) 462-6500; m.royall@adoptionattorneys.org

Harold C. Zuflacht; 12000 Huebner Rd., #200; San Antonio, TX 78230; (210) 349-9933; h.zuflacht@adoptionattorneys.org

LICENSED PRIVATE AGENCIES

ABC Adoption Agency, Inc.; San Antonio, TX; (210) 227-7820; (Dom)

Abrazo Adoption Associates (AAA); San Antonio, TX; (210) 342-5683; www.abrazo.org; (Dom)

Adoptation; Houston, TX; (713) 333-2232; www.adoptation.org; (Dom)

Adoption Access, Inc.; Dallas, TX; (214) 750-4847; www.adoptionaccess.com; (Dom)

Adoption Advisory, Inc.; Dallas, TX; (214) 520-0004; www.adoptadvisory.com; (Dom)

Adoption Advocates, Inc. (AAI); Austin, TX; (512) 477-1122; www.adoptionadvocates.net/index.html; (Dom) (Intl)

Adoption Affiliates, Inc.; San Antonio, TX; (210) 824-9939; (Dom)

Adoption—A Gift of Love; Denton, TX; (940) 243-0749; www.adoption-agol.org; (Intl) China, Mexico

Adoption Alliance; San Antonio, TX; (210) 349-3991; www.adoption-alliance.com; (Dom)

Adoption Angels, Inc.; San Antonio, TX; (210) 227-2229; www.adoptionangels.com; (Dom)

Adoption as an Option; Sugar Land, TX; (713) 468-1053; (Dom) (Intl)

Adoption Family Services, Inc. (AFS); Rockwall, TX; (972) 771-4491; www.adoptfamilyservices.com; (Dom)

Adoption Information and Counseling Services, Inc.; Houston, TX; (713) 529-4341; www.adoptquest.com; (Dom)

Adoption Services Associates (ASA); San Antonio, TX; (210) 699-6094; www.adoptionservicesassociates.org; (Dom)

Adoption Services, Inc.; Fort Worth, TX; (817) 921-0718; (Dom)

Adoption Services Worldwide, Inc.; San Antonio, TX; (210) 342-0444; www.babyasw.com; (Dom) (Intl)

AdoptionWorks, A Child Placing Agency of ChristianWorks for Children, Inc.; Dallas, TX; (972) 960-9981; www.adoptionworks.org; (Dom)

Adoptions International, Inc. (A.I.I.); Dallas, TX; (214) 342-8388; www.adoptmeinternational.org; (Intl) Guatemala, Kazakhstan, Russian Federation, Vietnam

Alternatives in Motion; Houston, TX; (281) 821-6508; www.aimadoptions.org; (Dom)

Andrel Adoptions (AAI); Austin, TX; (512) 448-4605; (Dom)

Angel Adoptions of the Heart; Houston, TX; (713) 523-2273; (Dom)

Buckner Adoption and Maternity Services; Dallas, TX; (214) 319-3426; www.buckneradoption.org; (Dom) (Intl)

Buckner International Adoption; Dallas, TX; (214) 381-1552; www.bucknerinternationaladoption.org; (Intl) China, Guatemala, Romania, Russian Federation

Caring Adoptions; Houston, TX; (281) 920-4300; www.caringadoptions.org; (Dom)

Catholic Family Service, Inc.; Amarillo, TX; (806) 376-4571; www.catholicfamilyservice.org; (Dom)

Catholic Social Services of Laredo; Laredo, TX; (210) 722-2443; (Dom)

Child Placement Center of Texas; Killeen, TX; (817) 690-5959; www.childplacement center.com; (Dom)

Children and Family Institute; Dallas, TX; (214) 337-9979; www.cfiadopt.org; (Dom)

Children's Home of Lubbock; Lubbock, TX; (806) 762-0481; www.childshome.org; (Dom)

Chosen Heritage Christian Adoption Services; Duncanville, TX; (972) 296-5111; (Dom) (Intl) China, Russian Federation, Ukraine

Christian Homes; Abilene, TX; (915) 677-2205; www.christianhomes.com; (Dom)

Counsel for Adoption Resource Exchange; Killeen, TX; (254) 690-2223; (Dom)

A Cradle of Hope; Dallas, TX; (214) 747-4500; (Intl)

Cradle of Life Adoption Agency; Beaumont, TX; (409) 832-3000; (Dom)

DePelchin Children's Center; Houston, TX; (713) 730-2335; www.depelchin.org; (Dom)

El Paso Adoption Services (EPAS); El Paso, TX; (915) 542-1086; www.epadoption.org; (Dom)

Gladney Center for Adoption; Fort Worth, TX; (817) 922-6000; www.adoptionsby gladney.com; (Dom) (Intl)

Great Wall China Adoption (GWCA); Austin, TX; (512) 323-9595; www.gwca.org; (Intl) China

Harrah's Adoption International Mission (AIM); Spring, TX; (281) 465-9990; www.hfsa dopt.org; (Intl) China

Homes of Saint Mark (HSM); Houston, TX; (713) 522-2800; www.homesofstmark .org; (Dom) (Intl) Mexico

Hope Adoption, Inc.; Dallas, TX; (214) 672-9399; www.hopeadoption.org; (Intl) Azerbaijan, Bulgaria, China, Ethiopia, Guatemala, Kazakhstan, Ukraine

Hope Cottage Pregnancy and Adoption Center; Dallas, TX; (214) 526-8721; www.hope cottage.org; (Dom) (Intl) China, El Salvador, Guatemala, India, Kazakhstan, Moldova, Romania, Ukraine

Inheritance Adoptions; Wichita Falls, TX; (817) 322-3678; www.inheritanceadoptions .org; (Dom)

International Child Placing Agency; Los Fresnos, TX; (210) 233-5705; (Intl)

International Family Services (IFS); Friendswood, TX; (281) 992-4677; www.ifservices .org; (Dom) (Intl) China, Guatemala, India, Russian Federation

J&B Kids, Inc., Placing Agency; Yorktown, TX; (361) 564-9780; (Dom)

LDS Family Services; Carrollton, TX; (972) 242-2182; (Dom)

Lena Pope Home, Inc.; Fort Worth, TX; (817) 731-8681; www.lenapopehome.org; (Dom)

Little Miracles International, Inc.; Amarillo, TX; (806) 351-1100; www.littlemiracles .org; (Intl) Azerbaijan, Bulgaria, Cambodia, China, Guatemala, Kazakhstan, Republic of Georgia, Romania, Ukraine

Los Ninos International Adoption Center (LNI); The Woodlands, TX; (281) 363-2892; www.losninos.org; (Intl) Brazil, Bulgaria, China, Colombia, El Salvador, Guatemala, Kazakhstan, Panama, Russian Federation, Ukraine

Loving Alternatives; Tyler, TX; (903) 581-7720; www.livalt.org/index.html; (Dom)

Lutheran Social Services of the South, Inc.; Austin, TX; (512) 459-1000; www.lsss.org; (Dom) (Intl)

Marywood Children and Family Services; Austin, TX; (512) 472-9251; www.marywood .org; (Dom)

Methodist Children's Home; Waco, TX; (254) 753-0181; www.methodistchildrens home.org; (Dom)

Methodist Mission Home; San Antonio, TX; (210) 696-2410; www.mmhome.org; (Dom) (Intl) China, Colombia, Ethiopia, Guatemala, India, Kazakhstan, Korea (South), Russian Federation

Smithlawn Maternity Home; Lubbock, TX; (806) 745-2574; www.door.net/smithlawn; (Dom)

Spaulding for Children; Houston, TX; (713) 681-6991; www.spauldingforchildren .org; (Dom)

Texas Baptist Home (An Act of Love); Waxahachie, TX; (972) 937-1321; www.tbhc.org; (Dom)

Unity Children's Home; Houston, TX; (281) 537-0437; (Dom) (Intl)

UTAH

STATE ADOPTION OFFICE: Utah Department of Human Services; Division of Child and Family Services; 120 North 200 West, Suite 225; Salt Lake City, UT 84103; (801) 538-4437; www.hsdcfs.utah.gov

ICPC ADMINISTRATOR: Utah Department of Human Services; 120 North 200 West, Suite 225; Salt Lake City, UT 84103; (801) 538-4100; www.dcfs.utah.gov

STATE ADOPTION EXCHANGE: Utah Adoption Exchange: (801) 265-0444; www.utdcfs adopt.org; ks@adoptex.org

UTAH STATE BAR: (801) 531-9077; www.utahbar.org

ANNUAL NUMBER OF ADOPTIVE ADOPTIONS FINALIZED IN STATE: 1,387

STATE LAWS AND PROCEDURES—FAST FACTS

Types permitted? Independent and agency (30% of newborns via independent).

Who can adopt in state? Residents, and nonresidents when child born in state or the agency making the placement is located in state.

How long after the child's placement to finalize the adoption in court? 6 months.

Is adoptive parent advertising (to find a birth mother) permitted? Yes.

Is a preplacement home study required? Yes.

Typical home study fee? $700 (agency fees usually higher if agency located child).

Can adoptive parents help birth mother with expenses? Yes: legal, medical, living.

Can child leave hospital with adoptive parents? Yes, with signed form.

When can birth mother sign her Consent to Adoption? 24 hours after birth.

Can the consent be revoked? No, irrevocable upon signing.

What are the putative father's rights? There is a registry. To block adoption he must normally file a paternity action, register notice of that action, and show he paid pregnancy costs prior to birth mother signing consent. If he lives outside of Utah he may be given an additional 20 days.

AMERICAN ACADEMY OF ADOPTION ATTORNEYS MEMBERS

Les F. England; 875 Iron Horse Dr., Suite F; Park City, UT 84068; (435) 649-0569; l.england@adoptionattorneys.org
Les England began practicing law in 1982.

Larry S. Jenkins; Wood Crapo, LLC; 60 E. South Temple St., #500; Salt Lake City, UT 84111; (801) 366-6060; www.woodcrapo.com; lsjenkins@woodcrapo.com
Larry Jenkins began practicing law in 1986. He has completed 2,000 adoptions in his career and last year completed 200. 90% are newborn placements His clients find their own birth mother.

A biography was not available for the following AAAA member:
Dale M. Dorius; 29 S. Main; Brigham City, UT 84302; (435) 723-5219; d.dorius@adoptionattorneys.org

LICENSED PRIVATE AGENCIES

A Act of Love/Alternative Options and Services for Children; Sandy, UT; (801) 572-1696; www.aactofloveadoptions.com; (Dom)

Adopt an Angel; Salt Lake City, UT; (801) 537-1622; www.adoptangel.org; (Dom)

Adoption Center of Choice, Inc.; Orem, UT; (801) 224-2440; (Dom)

Children's Aid Society of Utah; Ogden, UT; (801) 393-8671; www.casadoption.org; (Dom)

Children's Service Society of Utah; Salt Lake City, UT; (801) 355-7444; www.cssutah.org; (Dom)

A Child's Dream; West Valley City, UT; (360) 598-6533; (Dom)

Families for Children; Salt Lake City, UT; (801) 467-3413; (Dom)

Focus on Children; Logan, UT; (888) 801-7295; http://focusonchildren.com; (Intl)

A Guardian Angel Adoptions; Sandy, UT; (801) 755-9533; www.aguardianangel.com; (Dom)

Heart and Soul Adoptions, Inc.; Farmington, UT; (801) 451-9333; www.heartandsouladoptions.com; (Dom)

Heart to Heart Adoptions, Inc.; Sandy, UT; (801) 563-1000; www.hearttoheartadoptions.net; (Dom)

LDS Family Services; American Fork, UT; (801) 216-8000; (Dom)

LDS Family Services; Cedar City, UT; (435) 586-4479; (Dom)

LDS Family Services; Kearns, UT; (801) 969-4181; www.providentliving.org; (Dom)

LDS Family Services; Logan, UT; (435) 752-5302; www.providentliving.org; (Dom)

LDS Family Services; Ogden, UT; (801) 621-6510; www.ldsfamilyservices.org; (Dom)

LDS Family Services; Price, UT; (435) 637-2991; (Dom)

LDS Family Services; Provo, UT; (801) 422-7620; (Dom)

LDS Family Services; Richfield, UT; (435) 896-6446; (Dom)

LDS Family Services; Salt Lake City, UT; (801) 240-6500; www.ldsfamilyservices.org; (Dom)

LDS Family Services; Sandy, UT; (801) 566-2556; www.itsaboutlove.com; (Dom)
LDS Family Services; St. George, UT; (435) 673-6446; (Dom)
Legacy International Adoptions, LLC; Salt Lake City, UT; (801) 278-3066; (Intl)
A Nurture Adopt Adoption Agency; Cedar Hills, UT; (801) 772-0409; www.nurture adopt.org/anaaa; (Dom)
A TLC Adoption; Farmington, UT; (801) 451-9333; www.tlcadoption.com; (Dom)
Wasatch International Adoptions (WIA); Ogden, UT; (801) 334-8683; www.wiaa.org; (Intl) Bulgaria, China, Guatemala, Haiti, Kazakhstan, Vietnam
West Sands Adoptions; St. George, UT; (801) 377-4379; www.westsandsadoption.org; (Intl) China, Haiti, Kazakhstan, Marshall Islands, Ukraine

VERMONT

STATE ADOPTION OFFICE: Vermont Department for Child and Families; Family Services Division; 103 S. Main St., Osgood 3; Waterbury, VT 05671-2401; (802) 241-2669; www.projectfamilyvt.org

ICPC ADMINISTRATOR: Vermont Department for Children and Families (VDCF); (same as above); Agency of Human Services; (802) 241-2131; www.dcf.state.vt.us

STATE ADOPTION EXCHANGE: Vermont's Waiting Children: (802) 241-2122; www.projectfamilyvt.org

VERMONT BAR ASSOCIATION: (802) 223-2020; www.vtbar.org

ANNUAL NUMBER OF ADOPTIVE ADOPTIONS FINALIZED IN STATE: 407

STATE LAWS AND PROCEDURES—FAST FACTS
Types permitted? Independent and agency (40% of newborns via independent).
Who can adopt in state? Residents, and nonresidents when the agency making the placement is located in state.
How long after the child's placement to finalize the adoption in court? 7 months.
Is adoptive parent advertising (to find a birth mother) permitted? Yes.
Is a preplacement home study required? Yes.
Typical home study fee? $1,200 (agency fees usually higher if agency located child).
Can adoptive parents help birth mother with expenses? Yes: legal, medical, living.
Can child leave hospital with adoptive parents? Yes, with signed form.
When can birth mother sign her Consent to Adoption? 36 hours after birth.
Can the consent be revoked? Yes, for 21 days, then irrevocable.
What are the putative father's rights? There is a registry, initiated by a birth father filing a paternity action, at which time the court notifies the registry.

AMERICAN ACADEMY OF ADOPTION ATTORNEYS MEMBERS
Kurt M. Hughes; Murdoch, Hughes & Twarog, PC; PO Box 363; Burlington, VT 05402; (802) 864-9811; www.adoptvt.com; khughes@mhtpc.com
Kurt Hughes began practicing law in 1985. He has completed several hundred adoptions in his career and last year completed 50. 90% are newborn placements, 10% are toddlers or above. His clients find their own birth mother.

LICENSED PRIVATE AGENCIES

Acorn Adoption & Family Services; Burlington, VT; (802) 865-3898; (Dom)

Adoption Advocates, Inc.; Shelburne, VT; (802) 985-8289; (Intl)

Angels' Haven Outreach; Monkton, VT; (802) 453-5450; www.angels-haven.com; (Intl) China, Ethiopia, Guatemala, Korea (South), Liberia, Nepal, Sierra Leone

Casey Family Services; White River Junction, VT; (802) 649-1400; www.caseyfamily services.org; (Dom)

Friends in Adoption; Middletown Springs, VT; (802)-235-2373; www.friendsin adoption.org; (Dom)

Lund Family Center (LFC); Burlington, VT; (802) 864-7467; www.lundfamilycenter.org; (Dom) (Intl) China, Ghana, Guatemala, Kazakhstan, United States, Vietnam

Vermont Catholic Charities (VCC); Burlington, VT; (802) 658-6110; www.vermont catholic.org; (Dom)

Vermont Catholic Charities; Rutland, VT; (802) 658-6110; www.vermontcatholic.org/ vcc/vcc.html; (Dom) (Intl)

Vermont Children's Aid Society; Winooski, VT; (802) 655-0006; www.vtcas.org; (Dom) (Intl) China, Democratic People's Republic of Korea, Korea (South)

Wide Horizons for Children (WHFC); Monkton, VT; (802) 453-2581; www.whfc.org; (Dom) (Intl) China, Guatemala, Korea (South), Lithuania, Russian Federation, Ukraine

VIRGINIA

STATE ADOPTION OFFICE: Virginia Department of Social Services; Family Services, Adoption Unit; 7 N. 8th St.; Richmond, VA 23219; (804) 726-7575; www .dss.virginia.gov

ICPC ADMINISTRATOR: Virginia Department of Social Services; (804) 726-7581; www .dss.state.va.us

STATE ADOPTION EXCHANGE: Adoption Resource Exchange of Virginia (AREVA); (804) 726-7524; (804) 726-7499; www.adoptuskids.org/states/va

VIRGINIA STATE BAR: (804) 775-0500; www.vsb.org

ANNUAL NUMBER OF ADOPTIVE ADOPTIONS FINALIZED IN STATE: 2,301

STATE LAWS AND PROCEDURES—FAST FACTS

Types permitted? Independent and agency (75% of newborns via independent).

Who can adopt in state? Residents, and nonresidents when the birth parent consent is taken in state or the agency making the placement is located in state.

How long after the child's placement to finalize the adoption in court? 4–9 months.

Is adoptive parent advertising (to find a birth mother) permitted? Yes.

Is a preplacement home study required? Independent—no. Agency—yes.

Typical home study fee? $1,300–$2,100 (up to $18,000 if agency locating child).

Can adoptive parents help birth mother with expenses? Yes: legal, medical. Living assistance permitted if physician confirms she is unable to work.

Can child leave hospital with adoptive parents? Yes, with signed form.

When can birth mother sign her Consent to Adoption? Independent—3 days after birth (but consent not accepted until preplacement home study completed). Agency—anytime after birth.

Can the consent be revoked? Independent—yes, for 10 days, then irrevocable. Agency—yes, for 7 days, until child is placed with adoptive parents, or until child is 10 days old, whichever occurs later.

What are the putative father's rights? A new law is pending. If passed, it will require notice to him stating he has 10 days to register. If he fails to register, no further notice to him is needed. If he registers and objects, to block the adoption he must show best interests of child not served by adoption.

AMERICAN ACADEMY OF ADOPTION ATTORNEYS MEMBERS

Mark Eckman; 311 Maple Ave., Suite E; Vienna, VA 22180; (703) 242-8801; www .datzfoundation.org; markeckman@hotmail.com
Mark Eckman began practicing law in 1984. He has completed 1,000 adoptions in his career and last year completed 110. He has intercountry adoption programs in China, Guatemala, Russia. He speaks Spanish, French, German, and Italian.

Barbara C. Jones; 7016 Balmoral Forest Rd.; Clifton, VA 20124; (703) 222-1101; b.jones@adoptionattorneys.org
Barbara Jones began practicing law in 1988. She has completed 2,500 adoptions in her career and last year completed 100. 75% are newborn placements. Her clients find their own birth mother.

Robert H. Klima; 9256 Mosby St.; Manassas, VA 20110; (703) 361-5051; r.klima@ adoptionattorneys.org
Robert Klima began practicing law in 1978.

Darlis E. Moyer; 75 N. Mason St., #200; Harrisburg, VA 22802; (540) 434-9947; d.moyer@adoptionattorneys.org
Darlis Moyer began practicing law in 1980.

Thomas Nolan; Virginia Wills Trusts & Estates PLC; 215 Wayles Ln., #125; Charlottesville, VA 22911; (434) 817-4001; www.vepcharlottesville.com; tom@ vepcharlottesville.com
Thomas Nolan began practicing law in 1984. He has completed 150 adoptions in his career and last year completed 20. 95% are newborn placements. His clients find their own birth mother.

Betsy H. Phillips; 12576 Wards Rd.; Rustburg, VA 24588; (434) 821-5100; b.phillips@ adoptionattorneys.org
Betsy Phillips began practicing law in 1983.

Stanton Phillips; Adoption Legal Services; 1921 Gallows Rd., #110; Vienna, VA 22182; (703) 891-2400; www.babylaw.us; phillips@babylaw.us

Stanton Phillips began practicing law in 1980. He has completed 2,500 adoptions in his career and last year completed 100. 95% are newborn placements. 10% of his clients find a birth mother through his office. He is the recipient of 2006 Congressional Angel in Adoption Award.

Rodney M. Poole; Poole & Poole; 4901 Dickens Rd., #108; Richmond, VA 23230; (804) 358-6669; www.pooleandpoole.com; rpooleadop@aol.com
Rodney Poole began practicing law in 1973. He has completed 2,500 adoptions in his career and last year completed 56. 85% are newborn placements. 10% of his clients find a birth mother through his office. He is an adoptive parent and a past president of the American Academy of Adoption Attorneys.

Coleen M. Quinn; Cantor Arkema, PC; 1111 E. Main St., 16th Floor; Richmond, VA 23219; (804) 343-4375; www.virginia-adoption-attorney.com; cquinn@cantorarkema.com
Coleen Quinn began practicing law in 1988. She has completed 700 adoptions in her career and last year completed 50. 80% are newborn placements. 10% of her clients find a birth mother through her office.

Biographies were not available for the following AAAA members:
Gary B. Allison; 281 Independence Blvd., #310; Virginia Beach, VA 23462; (757) 518-8000; g.allison@adoptionattorneys.org;

Rosemary G. O'Brien; 109 S. Fairfax St.; Alexandria, VA 22314; (703) 549-5110; r.obrien@adoptionattorneys.org

Ellen S. Weinman; 111 E. Main St.; Salem, VA 24153; (540) 389-3825; e.weinman@adoptionattorneys.org

Please be aware than some AAAA members in neighboring states also practice in Virginia, including Mark McDermott (DC) and Peter Wiernicki (MD).

LICENSED PRIVATE AGENCIES

ABC Adoption Services; Roanoke, VA; (540) 989-2845; www.abcadoptions.org; (Dom) (Intl) Armenia, China, Guatemala, Korea (South), Moldova, Peru, Russian Federation, Vietnam

Adoption Center of Washington, Inc.; Alexandria, VA; (703) 549-7774; www.adoption center.com; (Intl) China, Guatemala, Kazakhstan, Russian Federation, Ukraine, Vietnam

Adoption Options/Jewish Social Service Agency, Inc. (Adoption Options); Fairfax, VA; (703) 204-9592; www.jssa.org; (Dom) (Intl)

Adoption Service Information Agency, Inc. (ASIA); Arlington, VA; (703) 312-0263; www.childrenshomeadopt.org/asia-adopt_org.html; (Dom) (Intl) China, Colombia, Ethiopia, Guatemala, India, Korea (South), Russian Federation, Thailand, Ukraine, Vietnam

Adoption Services, Inc.; Fairfax, VA; (717) 737-3960; http://adoptionservices.org; (Dom) (Intl) China, Guatemala, Russian Federation, Ukraine

Adoptions from the Heart; Chesapeake, VA; (757) 361-0008; www.adoptionsfromthe heart.org; (Dom) (Intl) China, Ecuador, Guatemala, India, Kazakhstan, Mongolia, Ukraine, Vietnam

Adoptions Together; Herndon, VA; (703) 689-0404; www.centerforadoptivefamilies .org; (Dom) (Intl)

Adoption with Love (JFS); Richmond, VA; (804) 282-5644; www.jfsrichmond.org; (Dom) (Intl) Belarus, China, Colombia, Guatemala, India, Russian Federation, Ukraine

America World Adoption Association, Inc. (AWAA); McLean, VA; (703) 356-8447; www .awaa.org; (Intl) China, Kazakhstan, Russian Federation, Ukraine

Autumn Adoptions, Inc.; Alexandria, VA; (703) 541-0697; www.autumnadoptions .org; (Dom) (Intl)

Barker Foundation; Falls Church, VA; (703) 536-1827; www.barkerfoundation.org; (Dom) (Intl) China, Colombia, El Salvador, India, Korea (South)

Bethany Christian Services, Inc.; Charlottesville, VA; (434) 979-9631; www.bethany .org/virginia; (Dom) (Intl)

Bethany Christian Services, Inc.; Fairfax, VA; (703) 385-5440; www.bethany.org/ virginia; (Dom) (Intl)

Bethany Christian Services, Inc.; Fredericksburg, VA; (540) 373-5165; www.bethany .org; (Dom) (Intl) Albania, China, Guatemala, Ukraine

Bethany Christian Services, Inc.; Virginia Beach, VA; (757) 499-9367; www.bethany .org; (Dom) (Intl)

Catholic Charities of Eastern Virginia, Inc.; Newport News, VA; (757) 875-0060; www .cceva.org; (Dom) (Intl)

Catholic Charities of Eastern Virginia, Inc.; Virginia Beach, VA; (757) 456-2366; www .cceva.org; (Dom)

Catholic Charities of Eastern Virginia, Inc.; Virginia Beach, VA; (757) 467-7707; www .cceva.org; (Dom)

Catholic Charities of Eastern Virginia, Inc.; Williamsburg, VA; (757) 253-2847; www .cceva.org; (Dom) (Intl)

Catholic Charities of the Diocese of Arlington—Children's Services (CCDA); Burke, VA; (703) 425-0100; www.ccda.net/children's services.html; (Dom)

Catholic Charities of the Diocese of Arlington, Inc.; Fredericksburg, VA; (540) 371-1124; www.ccda.net; (Dom)

Children's Home Society of Virginia, Inc.; Fredericksburg, VA; (540) 899-3441; www .chsva.org; (Dom)

Children's Home Society of Virginia, Inc.; Richmond, VA; (804) 353-0191; www.chsva .org; (Dom)

Children's Home Society of Virginia, Inc.; Roanoke, VA; (540) 344-9281; www.chsva .org; (Dom)

Children's Services of Virginia, Inc.; Manassas, VA; (703) 331-0075; www.childrens servicesofva.com; (Dom)

Children's Services of Virginia, Inc.; Winchester, VA; (540) 667-0116; www.childrens servicesofva.com; (Dom)

Children's Services of Virginia, Inc.; Woodbridge, VA; (703) 492-0463; www.csv-inc.com/tfc/index.htm; (Dom)

Commonwealth Catholic Charities, Inc.; Norton, VA; (276) 679-1195; www.cccofva.org; (Dom) (Intl)

Commonwealth Catholic Charities, Inc.; Richmond, VA; (804) 272-2235; www.cccofva.org/defaultHome.aspx; (Dom) (Intl)

Commonwealth Catholic Charities, Inc.; Roanoke, VA; (540) 344-5107; www.cccofvirginia.org; (Dom) (Intl)

Coordinators2inc; Richmond, VA; (804) 354-1881; www.c2adopt.org; (Dom) (Intl) China, Guatemala

Datz Foundation; Vienna, VA; (703) 242-8800; www.datzfound.com; (Dom) (Intl) China, Guatemala, Russian Federation, Ukraine

DePaul Family Services, Inc.; Abingdon, VA; (276) 623-0881; www.depaulfamilyservices.org; (Dom)

DePaul Family Services, Inc.; Charlottesville, VA; (434) 977-9847; www.depaulfamilyservices.org; (Dom)

DePaul Family Services, Inc.; Christiansburg, VA; (540) 381-1848; www.depaulfamilyservices.org; (Dom)

DePaul Family Services, Inc.; Danville, VA; (434) 793-5358; www.depaulfamilyservices.org; (Dom)

DePaul Family Services, Inc.; Lynchburg, VA; (434) 528-0184; www.depaulfamilyservices.org; (Dom)

DePaul Family Services, Inc.; Roanoke, VA; (540) 265-8923; www.depaulfamilyservices.org; (Dom)

Families United Through Adoption; Charlottesville, VA; (434) 923-8253; (Dom)

Family Life Services; Lynchburg, VA; (434) 845-5334; www.godparent.org; (Dom)

Forever Families Adoption Services, Inc.; Warrenton, VA; (540) 341-4679; http://ffasva.org; (Intl)

Frost International Adoptions, Inc.; Falls Church, VA; (703) 444-7912; www.frostadopt.org; (Intl) Kazakhstan, Russian Federation, Ukraine

Holston United Methodist Home for Children, Inc.; Bristol, VA; (276) 591-5301; www.holstonhome.org; (Dom) (Intl)

Holy Cross Child Placement Agency, Inc.; Alexandria, VA; (703) 356-8824; www.holycrosschild.org; (Dom) (Intl) Guatemala, India

Jewish Family Service of Tidewater, Inc.; Virginia Beach, VA; (757) 459-4640; www.jfsadoptionresources.org; (Dom) (Intl)

Jewish Family Services (JFS); Richmond, VA; (804) 282-5644; www.jfsrichmond.org; (Dom) (Intl)

LDS Family Services of Virginia, Inc.; Richmond, VA; (804) 743-0727; www.itsaboutlove.org; (Dom)

Loving Families, Inc.; Purcellville, VA; (703) 370-7140; www.alovingfamily.org; (Dom) (Intl) Ukraine

Lutheran Family Services, Inc.; Hampton, VA; (757) 722-4707; www.lfsva.org; (Dom)

Lutheran Family Services, Inc.; Wytheville, VA; (276) 228-5233; www.lfsva.org; (Dom)

Lutheran Family Services of Virginia; Bedford, VA; (540) 586-3623; www.lfsva.org; (Dom)

Lutheran Family Services of Virginia; Richmond, VA; (804) 288-0122; www.lfsva.org; (Dom) (Intl) China, Russian Federation, Ukraine

Lutheran Social Services of the National Captial Area, Inc.; Falls Church, VA; (703) 698-5026 ext. 117; www.lssnca.org; (Dom)

Miracles of Grace International; Ashburn, VA; (703) 729-3086; www.miraclesofgrace.com; (Intl)

Mother Goose Adoptions; Ashburn, VA; (703) 729-3086; www.mothergoose adoptions.com; (Dom)

People Places of Charlottesville; Charlottesville, VA; (434) 979-0335; www.people places.org; (Dom)

Phillips Teaching Homes; Annandale, VA; (703) 941-3471; www.phillipsprograms.org; (Dom)

SFI Adoption Services, LC; Winchester, VA; (703) 200-9099; www.sfiadopt.org; (Dom) (Intl) China, Guatemala, Kazakhstan, Romania, Russian Federation

Shore Adoption Services, Inc.; Virginia Beach, VA; (757) 687-8602; www.shore adoptionservices.org; (Dom) (Intl)

United Methodist Family Services of Virginia, Inc.; Alexandria, VA; (703) 941-9008; www.umfs.org; (Dom) (Intl)

United Methodist Family Services of Virginia, Inc.; Fredericksburg, VA; (540) 898-1773; www.umfs.org; (Dom) (Intl)

United Methodist Family Services of Virginia, Inc.; Lacross, VA; (434) 757-1065; www.umfs.org/index.html; (Dom) (Intl)

United Methodist Family Services of Virginia, Inc.; Richmond, VA; (804) 353-2334; www.umfs.org; (Dom) (Intl)

United Methodist Family Services of Virginia, Inc.; Virginia Beach, VA; (757) 490-9791; www.umfs.org; (Dom) (Intl)

Virginia Baptist Children's Home and Family Services; Richmond, VA; (804) 545-1200; www.vbchfs.org; (Dom)

Welcome House Adoption Program (of Pearl S. Buck International) (PSBI); Richmond, VA; (804) 740-7311; www.pearl-s-buck.org; (Intl)

WASHINGTON

STATE ADOPTION OFFICE: Washington Department of Social and Health Services (DSHS); Division of Children and Family Services; 1115 Washington St., SE— PO Box 45713; Olympia, WA 98504; (360) 902-7968; www1.dshs.wa.gov

ICPC ADMINISTRATOR: Washington Department of Social and Health Services; PO Box 45711; Olympia, WA 98504-5710; (360) 902-7984

STATE ADOPTION EXCHANGE: Washington Adoption Resource Exchange (WARE); (206) 441-7242; (206) 441-7281; www.warekids.org

WASHINGTON STATE BAR ASSOCIATION: (206) 443-9722; www.wsba.org

ANNUAL NUMBER OF ADOPTIVE ADOPTIONS FINALIZED IN STATE: 2,748

STATE LAWS AND PROCEDURES—FAST FACTS

Types permitted? Independent and agency (70% of newborns via independent).

Who can adopt in state? Residents, and nonresidents when child born in state or the agency making the placement is located in state.

How long after the child's placement to finalize the adoption in court? 2–3 months.

Is adoptive parent advertising (to find a birth mother) permitted? Yes, if have completed home study from a Washington agency.

Is a preplacement home study required? Yes.

Typical home study fee? $2,000 (agency fees usually higher if agency located child).

Can adoptive parents help birth mother with expenses? Yes: legal, medical, living, with court approval.

Can child leave hospital with adoptive parents? Yes, but some require a court order.

When can birth mother sign her Consent to Adoption? Before or anytime after the birth. If under age 18, the birth mother needs a guardian ad litem appointed.

Can the consent be revoked? Yes, until a court confirms the consent. This can occur no sooner than 48 hours after birth, or the signing of the consent, whichever is later.

What are the putative father's rights? There is no registry. Notice must be attempted. Usually the notice is 20 days, and he can only block adoption by proving adoption not in best interests of the child and that he did not fail to perform parental duties.

AMERICAN ACADEMY OF ADOPTION ATTORNEYS MEMBERS

David V. Andersen; 7016 35th Ave. NE; Seattle, WA 98115; (206) 267–7200; dvalaw@seanet.com

> *David Andersen began practicing law in 1981. He has completed 1,500 adoptions in his career and last year completed 88. 45% are newborn placements. 1% of his clients find a birth mother through his office.*

Rita L. Bender; Skellenger Bender, PS; 1301 5th Ave., #3401; Seattle, WA 98101; (206) 623-6501; www.skellengerbender.com; rbender@skellengerbendercom

> *Rita Bender began practicing law in 1968. She has completed 1,000 adoptions in her career and last year completed 50. 95% are newborn placements. 50% of her clients find a birth mother through her office.*

Mark M. Demaray; 145 3rd Ave. South, #201; Edmonds, WA 98020; (425) 771-6453; www.washingtonadoptionattorney.com; markdemaray@msn.com

> *Mark M. Demaray began practicing law in 1981. He has completed 3,000 adoptions in his career and last year completed 85. 95% are newborn placements. 20% of his clients find a birth mother through his office. He is an adoptive parent.*

J. Eric Gustafson; Lyon, Weigand & Gustafson, PS; 222 N. 3rd St.; Yakima, WA 98901; (509) 248-7220; www.northwestadoptions.com; egustafson@lyon-law .com
Eric Gustafson began practicing law in 1973. He has completed 800 adoptions in his career and last year completed 52. 90% are newborn placements. 90% of his clients find a birth mother through his office. He is an adoptive parent.

Michele Gentry Hinz; 33035 52nd Ave. South; Auburn, WA 98001; (253) 735-0928; michelehinz@hotmail.com
Michele Hinz began practicing law in 1981.

Margaret Holm; 2011 State Ave.; Olympia, WA 98506; (360) 943-6933; margaret holm@comcast.net
Margaret Holm began practicing law in 1983. She has completed 2,250 adoptions in her career and last year completed 100. 90% are newborn placements. 15% of her clients find a birth mother through her office.

Albert G. Lirhus; Dubuar, Lirhus & Engel, LLP; 720 Olive Way, #625; Seattle, WA 98101; (206) 728-5858; www.dle-law.com; lirhus@dle-law.com
Albert Lirhus began practicing law in 1973. He has completed 3,000 adoptions in his career and last year completed 235. 70% are newborn placements. 20% of his clients find a birth mother through his office.

Raegen N. Rasnic; 1301 5th Ave., #3401; Seattle, WA 98101; (206) 623-6501; r.rasnic@adoptionattorneys.org
Raegen Rasnic began practicing in 1995.

Joyce E. Robeson; 201 St. Helens Ave.; Tacoma, WA 98402; (253) 572-5104; j.robson@ adoptionattorneys.org
Joyce Robson began practicing law in 1988. She has completed 1,500 adoptions in her career and last year completed 162. 15% are newborn placements. 50% of her clients find a birth mother through her office. She is an adoptive parent.

Marie N. Tilden; 1014 Franklin St.; Vancouver, WA 98660; (360) 695-0290; www .marietilden.com; marie@marietilden.com
Marie Tilden began practicing law in 1985. She has completed 400 adoptions in her career and last year completed 28. 90% are newborn placements. 10% of her clients find a birth mother through her office. She is an adoptive parent.

Please be aware that some AAAA members located in neighboring states also practice in Washington, including: John Chally (OR) and Sandra Hodgson (OR).

LICENSED PRIVATE AGENCIES
Adoption Advocates International; Port Angeles, WA; (360) 452-4777; www.adoption advocates.org; (Dom) (Intl)
Adoption Resource Center of Children's Home Society; Spokane Valley, WA; (509) 747-4174; (Dom) (Intl) China

Amara Parenting and Adoption Services; Seattle, WA; (206) 260-1700; www.amara parenting.org; (Dom)

Americans Adopting Orphans; Seattle, WA; (206) 524-5437; www.orphans.com; (Intl) Cambodia, China, Ukraine, Vietnam

Bethany Christian Services; Seattle, WA; (206) 367-4604; www.bethany.org/washing ton; (Dom) (Intl)

Catholic Children and Family Service (CCFS); Walla Walla, WA; (509) 525-0572; (Dom) (Intl)

Catholic Community Services; Seattle, WA; (206) 328-5921; (Dom)

Catholic Community Services of Western Washington; Bellingham, WA; (360) 676-2164; www.ccsww.org/familyservices/northwest/whatcom/index.php; (Dom)

Catholic Family and Child Service; Richland, WA; (509) 946-4645; www.cfcs3cities .org/index.htm; (Dom)

Catholic Family and Child Service; Spokane, WA; (509) 358-4260; (Dom)

Catholic Family and Child Service of Yakima (CFCS); Yakima, WA; (509) 965-7100; www .cfcsyakima.org; (Dom)

Children's Home Society of Washington; Seattle, WA; (206) 695-3200; www.chs-wa .org; (Dom)

Children's Home Society of Washington; Tacoma, WA; (253) 472-3355; www.chs-wa .org; (Dom)

Children's Home Society of Washington, North Central Region; Wenatchee, WA; (509) 663-0034; www.chs-wa.org; (Dom)

Children's Home Society of Washington, Southwest Area; Vancouver, WA; (360) 695-1325; www.chs-wa.org; (Dom)

Children's Hope International (CHI); Issaquah, WA; (425) 391-9150; www.childrenshope .com; (Intl) China, Colombia, Kazakhstan, Russian Federation, Vietnam

Children's House International (CHI); Ferndale, WA; (360) 383-0623; (360) 383-0640; www.adopting.com/chi; (Intl) Bolivia, Bulgaria, Cambodia, China, Ecuador, Guatemala, Haiti, Hungary, India, Kazakhstan, Mexico, Moldova, Nepal, Peru, Romania, Russian Federation, Ukraine, Vietnam

A Child's Dream; Poulsbo, WA; (360) 589-6533; www.achildsdream.org; (Dom)

Faith International Adoptions; Tacoma, WA; (253) 383-1928; www.faithadopt.org; (Intl)

LDS Family Services; Spokane, WA; (509) 926-6581; http://ldsfamilyservices.org; (Dom)

Life's Vision International Adoption & Children's Humanitarian Aid (LVI); Bellevue, WA; (425) 614-3938 http://lifesvision.org; (Intl) China, Ghana, Guatemala, Haiti, Nepal

Lutheran Community Services North West; Seattle, WA; (206) 694-5700; www.lcsnw .org; (Dom)

Lutheran Social Services of Washington, Kennewick, WA; (509) 735-6446; (Dom)

New Hope Children and Family Agency; Seattle, WA; (206) 363-1800; www.newhope kids.org; (Dom) (Intl)

UJIMA Community Services (One Church, One Child of Washington State, Inc.); Seattle, WA; (206) 760-3456; www.ococujima.org; (Dom)

World Association for Children and Parents (WACAP); Seattle, WA; (206) 575-4550; www.wacap.org; (Dom) (Intl) China, India, Korea (South), Russian Federation, Thailand

WEST VIRGINIA

STATE ADOPTION OFFICE: West Virginia Department of Health and Human Resources; Office of Social Services; 350 Capitol St., Room 691; Charleston, WV 25301; (304) 558-3431; bobbyjmiller@wvdhhr.org

ICPC ADMINISTRATOR: West Virginia Department of Health and Human Resources; Bureau for Children and Families; (same address as above); (304) 558-1260; nchalhoub@wvdhhr.org

STATE ADOPTION EXCHANGE: West Virginia Adoption Resource Network; Bureau for Children and Families; (same address as above); (304) 558-2891; www .adoptawvchild.org; cstalnaker@wvdhhr.org

WEST VIRGINIA STATE BAR: (304) 558-2456; www.wvbar.org

ANNUAL NUMBER OF ADOPTIVE ADOPTIONS FINALIZED IN STATE: 908

STATE LAWS AND PROCEDURES—FAST FACTS

Types permitted? Independent and agency (50% of newborns via independent).
Who can adopt in state? Residents only.
How long after the child's placement to finalize the adoption in court? 6–9 months.
Is adoptive parent advertising (to find a birth mother) permitted? Yes.
Is a preplacement home study required? No.
Typical home study fee? $1,400 (agency fees usually higher if agency located child).
Can adoptive parents help birth mother with expenses? Yes: legal, medical, living.
Can child leave hospital with adoptive parents? Yes, with signed form.
When can birth mother sign her Consent to Adoption? 72 hours after birth.
Can the consent be revoked? There are two options. If an Irrevocable Consent form is used, it is irrevocable upon signing. If a Conditional Consent form is used, any period can be listed before finalization in which to revoke consent.
What are the putative father's rights? There is a registry. Notice must be attempted if he registered or is named by the birth mother.

AMERICAN ACADEMY OF ADOPTION ATTORNEYS MEMBERS
David Allen Barnette; Jackson Kelly, PLLC; PO Box 553; Charleston, WV 25322; (304) 340-1327; dbarnette@jacksonkelly.com
> *David Barnette began practicing law in 1979. He has completed 720 adoptions in his career and last year completed 45. 30% are newborn placements. 5% of his clients find a birth mother through his office.*

LICENSED PRIVATE AGENCIES
Adoption Services, Inc.; Berkley Springs, WV; (717) 737-3960; http://adoptionservices .org; (Dom) (Intl) China, Guatemala, Russian Federation

Adoptions from the Heart; Beaver, WV; (304) 763-5400; www.adoptionsfromtheheart
.org; (Dom) (Intl) China, Ecuador, Guatemala, India, Kazakhstan, Mongolia,
Ukraine, Vietnam

Braley and Thompson, Inc.; Dunbar, WV; (304) 722-1704; www.btkids.biz; (Dom)
(Intl) Ukraine

Burlington United Methodist Family Services; Grafton, WV; (304) 265-1338; www
.bumfs.org; (Dom)

Burlington United Methodist Family Services; Keyser, WV; (304) 788-2342; www.bumfs
.org; (Dom) (Intl)

Children's Home Society of West Virginia; Charleston, WV; (304) 345-3894; www
.childhswv.org; (Dom)

Children's Home Society of West Virginia; Martinsburg, WV; (304) 264-0225; www
.childhswv.org/index.htm; (Dom) (Intl)

Children's Home Society of West Virginia; Morgantown, WV; (304) 284-0992; www
.childhswv.org; (Dom) (Intl)

Children's Home Society of West Virginia; Princeton, WV; (304) 431-2424; www.child
hswv.org; (Dom) China, Romania

WISCONSIN

STATE ADOPTION OFFICE: Wisconsin Department of Health and Family Services; 1
W. Wilson St.; PO Box 8916; Madison, WI 53703; (608) 266-3595; www
.dhfs.state.wi.us

ICPC ADMINISTRATOR: Wisconsin Health and Family Services; Child Welfare and Family Violence Section, Bureau of Programs and Policies; (same address as above);
(608) 266-1489; (608) 264-6750

STATE ADOPTION EXCHANGE: Adoption Resources of Wisconsin; (414) 475-1246; www
.wiadopt.org; info@wiadopt.org

STATE BAR OF WISCONSIN: (608) 257-3838; www.wisbar.org

ANNUAL NUMBER OF ADOPTIVE ADOPTIONS FINALIZED IN STATE: 2,515

STATE LAWS AND PROCEDURES—FAST FACTS

Types permitted? Independent and agency (60% of newborns via independent).

Who can adopt in state? Residents only.

How long after the child's placement to finalize the adoption in court? 6 months.

Is adoptive parent advertising (to find a birth mother) permitted? Yes, with completed home study.

Is a preplacement home study required? Yes.

Typical home study fee? $6,000–$12,000 (agency fees usually higher if agency
located child).

Can adoptive parents help birth mother with expenses? Yes: legal, medical, living,
but living assistance can't exceed $5,000.

Can child leave hospital with adoptive parents? Yes, if licensed as foster parents.

When can birth mother sign her Consent to Adoption? Anytime after birth.
Can the consent be revoked? Yes. Consent made by filing a Petition for Voluntary Termination of Parental Rights. Prior to court order (usually scheduled 2–4 weeks postbirth), she has right to revoke consent. Once order signed, consent is irrevocable.
What are the putative father's rights? There is a registry option. Notice may be given of action to terminate his rights, or he can be noticed of right to file with registry within 14 days of birth or 21 days of notice, whichever is longer.

AMERICAN ACADEMY OF ADOPTION ATTORNEYS MEMBERS

Lynn J. Bodi; The Law Center for Children & Families; 434 S. Yellowstone Dr.; Madison, WI 53719; (608) 821-8212; www.law4kids.com; lbodi@law4kids.com
Lynn Bodi began practicing law in 1987. She has completed 200 adoptions in her career and last year completed 20. 95% are newborn placements. Her clients find their own birth mother.

Carol M. Gapen; The Law Center for Children & Families; 434 S. Yellowstone Dr.; Madison, WI 53719; (608) 821-8211; www.law4kids.com; egapen@law4kids .com
Carol Gapen began practicing law in 1988. She has completed 450 adoptions in her career and last year completed 27. 95% are newborn placements. Her clients find their own birth mother.

Stephen W. Hayes; 20800 Swenson Dr., #475; Waukesha, WI 53186; (262) 798-8220; www.tsglaw.com; swh@tsglaw.com
Stephen Hayes began practicing law in 1969. He has completed 3,200 adoptions in his career and last year completed 120. 85% are newborn placements. His clients find their own birth mother.

Theresa L. Roetter; Hill, Glowacki, Jaeger & Hughes, LLP; 2010 Eastwood Dr., #301; Madison, WI 53704; (608) 244-1354, ext. 325; www.hill-law-firm.com; troetter@ hill-law-firm.com
Theresa Roetter began practicing law in 1993. She has completed 350 adoptions in her career and last year completed 33. 95% are newborn placements. Her clients find their own birth mother.

Richard B. Schoenbohm; Schoenbohm & Schoenbohm, SC; 600 E. Northland Ave.; Appleton, WI 54911; (920) 735-5858; schoenbo@athernet.net
Richard Schoenbohm began practicing law in 1980. He has completed 225 adoptions in his career and last year completed 14. 90% are newborn placements. His clients find their own birth mother.

Victoria J. Schroeder; 2574 Sun Valley Dr., #200; Delafield, WI 53018; (262) 646-2054; vjsch@execpc.com
Victoria Schroeder began practicing law in 1980. She has completed 1,000 adoptions in her career and last year completed 50. 98% are newborn placements. Her clients find their own birth mother.

A biography was not available for the following AAAA member:
Judith Sperling-Newton; 434 S. Yellowstone Dr.; Madison, WI 53719; (608) 821-8210; j.sperling-newton@adoptionattorneys.org

Please be aware that some AAAA members located in neighboring states also practice in Wisconsin, including Gary Debele (MN).

LICENSED PRIVATE AGENCIES

Adoption Advocates, Inc.; Madison, WI; (608) 246-2844; www.madison.com/communities/adoptadvo; (Dom) (Intl)

Adoption Choice, Inc.; Milwaukee, WI; (414) 276-3262; www.adoptionchoiceinc.org; (Dom) (Intl) Azerbaijan, Bulgaria, China, Guatemala, Kazakhstan, Russian Federation, Ukraine

Adoption Option; Waukesha, WI; (262) 544-4278; (Dom) (Intl)

Adoption Services, Inc.; Appleton, WI; (920) 735-6750; www.adoptionservicesinc .com; (Dom) (Intl) China, Colombia, Ecuador, Guatemala, India, Kazakhstan, Korea (South), Peru, Russian Federation

Adoption Services, Inc.; Mequon, WI; (262) 241-8755; www.adoptionservicesinc .com; (Dom) (Intl)

Adoption Services, Inc.; Waukesha, WI; (262) 513-0443; www.adoptionservicesinc .com; (Dom) (Intl) China, Colombia, Ecuador, Guatemala, India, Kazakhstan, Korea (South), Marshall Islands, Peru, Russian Federation, Sierra Leone, Ukraine

Adoptions of Wisconsin, Inc.; Madison, WI; (608) 821-8220; www.adoptionsof wisconsin.com; (Dom) China

Bethany Christian Services of Wisconsin; Waukesha, WI; (262) 547-6557; www.bethany .org; (Dom) (Intl)

Catholic Charities—Diocese of Green Bay; Green Bay, WI; (920) 437-7531 ext. 8234; www.gbdioc.org; (Dom)

Catholic Charities, Inc. (CCDL); LaCrosse, WI; (608) 782-0704; www.catholiccharities lax.org; (Dom)

Catholic Charities—Madison; Madison, WI; (608) 833-4800; www.ccmadison.org; (Dom) (Intl)

Catholic Charities of the Archdiocese of Milwaukee; Milwaukee, WI; (414) 771-2881; www.ccmke.org; (Dom) (Intl) China, Guatemala, India, Poland, Russian Federation, Ukraine

Children and Families First, Inc.; Madison, WI; (608) 826-0498; www.cffwi.org; (Dom) (Intl)

Children's Service Society of Wisconsin; West Allis, WI; (414) 453-1400; www.cssw.org; (Dom)

Community Adoption Center (CAC); Manitowoc, WI; (920) 682-9211; http://community adoption.com; (Dom) (Intl)

Crossroads Adoption Services; Hudson, WI; (715) 386-5550; www.crossroadsadoption .com; (Dom) (Intl) China, Colombia, Guatemala, India, Nepal, Peru, Philippines, Russian Federation, Thailand, Ukraine

Evangelical Child and Family Agency of Wisconsin (ECFA); New Berlin, WI; (262) 789-1881; www.ecfawisc.org; (Dom) (Intl)

LDS Social Services; Madison, WI; (608) 238-5377; (Dom) (Intl)

Lifelink Adoption Services; Appleton, WI; (920) 882-8450; www.lifelinkadoption.org; (Intl) Bulgaria, China, Guatemala, India, Korea (South), Philippines, Russian Federation, Ukraine

Lifelink Adoption Services; Brookfield, WI; (262) 781-7781; www.lifelinkadoption.org; (Intl) Bulgaria, China, Guatemala, India, Korea (South), Philippines, Russian Federation, Ukraine

Lifelink Adoption Services; Fitchburg, WI; (608) 278-4011; www.lifelinkadoption.org; (Intl)

Lutheran Counseling and Family Services of Wisconsin (LCFS); Wauwatosa, WI; (414) 536-8333; www.lcfswi.org; (Dom) (Intl)

Lutheran Social Services of Wisconsin and Upper Michigan, Inc. (LSS); Milwaukee, WI; (414) 281-4400; www.lsswis.org; (Dom) (Intl)

PATH Wisconsin Inc.; Hudson, WI; (715) 386-1547; http://pathinc.org; (Dom)

Pauquette Adoption Services, Inc. (PAS); Portage, WI; (608) 742-8004; www.adoptpas.com; (Dom) (Intl) China, Colombia, Ecuador, Ethiopia, Guatemala, Haiti, India, Korea (South), Mexico, Russian Federation, Vietnam

Special Beginnings Adoption Services; Brookfield, WI; (262) 432-1055; www.voa-wi.org; (Dom) (Intl)

Special Children, Inc.; Elm Grove, WI; (262) 821-2125; www.specialchildreninc.com; (Dom) (Intl)

Sunshine International Adoption, Inc.; Elm Grove, WI; (262) 796-9898; www.sunshineadoption.org; (Intl) Bulgaria, China, Colombia, Guatemala, Kazakhstan, Russian Federation, Ukraine

WYOMING

STATE ADOPTION OFFICE: Wyoming Department of Family Services; 130 Hobbs Ave.; Cheyenne, WY 82009; (307) 777-3570; http://dfsweb.state.wy.us

ICPC ADMINISTRATOR: Wyoming Department of Family Services; (same address as above); (307) 777-3693; http://dfsweb.state.wy.us/adoption.html

STATE ADOPTION EXCHANGE: Wyoming Department of Family Services; (307) 473-3924; http://dfsweb.state.wy.us; rfry@state.wy.us

WYOMING STATE BAR: (307) 632-9061; www.wyomingbar.org

ANNUAL NUMBER OF ADOPTIVE ADOPTIONS FINALIZED IN STATE: 412

STATE LAWS AND PROCEDURES—FAST FACTS
Types permitted? Independent and agency (30% of newborns via independent).
Who can adopt in state? Residents only.
How long after the child's placement to finalize the adoption in court? 6 months.
Is adoptive parent advertising (to find a birth mother) permitted? Yes.

Is a preplacement home study required? No, in fact there is not even a requirement for a postplacement home study, unless one is ordered by the court.

Typical home study fee? $350–$550 (agency fees usually higher if agency located child).

Can adoptive parents help birth mother with expenses? Yes: legal, medical, living, usually with advance court approval.

Can child leave hospital with adoptive parents? Yes, with signed form.

When can birth mother sign her Consent to Adoption? Anytime after birth.

Can the consent be revoked? No, irrevocable upon signing.

What are the putative father's rights? There is a registry. Notice must be attempted if he is registered or named by birth mother. He has 30 days in which to file paternity action.

AMERICAN ACADEMY OF ADOPTION ATTORNEYS MEMBERS

Peter J. Feeney; 100 W. B St., #100; Casper, WY 82602; (307) 266-4422; p.feeney@adoptionattorneys.org
Peter Feeney began practicing law in 1974.

Douglas H. Reiniger; 25 S. Gros Ventre St.; Jackson, WY 83001; (307) 690-6625; reinigerlaw@wyoming.com
Douglas Reiniger began practicing law in 1981. He has completed 1,000 adoptions in his career and last year completed 18. 90% are newborn placements. His clients find their own birth mother. He is a past president of the American Academy of Adoption Attorneys.

LICENSED PRIVATE AGENCIES

ADOPPT, Inc.; Gillette, WY; (307) 687-7147; www.adopptinc.com; (Intl)

Adoption in the Tetons; Jackson, WY; (307) 733-5680; (Dom)

Casey Family Program; Cheyenne, WY; (307) 638-2564; www.casey.org; (Dom)

Catholic Charities of Wyoming; Cheyenne, WY; (307) 638-1530; www.dioceseof cheyenne.org; (Dom)

Focus on Children, Inc.; Cokeville, WY; (307) 279-3434; www.focusonchildrenadopt .org; (Dom) Brazil, Bulgaria, China, Guatemala, Kazakhstan, Pacific Islands, Russian Federation, Ukraine

Global Adoption Services, Inc.; Sheridan, WY; (307) 674-6606; www.adoptglobal.org; (Dom) (Intl) China, Russian Federation

LDS Family Services, Inc.; Sheridan, WY; (307) 637-5364; (Dom)

Wyoming Children's Society; Cheyenne, WY; (307) 632-7619; www.wyomingcs.org; (Dom) (Intl) Russian Federation

Recommended Reading

SUBJECT: ARE YOU READY TO ADOPT?

Adopting After Infertility by Patricia Irwin Johnston (Perspectives Press, 1994)

Adoption Without Fear by James Gritter (Corona Publishing, 1989)

SUBJECT: BEING AN ADOPTIVE PARENT

Adoption Nation by Adam Pertman (Basic Books, 2001)

Attaching in Adoption by Deborah Gray (Perspectives Press, 2002)

Inside Transracial Adoption by Gail Steniberg and Beth Hall (Perspectives Press, 2000)

Love and Logic Magic for Early Childhood: Practical Parenting from Birth to Age Six Years by Foster Cline and Jim Fray (Love and Logic Press, 2002) (Not an "adoption" book, just an excellent book on parenting)

The Open Adoption Experience by Lois Ruskai Melina and Sharon Kaplan Roszia (HarperCollins, 1993)

Raising Adopted Children by Lois Ruskai Melina (HarperCollins, 1998)

The Russian Word for Snow by Janis Cooke Newman (St. Martin's, 2002)

Twenty Things Adopted Kids Wish Their Adoptive Parents Knew by Sherie Eldridge (Delta, 1999)

SUBJECT: TALKING TO YOUR CHILD ABOUT ADOPTION

Dear Birthmother by Kathleen Silber and Phylis Speedlin (Corona Publishing, 1991)

Making Sense of Adoption by Lois Ruskai Melina (Solstice Press, 1989)

Talking to Your Child About Adoption by Patricia Dorner (British Association for Adoption and Fostering, 1998)

Talking with Young Children about Adoption by Mary Watkins and Susan Fisher (Yale University Press, 1995)

Telling the Truth to Your Adopted or Foster Child by Betsy Keefer and Joyce Schooler (Bergin & Garvey, 2000)

SUBJECT: OLDER-CHILD AND SPECIAL-NEEDS ADOPTION ISSUES

Adopting the Hurt Child: Families with Special Needs by Gregory Keck and Regina Kupecky (Navpress Publishing Group, 1998)

Parenting the Hurt Child: Helping Adoptive Families Heal and Grow by Gregory Keck and Regina Kupecky (Pinon Press, 2002)

Toddler Adoption: The Weaver's Craft by Mary Hopkins-Best (Perspectives Press, 1994)

ALL ADOPTION SUBJECTS

Adoptive Families magazine, a monthly publication, consistently has articles on each of the above subjects. Subscribe at (800) 372-3300 or visit its website at www.adoptivefamilies.com.

National and Regional Adoption Exchanges

NATIONAL EXCHANGE
Children's Bureau
Department of Health and Human Services
8015 Corporate Dr., Suite C
Baltimore, MD 21236
(888) 200-4005; www.adoptUSkids.org; info@adoptuskids.org

REGIONAL EXCHANGES
Adopt America Network
(800) 246-1731; www.adoptamericanetwork.org; mking@adoptamericanetwork.org

The Adoption Exchange
14232 E. Evans Ave.
Aurora, CO 80014
(303) 755-4756; www.adoptex.org; info@adoptex.org

Children Awaiting Parents, Inc. (The CAP Book)
595 Blossom Rd., #306
Rochester, NY 14610
(888) 835-8802; www.capbook.org; info@capbook.org

National Adoption Center
1500 Walnut St., #701
Philadelphia, PA 19102
(800) TO-ADOPT; www.adopt.org

Northwest Adoption Exchange
600 Stewart St., #313
Seattle, WA 98101; (800) 927-9411
www.nwae.org; hwae@nwresowce.org

STATE EXCHANGES
Chapter 15 (state-by-state review) lists each state's individual adoption exchange.

FOR GENERAL ASSISTANCE

Two nationally recognized and respected organizations are the North American Council on Adoptable Children (NACAC) and the Child Welfare League of America (CWLA). Each provides helpful information to those seeking to adopt special-needs and waiting children. Their contact information is provided in Appendix C.

Helpful Organizations, Publications, and Websites

Helpful Organizations

The American Adoption Congress
(202) 483-3399; www.americanadoptioncongress.org
The American Adoption Congress is dedicated to promoting legislation and public awareness regarding adoptee and birth parent access to indentifying information.

The Child Welfare Information Gateway
1250 Maryland Ave., SW, 8th Floor
Washington, DC 20023
(800) 384-3366; www.childwelfare.gov; info@childwelfare.gov
The Child Welfare Information Gateway was formerly known as the National Adoption Information Clearinghouse. It is a service of the U.S. Department of Health and Human Services. It offers a tremendous database of information on public and private adoption agencies, and well as general information on all types of adoption.

The Child Welfare League of America (CWLA)
440 1st St., NW, 3rd Floor; Washington, DC 20001
(202) 638-2952; www.cwla.org
The Child Welfare League of America is the nation's oldest and largest membership-based child welfare organization, committed to promoting the well-being of children and their families, and protecting every child from harm. It is an association of more than 900 public and private nonprofit agencies that assist more than 2.5 million abused and neglected children and their families each year.

Concerned United Birthparents, Inc. (CUB)
PO Box 503475; San Diego, CA 92510
(800) 822-2777; www.cubirthparents.org
Concerned United Birthparents is a national organization focusing on the needs and concerns of birth parents, and their sometimes overlooked role in the adoption process.

The Evan B. Donaldson Adoption Institute
525 Broadway, 6th Floor; New York, NY 10012
(212) 925-4089; www.adoptioninstitute.org; info@adoptioninstitute.org

The Evan B. Donaldson Adoption Institute provides leadership to improve adoption laws, policies, and practices through detailed research and advocacy. Its goal is to translate policy into action, achieving ethical and legal reforms.

National Council for Adoption
225 N. Washington St.; Alexandra, VA 22314
(703) 299-6633; www.adoptioncouncil.org; ndfa@adoptioncouncil.org
The National Council for Adoption is devoted to serving the best interests of children through adoption and has championed this cause since its founding in 1980. It is an advocate for state laws that promote sound adoption policy (serving the interests of adoptive parents, birth parents, and adoptees) and is a resource for state and federal lawmakers. Helpful statistics are provided via its website. It was responsible for the nation's first photolisting of waiting children, now done by www.adopt uskids.org.

North American Council for Adoptable Children (NACAC)
970 Raymond Ave., #106; St. Paul, MN 55114
(651) 644-3036; www.nacac.org; info@nacac.org
The North American Council for Adoptable Children believes every child has the right to a permanent, nurturing, and culturally sensitive family. Founded in 1974 by adoptive parents, NACAC is committed to the needs of waiting children and the families who adopt them. Its website provides adoptive parent support groups for those who have adopted waiting and special-needs children.

RESOLVE
7910 Woodmont Ave., Suite 1350
Bethesda, MD 20814; (301) 652-8585
www.resolve.org; info@resolve.org
Resolve is a highly respected, nonprofit national infertility organization. Since 1974 it has been dedicated to providing education, support, and advocacy for those dealing with infertility. There are regional chapters throughout the United States. Adoption is a topic often covered in their publications and seminars.

PUBLICATIONS
Adoptive Families Magazine
39 W. 37th St., 15th Floor; New York, NY 10018
(800) 372-3300; www.adoptivefamilies.com
Adoptive Families is an excellent magazine offering articles of tremendous assistance to both new adoptive parents, as well as those whose adopted chidren are now adults. In addition, it offers a very helpful website with articles on all types of adoptions, and such diverse offerings as open adoption records, adoptive parent support groups, listings of adoption agencies and attorneys, and even an adoption bookstore.

Note: Most of the above organizations provide a magazine or journal as part of their membership, although none are as broad-based as *Adoptive Families* magazine.

WEBSITES

Adoption.com
A highly commercial site with dozens of URLs leading to it. Despite the many advertisements it carries, there are many excellent articles and other helpful information provided, viewable at no cost, making it a helpful resource.

Adoption101.com
Free online articles on adoption in an advertising-free setting. It also offers preprinted adoption networking mailing labels for every state, limited to recipients in professions likely to be have contact with birth mothers.

Sample Photo-Résumé Letter

(Photo)

Hi,

We're Brian and Shelly and we are hoping with all our hearts to adopt. Dealing with infertility has only strengthened our resolve to have a family.

We live in a wonderful surburban community in Southern Calfornia. Our neighbors are some of our best friends and many of them have young children or are just starting their families. We are about five minutes to the ocean and we love to spend weekends at the beach. Brian likes to bodysurf while I prefer to sit under an umbrella and read a good book. What we'd really love to be doing is building sand castles with our child, but we know that day will come. Besides the beach, Brian likes to barbeque in our backyard (he planted all the plants and trees, and did all the landscaping himself—building our own backyard "paradise") and also enjoys playing softball and doing home projects. I like sports like jogging and tennis, but I also like being a homebody and just relaxing at home with Brian. Sunday mornings we do the crossword puzzle together and see who can get the most answers—winner gets a massage. (Sometimes I even let him win!)

Brian is a fireman and loves his job. He also feels good about having a job where he can help people and make a difference in our town. My job is not so exciting. I'm the assistant manager of a clothing boutique, but I have fun helping people choose clothes that make them feel good about themselves. When we are lucky enough to be picked as adoptive parents, we plan for me to stop working and be a full-time mom.

We want your pregnancy to be a safe and comfortable one, and we are able to help with pregnancy-related expenses allowed by law. To help us all do everything correctly, we have hired an adoption attorney/agency, William Smith/XYZ Adoption Center. To learn more about us, you can call him/them toll-free at 1-800-756-6757. Many adoptions nowadays are open, allowing us to meet, share identities, and get to know each other, so you can be sure you are picking the right parents for your baby. If you think that might be us, we can't wait to meet you!

Brian and Shelly

Sample "Traditional" Networking Cover Letter

Hi!

We are hoping to adopt a baby. We are sending you our photo-résumé letter with the hope you will keep it on hand, and when the time comes, that you will pass it along to a woman who is facing an unplanned pregnancy and might be considering adoption as a loving option for her child. We want her pregnancy to be a comfortable and healthy one and are able to help with pregnancy-related expenses.

We have selected "open" adoption because it allows adoptive and birth parents to get to know each other before the birth, with no hidden identities. We've also selected an adoption attorney/agency, Jane Smith/XYZ Adoption Agency, to help us do everything right.

Please keep our letter on hand for when the time comes that you know of someone who may wish to call us.

Thank you!

Hi!

We are hoping to adopt a baby. We are sending you our photo-résumé letter with the hope you will keep it on hand, and when the time comes, that you will pass it along to a woman who is facing an unplanned pregnancy and might be considering adoption as a loving option for her child. We want her pregnancy to be a comfortable and healthy one and are able to help with pregnancy-related expenses.

We have selected "open" adoption because it allows adoptive and birth parents to get to know each other before the birth, with no hidden identities. We've also selected an adoption attorney/agency, Jane Smith/XYZ Adoption Agency, to help us do everything right.

Please keep our letter on hand for when the time comes that you know of someone who may wish to call us.

Thank you!

Note: printing two cover letters per page will allow you to cut it in half, giving you two copies. Then affix one to each photo-résumé letter, allowing half of the cover letter to show from behind it.

Sample "Personal"
Neworking Cover Letter

Dear Friends:

We are hoping to adopt a baby and we hope that you can help us. As you may know, there are many couples like us unable to conceive a child who turn their hopes to adoption. Unfortunately, there are more couples waiting to adopt than there are babies. Nowadays, most adoptions are started by the baby's biological mother, learning of a couple who is hoping to adopt, usually from one of her health-care providers or a friend.

The process is very open and women considering adoption can meet us in person to decide if they would like to select us as the adoptive parents. That's where you come in! We hope you will help us by personally giving a copy of our résumé letter (we've enclosed five) to people you know who will keep it on hand for when they may come into contact with a woman with an unplanned pregnancy. Specifically, please give one directly to your family doctor the next time you have an appointment, as well as your ob-gyn. Not their receptionist, but directly to the doctor. Other people you could give it to could be your minister, and any friends you have who work in medical clinics, as counselors, etc. Even where you get your hair and nails done can be great places to get the word out. If you have any questions about giving out our letter, or how adoption works, please call us. We have an adoption attorney/agency helping us to be sure we do everything correctly.

There is nothing more important to us than having a family, and we thank you for helping us create ours.

Ryan and Robin

INDEX

Page numbers in **bold** indicate tables.

About the Author

Randall Hicks is a successful adoption attorney now in his twentieth year of practice. He has completed more than 900 adoptions, both domestic and international. He is a member of the American Academy of Adoption Attorneys and has served as an advisor to the California state legislature. His victories in the appellate courts have helped create precedent protecting the right of adoptive parents, litigating cases as high as the U.S. Supreme Court.

He is the author of previous highly acclaimed how-to adoption books, as well as a children's book showing adoption is a loving and natural way to join a family. He has been a featured guest on many national televison programs and was the host of the PBS educational series *Adoption Forum*. In his youth, prior to becoming an attorney, he was a TV and film actor, appearing on *General Hospital*, in several TV movies, and in the role of Billy Hayes in the television series version of the feature film *Midnight Express*.

In Randy's spare time he is a mystery author, creating a lighthearted mystery series featuring Toby Dillon, an adoption attorney and part-time county club tennis pro. His debut mystery, *The Baby Game*, won the 2006 Gumshoe Award for Best Debut Mystery, and was a finalist for the Anthony, Barry, and Macavity Awards. Visit www.tobydillon.com.

Randy lives on a small farm in southern California where he pretends he is a farmer and rancher. He also enjoys carpentry and trying to add a consistent topspin backhand to his tennis game.